T0330320

The Global Urban Competitiveness Report – 2013

The Global Urban Competitiveness Report – 2013

Edited by

Pengfei Ni

Professor of Economics, Chinese Academy of Social Sciences, China

Peter Karl Kresl

Professor of Economics Emeritus, Bucknell University, USA

Wei Liu

Researcher, Chinese Academy of Social Sciences, China

IN ASSOCIATION WITH THE CHINESE ACADEMY OF SOCIAL SCIENCES

Cheltenham, UK • Northampton, MA, USA

© Pengfei Ni, Peter Karl Kresl and Wei Liu 2015

All rights reserved. No part of this publication may be reproduced, stored in a retrieval system or transmitted in any form or by any means, electronic, mechanical or photocopying, recording, or otherwise without the prior permission of the publisher.

Published by
Edward Elgar Publishing Limited
The Lypiatts
15 Lansdown Road
Cheltenham
Glos GL50 2JA
UK

Edward Elgar Publishing, Inc.
William Pratt House
9 Dewey Court
Northampton
Massachusetts 01060
USA

A catalogue record for this book
is available from the British Library

Library of Congress Control Number: 2014954940

This book is available electronically in the **Elgar**online
Economics subject collection
DOI 10.4337/9781782548034

MIX
Paper from
responsible sources
FSC
www.fsc.org   FSC® C013056

ISBN 978 1 78254 802 7 (cased)
ISBN 978 1 78254 803 4 (eBook)

Printed and bound in Great Britain by T.J. International Ltd, Padstow

Contents

Group members		vii
Global Urban Competitiveness Assessment Team		ix
Prologue		xi

PART I   GENERAL ANALYSIS

1   Conceptual framework and analytical methods   3
    Pengfei Ni, Xiaolan Yang and Peter Karl Kresl
2   Global urban sustainable competitiveness index   15
    Wei Liu, Mian Li, Jie Yang and Shaokun Wei
3   Global urban sustainable competitiveness: a comprehensive analysis   28
    Jie Wei and Pengfei Ni
4   Global urban sustainable competitiveness: a regional analysis   47
    Jie Yang and Kai Liu
5   Global urban sustainable competitiveness and urban GDP per capita   69
    Anquan Zhang
6   Global urban sustainable competitiveness and urban population size   83
    Chao Li
7   Global urban sustainable competitiveness: characteristics of functional centers   99
    Qingbin Li

PART II   SPECIALIZED ANALYSIS

8   The specialized differences: one key vector in urban competitiveness   117
    Saskia Sassen
9   Social and technological innovations in the competitiveness of cities   127
    Banji Oyelaran-Oyeyinka
10 Green cities: examples of governing for green growth from OECD countries   161
    Lamia Kamal-Chaoui, Margo Cointreau and Xiao Wang
11 Institutions and urban competitiveness – a Doing Business perspective   172
    Doing Business Group in the World Bank
12 The challenge of world city network pattern changes on the world city network analysis   181
    Peter J. Taylor

13 Population aging and urban competitiveness   194
    Peter Karl Kresl
14 Driving factors of urban prosperity: an empirical analysis of global cities   207
    Pengfei Ni
15 Patterns of the global cities: present and future   234
    Pengfei Ni and Peter Karl Kresl

PART III   INDEX REPORT

16 The state of sustainable competitiveness of 500 cities   245
    Global Urban Competitiveness Assessment Team

Group members

CONSULTANTS

Weiguang Wang (President of Chinese Academy of Social Sciences (CASS))
Yang Li (Vice President of Chinese Academy of Social Sciences)
Changhong Pei (Director of Institute of Economics, CASS)
Peiyong Gao (Director of National Academy of Economic Strategy of Chinese Academy of Social Sciences)
Gang Fan (Vice President of China Society of Economic Reform, Director of Institute of the Chinese Eonomy)
Xiaoxi Li (Convener of Economy Division under Chinese Ministry of Education)
Peter Hall (Professor, Bartlett School of Architecture and Planning, University College of London)
Saskia Sassen (Professor of Columbia University, USA)
Peter J. Taylor (Academician of UK Royal Academy of Social Science, Director of the Globalization and World Cities Research Network)
Edward Blackley (Academician of US Academy of Public Management)

AUTHORS AND CONTRIBUTORS

Pengfei Ni (Center for City and Competitiveness, CASS)
Peter Karl Kresl (Bucknell University, USA)
Peter J. Taylor (Royal Academy of Social Science, Director of the Globalization and World Cities Research Network)
Saskia Sassen (Professor of Columbia University)
Banji Oyelaran-Oyeyinka (Director of the Monitoring and Research Division of UN-Habitat, researcher of Research and Training Department of UN- HABITAT)
Lamia Kamal-Chaoui (Head of Urban Development Programme, OECD)
Margo Cointreau (Urban Development Programme, OECD)
Xiao Wang (Urban Development Programme, OECD)
Wei Liu (Center for City and Competitiveness, CASS)
Yingwei Zhao (Graduate School, Chinese Academy of Social Sciences)
Heng Zhao (Graduate School, Chinese Academy of Social Sciences)
Jie Yang (Graduate School, Chinese Academy of Social Sciences)
Xiaolan Yang (School of Economics, Central University of Finance and Economics, China)
Kai Liu (Zhongnan University)
Jie Wei (School of Economics and Management, Northwest University)
Chao Li (National Academy of Economic Strategy, Chinese Academy of Social Sciences)

Qingbin Li (Institute of Economic Research, National Development and Reform Commission)
Anquan Zhang (School of Economics, Southwestern University of Finance and Economics)
Mian Li (Graduate School, Chinese Academy of Social Sciences)
Shaokun Wei (Department of Policy Research, China Center for Urban Development)

ACADEMIC ASSISTANTS

Wei Liu (Graduate School, Chinese Academy of Social Sciences)
Shaokun Wei (Department of Policy Research, China Center for Urban Development)

MEMBERS OF EDITORIAL BOARD

Peter J. Taylor (Academician of UK Royal Academy of Social Sciences, Professor of
      Loughborough University, UK)
Peter Karl Kresl (Professor of Bucknell University)
Saskia Sassen (Professor of Columbia University)
Lamia Kamal Chaoui (Head of Urban Development Programme, OECD)
Banji Oyelaran Oyeyinka (Director of the Monitoring and Research Division of UN-
      HABITAT, researcher of Research and Training Department of UN University)
Lihong Wang (Expert of Chinese Division of World Bank)
Richard LeGates (Professor of San Francisco State University)
David Maurrassee (Professor of Columbia University, US)
William Lever (Professor of University of Glasgow, UK)
Dong Sungcho (Professor of Seoul National University)
Jaime Sobrino (Professor of College of Mexico)
Guido Ferrari (Professor of University of Florence)
Kathy Pain (Professor of Research Centre of City and Real Estate of Reading University)
Peter Brain (President of Australian Institute of Industrial and Economy)
Francois Gipoulou (Director of Research Centre of French Academy)
Stefano Mollica (Chairman of Italian Regional Development Association)
Berg Van den Leo (Professor of Erasmus University, Netherlands)
Jianfa Shen (Professor of the Chinese University of Hong Kong)
Shen Wei (Associate Professor of Ecole de Supérieure des Sciences Commerciales d'Angers)
Pengfei Ni (Professor of Economics, Director of Center for City and Competitiveness of
      CASS)
Shaokun Wei (Department of Policy Research, China Center for Urban Development)

Global Urban Competitiveness Assessment Team

DIRECTORS

Pengfei Ni, Peter Karl Kresl and Wei Liu

TEAM MEMBERS

Shaokun Wei (Department of Policy Research, China Center for Urban Development)
Pengfei Bu (Capital University of Economics and Business)
Yingwei Zhao (Graduate School, Chinese Academy of Social Sciences)
Heng Zhao (Graduate School, Chinese Academy of Social Sciences)
Jie Wei (School of Economics and Management, Northwest University)
Jingyu Qiao (China Foreign Affairs University)
Kai Liu (Zhongnan University of Economics and Law of China)
Chao Li (National Academy of Economic Strategy, Chinese Academy of Social Sciences)
Qingbin Li (Institute of Economic Research, National Development and Reform Commission)
Anquan Zhang (School of Economics, Southwestern University of Finance and Economics)

Prologue

Today, over half of the population of earth lives in cities where globalization and informationization are growing dramatically. Cities have become significantly important in the development of the world and competition among them has been increasingly fierce, a situation which has drawn the attention of global policy-makers, bringing more and more research institutes and researchers to study this issue. Since the Global Urban Competitiveness Project was founded in 2005, with support from the Chinese Academy of Social Sciences and National Academy of Economic Strategy, it has got together related experts globally to carry out research studies and seminars, based on which articles and works have been composed and the Report on Global Urban Competitiveness (biannual report) has been released four times. With the aim of becoming one of the world-class academic brands in the field of world urban research, we have maintained unremitting endeavor. Compared with past reports, this year's has been considerably adjusted and significantly improved in content, structure and quality.

The report is composed of three parts. The analysis on global urban competitiveness is incorporated into the first part in which the impact of the financial crisis on global urban competitiveness is analyzed by using the latest data (2001-2009), demonstrating the ongoing adjustment of global urban competitiveness structure accelerated by the financial crisis, and conducting primary research on the competitiveness of 500 city groups over the world. This year, a long-lasting wish has been fulfilled by inviting the urban research team from international organizations and other world renowned expert teams, together with experts from GUCP, to co-author this report. And typical cities' competitiveness strategies are analyzed to provide experience to other cities. In the second part, a brilliant discussion on the structure, trend and determinants of global urban development, prosperity and competitiveness is presented by the team led by Banji Oyelaran-Oyeyinka, director of Global Urban Evaluation and Research Department of the UN Human Settlement Programme, the team led by Lamia Kamal-Chaoui, head of the OECD Development Programme, the GAWC team led by Peter Taylor, global renowned urban researcher and an academician of the UK Academy of Social Sciences, the GUCP team led by Peter Karl Kresl and Pengfei Ni, and Saskia Sassen, a global renowned economist and professor of Columbia University. Moreover, a dominant opinion has formed on global urban development through email interviews with a number of experts all over the world by the project team.

It is gratifying that after years of constant endeavor, the project team has built up a comprehensive and concise index system and valuation method, discovered sustainable and reliable data collection channels and methods, and obtained true, reliable and stable data, an accurate reflection of many aspects of a city and its competitiveness, the combination of which lays a solid foundation of data that makes this project a world-class academic brand of world urban research.

The composition of this report is a demanding and challenging task, especially the work on completion of re-evaluating global urban competitiveness. Under the leadership of Pengfei Ni, with the organization and coordination of Liu Wei, the team gathered nearly 100 experts and implemented a two-year task of data collection, organization, verification and comparison, improving the index system and evaluation method, quantitative analysis and empirical testing. The project team members conducted a considerable number of studies and discussions, communicated with many experts from countries around the world, and contacted several city governments for field research in different countries. The theoretical base, index system, research structure and key conclusions are the contributions of Pengfei Ni. Doctor Qinghu Hou is responsible for quantitative technical direction. Doctor Chao Li and Doctor Jie Wei are responsible for detailed measurement and calculation. Wei Liu is responsible for data collection and compilation, material gathering, measurement analysis as well as drafting and coordination and other tasks. Data entry was done by Ze Yu, Yanan Si, Xiaomeng Mei, Jing Cui and other students.

This research has received strong support from many cities around the world and international experts. During the period of raw data collection as well as the later analysis, study and composition, the project team was supported by many city governments all over the world. Meanwhile, a number of international experts and researchers offered great support and help. Hereby, we, the project team, would like to express our heartfelt appreciation to those friends who supported and cared about this project.

This report has received passionate and altruistic support from report consultants, leaders and colleagues from the Chinese Academy of Social Sciences and National Academy of Economic Strategy. Mr. Xie Shouguang and his colleagues offered their strong support to the publication of the Chinese version of this report. The English version has been published with the great support from Mr. Edward Elgar and his team at Edward Elgar Publishing. We would like to express our sincere gratitude to them.

Peter Karl Kresl
President of Global Urban Competitiveness Project
Professor of Economics (Emeritus), Bucknell University (USA)

Pengfei Ni
Secretary-General of Global Urban Competitiveness Project
Director of Center for City and Competitiveness, Chinese Academy of Social Sciences

Part I

General Analysis

1. Conceptual framework and analytical methods

Pengfei Ni,[1] Xiaolan Yang[2] and Peter Karl Kresl[3]

BACKGROUND: URBAN SUSTAINABLE COMPETITIVENESS AND ITS MEASUREMENT

Sustainable urban competitiveness is a hot topic increasingly attracting attention from city managers, social organizations, and city experts. Over a decade ago, Saskia Sassen asserted, 'The city belongs to the twenty-first century more than the nation.' Accompanying the advanced development in science and technology, newly industrialized countries have been rising sharply, and the urbanization process has expanded around the world. On the one hand, being growth engines, cities are playing an increasingly important role as key platforms for human beings and the centers of power and decision-making. On the other hand, cites in the world are confronting a number of common problems and challenges. First, with the free flow of production factors, goods, and services globally, fierce competition among cities is increasing. Second, there is an increasing number of problems related to the future development of cities, including increasing popular consciousness of civil rights among citizens, diminishing motivation for creation, readjustment of the power structure, contradictions from a diversified culture, social class divergence, source deficiency, environmental pollution and climate change. All the problems confronted by cities lead to the transfer of urban development objectives: from 'competing for wealth' to 'creating and providing more complex and advanced social wellbeing'. Of course, all these socioeconomic challenges and problems make it necessary to propose the concept of sustainable competitiveness rather than only competitiveness. Additionally, it is necessary to provide for an understanding of this concept in order to achieve a broad concentration on 'sustainable competitiveness' in urban management practices. The evaluation of urban sustainable competitiveness is the best starting point for putting theoretical research into practice.

Two streams of research have always been popular. The first stream regards sustainable

1   Pengfei Ni, Center of City and Competitiveness, CASS, No. 2 yuetanbeixiaojie, Xicheng District, Beijing, China, post code: 100836, Tel: 8610-68063478.
    Email: ni_pengfei@163.com.

2   Xiaolan Yang, School of Economics, Central University of Finance and Economics, China, post code: 100081, Tel: 8610-68063478.

3   Peter Karl Kresl, Bucknell University, Lewisburg, PA, USA 17837, Tel: 570-490-5193.
    Email: kresl@bucknell.edu.

development. Sustainable development of cities has always been a popular term attracting regular and sustained attention from environmental studies and city experts (Burton et al. 2013, Wheeler and Beatley 2004, Satterthwaite 1999, Breheny 1992). The other stream consists of studies on urban competitiveness. Since the 1990s, urban competitiveness has become a popular topic considered by geographers, economists, and city mangers (Huggins and Clifton 2011, Martin and Simmie 2008, Ache et al. 2008, Wolff et al. 2007, Thompson and Ward 2005, Budd and Hirmis 2004, Porter et al. 2004, Turok 2004, Garden and Martin 2003, Camagni 2002, Rogerson 1999, Begg 1999, Kresl 1995). However, 'sustainable development' is newly attracting broad attention from researchers and related organizers. Typically, it is believed that cities are the key source of climate change, as well as the solution, so cities should mitigate climate change through 'climate-conscious' urban planning and management on the one hand and sustain 'green growth' on the other hand (Kamal-Chaoui and Roberts 2009, Kern et al. 2008, OECD 2008). The European Commission (EC) (2010) proposes a new European Union strategy for 'smart, sustainable and inclusive growth'. Balkyte and Tvaronavičiene (2010) introduce the concept of 'sustainable competitiveness' by focusing on how competitiveness and sustainability interact with each other. Berg et al. (2014) trace 'competitiveness-oriented' urban policies in eight European cities over as long as two decades, indicating the major challenge in cities is to balance economic competitiveness with social progress and prevention of environmental deterioration. The recent 'Global Competitiveness Report 2013-2014' by the World Economic Forum (2013) modified its indicators to match a more sustainable and resilient method of growth. Almost at the same time, there has been consensus among the committee members of the Global Urban Competitiveness Project (GUCP) that the competitiveness of cities should be sustainable. In the recent 2014 GUCP conferences held in Amsterdam, one major topic was to establish proper indicators to evaluate and examine the sustainable competitiveness of cities. Ni (2013) proposed the concept of 'urban sustainable competitiveness' and tried to explain this concept with seven subgroup indicators. This indicator system has been applied in measuring 294 Chinese cities at the prefectural level and above in the 'Chinese Urban Competitiveness Report 2013'. Obviously, how to keep and retain a city's competitiveness while realizing sustainable growth is the first major question that every mayor and city manager needs to consider.

Concepts of Urban Sustainable Competitiveness

Urban sustainable competitiveness is the ability for a city to promote its advantages in technology, economy, society, environment, culture, management, and global connections and to search for systematic optimization in order to continually satisfy the complex and demanding social wellbeing needs of citizens. A qualified city with sustainable competitiveness synthesizes the natures of the following cities:

- The economic dynamic city;
- The innovation-driven city;
- The socially cohesive city;
- The environment-friendly city;
- The culture-diversified city;
- The open international city;
- The well-managed city.

We do not mean that a city should perfectly meet all the standards for these seven aspects. Instead, this term indicates a comprehensive understanding of future cities and provides a general perception that cities strive to approach.

Economic dynamic city. Persistent economic growth has always been pursued by cities, as it is the base for social cohesion, technological progress and human development. A city that could attract high value added, high creative firms and could retain the innovative and enterprising talents, would achieve persistent growth in productivity and wealth. Diversified labor division and cooperation made cities the centers of knowledge accumulation and creation (Jacobs 1969). The diversity in a city also affects the level of output and the level of wellbeing achievable in that city (Quigley 1998). An ideal competitive city should be a place where foreign firms would like to invest, where new firms emerge endlessly, where both small and large businesses coexist and compete in the market, where the entrepreneurship is rich, and where there is full employment and people work hard. A sustainable competitive city should perform well economically with a relative high economic growth rate.

Innovation-driven city. Innovation is an unlimited driving force for the persistent socioeconomic development of cities. Innovation is the most advanced form of competitiveness (Storper 1997). Innovation is the most important capability needed for a city to succeed within global competition and for cities to cultivate innovation-led growth through the accumulation of knowledge (Lever 2002a, Lever 2002b). 'In a globalized economy, the key resources for regional and urban competitiveness depend on localized processes of knowledge creation, in which people and firms learn about new technology, learn to trust each other, and share and exchange information' (Malecki, 2003). Kitson et al. (2004) argue that the presence of an innovative and creative class is a key factor 'supporting and underpinning an efficient productive base for the regional economy in the form of regional externalities'. Malecki (1997) proves the positive linear relationship between innovation, knowledge creation, and economic growth. An ideal city should be an innovation-driven society, where economic progress is advanced by knowledge accumulation and where knowledge industries make up a dominant portion of the local economy. In other words, knowledge is both an important input as well as a major output.

Socially cohesive city. A fair social system and compatible social spirit are necessary to guarantee the sustained growth and orderly operation of a city. Social cohesion and urban competitiveness have been recognized as two major issues in cities in the globalized world since the 1980s (Ache et al. 2008). In a study of Canadian cities, Ranci (2011) finds a high correlation coefficient between social cohesion and economic downturn in a study of European cities. Kitchen and Williams (2010) find that social conditions affect the expectations of residents on crime rate and security, thus affecting productivity. Ellen and O'Regan (2010) explore the influence of crime rates on urban populations and find that they lead to changes in urban growth. An ideal city should be a place where people live together with peace and fairness, where social conflict can be resolved through a rational judgment mechanism, and where the social mechanism can consider different opinions to balance competing interests.

Environment-friendly city. There seems to be a conflict between realizing economic growth, social cohesion, and technological innovation while protecting the quality of the environment in the short run, but this conflict can be resolved in the long term. Environmental pollution is an important factor affecting economic growth. Quality of life and urban amenities have been found to matter in the location decisions of high-human-capital households (Glaeser and Shapiro 2001). According to Porter (1998), 'strict environmental policy will inevitably enhance competitive advantages against foreign rivals'. Thus, the competitive advantages embodied in combining industry with strict environmental conditions become competitive advantages of a city. An observation of cities that promote their prosperity with scientific and technological innovations shows that many also have the world's best urban ecological environments and quality of life, such as San Jose, Vienna, Stockholm, Helsinki, Seattle, and Singapore. A good environment is a factor that enhances the attractiveness of a city (Ni et al. 2014). An ideal city should be a livable place, where people and nature coexist in harmony, where the production process and other human activities perform as one part of a natural cycle coordinating with other circular systems in nature, where the economy is operated according to a low-carbon model, where the ecological and environmental construction play an indispensable part, and where the artificial environment and natural environment are integrated.

Culture-diversified city. The cultural environment of a city is important for attracting people. The integration of different cultures enhances the competitive advantage of cities. Culture directly influences individual behavior through its impact on values and preferences (Rabin 1993). It is the dominant resource and decisive factor of production (Flarey 1996). It can be translated as the social norms and the individual beliefs that sustain Nash equilibrium as focal points in repeated social interactions (e.g. Myerson 2013, Schotter 2008, Greif 1994). The correlation coefficient for the basic talent index and cultural amenities is positive and significant (Florida 2002). The range and quality of cultural facilities and assets serve to support and underpin an efficient, productive base for the regional economy in the form of regional externalities (Kitson et al. 2004). An ideal culturally diverse city should be an open space where people and business adore the open and free cultural environment, and where old and new cultures merge into a splendid cultural picture.

Open international city. Castells (2011) points out that a city 'is not a place but a process', indicating that cities exist in interrelated global networks. A number of researchers hold the view that global connection is even more important than local connection, since it is an essential way to improve and upgrade a city's capabilities by participating in the global value chain (Markgren 2001, Angel and Engstrom 1995, Ni and Pan 2010). Bathelt et al. (2004) conclude that innovation and new knowledge are best understood as a combination of local and global interactions. An ideal open international city is where the efficient exchanges of information and material flows happen. Due to the wide applications of ICT, cities become smart cities which are categorized, on the one hand, by the ICT-enabled production and living system, and on the other hand, by innovations in public management and services due to the broad participation of citizens.

Well-managed city. Government plays an indispensable but challenging role in the promotion of urban prosperity. Among other things, it can help compensate for market failure. Well-administered and well-governed cities that are open to new ideas, cultures, and technologies can act as a nation's best catalyst of economic growth and human development (UN-Habitat 2010). An ideal well-managed city should provide efficient public services for citizens and firms in order to enable citizens to live and work freely in the city, to protect their legal rights, and to satisfy the requirement of firms for a free market environment. The legal appeals of firms and citizens could be expressed and realized with respect.

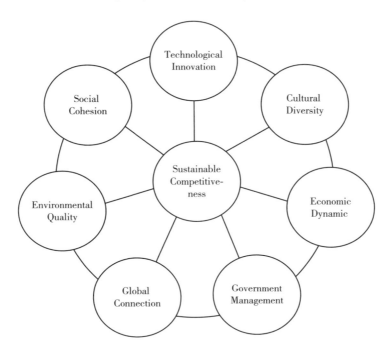

Figure 1.1   Analysis Framework of Urban Sustainable Competitiveness

Generally, economic dynamic, technological innovation, environmental quality, social cohesion, cultural diversity, global connection and government management comprise the different elements of sustainable development. They go hand in hand, interacting and reinforcing each other.

Based on the above perceptions, we measured urban competitiveness of a city from the seven perspectives: economic dynamic, technological innovation, environmental quality, social cohesion, cultural diversity, global connection and government management. The sustainable competitiveness is obtained by integrating the seven subgroup components.

Applied Sustainable Competitiveness Indicator

Based on the discussion of the important factors in deciding sustainable development, we choose typical indicators to measure the competitiveness components, which construct the sustainable competitiveness indicator system.

Economic Dynamic: GDP per capita and GDP growth rate. GDP per capita is GDP divided by the city population. It represents short-term economic efficiency. GDP growth rate is the average value of the GDP growth rate from 2001 to 2009, indicating long-term growth potential.

Technological Innovation: patent applications per 10,000 people, which is the total number of patents divided by the urban population. Patent applications are a direct expression of innovation. They are also an important indicator of a knowledge-based economy (Bontis 2004, Ni 2012).

Social Cohesion: inverse crime rate. As mentioned above, the crime rate is the most popular variable to represent social order. The higher the crime rate is, the worse the social environment. To keep consistent direction with other indicators, we used the inverse of the crime rate.

Environmental Quality: inverse carbon dioxide (CO_2) emissions per capita, total carbon dioxide emissions divided by the population. Among the variety of indicators referring to environment, carbon dioxide is an important indicator available for cities. It reflects energy conservation, environmental pollution, and climate change. Similarly, the inverse value was used here to keep accordance with other indicators.

Cultural Diversity: the languages used in international restaurants. Generally speaking, the best indicator to reflect diversity in culture is to count the people from different countries and races. The more diverse the nationalities of residents that are included in one city or the more diverse their races, the more colorful the culture is, and the more compatible a city is. However, it is hard to obtain the exact data on nationality and race, so we had to take the languages used in international restaurants as an alternative.

Global Connection: Global Network Connectivity. Cities are connected globally through a variety of forms, including business flows, material flows, information flows, and transport infrastructure. However, in the area of globalization, the connections derived from multinational advanced producer services best reflect the nature of increasing connectivity among cities (Taylor 2004). This indicator was constructed based on Taylor's method for determining a world city's global connectivity (Taylor et al. 2001, Taylor 2001). The method and data source are specified in the next section.

Government Management: Doing Business Index. The doing business index focuses on measuring the various costs a firm must bear to start a business in a city. It is a synthesis of the time and money that a firm uses to obtain official legal approval. It is a proper reflection of government efficiency and the degree of interpretation from government. Managed by the World Bank, this indicator was set up through a broad yearly survey of the largest cities of more than one hundred countries.

Theoretically, the perfect indicator to evaluate performance on sustainable competitiveness should be one that can reflect agglomeration and changes in a city's size, for example population data. However, the research methods deny the use of population data. First, cities should pursue an optimal size rather than use the thinking of 'the larger the better'. Second, there are restrictions on population movement across countries. Third, the resource and factor agglomeration process can be manipulated by official power in some countries, especially developing countries. Therefore, we did not directly use population data to measure sustainable competitiveness.

THE SELECTION OF SAMPLE CITIES

City Definition

In this report a city refers to the concentrated residential area under the governance of an administrative management center, including not only the urbanized area, but the affiliated suburbs and villages. From this definition, it can be seen clearly that the city we refer to is a city in the administrative sense. But the following terms need to be distinguished.

City and region: since the supreme administrative organization of the city governs some lower level administered places which are also called cities, a city only refers to the district itself, excluding other lower level cities under it. For example, some county-level cities are registered and managed under the prefectural-level cities, but here they are excluded.

City and urbanized area: the difference between city and urbanized area is that city is a region in the administrative sense, while urbanized area refers to a region in the social and economic sense, so that urbanized area means an urbanized region excluding the surrounding villages.

City and metropolitan area: due to the accessibility of data, some cities adopt the concept of urbanized area, while others adopt the concept of metropolitan area. We have provided explanations in these cases, cities without explanations are cities in the administrative sense.

Sample Selection

Five hundred cities across the world were selected as research targets. They are chosen based on a few steps and each step follows some rule. Firstly, we searched from one continent to another, from one country to another, and we made a rough list of possible cities from major countries. Secondly, the number of candidates in each country or region was identified according to their relative population and income per capita. Thirdly, specific sample cities were selected in each country or region sequentially according to their size and relative positions in their countries. Fourthly, evaluation was made for candidate cities in each country with consideration of the availability, accuracy and standardization of the statistical data of each city. Eventually, those with more standard and accurate data available were selected as sample cities.

City Distribution

In terms of geographical distribution, the 500 cities selected through the above steps are located in about 130 countries or regions in 6 continents. Specifically, 187 of the cities are in Asia, 136 in Europe, 107 in North America, 33 in Africa, 28 in South America, 33 in Africa, 28 in South America and 9 in Oceania. In terms of development stage, the 500 cities may be divided into 6 groups by the standard of GDP per capita (based on official exchange rates of 2005). Forty-nine of the sample cities have a GDP per capita of more than 500,000 dollars, 58 between 400,000 and 49,999 dollars, 66 between 30,000 and 39,999 dollars, 81 between 10,000 and 29,999 dollars, 90 between 5,000 and 9,999 dollars and 156 less than 5,000 dollars. In general, these 500 cities represent the economic efficiency of different regions.

Data Source and Data Collection

Population: Some cities only provide residential population data, but some provide permanent population or temporary population data too. In our study, cities' population has been unified with the permanent account. The data sources for population data are various, including official websites of cities, states or countries, and statistical yearbooks of cities, countries and regions.

GDP data are from the official statistics, which are loaded from the following sources: the websites of statistics bureaux of cities, regions or states, the statistical yearbooks of cities, regions or states in each country, EU statistical reports and the related websites. If only the GVA data were available, we could then calculate the country's or the city's GDP in accordance with its similar quantitative relationship with its GVA.

Some cities' GDP data was estimated based on country data. Estimation is an approach that uses the statistics of a nation to estimate the figure for a city and it was applied in data collection for cities in Latin America and Africa. As the GDP data of some cities in South America and Africa are hard to obtain, we can only make reference to the GDP data of the country or other cities in the country; we estimated the GDP data of such cities on the basis of the relevant information or some researcher's experience.

Patent application data has been collected from the World Intellectual Property Organization (WIPO) which could be downloaded from the WIPO website.[4]

Data on crime rates were from official statistics and reports which were obtained from bureaux websites of related cities, countries and regions, the statistics yearbooks of related cities, countries and regions, the EU statistical reports, the wikipedia website,[5] the population ranking list of the World Bank, the websites of mayors and related public news media.

Carbon dioxide emissions data of the 500 cities were downloaded from the website of UNSD.[6]

Doing business index results were sourced from the 'Doing Business Report' (2013). The Doing Business report series includes annual reports going back to 2004, a wide variety of subnational studies, and a number of special reports dealing with regions in which the doing business environment in various of countries, cities or regions has been evaluated.[7]

Global network connectivity: the global network connectivity index was constructed following Taylor's global world city connectivity (GNC). According to Taylor (Taylor et al. 2002), cities are firstly coded using a six-point scale service value system according to the location strategies of multinational financial companies. If a city was scored '0' by a firm, it means that this firm did not locate any office in the city. If a city was scored '5', it means that the firm has located its headquarters in this city. Secondly, connectivity between two cities was calculated by multiplying the service values of the same firm in two cities. For example, service values of firm j in city a and city b are defined as v_{aj} and v_{bj} respectively. The city-dyad connectivity is $C_{abj} = v_{aj} \cdot v_{bj}$. Thirdly, the total world city connectivity between city a and city b is obtained by aggregating the city-dyad connectivity of all the firms. The function is as below:

$$CDC_{a \leftrightarrow b} = \sum_j CDC_{ab.j} = \sum_j V_{aj} \times V_{bj} \text{ (where } a \neq b)$$

Therefore, the total global network connectivity for city a follows the below equation:

$$GNC_a = GNC_b = \sum_b CDC_{ab} \text{ (where } a \neq b)$$

Our global connectivity is distinguished from the original vision, as we take economic connections created by multinational corporations covering a variety of sectors instead of financial services. The multinational corporations were sourced from Forbes 2000.

Based on a study of the indices and standards of the United Nations Statistical Division

---

4   http://www.wipo.int/.

5   http://en.wikipedia.org/wiki/Main_Page.

6   http://unstats.un.org/unsd/ENVIRONMENT/qindicators.htm.

7   http://www.doingbusiness.org/reports/.

(UNSD), World Bank World Development Indexes, OECD Database and other international organizations, we determined an approach for the conversion of data of each country and set up the most appropriate, comparable and widely used statistical standards for data collection and processing. Eventually, we were able to build a uniform database to cover the 500 international cities.

ASSESSMENT AND CALCULATION METHODS

Since the data representing different competitiveness components are various in unit, non-dimensionalization processing has been conducted to convert data into non-unit values. The rescaling of the six variables follows the standardized equations as below:

(1) z-score rescaling

$$X_i = \frac{(x_i - \bar{x})}{Q^2}$$

where x_i is the original data, $\bar{x}$ is the mean value, Q^2 is the standard deviation and X_i is the standardized data.

(2) Exponential rescaling

$$X_i = \frac{x_i}{x_{0i}}$$

where x_i is value of the original data, x_{0i} is the maximum value and X_i represents the transferred data.

(3) 0-1 scaling

$$X_i = \frac{(x_i - x_{min})}{(x_{max} - x_{min})}$$

where X_i is the transferred value of x_i, x_i is the original data, x_{max} is the maximum value of the data set and x_{min} is the minimum value.

Each of the six sustainable competitiveness components referring to Social Cohesion, Environmental Quality, Cultural Diversity, Technological Innovation, Global Connection and Government Management has been represented by one single variable. Different standardized methods have been used according to the characteristics of different variables.

Economic Dynamic is composed of GDP per capita and GDP growth rate. These two variables have been standardized individually and then synthesized together with weightings of 1/3 and 2/3 respectively.

The comprehensive Sustainable Competitiveness index was synthesized with equal weighting methods.

$$Z_i = \sum_l z_{il}$$

where Z_i represents the sustainable competitiveness index and z_{il} represents the seven competitiveness component subgroups.

REFERENCES

Ache, P., H. T. Andersen, T. Maloutas, M. Raco and T. Tasan-Kok (2008), *Cities Between Competitiveness and Cohesion: Discourses, Realities and Implementation*, Springer.

Angel, D. P. and J. Engstrom (1995), Manufacturing systems and technological change: the US personal computer industry, *Economic Geography*, 79–102.

Balkyte, A. and M. Tvaronavičiene (2010), Perception of competitiveness in the context of sustainable development: facets of 'sustainable competitiveness', *Journal of Business Economics and Management*, 11, 341–365.

Bathelt, H., A. Malmberg and P. Maskell (2004), Clusters and knowledge: local buzz, global pipelines and the process of knowledge creation, *Progress in Human Geography*, 28, 31–56.

Begg, I. (1999), Cities and competitiveness, *Urban Studies*, 36, 795–809.

Berg, L. v. d., J. v. d. Meer and L. Carvalho (2014), *Cities as Engines of Sustainable Competitiveness*, Ashgate Pub. Co.

Bontis, N. (2004), National intellectual capital index: a United Nations initiative for the Arab region, *Journal of Intellectual Capital*, 5, 13–39.

Breheny, M. J. (1992), *Sustainable Development and Urban Form*, Pion.

Budd, L. and A. Hirmis (2004), Conceptual framework for regional competitiveness, *Regional Studies*, 38, 1015–1028.

Burton, E., M. Jenks and K. Williams (2013), *Achieving Sustainable Urban Form*, Routledge.

Camagni, R. (2002), On the concept of territorial competitiveness: sound or misleading? *Urban Studies*, 39, 2395–2411.

Castells, M. (2011), *The Rise of the Network Society: The Information Age: Economy, Society, and Culture*, John Wiley & Sons.

Ellen, I. G. and K. O'Regan (2010), Crime and urban flight revisited: the effect of the 1990s drop in crime on cities, *Journal of Urban Economics*, 68, 247–259.

European Commission (2010), *Europe 2020: A Strategy for Smart, Sustainable and Inclusive Growth*, Brussels: European Commission.

Flarey, D. L. (1996), Managing in a time of great change, *Journal of Nursing Administration*, 26, 16–17.

Florida, R. (2002), The economic geography of talent, *Annals of the Association of American Geographers*, 92, 743–755.

Garden, C. and R. L. Martin (2003), A study on the factors of regional competitiveness, In a draft final report for The European Commission Directorate-General Regional Policy.

Glaeser, E. L. and J. M. Shapiro (2001), *City Growth and the 2000 Census: Which Places Grew, and Why*, Brookings Institution, Center on Urban and Metropolitan Policy.

Greif, A. (1994), Cultural beliefs and the organization of society: a historical and theoretical reflection on collectivist and individualist societies, *Journal of Political Economy*, 912–

950.

Huggins, R. and N. Clifton (2011), Competitiveness, creativity, and place-based development, *Environment and Planning-Part A*, 43, 1341.

Jacobs, J. (1969), *The Economy of Cities*, New York: Random House.

Kamal-Chaoui, L. and A. Roberts (eds) (2009), Competitive cities and climate change, OECD Regional Development Working Papers No. 2, OECD Publishing.

Kern, K., G. Alber and S. Energy (2008), Governing climate change in cities: modes of urban climate governance in multi-level systems, *Competitive Cities and Climate Change*, 171.

Kitchen, P. and A. Williams (2010), Quality of life and perceptions of crime in Saskatoon, Canada, *Social Indicators Research*, 95, 33–61.

Kitson, M., R. Martin and P. Tyler (2004), Regional competitiveness: an elusive yet key concept? *Regional Studies*, 38, 991–999.

Kresl, P. K. (1995), The determinants of urban competitiveness: a survey, in P. K. Kresl and G. Gappert (eds), *North American Cities and the Global Economy*, Thousand Oaks, CA: Sage, pp. 45–68.

Lever, W. F. (2002a), Correlating the knowledge-base of cities with economic growth, *Urban Studies*, 39, 859–870.

Lever, W. F. (2002b), The knowledge base and the competitive city, in I. Begg (ed.), *Urban Competitiveness: Policies for Dynamic Cities*, The Policy Press.

Malecki, E. (1997), *Technology and Economic Development: The Dynamics of Local, Regional, and National Change* (2nd edn), New York: John Wiley.

Markgren, B. (2001), Is proximity a geographical question in business relationships? Working Papers, Uppsala: Uppsala University, Department of Business Studies.

Martin, R. and J. Simmie (2008), The theoretical bases of urban competitiveness: does proximity matter? *Revue d'Économie Régionale & Urbaine*, 333–351.

Myerson, R. B. (2013), *Game Theory*, Harvard University Press.

Ni, P. (2012), *The Global Urban Competitiveness Report - 2011*, Edward Elgar Publishing.

Ni, P. (2013), *The Global Urban Competitiveness Report - 2013*, Social Science Documentation Publishing House.

Ni, P., P. Kresl and X. Li (2014), China urban competitiveness in industrialization: based on the panel data of 25 cities in China from 1990 to 2009, *Urban Studies*.

Ni, P. and W. Pan (2010), The strategic outline for building Chengdu into a world-class modern garden city, *Urban Insight* (in Chinese), 4, 110–124.

OECD (2008), Competitive cities in a changing climate: an issues paper, *in Competitive Cities and Climate Change*, OECD Conference Proceedings, Milan, 9–10 October 2008, Paris: OECD Publications.

Porter, M. E. (1998), Clusters and the new economics of competition, *Harvard Business Review*, November, 77–90.

Porter, M. E., C. H. Ketels, K. Miller and R. Bryden (2004), *Competitiveness in Rural US Regions: Learning and Research Agenda*, Boston, MA: Harvard Business School Institute for Strategy and Competitiveness.

Quigley, J. M. (1998), Urban diversity and economic growth, *Journal of Economic Perspectives*, 12, 127–138.

Rabin, M. (1993), Incorporating fairness into game theory and economics, *Advances in Behavioral Economics*, 297.

Ranci, C. (2011), Competitiveness and social cohesion in western European cities, *Urban Studies*, 48, 2789–2804.

Rogerson, R. J. (1999), Quality of life and city competitiveness, *Urban Studies*, 36, 969–985.

Satterthwaite, D. (1999), *The Earthscan Reader in Sustainable Cities*, London: Earthscan.

Schotter, A. (2008), *The Economic Theory of Social Institutions*, Cambridge: Cambridge University Press.

Storper, M. (1997), *The Regional World: Territorial Development in a Global Economy*, New York: Guilford Press.

Taylor, P. J. (2001), Specification of the world city network, *Geographical Analysis*, 33, 181–194.

Taylor, P. J. (2004), *World City Network: A Global Urban Analysis*, New York: Routledge.

Taylor, P. J., G. Catalano and D. R. F. Walker (2002), Measurement of the world city network, *Urban Studies*, 39, 2367–2376.

Taylor, P. J., M. Hoyler, D. R. Walker and M. J. Szegner (2001), A new mapping of the world for the new millennium, *The Geographical Journal*, 167, 213–222.

Thompson, N. and N. Ward (2005), Rural areas and regional competitiveness, Report to Local Government Rural Network, Centre for Rural Economy, University of Newcastle upon Tyne.

Turok, I. (2004), Cities, regions and competitiveness, *Regional Studies*, 38, 1069–1083.

UN-Habitat (2010), *The State of African Cities 2010: Governance, Inequality and Urban Land Markets*, United Nations.

Wheeler, S. M. and T. Beatley (2004), *The Sustainable Urban Development Reader*, New York: Routledge.

Wolff, F., K. Schmitt and C. Hochfeld (2007), Competitiveness, innovation and sustainability: clarifying the concepts and their interrelations, Berlin: Öko-Institut, retrieved November 26, 2008.

World Bank (2013), *Doing Business 2013: Smarter Regulations for Small and Medium-Size Enterprises*, World Bank.

2. Global urban sustainable competitiveness index

Wei Liu,[1] Mian Li,[2] Jie Yang[3] and Shaokun Wei[4]

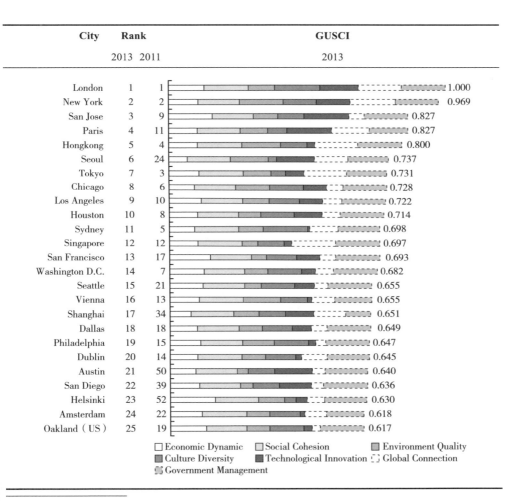

City	Rank 2013	Rank 2011	GUSCI 2013
London	1	1	1.000
New York	2	2	0.969
San Jose	3	9	0.827
Paris	4	11	0.827
Hongkong	5	4	0.800
Seoul	6	24	0.737
Tokyo	7	3	0.731
Chicago	8	6	0.728
Los Angeles	9	10	0.722
Houston	10	8	0.714
Sydney	11	5	0.698
Singapore	12	12	0.697
San Francisco	13	17	0.693
Washington D.C.	14	7	0.682
Seattle	15	21	0.655
Vienna	16	13	0.655
Shanghai	17	34	0.651
Dallas	18	18	0.649
Philadelphia	19	15	0.647
Dublin	20	14	0.645
Austin	21	50	0.640
San Diego	22	39	0.636
Helsinki	23	52	0.630
Amsterdam	24	22	0.618
Oakland (US)	25	19	0.617

□ Economic Dynamic □ Social Cohesion ■ Environment Quality
■ Culture Diversity ■ Technological Innovation ⸬ Global Connection
▒ Government Management

1   Wei Liu, Center of City and Competitiveness, CASS. No. 2 yuetanbeixiaojie, Xicheng District, Beijing, China, post code: 100836, Tel: 8610-68063478. Email: lwcass@163.com.

2   Mian Li, Center of City and Competitiveness, CASS. No. 2 yuetanbeixiaojie, Xicheng District, Beijing, China, post code: 100836, Tel: 8610-68063478. Email: limian_plan@163.com.

3   Jie Yang, Center of City and Competitiveness, CASS. No. 2 yuetanbeixiaojie, Xicheng District, Beijing, China, post code: 100836, Tel: 8610-68063478. Email: j. yang. sec@163.com.

4   Shaokun Wei, Department of Policy Research, China Center for Urban Development, Beijing, China, post code: 100836, Tel: 8610-68063478. Email: weishaokun@sina.com.

City	Rank	GUSCI
	2013 2011	2013

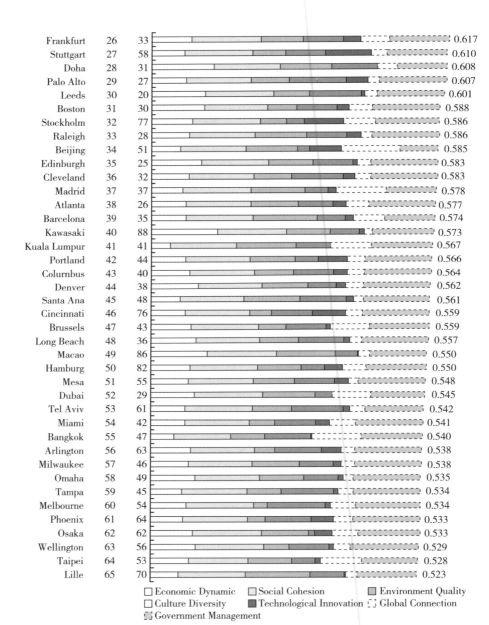

City	2013	2011	GUSCI 2013
Frankfurt	26	33	0.617
Stuttgart	27	58	0.610
Doha	28	31	0.608
Palo Alto	29	27	0.607
Leeds	30	20	0.601
Boston	31	30	0.588
Stockholm	32	77	0.586
Raleigh	33	28	0.586
Beijing	34	51	0.585
Edinburgh	35	25	0.583
Cleveland	36	32	0.583
Madrid	37	37	0.578
Atlanta	38	26	0.577
Barcelona	39	35	0.574
Kawasaki	40	88	0.573
Kuala Lumpur	41	41	0.567
Portland	42	44	0.566
Columbus	43	40	0.564
Denver	44	38	0.562
Santa Ana	45	48	0.561
Cincinnati	46	76	0.559
Brussels	47	43	0.559
Long Beach	48	36	0.557
Macao	49	86	0.550
Hamburg	50	82	0.550
Mesa	51	55	0.548
Dubai	52	29	0.545
Tel Aviv	53	61	0.542
Miami	54	42	0.541
Bangkok	55	47	0.540
Arlington	56	63	0.538
Milwaukee	57	46	0.538
Omaha	58	49	0.535
Tampa	59	45	0.534
Melbourne	60	54	0.534
Phoenix	61	64	0.533
Osaka	62	62	0.533
Wellington	63	56	0.529
Taipei	64	53	0.528
Lille	65	70	0.523

☐ Economic Dynamic   ☐ Social Cohesion   ▨ Environment Quality
☐ Culture Diversity   ■ Technological Innovation   ⫶ Global Connection
▨ Government Management

City	Rank		GUSCI
	2013	2011	2013

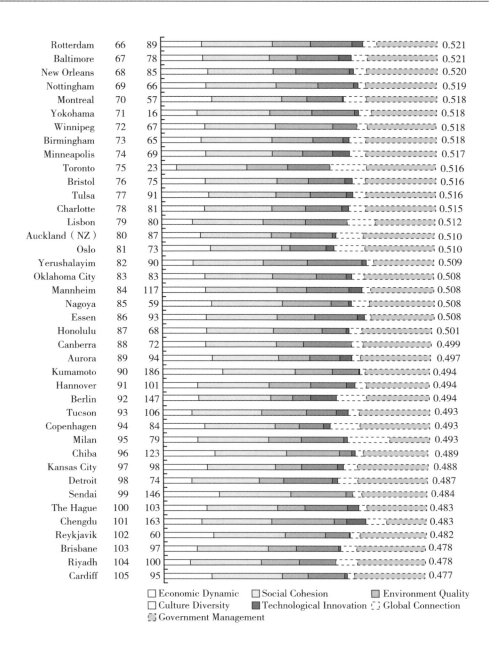

City	2013	2011	GUSCI 2013
Rotterdam	66	89	0.521
Baltimore	67	78	0.521
New Orleans	68	85	0.520
Nottingham	69	66	0.519
Montreal	70	57	0.518
Yokohama	71	16	0.518
Winnipeg	72	67	0.518
Birmingham	73	65	0.518
Minneapolis	74	69	0.517
Toronto	75	23	0.516
Bristol	76	75	0.516
Tulsa	77	91	0.516
Charlotte	78	81	0.515
Lisbon	79	80	0.512
Auckland (NZ)	80	87	0.510
Oslo	81	73	0.510
Yerushalayim	82	90	0.509
Oklahoma City	83	83	0.508
Mannheim	84	117	0.508
Nagoya	85	59	0.508
Essen	86	93	0.508
Honolulu	87	68	0.501
Canberra	88	72	0.499
Aurora	89	94	0.497
Kumamoto	90	186	0.494
Hannover	91	101	0.494
Berlin	92	147	0.494
Tucson	93	106	0.493
Copenhagen	94	84	0.493
Milan	95	79	0.493
Chiba	96	123	0.489
Kansas City	97	98	0.488
Detroit	98	74	0.487
Sendai	99	146	0.484
The Hague	100	103	0.483
Chengdu	101	163	0.483
Reykjavik	102	60	0.482
Brisbane	103	97	0.478
Riyadh	104	100	0.478
Cardiff	105	95	0.477

□ Economic Dynamic □ Social Cohesion ▨ Environment Quality
□ Culture Diversity ■ Technological Innovation ⊡ Global Connection
▨ Government Management

City	Rank		GUSCI
	2013	2011	2013

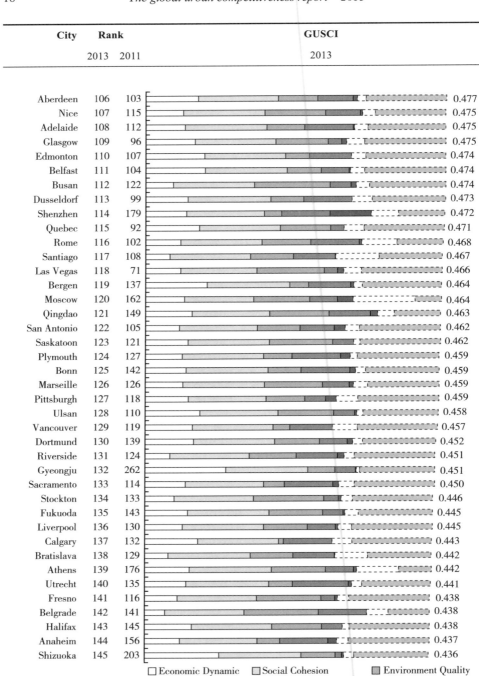

City	2013	2011	GUSCI 2013
Aberdeen	106	103	0.477
Nice	107	115	0.475
Adelaide	108	112	0.475
Glasgow	109	96	0.475
Edmonton	110	107	0.474
Belfast	111	104	0.474
Busan	112	122	0.474
Dusseldorf	113	99	0.473
Shenzhen	114	179	0.472
Quebec	115	92	0.471
Rome	116	102	0.468
Santiago	117	108	0.467
Las Vegas	118	71	0.466
Bergen	119	137	0.464
Moscow	120	162	0.464
Qingdao	121	149	0.463
San Antonio	122	105	0.462
Saskatoon	123	121	0.462
Plymouth	124	127	0.459
Bonn	125	142	0.459
Marseille	126	126	0.459
Pittsburgh	127	118	0.459
Ulsan	128	110	0.458
Vancouver	129	119	0.457
Dortmund	130	139	0.452
Riverside	131	124	0.451
Gyeongju	132	262	0.451
Sacramento	133	114	0.450
Stockton	134	133	0.446
Fukuoda	135	143	0.445
Liverpool	136	130	0.445
Calgary	137	132	0.443
Bratislava	138	129	0.442
Athens	139	176	0.442
Utrecht	140	135	0.441
Fresno	141	116	0.438
Belgrade	142	141	0.438
Halifax	143	145	0.438
Anaheim	144	156	0.437
Shizuoka	145	203	0.436

☐ Economic Dynamic   ☐ Social Cohesion   ☐ Environment Quality
☐ Culture Diversity   ☐ Technological Innovation   ☐ Global Connection
☐ Government Management

City	Rank		GUSCI
	2013	2011	2013

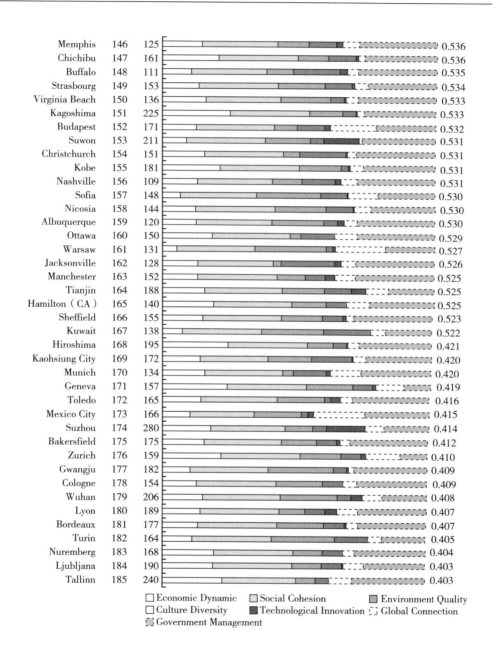

City	2013	2011	GUSCI 2013
Memphis	146	125	0.536
Chichibu	147	161	0.536
Buffalo	148	111	0.535
Strasbourg	149	153	0.534
Virginia Beach	150	136	0.533
Kagoshima	151	225	0.533
Budapest	152	171	0.532
Suwon	153	211	0.531
Christchurch	154	151	0.531
Kobe	155	181	0.531
Nashville	156	109	0.531
Sofia	157	148	0.530
Nicosia	158	144	0.530
Albuquerque	159	120	0.530
Ottawa	160	150	0.529
Warsaw	161	131	0.527
Jacksonville	162	128	0.526
Manchester	163	152	0.525
Tianjin	164	188	0.525
Hamilton（CA）	165	140	0.525
Sheffield	166	155	0.523
Kuwait	167	138	0.522
Hiroshima	168	195	0.421
Kaohsiung City	169	172	0.420
Munich	170	134	0.420
Geneva	171	157	0.419
Toledo	172	165	0.416
Mexico City	173	166	0.415
Suzhou	174	280	0.414
Bakersfield	175	175	0.412
Zurich	176	159	0.410
Gwangju	177	182	0.409
Cologne	178	154	0.409
Wuhan	179	206	0.408
Lyon	180	189	0.407
Bordeaux	181	177	0.407
Turin	182	164	0.405
Nuremberg	183	168	0.404
Ljubljana	184	190	0.403
Tallinn	185	240	0.403

☐ Economic Dynamic   ☐ Social Cohesion   ▨ Environment Quality
☐ Culture Diversity   ■ Technological Innovation   ⌐⌐ Global Connection
▨ Government Management

City	Rank		GUSCI
	2013	2011	2013

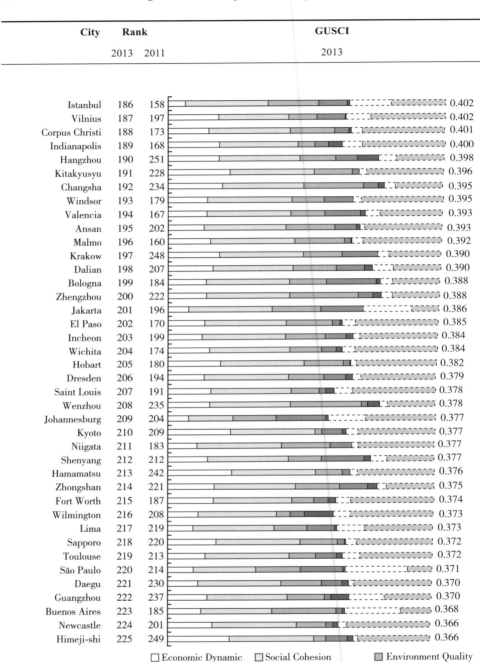

City	Rank 2013	Rank 2011	GUSCI 2013
Istanbul	186	158	0.402
Vilnius	187	197	0.402
Corpus Christi	188	173	0.401
Indianapolis	189	168	0.400
Hangzhou	190	251	0.398
Kitakyusyu	191	228	0.396
Changsha	192	234	0.395
Windsor	193	179	0.395
Valencia	194	167	0.393
Ansan	195	202	0.393
Malmo	196	160	0.392
Krakow	197	248	0.390
Dalian	198	207	0.390
Bologna	199	184	0.388
Zhengzhou	200	222	0.388
Jakarta	201	196	0.386
El Paso	202	170	0.385
Incheon	203	199	0.384
Wichita	204	174	0.384
Hobart	205	180	0.382
Dresden	206	194	0.379
Saint Louis	207	191	0.378
Wenzhou	208	235	0.378
Johannesburg	209	204	0.377
Kyoto	210	209	0.377
Niigata	211	183	0.377
Shenyang	212	212	0.377
Hamamatsu	213	242	0.376
Zhongshan	214	221	0.375
Fort Worth	215	187	0.374
Wilmington	216	208	0.373
Lima	217	219	0.373
Sapporo	218	220	0.372
Toulouse	219	213	0.372
São Paulo	220	214	0.371
Daegu	221	230	0.370
Guangzhou	222	237	0.370
Buenos Aires	223	185	0.368
Newcastle	224	201	0.366
Himeji-shi	225	249	0.366

□ Economic Dynamic ☐ Social Cohesion ▨ Environment Quality
□ Culture Diversity ■ Technological Innovation ⌐⌐ Global Connection
▨ Government Management

City	Rank		GUSCI
	2013	2011	2013

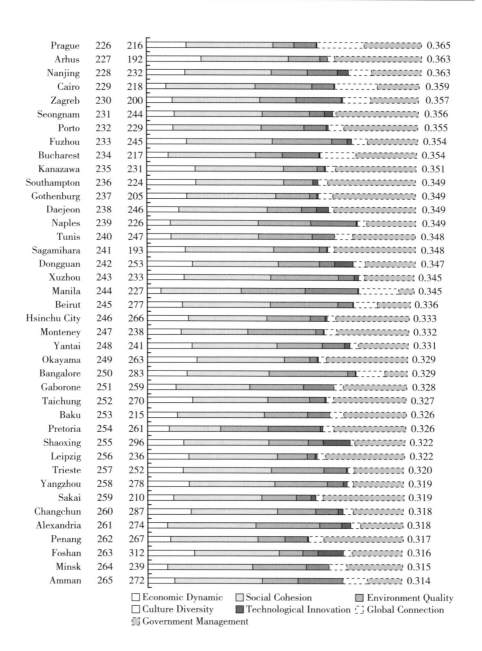

City	2013	2011	GUSCI 2013
Prague	226	216	0.365
Arhus	227	192	0.363
Nanjing	228	232	0.363
Cairo	229	218	0.359
Zagreb	230	200	0.357
Seongnam	231	244	0.356
Porto	232	229	0.355
Fuzhou	233	245	0.354
Bucharest	234	217	0.354
Kanazawa	235	231	0.351
Southampton	236	224	0.349
Gothenburg	237	205	0.349
Daejeon	238	246	0.349
Naples	239	226	0.349
Tunis	240	247	0.348
Sagamihara	241	193	0.348
Dongguan	242	253	0.347
Xuzhou	243	233	0.345
Manila	244	227	0.345
Beirut	245	277	0.336
Hsinchu City	246	266	0.333
Monteney	247	238	0.332
Yantai	248	241	0.331
Okayama	249	263	0.329
Bangalore	250	283	0.329
Gaborone	251	259	0.328
Taichung	252	270	0.327
Baku	253	215	0.326
Pretoria	254	261	0.326
Shaoxing	255	296	0.322
Leipzig	256	236	0.322
Trieste	257	252	0.320
Yangzhou	258	278	0.319
Sakai	259	210	0.319
Changchun	260	287	0.318
Alexandria	261	274	0.318
Penang	262	267	0.317
Foshan	263	312	0.316
Minsk	264	239	0.315
Amman	265	272	0.314

☐ Economic Dynamic　☐ Social Cohesion　▨ Environment Quality
☐ Culture Diversity　■ Technological Innovation　⌐⌐ Global Connection
▨ Government Management

City	Rank		GUSCI
	2013	2011	2013

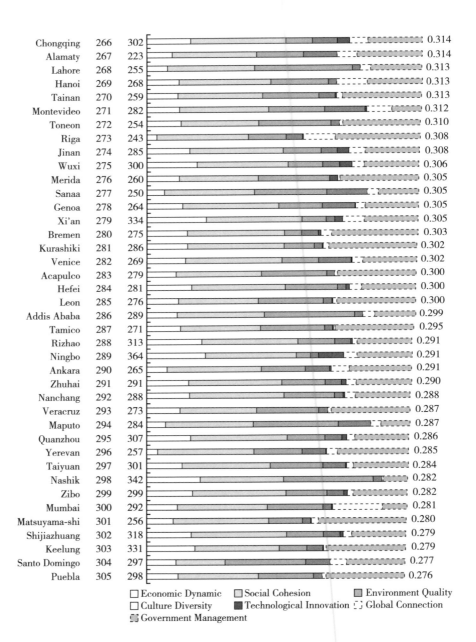

City	2013	2011	GUSCI 2013
Chongqing	266	302	0.314
Alamaty	267	223	0.314
Lahore	268	255	0.313
Hanoi	269	268	0.313
Tainan	270	259	0.313
Montevideo	271	282	0.312
Toneon	272	254	0.310
Riga	273	243	0.308
Jinan	274	285	0.308
Wuxi	275	300	0.306
Merida	276	260	0.305
Sanaa	277	250	0.305
Genoa	278	264	0.305
Xi'an	279	334	0.305
Bremen	280	275	0.303
Kurashiki	281	286	0.302
Venice	282	269	0.302
Acapulco	283	279	0.300
Hefei	284	281	0.300
Leon	285	276	0.300
Addis Ababa	286	289	0.299
Tamico	287	271	0.295
Rizhao	288	313	0.291
Ningbo	289	364	0.291
Ankara	290	265	0.291
Zhuhai	291	291	0.290
Nanchang	292	288	0.288
Veracruz	293	273	0.287
Maputo	294	284	0.287
Quanzhou	295	307	0.286
Yerevan	296	257	0.285
Taiyuan	297	301	0.284
Nashik	298	342	0.282
Zibo	299	299	0.282
Mumbai	300	292	0.281
Matsuyama-shi	301	256	0.280
Shijiazhuang	302	318	0.279
Keelung	303	331	0.279
Santo Domingo	304	297	0.277
Puebla	305	298	0.276

□ Economic Dynamic □ Social Cohesion ▨ Environment Quality
□ Culture Diversity ■ Technological Innovation ⊡ Global Connection
▨ Government Management

City	Rank		GUSCI
	2013	2011	2013

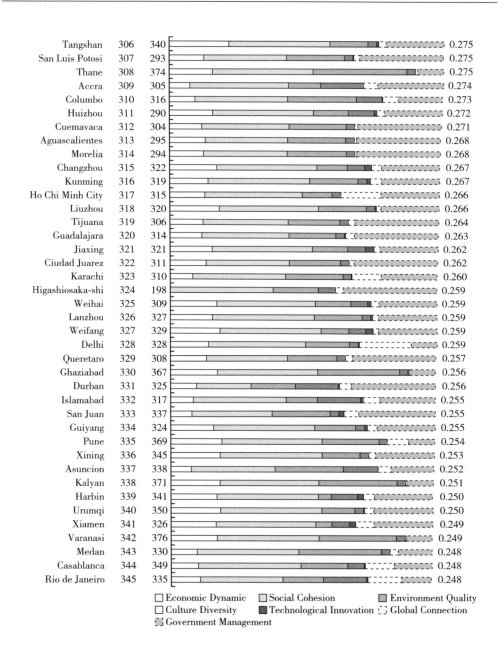

City	2013	2011	GUSCI 2013
Tangshan	306	340	0.275
San Luis Potosi	307	293	0.275
Thane	308	374	0.275
Accra	309	305	0.274
Columbo	310	316	0.273
Huizhou	311	290	0.272
Cuemavaca	312	304	0.271
Aguascalientes	313	295	0.268
Morelia	314	294	0.268
Changzhou	315	322	0.267
Kunming	316	319	0.267
Ho Chi Minh City	317	315	0.266
Liuzhou	318	320	0.266
Tijuana	319	306	0.264
Guadalajara	320	314	0.263
Jiaxing	321	321	0.262
Ciudad Juarez	322	311	0.262
Karachi	323	310	0.260
Higashiosaka-shi	324	198	0.259
Weihai	325	309	0.259
Lanzhou	326	327	0.259
Weifang	327	329	0.259
Delhi	328	328	0.259
Queretaro	329	308	0.257
Ghaziabad	330	367	0.256
Durban	331	325	0.256
Islamabad	332	317	0.255
San Juan	333	337	0.255
Guiyang	334	324	0.255
Pune	335	369	0.254
Xining	336	345	0.253
Asuncion	337	338	0.252
Kalyan	338	371	0.251
Harbin	339	341	0.250
Urumqi	340	350	0.250
Xiamen	341	326	0.249
Varanasi	342	376	0.249
Medan	343	330	0.248
Casablanca	344	349	0.248
Rio de Janeiro	345	335	0.248

☐ Economic Dynamic ☐ Social Cohesion ▦ Environment Quality
☐ Culture Diversity ■ Technological Innovation ⌐⌐ Global Connection
▥ Government Management

City	Rank		GUSCI
	2013	2011	2013

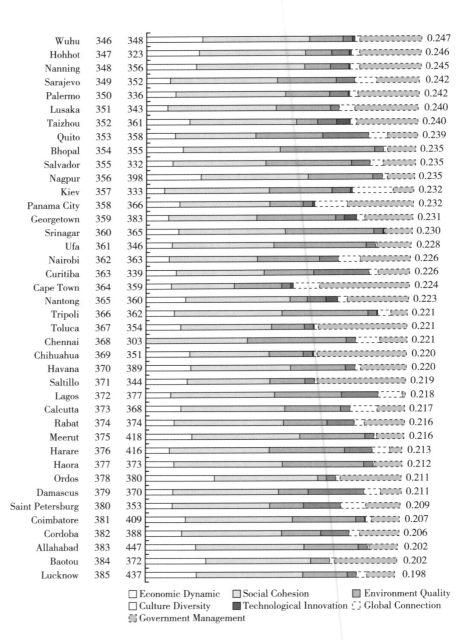

City	2013	2011	GUSCI 2013
Wuhu	346	348	0.247
Hohhot	347	323	0.246
Nanning	348	356	0.245
Sarajevo	349	352	0.242
Palermo	350	336	0.242
Lusaka	351	343	0.240
Taizhou	352	361	0.240
Quito	353	358	0.239
Bhopal	354	355	0.235
Salvador	355	332	0.235
Nagpur	356	398	0.235
Kiev	357	333	0.232
Panama City	358	366	0.232
Georgetown	359	383	0.231
Srinagar	360	365	0.230
Ufa	361	346	0.228
Nairobi	362	363	0.226
Curitiba	363	339	0.226
Cape Town	364	359	0.224
Nantong	365	360	0.223
Tripoli	366	362	0.221
Toluca	367	354	0.221
Chennai	368	303	0.221
Chihuahua	369	351	0.220
Havana	370	389	0.220
Saltillo	371	344	0.219
Lagos	372	377	0.218
Calcutta	373	368	0.217
Rabat	374	374	0.216
Meerut	375	418	0.216
Harare	376	416	0.213
Haora	377	373	0.212
Ordos	378	380	0.211
Damascus	379	370	0.211
Saint Petersburg	380	353	0.209
Coimbatore	381	409	0.207
Cordoba	382	388	0.206
Allahabad	383	447	0.202
Baotou	384	372	0.202
Lucknow	385	437	0.198

☐ Economic Dynamic   ☐ Social Cohesion   ▨ Environment Quality
☐ Culture Diversity   ■ Technological Innovation   ⸽⸽ Global Connection
▨ Government Management

City	Rank		GUSCI
	2013	2011	2013

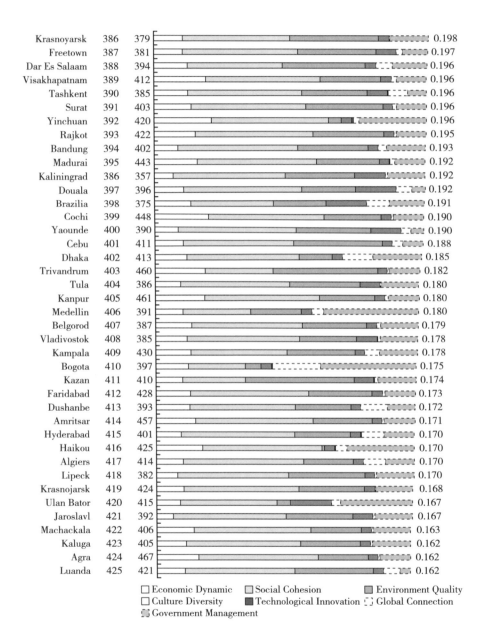

City	2013	2011	GUSCI 2013
Krasnoyarsk	386	379	0.198
Freetown	387	381	0.197
Dar Es Salaam	388	394	0.196
Visakhapatnam	389	412	0.196
Tashkent	390	385	0.196
Surat	391	403	0.196
Yinchuan	392	420	0.196
Rajkot	393	422	0.195
Bandung	394	402	0.193
Madurai	395	443	0.192
Kaliningrad	386	357	0.192
Douala	397	396	0.192
Brazilia	398	375	0.191
Cochi	399	448	0.190
Yaounde	400	390	0.190
Cebu	401	411	0.188
Dhaka	402	413	0.185
Trivandrum	403	460	0.182
Tula	404	386	0.180
Kanpur	405	461	0.180
Medellin	406	391	0.180
Belgorod	407	387	0.179
Vladivostok	408	385	0.178
Kampala	409	430	0.178
Bogota	410	397	0.175
Kazan	411	410	0.174
Faridabad	412	428	0.173
Dushanbe	413	393	0.172
Amritsar	414	457	0.171
Hyderabad	415	401	0.170
Haikou	416	425	0.170
Algiers	417	414	0.170
Lipeck	418	382	0.170
Krasnojarsk	419	424	0.168
Ulan Bator	420	415	0.167
Jaroslavl	421	392	0.167
Machackala	422	406	0.163
Kaluga	423	405	0.162
Agra	424	467	0.162
Luanda	425	421	0.162

☐ Economic Dynamic　☐ Social Cohesion　▨ Environment Quality
☐ Culture Diversity　■ Technological Innovation　⁚⁚ Global Connection
▥ Government Management

City	Rank		GUSCI
	2013	2011	2013

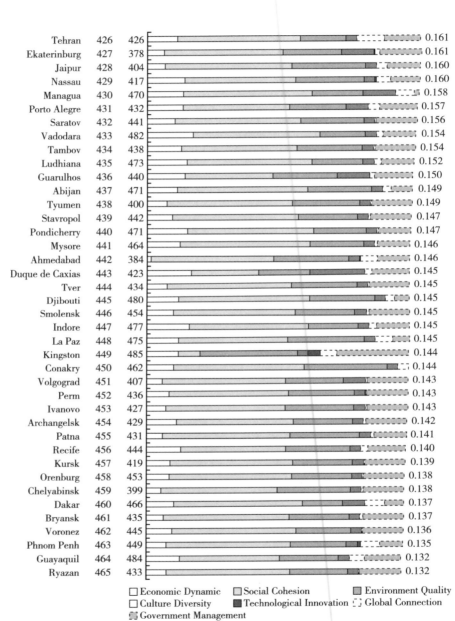

City	Rank 2013	Rank 2011	GUSCI 2013
Tehran	426	426	0.161
Ekaterinburg	427	378	0.161
Jaipur	428	404	0.160
Nassau	429	417	0.160
Managua	430	470	0.158
Porto Alegre	431	432	0.157
Saratov	432	441	0.156
Vadodara	433	482	0.154
Tambov	434	438	0.154
Ludhiana	435	473	0.152
Guarulhos	436	440	0.150
Abijan	437	471	0.149
Tyumen	438	400	0.149
Stavropol	439	442	0.147
Pondicherry	440	471	0.147
Mysore	441	464	0.146
Ahmedabad	442	384	0.146
Duque de Caxias	443	423	0.145
Tver	444	434	0.145
Djibouti	445	480	0.145
Smolensk	446	454	0.145
Indore	447	477	0.145
La Paz	448	475	0.145
Kingston	449	485	0.144
Conakry	450	462	0.144
Volgograd	451	407	0.143
Perm	452	436	0.143
Ivanovo	453	427	0.143
Archangelsk	454	429	0.142
Patna	455	431	0.141
Recife	456	444	0.140
Kursk	457	419	0.139
Orenburg	458	453	0.138
Chelyabinsk	459	399	0.138
Dakar	460	466	0.137
Bryansk	461	435	0.137
Voronez	462	445	0.136
Phnom Penh	463	449	0.135
Guayaquil	464	484	0.132
Ryazan	465	433	0.132

☐ Economic Dynamic   ☐ Social Cohesion   ▨ Environment Quality
☐ Culture Diversity   ■ Technological Innovation   ⸬ Global Connection
▨ Government Management

City	Rank		GUSCI
	2013	2011	2013

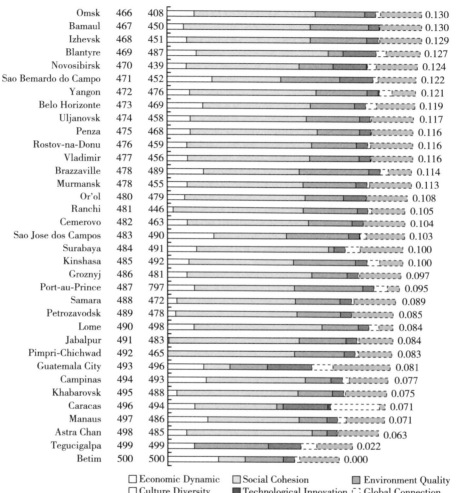

City	2013	2011	GUSCI 2013
Omsk	466	408	0.130
Bamaul	467	450	0.130
Izhevsk	468	451	0.129
Blantyre	469	487	0.127
Novosibirsk	470	439	0.124
Sao Bemardo do Campo	471	452	0.122
Yangon	472	476	0.121
Belo Horizonte	473	469	0.119
Uljanovsk	474	458	0.117
Penza	475	468	0.116
Rostov-na-Donu	476	459	0.116
Vladimir	477	456	0.116
Brazzaville	478	489	0.114
Murmansk	478	455	0.113
Or'ol	480	479	0.108
Ranchi	481	446	0.105
Cemerovo	482	463	0.104
Sao Jose dos Campos	483	490	0.103
Surabaya	484	491	0.100
Kinshasa	485	492	0.100
Groznyj	486	481	0.097
Port-au-Prince	487	797	0.095
Samara	488	472	0.089
Petrozavodsk	489	478	0.085
Lome	490	498	0.084
Jabalpur	491	483	0.084
Pimpri-Chichwad	492	465	0.083
Guatemala City	493	496	0.081
Campinas	494	493	0.077
Khabarovsk	495	488	0.075
Caracas	496	494	0.071
Manaus	497	486	0.071
Astra Chan	498	485	0.063
Tegucigalpa	499	499	0.022
Betim	500	500	0.000

☐ Economic Dynamic   ☐ Social Cohesion   ▨ Environment Quality
☐ Culture Diversity   ■ Technological Innovation   ⌐⌐ Global Connection
▨ Government Management

3. Global urban sustainable competitiveness: a comprehensive analysis

Jie Wei[1] and Pengfei Ni[2]

In the era of the city, urban development is of utmost importance to peoples, companies, regions, and nations. Economic crisis, social exclusion, resource scarcity, climate change, environmental pollution, demographic changes, public awakening, and political confrontation mean that the city and the world not only face the threat of competition with each other, but they also face challenges to sustainable development. To create a better future for the world, we must enhance the sustainable competitiveness of its cities.

We selected 500 sample cities (see Chapter 16) and seven key indicators, including economic power, technological innovation, social cohesion, environment, global linkages, government management, and cultural diversity to create Global Urban Sustainable Competitiveness Indices (GUSCI) for 2011and 2013. Using these GUSCI, this report analyzes the development structure, development characteristics, development trends, and reasons for the sustainable competitiveness of cities around the world.

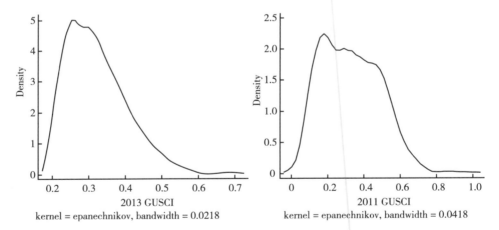

Figure 3.1   *Comparison of GUSCI Distributions for 2011 and 2013*

1   Jie Wei, School of Economics and Management, No. 1 Xuefu Avenue, Changan District, Xian, China. Email: winnie19860115@163.com.

2   Pengfei Ni, Center of City and Competitiveness, CASS. No. 2 yuetanbeixiaojie, Xicheng District, Beijing, China, post code: 100836, Tel: 8610-68063478. Email: ni_pengfei@163.com.

GENERAL FINDINGS: GLOBAL URBAN COMPETITIVENESS INCREASED OVERALL; EMERGING ECONOMY CITIES WERE A HIGHLIGHT

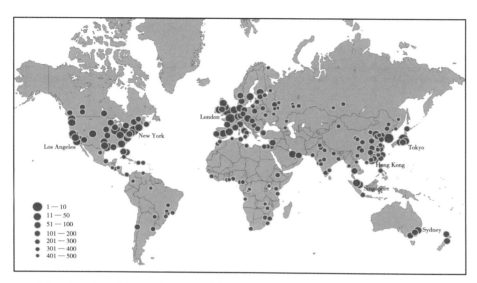

Figure 3.2   Regional Distribution of GUSCI Cities 2013

Pattern: Usual Suspects Continued to Do Well; Emerging Market Urban Competitiveness Increased

Analysis of the 2013 GUSCI shows a basic trend: the usual suspects in developed countries remained strong, while emerging market cities accelerated their pace of advance and urban competitiveness increased significantly. We have four exhibits to demonstrate this pattern.

Exhibit 1: Secondary Cities of Developed Countries Performed Well; Capitals of Emerging Market Countries Played Leading Roles

European and American metropolises, by virtue of their great social, economic, and cultural advantages, as well as their soft and hard environmental aspects accumulated over the years, are still at the top end of the global competitiveness rankings. The top ten cities in the 2013 GUSCI rankings (see Table 3.1) are all capitals or economic and financial centers of developed countries, with the exception of Seoul. Looking at the changes from 2011 to 2013, San Jose on America's west coast is undoubtedly the biggest bright spot. Relying on California's advantages in technology, San Jose has developed a strong comparative advantage in computers, aerospace equipment, and other high-tech industries. At the same time, San Jose's strong points, such as being America's safest city, have propelled it into the top three in the competitiveness rankings. The development potential and charm of America's small and medium cities can be seen at a glance in San Jose.

Another bright spot in the GUSCI top ten is Seoul, whose ranking rose 18 places between 2011 and 2013 to tenth. South Korea has been a fast-growing emerging market economy in the past few years and Seoul, as the country's capital and largest city, has harnessed the opportunity to enhance its competiveness. Its large and prosperous business district, position as one of East Asia's financial centers, and high degree of digitization have made Seoul a leader among emerging market cities and have led the city's own development.

Table 3.1   Top Ten GUSCI Rankings and Changes

	London	New York	San Jose	Paris	Hong Kong	Seoul	Tokyo	Chicago	Los Angeles	Houston
2013	1	2	3	4	5	6	7	8	9	10
2011	1	2	9	11	4	24	3	6	10	8
Change	0	0	+6	+7	-1	+18	-4	-2	+1	-2

Exhibit 2: Urban Competitiveness in East Asian Emerging Economies Increased Significantly Assisted by High Incomes

From changes to their competitiveness rankings between 2011 and 2013, one can see that Asian cities rose most in the rankings (see Figure 3.2): South Korea (one spot), China (five spots), Japan (three spots), and India (one spot). Emerging market economies represented by Asia have used the international division of labor to play to their advantage and increase their manufacturing capabilities, increasingly becoming important destinations for global capital. Cities in emerging market economies have likewise harnessed this development. At the same time we also discover a basic fact: the enhancement of competitiveness in emerging cities increases the income level of residents, and concern for the welfare of the people is an important advance.

Table 3.2   Top Ten Highest Risers in the GUSCI Rankings 2013

City	Region	Size	Income	2013	2011	Change
Gyeongju	Asia	Small	High	132	262	+130
Suzhou	Asia	Very Large	Medium	174	280	+106
Kumamoto	Asia	Medium	Higher	90	186	+96
Ningbo	Asia	Very Large	Medium	289	364	+75
Kagoshima	Asia	Medium	High	151	225	+74
Shenzhen	Asia	Very Large	Middle	114	179	+65
Allahabad	Asia	Large	Low	383	447	+64
Chengdu	Asia	Very Large	Lower	101	163	+62
Hangzhou	Asia	Very Large	Middle	190	251	+61
Shizuoka	Asia	Medium	High	145	203	+58

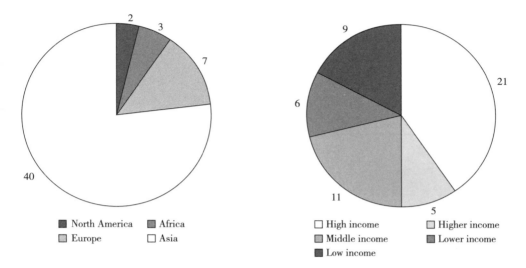

Figure 3.3   Regional Distribution and Income Distribution of Top 50 Highest Risers in the GUSCI Rankings 2013[3]

Exhibit 3: There is Serious Divergence Among Japanese Cities; Larger Does Not Necessarily Mean More Competitive

Looking at the ten cities with the largest declines in GUSCI rankings between 2011 and 2013, one first sees that Japanese cities have a serious divergence in competitiveness. Although Japan has three of the top ten highest-rising cities, it also has four in the top ten declining cities: Higashi-Osaka, Yokohama, Sakai, and Sagamihara. From the divergence in the development of Japanese cities and the cities with the largest declines in competitiveness, one can see that the proportion occupied by giant cities, very large cities, and large cities among the 50 cities with the largest declines in competitiveness was 37.5 percent. This is a wakeup call for urban development to recognize increasingly serious "urban diseases." More important than increasing the size of cities may be increasing innovation in urban planning.

Table 3.3   Top Ten Cities for Declining GUSCI Rankings 2013

City Name	Region	Size	Income	2013	2011	Change
Higashi-Osaka (Japan)	Asia	Small	Higher	324	198	-126
Chennai (India)	Asia	Very Large	Low	368	303	-65
Chelyabinsk (Russia)	Europe	Large	Lower	459	399	-60
Omsk (Russia)	Europe	Large	Lower	466	408	-58
Ahmedabad (India)	Asia	Very Large	Low	442	384	-58
Yokohama (Japan)	Asia	Very Large	Higher	71	16	-55

---

3   There are repeat listings in the number of risers, so 52 cities are included here.

Table 3.3   (continued)

City Name	Region	Size	Income	2013	2011	Change
Toronto (Canada)	North America	Giant	Lower	75	23	-52
Ekaterinburg (Russia)	Europe	Large	Lower	427	378	-49
Sakai (Japan)	Asia	Medium	Higher	259	210	-49
Sagamihara (Japan)	Asia	Medium	Higher	241	193	-48

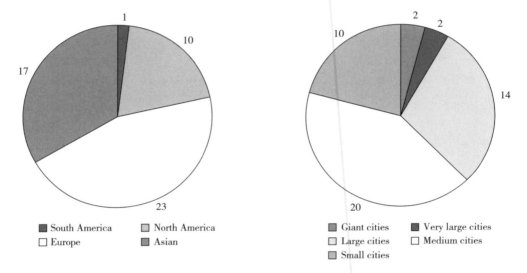

Figure 3.4   Regional Distribution and City-size Distribution of the Top 50 Cities with Declining GUSCI Rankings[4]

Exhibit 4: Most and Least Competitive Cities Were Stable; Number of Functions Is Key to Urban Competitiveness

Comparing the 2013 and 2011 rankings, one finds that nineteen cities had rankings that did not change (see Table 3.4). The positive city and reciprocal city did not change, nor did frontrunners including Singapore and Dallas, nor the least competitive cities such as Tehran. This indicates a certain degree of solidification in competitiveness among the most and least competitive cities.

Meanwhile, we compared the average number of city functions of the 19 cities with the largest rises and largest declines in urban competitiveness with the 19 cities whose rankings did not change (see Figure 3.5) and discovered the more functions a city has, the easier it is for it to maintain its position in the global competitiveness rankings. In addition to the first and second-place London and New York, Madrid, Osaka, Singapore, and Kuala Lumpur also had five functions.

---

4   Like the above, due to overlap, there is a total of 48 cities.

Table 3.4   Cities with Stable GUSCI Rankings from 2011 to 2013

City	London	New York	Singapore	Dallas	Madrid	Kuala Lumpur	Osaka	Oklahoma City	Marseille	Bakersfield
Ranking	1	2	12	18	37	41	62	83	126	175

City	Shenyang	Zhuhai	Zibo	Jiaxing	Delhi	Rabat	Tehran	Tegucigalpa	Betim
Ranking	212	291	299	321	328	374	426	499	500

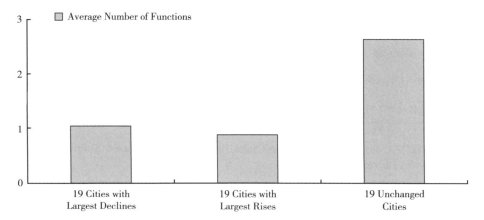

Figure 3.5   Average Number of Functions for the 19 Top Declining Cities, Rising Cities, and Stable Cities in the Competitiveness Rankings

Growth and Differences: Overall Competitiveness Increased; Lagging Cities Narrowed the Gap

Through analysis of the mean and coefficient of variation of the 2013 GUSCI, one finds that global competitiveness overall exhibited a significant rising trend. At the same time, the trend of cities in backward countries represented by Brazil, India, Russia, and China (BRIC) narrowing the gap is increasingly clear. We have three exhibits to prove this finding.

Exhibit 1: Average GUSCI Increased; Gap Has Narrowed

We compared the average and coefficient of variation of the GUSCI for 500 cities. In 2013, the average GUSCI was 4.9 percent higher than in 2011. The coefficient of variation fell 3.7 percent over the same period, signifying that the gap between cities had shrunk as cities competed with each other.

We compared the GUSCI averages and coefficients of variation for five levels of cities for 2011 and 2013 (see Table 3.5). One can see that the 2013 averages for middle-competitive, less-competitive, and least-competitive cities rose rather significantly, clearly more than in the most competitive and more competitive cities. In terms of the coefficient of variation, the decline was greatest among the least-competitive cities, followed by less competitive cities and middle-competitive cities. Such data reflect the optimum conclusion: cities with relatively lagging competitiveness, faced with increasingly intense global competition, are narrowing the gap with more competitive cities by improving their software and hardware and accelerating development. At the same time, the gap among lagging cities has narrowed. This further shows that in the midst of fierce global competition, striving to develop and catch up has become a major trend.

Table 3.5   Changes from 2011 to 2013 in Each Level of City

		2013	2011	Change
Most Competitive (Top 100)	Mean	0.353	0.337	0.016
	Coefficient of Variation	0.465	0.478	-0.013
More Competitive (100-200)	Mean	0.352	0.336	0.016
	Coefficient of Variation	0.457	0.470	-0.013
Middle Competitive (200-300)	Mean	0.345	0.328	0.017
	Coefficient of Variation	0.464	0.479	-0.015
Less Competitive (300-400)	Mean	0.325	0.308	0.017
	Coefficient of Variation	0.489	0.510	-0.021
Least Competitive (400-500)	Mean	0.320	0.303	0.017
	Coefficient of Variation	0.506	0.528	-0.022

Exhibit 2: South American and African Cities Presented a "Pyramid Shape;" Asian City Competitiveness Increased Most

In Figure 3.7, we show the 2013 average GUSCI values for cities according to continent. In descending order, they are Australia, North America, Europe, Asia, Africa, and South America. In separating each continent's cities into the categories of most competitive, more competitive, middle competitive, less competitive, and least competitive (see Figure 3.6), we found that Australia and North America presented "upside-down pyramids," with a greater number of more competitive cities. Europe, the third-most competitive continent, presented a "dumbbell" shape, with more cities in the more competitive and less competitive categories. Asia presented an "olive-shaped" trend, with few cities on the ends and middle-competitive cities making up the most. Africa and South America, the least competitive continents, presented "pyramid shaped," with less competitive and least competitive cities being more numerous.

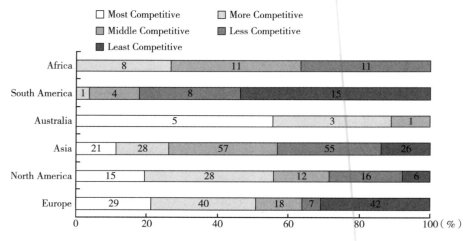

Figure 3.6   Distribution among Various Levels of Competitiveness for Cities by Continent

Comparing GUSCI scores for 2011 and 2013, Africa had the highest growth rate, followed by Asia, and then South America. At the same time, the coefficients of variation for these three continents fell overall in 2013, indicating that relatively backward cities represented on these three continents were leaders in increasing competitiveness, and the overall gap between cities narrowed. Growth in competitiveness was slower for already more competitive Europe, North America, and Australia, and the coefficients of variation also experienced varying degrees of growth. This all goes to show that the competitiveness gap among cities is narrowing, and cities in emerging economies are accelerating the development of their competitiveness.

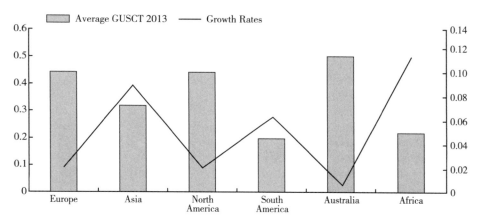

Figure 3.7   Average GUSCI Values and their Growth Rates 2013

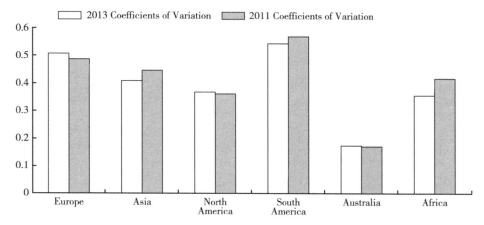

Figure 3.8   Coefficients of Variation by Continent for 2013 and 2011

Exhibit 3: BRICS City Competitiveness Increased Significantly; Gap Narrowed Faster Than World Average

Comparing the average GUSCI values for Brazil, Russia, India, China, and South Africa (BRICS) in 2013 and 2011, with the exception of Russia, which saw a slight decline, competitiveness in the other four countries grew significantly. India's grew the fastest, followed by China and South Africa. In terms of a horizontal comparison (see Figure 3.10), the BRICS GUSCI growth rate was significantly higher than those of the Big Five developed countries (the U.S., Japan, England, Germany, and France) and the world average, and the decline in the coefficient of variation was far greater than among developed countries and the world average. This shows that competitiveness in emerging economy cities has increased relatively quickly, while at the same time the gap between these cities has narrowed, strengthening the group's advantage.

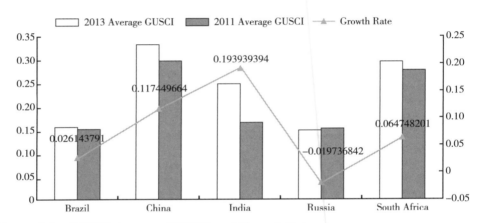

Figure 3.9   BRICS Average GUSCI and Growth Rate

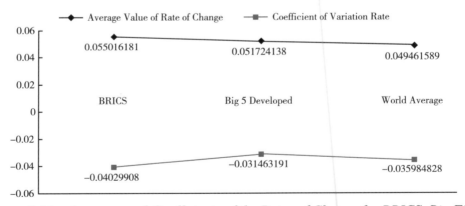

Figure 3.10   Averages and Coefficients of the Rates of Change for BRICS, Big Five Developed Countries, and World Average

REASON: INNOVATION IS AN INEXHAUSTIBLE DRIVING FORCE OF URBAN COMPETITIVENESS; KEY TO DEVELOPMENT LIES IN ABILITY TO IMPROVE GOVERNANCE

To analyze the pattern presented by global competitiveness and the reasons for growth and changes, we must mainly look at the seven dimensions of the GUSCI: economic dynamic, environmental quality, social cohesion, technological innovation, global linkages, cultural diversity, and governance.

1. Economic Cause: Per Capita GDP Most Important Factor in Improving Competitiveness; China's GDP Growth Has Been Eye-Catching

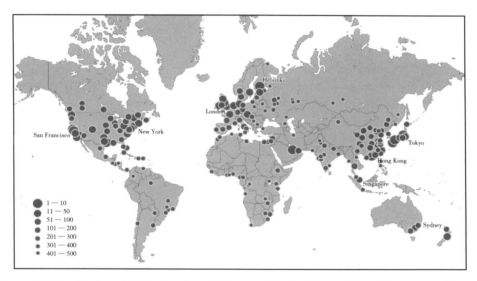

Figure 3.11   Regional Distribution of Economically Flourishing, Dynamic Cities 2013

By plotting points and fitting curves for the GUSCI and per capita GDP of the 500 sample cities, one finds that per capita GDP and GUSCI exhibit a significant positive relationship. This means that in today's rapidly urbanizing world, although the factors affecting cities are more and more numerous, economic development is still the most important. The top ten cities by per capita GDP were: London, Leeds, Geneva, Helsinki, Gyeongju, Washington D.C., Boston, San Francisco, San Jose, and Oakland. The top ten cities by GDP growth rate were: Suzhou, Hangzhou, Ningbo, Xi'an, Rizhao, Changsha, Tangshan, Ordos, Kawasaki, and Kumamoto, eight of which are Chinese and two of which are Japanese. This illustrates that cities in emerging economies represented by China are relying on the rapidly increasing economic strength of their countries to constantly accumulate per capita GDP through high GDP growth rates, further enhancing urban competitiveness, and narrowing the urban competitiveness gap with developed countries.

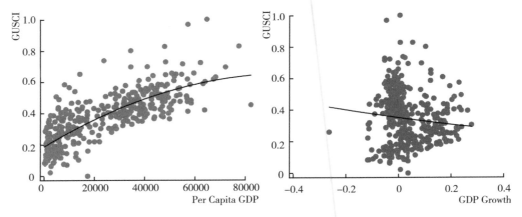

Figure 3.12   Scatter Plots for Per Capita GDP, GDP Growth Rates, and GUSCI for 500 Sample Cities

2. Social and Environmental Causes: Middle-Competitive Cities Most Restricted by Social Cohesion; Lagging Cities Need to Resolve Environmental Problems

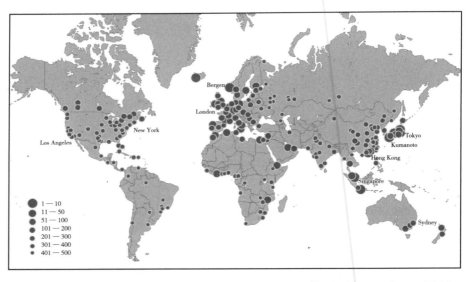

Figure 3.13   Regional Distribution of Inclusive, Socially Cohesive Cities 2013

We obtained the correlation coefficients of the remaining six dimensions and GUSCI. One can see that environmental and social indicators such as "per capita CO_2 emissions" and the "crime rate" are negatively correlated with urban competitiveness. So the health and sound development of the environment and society are fundamental constraints to enhancing competitiveness.

Table 3.6   Correlation between GUSCI and Various Indicators

	Environment	Society	Science and Technology	Linkages	Culture	Government Control
GUSCI	-0.1148	-0.3228	0.6224	0.646	0.7333	0.7853

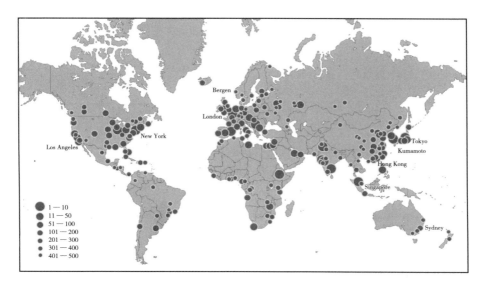

Figure 3.14   Regional Distribution of Eco-Friendly Cities 2013

Comparing the average per capita CO_2 emissions and crime rates for the five levels of cities (see Figure 3.14), we find that middle-competitive cities are equivalent to the more competitive categories of cities in environmental aspects, but crime rates are significantly higher than in more competitive cities–5.8 percent higher than in the most competitive and more competitive cities. This indicates that there is a gap between midstream cities and cities with good performance in social construction and competitiveness. Second, the least competitive cities had per capita CO_2 emissions 8.7 percent higher and crime rates 21.05 percent higher than the most competitive cities. The ten cities with the worst environmental quality were: Atrakhan, Baotou, Haikou, Ordos, Yinchuan, Kyoto, Bandung, Jacksonville, Kharkhari, and Caracas. The ten cities with the worst social circumstances were: Tegucigalpa, Guatemala City, Kingston, Santo Domingo, Betim, Duque de Caxias, São Bernardo do Campo, Bogota, Johannesburg, and Durban. Most are less developed cities in Asia, South America, and Africa. The ten cities with poor social situations in particular are low-income cities. But the top ten cities with poor environmental quality include Kyoto and Kharkhari, both high-income cities. This shows that all cities must attach importance to resolving environmental issues, particularly constructing eco-friendly, environmentally cohesive cities.

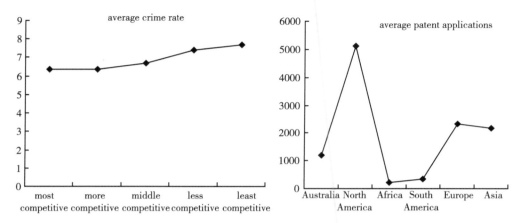

Figure 3.15   Average Per Capita CO₂ Emissions and Crime Rates for Five Levels of Cities 2013

3. Technological Cause: Recent Technological Innovation Has Not Been Satisfactory; North America Still Technologically Strongest

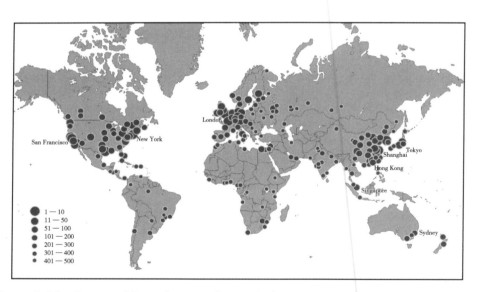

Figure 3.16   Regional Distribution of Knowledge Cities Driven by Technological Innovation 2013

Comparing the average number of patent applications for the 500 sample cities in 2013 and 2011, one finds that cities applied for an average of 2,600 patents in 2013, down 30 percent from 2011. Technology is increasingly an important endogenous force for enhancing urban competitiveness, but technological innovation measured by the number of patent applications performed unsatisfactorily in 2013.

Comparing the average number of patent applications for each continent (see Figure 3.16), North America, made up primarily of the U.S. and Canada, has the strongest ability for technological innovation, with more than twice the patent applications of second-place Europe. The top ten strongest technological innovators were: London, Paris, Stuttgart, Shanghai, Seoul, New York, Houston, San Jose, San Diego, and Austin. Shanghai and Seoul's performances are noteworthy, not only forming a strong challenge to the innovation capabilities of European and American cities, but also showing the gradual enhancement of economic quality in cities in emerging market economies. Technology is becoming the main force in economic development and competitiveness.

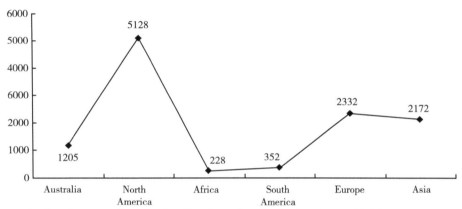

Figure 3.17   Average Patent Applications for Each Continent 2013

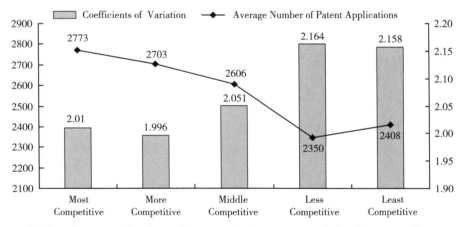

Figure 3.18   Average Number of Patent Applications and Coefficients of Variation for Five Levels of Cities 2013

4. Linkages and Culture: Global Linkages and City's Global Position Closely Related; Urban Sustainable Competitiveness Depends on Inclusiveness of Culture

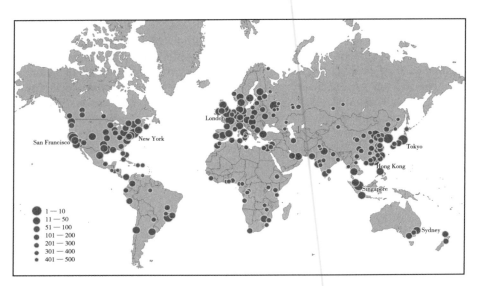

Figure 3.19   Regional Distribution of Open Cities with Global Linkages 2013

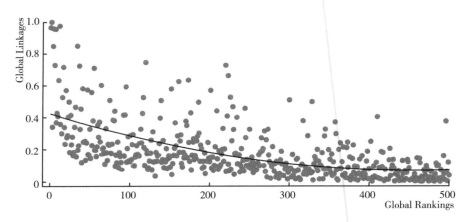

Figure 3.20   Scatter Graph of Global Linkages and Global Rankings

For global linkages, we use the "multinational companies linkage" indicator. For culture, we use the "multinational language index." Because these two indicators are relatively fixed, there were not too many new changes in 2013. GUSCI rankings are closely related to global linkages. Cities with high GUSCI rankings also have high degrees of global linkage, and vice versa.

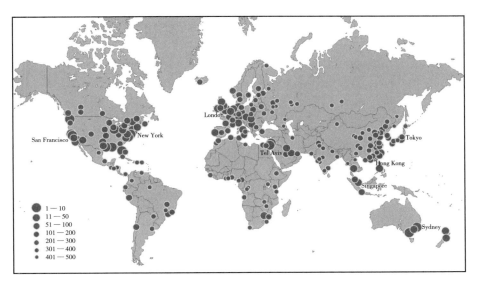

Figure 3.21   Regional Distribution of Cities with Diverse Cultures 2013

In terms of culture, through the "multinational language index," we divide the GUSCI rankings by the number of languages spoken (from 1 to 13, of which 12 is blank). In ascending order, the number of cities in which each number of languages are spoken, from 1 to 13, are: 1, 181, 77, 62, 43, 27, 31, 46, 15, 13, 2, 0, 2. In 36 percent of cities, two languages are spoken. One can also see that cities where more languages are spoken are more inclusive, more integrated, and have higher GUSCI rankings (see Figure 3.22).

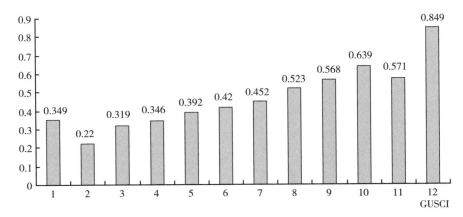

Figure 3.22   Average GUSCI Scores for Cities Speaking Different Numbers of Languages

5. Governance Cause: Governance Capacity Better in Small and Medium Cities, Forming Huge Potential for Long-Term Development

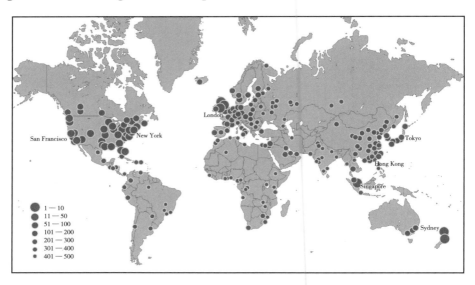

Figure 3.23 Regional Distribution of Cities with Effective Governance

Government is in a dominant position in urban development. Good governance mechanisms and sufficient impetus for innovation are key to long-term, healthy, and sustainable development. From the scatter plots and curve fitting for governance, represented by the business environment index, and GUSCI scores, one can see that governance and GUSCI are positively related. The quality of governance determines the level of urban competitiveness.

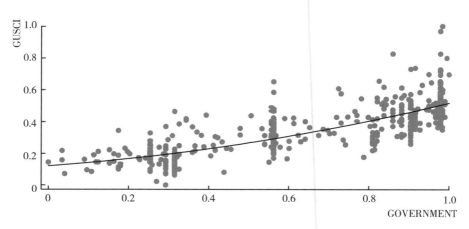

Figure 3.24 Scatter Chart for Governance and GUSCI for 500 Sample Cities

In terms of governance, from a regional point of view, Australia and North America rank first. Open and transparent government operations provide cities in these regions with positive operating environments, and cities from these regions thereby rank as highly competitive. On the other hand, governance is problematic in South America and Africa, and urban competitiveness is constrained by poor government management capabilities. In terms of city size, it is small and medium cities that have better governance capabilities. Large cities, due to high populations and increasingly prominent structural issues, present new challenges for governance. Here the advantages of small and medium cities stand out.

Table 3.7   Compilation of Business Environments for Cities by Size and Continent

City Size	Average Business Environment Index	Region	Average Business Environment Index
Giant	0.596	Australia	0.963
Very Large	0.569	North America	0.891
Large	0.528	Europe	0.636
Medium	0.718	Asia	0.571
Small	0.784	South America	0.362
		Africa	0.351

CASE: SEEKING A PARADIGM FOR FUTURE URBAN DEVELOPMENT

A. Seoul: A Microcosm of Cities in Emerging Market Economies

Seoul is located in the Han River basin in northwest South Korea. With a population of more than 10 million, it is South Korea's capital and political, economic, technological, and cultural center. In 2013, Seoul's GUSCI rank rose 18 places from 2011, leaping into the top ten, an eye-catching performance in the latest competiveness rankings. Seoul's economy began developing rapidly in the 1960s when it implemented an export-oriented economic development strategy and vigorously developed its export processing industry. Seoul has collected 29.7 percent of companies in South Korea and accounts for 21 percent of South Korea's GDP.

Seoul's performance on three competitiveness indicators is worth mentioning. First, CO_2 emissions per capita were only 0.0002 cubic meters, putting the city in the top twenty worldwide. With its skyscrapers, ancient palaces, blue rivers and towering mountains, the city has developed a tourism industry and hosted the 1988 summer Olympics and 2002 World Cup. Its beautiful environment and cohesive ecology are some of its distinguishing characteristics, and it is known as one of the world's most beautiful cities. Second, it has strong technological innovation capabilities. In 2013, the city had 33,053 patent applications, ranking it third in the world. Seoul is South Korea's educational and cultural center and is home to 34 universities including Seoul National University, representing 50 percent of total tertiary institutions in the nation. Third, its multinational company linkages rank tenth in the world. Seoul is a world trade center, and South Korea's most well-known companies, like Samsung, LG, Hyundai, KIA, and SK are all headquartered in Seoul. Numerous multinationals make their headquarters in Seoul, and international banks all have branches in the city.

Seoul rolls many functions into one city. Relying on South Korea's national development, it has strong technological innovation capabilities in its research institutions and well-known companies. At the same time, the multitude of multinational companies has significantly increased Seoul's global linkages. Together, these have made Seoul an outstanding representative and a microcosm of flourishing cities in emerging economies.

B. San Jose: The Future of Small Cities in Developed Countries

San Jose is a city in western California, located in the Santa Clara Valley south of San Francisco Bay. It is close to the Coyote River and 64 kilometers from San Francisco. With a population of 948,300 (2009), it is the third-largest city in California and the third largest in the U.S. The city held a top-ten GUSCI score in both 2011 and 2013 and improved by six places between the two periods, leaping to third. Among competitiveness indicators, San Jose's per capita GDP was US$ 77,401.91, ranking it second worldwide. The basis for this high income is San Jose's strong technological innovation. Its 38,209 patent applications ranked it second in the world, and the city is known as the capital of Silicon Valley. In the 1990s, along with the rise of the IT industry in Silicon Valley, San Jose drove innovation and industrial development in personal computers, the Internet, and biotechnology and enjoyed a rapidly growing economy. Today, San Jose is home to some 7,300 high-tech companies concentrated in semiconductors, computers, networking, software, information services, and biomedicine, making it the world's largest gathering place of high-tech knowledge. Many of the world's most well-known high-tech companies, such as Adobe, Cisco, and eBay, all have headquarters in the city, and more than a hundred well-known companies, such as IBM, Acer, Fujitsu, Hitachi, Infineon, Samsung, Siemens, and Sony Electronics, have set up branches or R&D centers there. San Jose is truly a high-tech city.

San Jose has taken aim at the trend of world economic and technological development to form unparalleled advantages in technology, innovation, knowledge, entrepreneurialism, and talent. It is one of the most productive and creative places in the world, standing proudly at the forefront of the development of the knowledge economy and new economy. High incomes, high technology, and high quality have also created a favorable safety environment and a stable society. According to 2004 statistics from the Federal Bureau of Investigation, San Jose is America's safest city with a population over 500,000. As a small or medium city, San Jose's use of innovation and technology to improve its global competitiveness ranking provides a good template for the development of other cities around the world.

4. Global urban sustainable competitiveness: a regional analysis

Jie Yang[1] and Kai Liu[2]

Cities have vastly different levels of competitiveness due to differences in their own economic, social, and environmental factors. But because cities within a country or region have clear similarities in economic, social, and environmental aspects, global urban sustainable competitiveness has clear regional characteristics and national context. This report conducts an analysis of the patterns, characteristics, and context of the urban sustainable competitiveness of major countries and regions.

Although the global financial crisis had a major impact on the development of cities around the world, including major changes to economic dynamism and innovation activities, no fundamental change occurred to the regional pattern of global urban sustainable competitiveness. In 2013, Oceania and North America were still far ahead in urban sustainable competitiveness, followed by European and Asian cities, with cities in underdeveloped Africa and South America bringing up the rear.

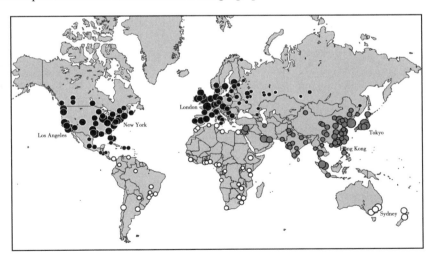

Figure 4.1   Regional Distribution of Global Urban Sustainable Competitiveness for 2013

1   Jie Yang, Center of City and Competitiveness, CASS. No. 2 yuetanbeixiaojie, Xicheng District, Beijing, China, post code: 100836, Tel: 8610-68063478.
Email: j. yang. sec@163.com.

2   Kai Liu, School of Business Administration, Zhongnan University of Economics and Law, 182 Nanhu Avenue, Eastlake High-tech Development Zone, Wuhan 430073, China.
Email: jxmylk24@163.com.

NORTH AMERICAN URBAN SUSTAINABLE COMPETITIVENESS: FAR AHEAD OVERALL; LARGE INTRA-REGIONAL DIFFERENCES

From a global perspective, North American cities have been in a leading sustainable competitive position for some time, and North America has some of the strongest GUSCI performers. In technological innovation in particular, North American cities show superior strength. In 2013, North American cities had the highest average number of patent applications, 5,128, far surpassing second-place Europe's average of 2,332 and Asia's of 2,172. But under the impact of the global financial crisis, the economic dynamism of North American cities fell slightly, with average urban per capita GDP falling from US$ 37,322 in 2011 to US$ 34,775 in 2013. The average economic growth rate fell from 4 percent to negative 1 percent over the same period. There are also significant differences in the sustainable competitiveness of cities within the region. In 2013, North America had five cities in the top ten GUSCI rankings, but all were United States (U.S.) cities. Neither of the other two North American countries, Canada and Mexico, had a city in the top ten.

Table 4.1   GUSCI Rankings for North American Countries 2011-2013

Year	Region	Country	Top 10	11-100	101-200	201-300	301-400	401-500	Total	Average Score
2013	North America	Total	5	40	28	12	12	0	97	0.471
		U.S.	5	37	18	5	0	0	65	0.531
		Canada	0	3	9	0	0	0	12	0.462
		Mexico	0	0	1	7	12	0	20	0.280
2011	North America	Total	6	40	31	12	8	0	97	0.464
		U.S.	6	36	22	1	0	0	65	0.520
		Canada	0	4	8	0	0	0	12	0.471
		Mexico	0	0	1	11	8	0	20	0.278

American Urban Sustainable Competitiveness: Opportunity within Crisis

Due to their large number and complex situations, the development of American cities has always been diverse. The country is home to cities consistently ranking in the forefront of the sustainable competitiveness index, fading star cities, rising emerging cities, and cities that have experienced major ups and downs over the years. But overall, American cities found opportunities for improving sustainable competitiveness in 2013.

As the source of the financial crisis, the sustainable competitiveness of some American cities fell in either absolute or relative terms during the crisis, while other cities managed to increase their competitiveness. Washington D.C. fell from seventh place in 2011 to fourteenth in 2013, while San Jose leapt from ninth to third. Overall, although 36 of the 65 U.S. sample cities fell in the GUSCI rankings, the average GUSCI score for U.S. cities rose slightly from 0.520 in 2011 to 0.531 in 2013.

In 2013, the average GDP per capita and economic growth rate in U.S. cities presented a downward trend, from US\$ 48,564 and 2.9 percent in 2011 to US\$ 44,414 and negative 3 percent in 2013. Only technological innovation continued to rise, with average patent applications increasing from 7,957 to 8,253 over the same period. One can see that even with general weakness in the U.S. economy, science and technology research and development did not slow, but accelerated. This will provide an important support for the maintenance of sustainable competitiveness in American cities.

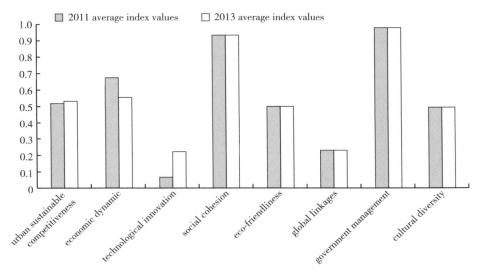

Figure 4.2   American Urban Sustainable Competitiveness and Average Indicator Values

Canadian Urban Sustainable Competitiveness: A Clear Downward Trend

Canada is a wealthy, high-tech industrial country. It is rich in natural resources, eco-friendly and has strong scientific and technological innovation capabilities and an inclusive society. But Canada's economy is in a stage of high-production, low inflation, falling unit labor costs, and dramatically rising exports. It also has a healthy business and investment environment.

However, during the global financial crisis, a downward trend was evident in the sustainable competitiveness of Canadian cities. Among twelve sample cities, compared to 2011, eleven had lower GUSCI rankings in 2013. In the post-financial-crisis era, city economies have recovered slowly. After the crisis, the thriving scene in Toronto was no more. Main cities now have rankings concentrated around 150. In 2011, Toronto ranked twenty-third globally, but by 2013, the highest-ranked Canadian city was Montreal at seventieth. This shows that Canada is still feeling the "aftershocks" of the financial crisis.

In 2013, the average GUSCI score of Canadian cities was 0.462, lower than the 0.471 average in 2011. Among the indicators, average per-capita urban GDP and economic growth rates fell significantly, from US$ 41,786 and 3.1 percent in 2011 to US$ 40,148 and 1.3 percent in 2013. Technological innovation fell even more, with the average number of patent applications filed in Canadian cities falling from 6,436 in 2011 to 76 in 2013. As one of the most important drivers of social development, the significant weakening of Canadian technological innovation makes for bleak prospects for recovery.

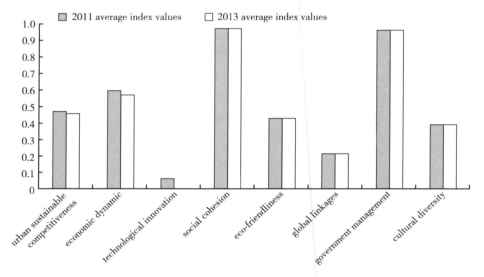

Figure 4.3   Canadian Urban Sustainable Competitiveness and Average Indicator Values

Mexican Urban Sustainable Competitiveness: Stagnation

Mexico is a developing country in Latin America. On the one hand, excessive urbanization has brought about a number of structural imbalances, while on the other hand, economic integration with North America has weakened the country's comparative advantage. The global financial crisis has further threatened the country's sustainable competitiveness.

Mexican cities overall fall in the middle and lower end of the GUSCI rankings. In 2013, of 20 Mexican sample cities, all but Mexico City at 179th ranked below 200th. Eighteen of these ranked below 250th. Although Mexico City's GUSCI score rose from 0.278 in 2011 to 0.280 in 2013, rankings for the other cities all fell. Overall, sustainable competiveness in Mexican cities remained stagnant.

In 2013, Mexico's per capita urban GDP increased slightly compared to 2011, from US$ 13,283 to US$ 13,665.But at the same time, due to the impact of the financial crisis, the average urban economic growth rate dropped significantly, from 8.6 percent to 2.6 percent. Although technological innovation increased, with the average number of patent applications growing from 202 to 225, in terms of social cohesion, the crime rate remained high, with the average number of criminal cases per 10,000 people remaining at 18.3, much higher than

5.9 in the U.S. and 1.8 in Canada. One can see that on the one hand Mexican cities have striven to regain economic growth momentum after the financial crisis and have continued to strengthen technological innovation. On the other hand, what's more important is focusing on enhancing social cohesion in cities in order to reverse the stagnation in urban sustainable competitiveness.

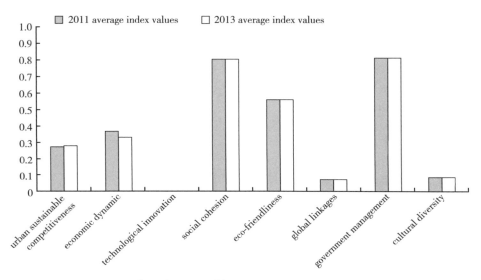

Figure 4.4   *Mexican Urban Sustainable Competitiveness and Average Indicator Values*

EUROPEAN URBAN SUSTAINABLE COMPETITIVENESS: SERIOUS OVERALL IMPACT; MORE DIVERGENCE INTERNALLY

In recent years, productivity and economic growth have been low in Europe, and the aging population has become a major obstacle. Coordination policies among European Union (E.U.) countries are diverse and complex, and emerging countries are challenging Europe's competitiveness.

In terms of urban sustainable competitiveness, the global financial crisis wounded European cities no less than American cities where the crisis originated and far more than Asian cities. Although average GUSCI scores in major European countries remained stable, at 0.298 in 2011 and 0.303 in 2013, the average per capita GDP and economic growth rate in European cities fell from US$ 25,069 and 4.6 percent in 2011 to US$ 24,639 and negative 0.9 percent, respectively, in 2013.Average patent applications also fell from 3,040 to 2,332, a relatively large drop. Compared to Asian cities, which in 2013 maintained average urban economic growth of 8.9 percent, and American cities, which have maintained strong technological innovation capabilities, European cities have been seriously wounded. Among countries within the region, GUSCI scores diverged. Compared to 2011, cities in Western

Europe, Northern Europe, and Central Europe saw their average scores increase by 0.011, 0.012, and 0.018, respectively, while average scores in cities in southern Europe increased by only 0.009 and fell by 0.0003 in Eastern Europe. In addition, GUSCI levels also diverged among the cities of major countries in the region.

Table 4.2   GUSCI Ranking Distribution among Major European Countries 2011-2013

Year	Region	Country	Top 10	11-100	101-200	201-300	301-400	401-500	Total	Average Score
2013	Europe	Total	2	13	20	6	4	42	87	**0.303**
		UK	1	5	8	2	0	0	16	0.507
		France	1	1	5	1	0	0	8	0.488
		Germany	0	7	6	3	0	0	16	0.463
		Russia	0	0	1	0	4	42	47	0.149
2011	Europe	Total	1	14	21	5	12	34	87	**0.298**
		UK	1	7	6	2	0	0	16	0.506
		France	0	2	5	1	0	0	8	0.455
		Germany	0	5	9	2	0	0	16	0.441
		Russia	0	0	1	0	12	34	47	0.152

Urban Sustainable Competitiveness in the U.K.: Increasingly Divergent

As a highly developed economy, the U.K. has similar advantages and problems to other developed economies. But it is different in the spatial location of its development: i.e. binary structure and polarization. This is also reflected on the pattern of its urban sustainable competitiveness.

Overall, U.K. cities are leaders in urban sustainable competitiveness, but differences among cities are growing starker. In 2013, average GUSCI score was 0.507, essentially flat with 0.506 in 2011. Of the 16 sample cities, only London maintained its number one spot in the rankings between 2011 and 2013. Plymouth rose slightly, while the other fourteen cities all fell to varying degrees. Among them, seven cities ranking relatively highly in 2011 fell an average of 6.4 places in 2013, while seven cities ranking relatively low in 2011 fell an average of 11.9 places, showing an increasing divergence in competitiveness of cities in the U.K.

Among 16 British sample cities in 2013, besides London and Birmingham, the other 14 cities had negative economic growth rates. Besides London, where per capita GDP rose slightly from US\$ 61,613 in 2011 to US\$ 64,701 in 2013, per capita GDP in the other 15 cities fell to varying degrees. In addition, the overall decrease in technological innovation and the slight increase in the crime rate impacted the sustainable competitiveness of cities to varying degrees. The average number of patent applications in British cities fell from 10,735 in 2011 to 4,290 in 2013, and the average number of criminal cases per 10,000 people increased slightly from 1.5 to 1.6. In terms of changes to GUSCI rankings, these shocks exacerbated the divergence in sustainable competitiveness among British cities.

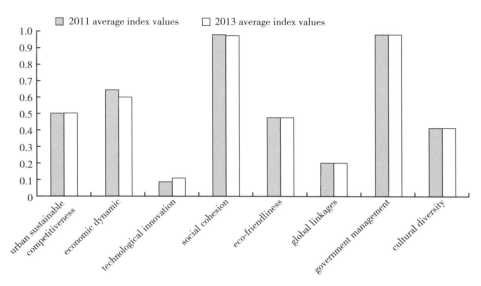

Figure 4.5   British Urban Sustainable Competitiveness and Average Indicator Values

French Urban Sustainable Competitiveness: Steady Progress

With the weakening of the national economy and the rise of emerging countries, France's current economic competitiveness has declined. But due to prominent advantages in large businesses, highly sophisticated technology, and the green energy industry, its long-term sustainable competitiveness remains strong.

France's eight sample cities rank in the middle to upper levels of the GUSCI rankings, and performance is stable. In 2013, France's average GUSCI score was 0.488, increasing slightly from 0.455 in 2011. Comparing the two years, Marseille's ranking remained unchanged, Toulouse and Bordeaux fell slightly, and the other five rose to varying degrees. Paris, which ranked eleventh in 2011, rose seven places to fourth in 2013.

While France was also seriously impacted by the financial crisis, and average urban per capita GDP and economic growth rate in France declined slightly from US$ 34,082 and 1.2 percent in 2011 to US$ 32,764 and negative 1.2 percent in 2013, at the same time, technological innovation became more dynamic, with the average number of patents rising from 4,443 to 6,539. Social cohesion also increased, with the average number of criminal cases per 10,000 people falling from 1.2 to 1.1. As a result, France made some progress in urban sustainable competitiveness while mostly remaining stable.

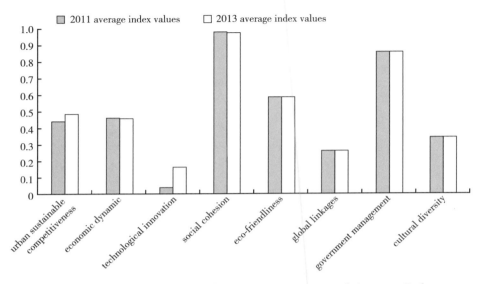

Figure 4.6   French Urban Sustainable Competitiveness and Average Indicator Values

German Urban Sustainable Development: Subtle Divergence

Compared with other countries, Germany is distinctive. German cities are small and competitive in manufacturing. German sustainable development has been at the forefront of the world. The financial crisis resulted in only subtle changes to the urban pattern in Germany.

In 2013, of sixteen German sample cities, seven entered the top 100 GUSCI rankings, and thirteen were within the top 200, overall demonstrating relatively strong sustainable competitiveness. But compared to France and the U.K., Germany lacks a world-leading city like London or Paris, with no cities in the top ten. After the financial crisis, sustainable competitiveness scores among German cities diverged slightly. Compared with 2011, of the ten German cities in the top 150 GUSCI scores, only Dusseldorf's rank declined. The rankings of the remaining nine cities rose to varying degrees. The six cities ranked below 150th, however, saw their rankings fall.

Average GDP ten German cities rose from US$ 38,551 in 2011 to US$ 38,735, while the economic growth rate fell from 2.3 percent to basically zero over the same period. For the other six cities, the average GDP and economic growth rate fell from US$ 36,119 and 3.1 percent, respectfully, in 2011 to US$ 34,264 and negative 1.5 percent in 2011, a relatively large decline. In terms of social cohesion, the average number of criminal cases per 10,000 people for the top ten German cities fell from 0.82 to 0.69, while the same indicator fell from 0.84 to 0.83 in the bottom six cities. In terms of technological innovation, the average number of patent applications for the top ten German cities rose from 6,406 to 7,910, while the same indicator fell from 4,010 to 1,182 for the bottom six cities. These all demonstrate the slight divergence among the urban sustainable competitiveness levels of German cities.

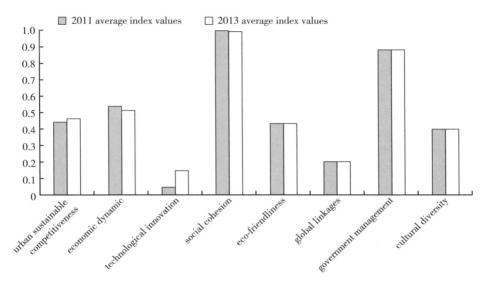

☐ 2011 average index values   ☐ 2013 average index values

Figure 4.7   German Urban Sustainable Competitiveness and Average Indicator Values

Russian Urban Sustainable Competitiveness: World's Weakest

Although Russia has rich natural resources and a strong military and is one of the BRIC countries, on both the national and city level, the country faces numerous problems in demographic structure, economic power, social cohesion, and technological innovation. Its prospects for the development of urban sustainable competitiveness are woeful.

In 2013, of the 500 sample cities assessed in this report, 42 of the 100 worst-ranked cities were Russian, accounting for 90 percent of the 47 Russian cities in the report. Of the remaining five cities, only Moscow ranked in the top 200. The other four cities fell between 300th and 400th. In 2013, eight more cities fell into the bottom 100, indicating further weakening. Russia's average GUSCI score fell from 0.152 in 2011 to 0.149 in 2013, making it one of the weakest countries in urban sustainable competitiveness.

In 2013, average per capita GDP among Russian sample cities was US$ 4,572, far lower than the level in major European countries. The average economic growth rate was negative 2 percent. In terms of social cohesion, the average number of criminal cases per 10,000 people remained around from 2011 to 2013, higher than the average of 6.6 for the 500 sample cities overall, and far higher than the level of one to two in other European countries. In terms of technological innovation, the average number of patent applications among Russian cities was less than 200 in both 2011 and 2013, lower than the average of 2,600 for all 500 sample cities. Among BRIC countries, Russia surpassed only Brazil. All of these factors have been a drag on Russia's urban sustainable competitiveness.

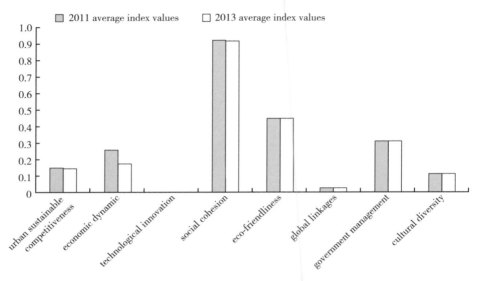

Figure 4.8   Russian Urban Sustainable Competitiveness and Average Indicator Values

ASIAN URBAN SUSTAINABLE COMPETITIVENESS: BETTER OVERALL, CHANGING PATTERN WITHIN THE REGION

Asia's population is huge, and many countries are in a phase of accelerated urbanization and industrialization. While Asian cities were also affected by the global financial crisis, compared to the cities of other regions, they still maintained good development momentum, and urban sustainable competitiveness has risen overall.

The average GUSCI score for China, Japan, Korea, and India rose from 0.280 to 0.312. Of these, Chinese, Korean, and Indian cities had the most outstanding performance. Among 61 Chinese sample cities, 46 rose in the GUSCI rankings from 2011 to 2013. Among 41 Indian sample cities, 29 rose in the GUSCI rankings in the same period, demonstrating increasing urban sustainable competitiveness in major Asian countries. In 2013, the average GUSCI value for Korean cities was 0.438, surpassing an average score of 0.422 for Japanese cities, and making Korea the leader in Asia. The pattern of urban sustainable competitiveness in the region is undergoing significant changes.

Table 4.3   Ranking Distribution of Major Asian Countries 2011-2013

Year	Region	Country	Top 10	11-100	101-200	201-300	301-400	401-500	Total	Average Rank
		Total	3	11	24	45	47	18	140	0.312
		China	0	2	10	25	23	1	61	0.319
2013	Asia	Japan	1	7	7	10	2	0	27	0.422
		Korea	1	0	6	4	0	0	11	0.438
		India	0	0	0	3	21	17	41	0.197
		Total	2	9	19	48	42	28	140	0.280
		China	0	2	4	25	28	2	61	0.283
2011	Asia	Japan	1	4	10	12	0	0	27	0.405
		Korea	0	1	4	6	0	0	11	0.389
		India	0	0	0	2	13	26	41	0.165

Chinese Urban Sustainable Competitiveness: Steady Improvement

As one of the BRICS countries, China on the one hand is experiencing rapid economic development and improvement in technological innovation. On the other hand, its ecological social environments are deteriorating, challenging the sustainability of its competitiveness. Additionally, China is in a period of accelerated urbanization, and urban economies and infrastructure are in the process of rapid development, producing many social and environmental issues.

But during the global financial crisis, the trend of steady improvement in urban sustainable competitiveness in China did not change. The average GUSCI score for the 61 Chinese sample cities excluding Hong Kong, Macau, and Taiwan rose from 0.283 in 2011 to 0.319 in 2013. And while only two Chinese cities were in the top 100 in 2013, the number ranking between 100th and 200th increased from four to ten, the number between 200th and 300th remained at 25, the number between 300th and 400th fell from 28 to 23, and the number between 400th and 500th fell from 2 to 1. One can see that Chinese urban sustainable competitiveness rankings improved overall, showing the steady improvement of the level of urban competitiveness among Chinese cities.

The economic dynamism of China's cities increased further in 2013, with average per capita GDP growing from US$ 6,636 to US$ 7,642, and average economic growth increasing from 15.3 percent to 16.5 percent. Technological innovation was also active, with average patents filed growing from 3,733 to 4,270 during the same period. Meanwhile, social cohesion has been steady, with around 3.2 criminal cases per 10,000 people, lower than India's level of around 3.8 and much lower than Russia at 7, Brazil at 29, and South Africa at 41. Among the BRICS, China has the highest level of social cohesion. These all form the foundation of China's steadily increasing sustainable competitiveness.

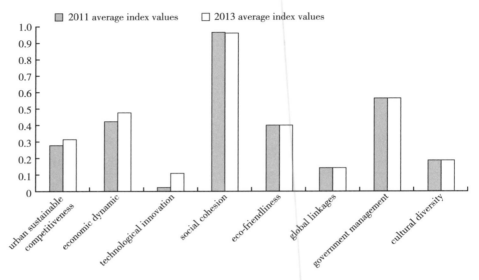

Figure 4.9   Chinese Urban Sustainable Competitiveness and Average Indicator Values

Japanese Urban Sustainable Competiveness: Serious Divergence

As a developed country, Japan has many advantages in sustainable competitiveness. It is a technological powerhouse, has a stable social system, has good and efficient social governance, and has a good ecological environment. However, it has lacked economic vigor for some time, its population is aging and declining, commercialization is poor, the educational system lacks creativity, the culture is closed, and resources are scarce.

On the level of the city, Japan leads Asia in urban sustainable competitiveness. But under the impact of the financial crisis, its cities have diverged seriously. Although sustainable competitiveness in Japan's city's rose overall in 2013 compared to 2011, with the average GUSCI score rising from 0.405 to 0.422, among 27 Japanese sample cities, sixteen rose in the rankings, one stayed the same, and ten fell. The risers on average rose 33.5 places, while decliners fell an average of 38.6 places. One can see that while sustainable competitiveness has increased in a portion of Japanese cities, it has also fallen significantly in another portion. Divergence in sustainable competitiveness is severe.

In 2013, the average per capita GDP and growth rate for the sixteen rising cities increased from US$ 32,793 and 1 percent, respectively, in 2011 to US$ 40,702 and 1.09 percent in 2013. Meanwhile, average per capita GDP and economic growth among the ten falling cities fell from US$ 37.231 and 1.5 percent to US$ 35,426 and negative 4.6 percent. In technological innovation, average patent applications in the 16 rising cities fell from 7,754 in 2011 to 651 in 2013, while among the declining cities it fell from 25,340 to 2,346. Clearly, the financial crisis has had a greater impact on innovative Japanese cities.

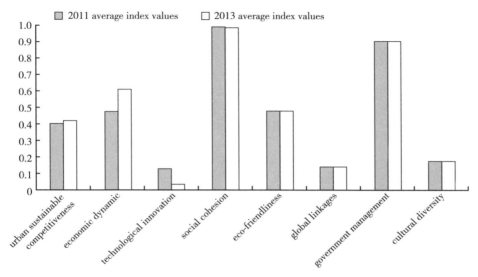

Figure 4.10   Japanese Urban Sustainable Competitiveness and Average Indicator Values

Korean Urban Sustainable Competitiveness: Leading Asia

South Korea is a thriving newly industrialized country. In recent years, it has had clearly increasing performance in technological innovation, economic development, social cohesion, and the ecological environment. In the context of the global financial crisis, compared to Japanese cities, Korean cities have performed well overall. Among 11 Korean sample cities, nine rose in the GUSCI rankings in 2013 compared to 2011, among which Seoul leapt 18 points and into the top ten. Korea's average GUSCI score rose from 0.389 to 0.438 over the same period, surpassing Japan to become the leader in urban sustainable competitiveness in Asia.

The outstanding performance of South Korean cities is mainly due to the country withstanding the impact of the financial crisis. Technological innovation in 2013 was still relatively vigorous, with the average number of patents in South Korean cities falling from 6,485 in 2011 to 6,350 in 2013. Compared with Japan's drop from 15,486 to 1,606 over the same period, Korea's level of technological innovation was relatively stable. At the same time, Korea's average per capita GDP increased from US$ 20,271 in 2011 to US$ 26,831 in 2013. Although the average economic growth rate fell from 3.4 percent to 1 percent, the economies of Korean cities overall still grew, solidifying the foundation for enhancing the level of sustainable urban competitiveness.

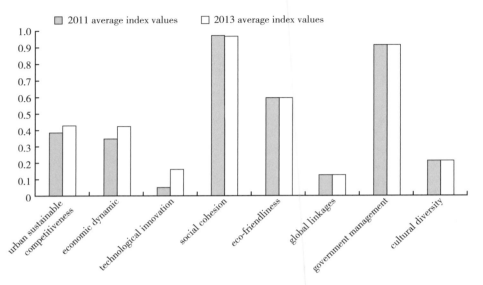

*Figure 4.11   South Korean Urban Sustainable Competitiveness and Average
            Indicator Values*

Indian Urban Sustainable Competitiveness: Significant Increase

India is a developing country with a large population that has now entered a phase of accelerated urbanization. Its level of urban development is low, but growth is rapid. Its cities, and especially large cities, are home to a large amount of high-end talent and other high-end elements, and India has huge middle class consumer demand. On the other hand, it faces many "urban diseases" and other unsustainable problems.

   On the city level, although, compared to 2011, India still had no city enter the ranks of the top 200 GUSCI scores in 2013 and the number in the top 300 fell from 3 to 2, this did not hinder the significant overall increase in Indian urban sustainable competitiveness. In 2013, India had an average GUSCI of 0.197, up nearly 19.4 percent from 0.165 in 2011, significantly higher than the increase of 12.7 percent in China and 12.6 percent in Korea, and far higher than 4.2 percent in Japan. Therefore, although India's urban sustainable competitiveness is still the lowest among major Asian countries, it undoubtedly improved the fastest in 2013.

   Given that social cohesion, eco-friendliness, global linkages, governance, and cultural diversity remained relatively constant in Indian cities, the majority of the increase in competitiveness came from economic dynamic. India's average per capita urban GDP rose from US$ 1,202 in 2011 to US$ 2,044 in 2013, and the average urban economic growth rate rose from 7.4 percent to 9.3 percent, demonstrating strong economic vitality. At the same time, India's urban innovation activities showed a sharp decline, with average patent applications falling from 356 to 46 over the same period. This casts a shadow over India's prospects for maintaining economic vitality and thus enhancing urban sustainable competitiveness.

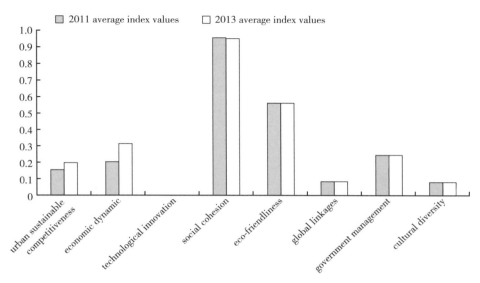

Figure 4.12　Indian Urban Sustainable Competitiveness and Average Indicator Values

RISING AND FALLING URBAN SUSTAINABLE COMPETITIVENESS IN OCEANIA, SOUTH AMERICA, AND AFRICA

Oceania, South America, and Africa have different levels of economic, social, and environmental development but a general decline in urban sustainable competitiveness. Oceania's level of urban sustainable competitiveness was relatively high and remained basically stable, with the average GUSCI score falling from 0.504 to 0.501 from 2011 to 2013. Africa had the largest decline in GUSCI, reaching 11.8 percent, with the average GUSCI score falling from 0.220 to 0.197.Second was South America at 6.2 percent, with the average GUSCI score falling from 0.197 to 0.185, mainly due to the impact of the financial crisis. Urban economic growths rate in the three continents fell significantly overall. In Oceania, the average urban economic growth rate fell from 3.3 percent in 2011 to 0.3 percent in 2013. In South America, the average growth rate fell from 7.7 percent to 3.2 percent over the same period, and in Africa, from 5 percent to 3.1 percent. Even so, compared to the negative average growth rates in European and American cities, cities on these three continents exhibited good economic vitality. Especially in cities in some major countries, sustainable competitiveness is still gradually improving.

Table 4.4   GUSCI Ranking Distributions for Major Countries in Oceania, South America, and Africa, 2011-2013

Year	Region	Country	Top 10	11-100	101-200	201-300	301-400	401-500	Total	Average Score
	Oceania	Australia	0	3	2	1	0	0	6	0.511
2013	South America	Brazil	0	0	0	1	4	10	15	0.157
	Africa	South Africa	0	0	0	2	2	0	4	0.296
	Oceania	Australia	1	3	2	0	0	0	6	0.512
2011	South America	Brazil	0	0	0	1	4	10	15	0.153
	Africa	South Africa	0	0	0	2	2	0	4	0.278

Australian Urban Sustainable Competitiveness: Decreasing Slightly from a High Level

Australia is the southern hemisphere's most economically developed country. It has vast land, a beautiful environment, cultural diversity, and a highly urbanized population. Many of its cities have been named some of the most livable places in the world. Both in terms of the country and its cities, Australia ranks high in sustainable competitiveness.

However, under the impact of the financial crisis, the overall level of sustainable urban competitiveness in Australian cities fell slightly. Of six Australian sample cities, five had declining GUSCI rankings between 2011 and 2013, with only Adelaide rising. Sydney also fell out of the top ten to eleventh. But overall, the average GUSCI score fell only marginally from 0.512 to 0.511.

Due to the financial crisis, the economic vitality of Australian cities declined significantly, with average urban per capita GDP and economic growth rate falling from US$ 41,517 and 3 percent, respectively, in 2011 to US$ 38,756 and negative 0.16 percent in 2013. Social cohesion also fell slightly, with the average number of criminal cases per 10,000 people rising from 1.31 to 1.36 over the same period. But technological innovation remained brisk, with average patent applications rising slightly from 1,037 to 1,067, providing strong support for the sustainable competitiveness of Australia's cities and allowing them to basically maintain their level of sustainable competitiveness under the impact of the financial crisis, falling only slightly.

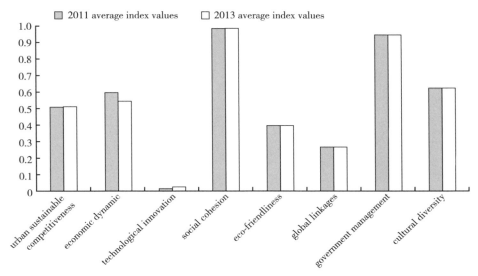

Figure 4.13   Australian Urban Sustainable Competitiveness and Average Indicator Values

Brazilian Urban Sustainable Competitiveness: Slight Rise from a Low Level

As one of the BRICS countries, as well as an over-urbanized country, Brazil has the world's richest biodiversity resources and is one of the world's fastest growing countries. But economic structural imbalances, single growth model, poor infrastructure, large income gap, and high crime rates lend significant uncertainty to the country's sustainable competitiveness.

In 2013, not one of 15 Brazilian cities had entered the ranks of the top 200 GUSCI scores. Compared to 2011, rankings for 11 cities fell, and 500th-ranked Betim remained unchanged. Only 3 cities ranked higher than 400th rose slightly, but the best-performing city climbed only seven places. Therefore, although Brazil's average GUSCI score rose slightly from 0.153 in 2011 to 0.157 in 2013, the sustainable competitiveness of Brazilian cities did not in fact achieve a strong increase.

Economic dynamism in Brazilian cities fell slightly between 2011 and 2013. Although average urban per capita GDP increased from US$ 8,470 to US$ 8,572, the average urban economic growth rate fell from 9.7 percent to 3.6 percent. Correspondingly, the average economic dynamic score dropped from 0.339 to 0.300.At the same time, Brazilian cities still lack vigorous technological innovation, with the average number of patents filed rising from 148 to 159, higher only than the average of 46 among Indian cities, lower than Russia's 197 and South Africa's 776, and far lower than China's 4,270. Social cohesion also remained at a relatively low level, with average criminal cases per 10,000 people of 29 in both 2011 and 2013. Among major countries, this better than only South Africa's 41.These have all caused overall weakness in improvement of the sustainable competitiveness of Brazilian cities.

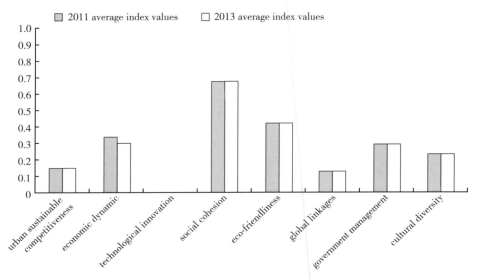

Figure 4.14   Brazilian Urban Sustainable Competitiveness and Average Indicator
Values

South African Urban Sustainable Competiveness: Crisis in Opportunity

As one of the BRICS countries, South Africa is the largest economy in Africa, as well as the best economy in Africa, despite its rapid growth in recent years. Although economic development has many advantages, the country's rich-poor divide, xenophobic tendencies, crime and corruption, and public health and social problems seriously restrict the improvement of sustainable competitiveness.

Although only one of the four South African sample cities rose in the sustainable competitiveness rankings from 2011 to 2013 and the remaining cities declined, overall, South African urban sustainable competitiveness increased. In 2013, South Africa's average GUSCI score was 0.296, up 6.5 percent from 0.278 in 2011.

Although also impacted by the financial crisis, South African cities maintained their economic dynamism. Average per capita urban GDP fell only slightly from US\$ 6,262 in 2011 to US\$ 6,260 in 2013, essentially unchanged. Although the average urban economic growth rate fell from 4.3 percent to 0.9 percent over the same period, growth was still positive. Overall, South African cities maintained their economic dynamism, with the average index rank rising from 0.211 to 0.238 between 2011 and 2013. At the same time, technological innovation remained brisk. The average number of patent applications grew from 731 to 776, lower only than China among BRICS countries and far higher than Russia, Brazil, and India. These are all factors in the improvement in South Africa's urban sustainable development. However, low social cohesion has always been a major issue vexing improvement to South Africa's urban sustainable competitiveness. Average criminal cases per 10,000 people remained high at 41 in both 2011 and 2013, far higher than developed countries and BRICS countries. Without improvement, further enhancement of urban sustainable competitiveness in South Africa will be restricted.

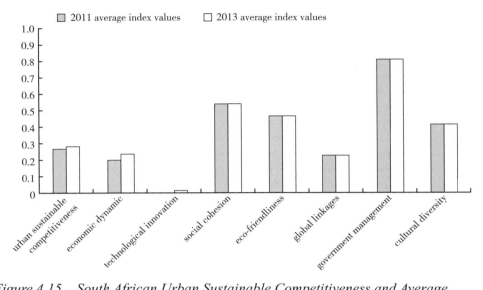

Figure 4.15   South African Urban Sustainable Competitiveness and Average Indicator Values

URBAN SUSTAINABLE COMPETITIVENESS CASE STUDIES: SHANGHAI AND NANTONG

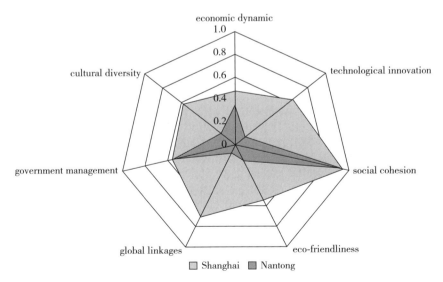

Figure 4.16   Comparison of GUSCI Indicators for Shanghai and Nantong

The Yangtze River Delta is the leading pioneer in China's economic development, and Shanghai and Nantong are the two shining eyes of the dragon, leading the rapid development of the region. Shanghai is located in the Yangtze River estuary, with the East China Sea to the east and Jiangsu and Zhejiang Provinces to the west. Together with Shanghai, these three areas constitute the "Pearl River Delta Economic Circle" leading China's economic development. As one of China's largest cities, Shanghai is not only China's economic, transportation, scientific and technological, industrial, financial, trade, conference, and shipping center, it is China's first free trade zone. Shanghai holds a prominent position in China's global strategy. Shanghai's urban sustainable competitiveness has increased rapidly, with the city rising from 34th-ranked to 17th-ranked between 2011 and 2013. Nantong is located across the river from Shanghai. It is a core city of the northern wing of the Yangtze River Delta and a key area in the development of coastal Jiangsu. It enjoys a reputation as "North Shanghai" and is one of the 14 coastal cities opened to the outside world. In recent years, Nantong has adhered to the development thinking of "relying on the river and sea, rising in central Jiangsu, merging into southern Suzhou, linking with Shanghai, going out into the world, being fully moderately well-off." The regional economy has maintained strong growth momentum, living standards have steadily improved, and the city's GUSCI rank has been essentially stable at around 360th.

Shanghai and Nantong have made great achievements in enhancing their sustainable competitiveness. But overall, Shanghai has been a leader in sustainable competitiveness in China, and it is far stronger than Nantong.

In terms of economic dynamism, in 2013, Shanghai's economic growth rate was 12.3 percent, quicker than Nantong's 11.2 percent. Its per capita GDP of US$ 14,213 was 3.9 times that of Nantong. But Nantong's Shanghai-led economic development has also exhibited a positive trend. In terms of social cohesion, Shanghai's development model is increasingly mature, and the crime rate has been steady but decreasing. Nantong's crime rate in 2011 was lower than Shanghai's, but with accelerated population movement into the city, it increased slightly in 2013.In terms of eco-friendliness, because Shanghai has entered the post-industrialization era, per capita CO_2 emissions overall are at a relatively low level. Nantong, on the other hand, is a manufacturing city that has just entered the industrialization stage. Per capita CO_2 emissions are high overall, and the development of the city has inevitably hurt the sustainability of the environment. In terms of cultural diversity, as an international metropolis, Shanghai has relatively strong cultural inclusion. In 2013, its multi-country language index score was 0.583, ranking it third among the 500 sample cities. Nantong's score was 0.167, ranking it 242nd. In terms of technological innovation, Shanghai's patent applications per 10,000 people far exceed those of Nantong, but Nantong is growing quickly in this area. In 2011, Shanghai had 34,481 patent applications, while Nantong had only 1,756. In 2013, Shanghai's patent applications had fallen to 24,468, while Nantong's had more than doubled to 4,102, indicating improved technological innovation. In global linkages, Shanghai receives investment from companies from around the world, making for a large-scale headquarters economy. In terms of global linkages, Shanghai performs extremely well. In 2013, its multinational company linkage index score was 0.716, ranking twelfth among the 500 sample cities and placing Shanghai in a network control node. By contrast, Nantong's global linkages are very weak, with the city scoring only 0.082 on the index and ranking 339th. But with the increasing expansion of Shanghai's headquarters economy, the city must transfer industry to surrounding cities. Therefore, if Nantong works to attract investment and prepares to receive industry from Shanghai, attracting foreign companies, especially well-known multinationals, will be favorable to enhancing the city's global linkages.

With the above comparisons, one can see that Shanghai's sustainable competiveness is overall stronger than Nantong, with unshakable advantages in many areas, especially economic dynamism, eco-friendliness, cultural diversity, and global linkages. But at the same time, Nantong is closing the gap with Shanghai in the areas of social cohesion and technological innovation. In a joint business environment, the two cities are both facing competitive pressure from at home and abroad. Through integration and wider cooperation, they can share strengths and develop in concert to build a Greater Shanghai that would be the true center of the Chinese economy and an important center for the world, playing a greater role in the sustainable competitiveness of China and the world.

ASSESSMENT AND CALCULATION METHODS

Since the data representing the different components of competitiveness employ various units, we remove dimensions to convert data into non-unit values. The rescaling of the six variables follows the standardized equations as follows:

Z-score rescaling

$$X_i = \frac{(x_i - \bar{x})}{Q^2}$$

where x_i is the original data, $\bar{x}$ is the mean value, Q^2 is the standard deviation and X_i is the standardized data.

Exponential rescaling

$$X_i = \frac{x_i}{x_{0i}}$$

where x_i is value of the original data, x_{0i} is the maximum value and X_i represents the transferred data.

0-1 scaling

$$X_i = \frac{(x_i - x_{min})}{(x_{max} - x_{min})}$$

where X_i is the transferred value of x_i, x_i is the original data, x_{max} is the maximum value of the data set and x_{min} is the minimum value.

Each of the six sustainable competitiveness components referring to Social Cohesion, Environmental Quality, Cultural Diversity, Technological Innovation, Global Linkages and Government Management has been represented by a single variable. Different standardized methods have been used according to the characteristics of different variables.

Economic Dynamic is composed of GDP per capita and the GDP growth rate. These two variables have been standardized individually and synthesized together with weightings of 1/3 and 2/3 respectively.

The comprehensive Sustainable Competitiveness index was synthesized with equal weighting methods.

$$Z_i = \sum_l z_{il}$$

where Z_i represents the sustainable competitiveness index and z_{il} represents the seven competitiveness component subgroups.

5. Global urban sustainable competitiveness and urban GDP per capita

Anquan Zhang[1]

Urban economic development is an important foundation for sustainable urban competitiveness, as well as an important manifestation of sustainable competitiveness. In cities at different levels of development, sustainable competitiveness is manifested differently, and these cities have different strengths and face different challenges. Using per capita GDP, this chapter divides 500 sample cities across 130 countries on five continents into five groupings for comparative analysis: high-income, higher-income, middle-income, lower-income, and low-income.[2]

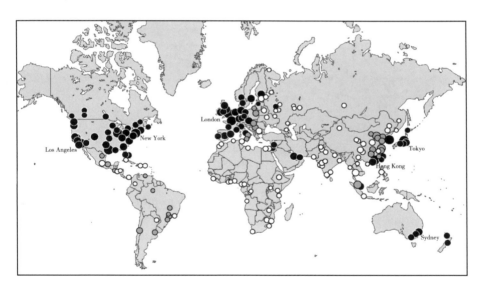

Figure 5.1   Distribution of the Sustainable Competitiveness of Global Cities by Income Level

1   Anquan Zhang, School of Economics, Southwestern University of Finance and Economics, 555 Liutai Avenue, Wenjiang, Chengdu, Sichuan, China, 611130.
Email: yx_cheung@126.com.

2   Classification criteria: high-income, US$ 40,000 and above; higher-income, US$ 20,000-40,000; middle-income, US$ 7,000-20,000; lower-income, US$ 3,000-7,000; low-income, US$ 3,000 and below.

PER CAPITA GDP SIGNIFICANTLY INFLUENCES A CITY'S SUSTAINABLE COMPETIVENESS

Background: In today's world, regardless of their level of development, almost all cities will face two problems: the need to develop in a comprehensive, balanced manner, while breaking through the crux of their development. No city that has not successfully grasped this principle can achieve the sustained upgrading of sustainable urban competitiveness.

Manifestation: There is a significant positive correlation between per capita GDP and sustainable competitiveness. The lower the income level, the more significant the correlation between urban sustainable competition and income.

From Figure 5.2 one can see that the urban sustainable competitiveness index is significantly positively correlated with the level of the urban economy. Among the top ten and top 100 cities globally, approximately 70 percent are high-income cities, and 30 percent are higher-income cities. These cities are mainly concentrated in developed countries. Only a minority of cities such as Hong Kong in China and Seoul in South Korea are located in emerging economies.

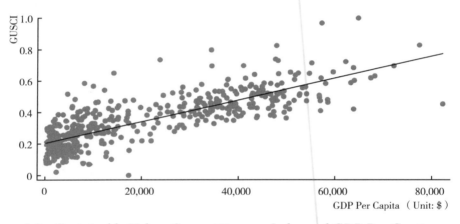

Figure 5.2   Sustainable Urban Competitiveness Index and GDP Per Capita

Reason: Income largely determines scientific and technological innovation, quality of the environment, social harmony, cultural diversity, global linkages, and governance, and thus also largely determines sustainable competitiveness.

Looking at the kernel density curves (Figure 5.3) of the Global Urban Sustainable Development Index (GUSCI) and per capita GDP, the two both appear on the left side, indicating that a large proportion of cities around the world have low levels of economic development and GUSCI. It should be noted that in contrast to the GUSCI kernel density curve, the per capita GDP kernel density curve is not a pure U-shaped curve but a double-peaked curve. This indicates that in low-income cities, the urban economy is the main factor determining urban sustainable competitiveness, but as the economy improves, the economy alone no longer determines sustainable competitiveness, and technological, environmental, social, and cultural factors all play a role.

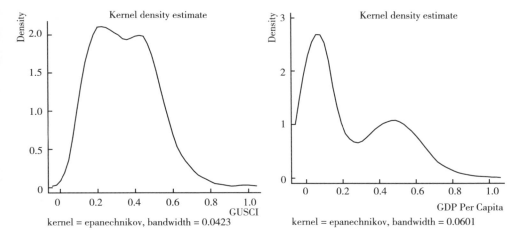

Figure 5.3   GUSCI and GDP Per Capita Kernel Density Curves for 500 Cities

However, scientific and technological, environmental, social, and cultural competitiveness are endogenous to economic growth—only after progressing to a certain degree of economic development is a city likely to make progress in these areas. From the different competitive situations in various aspects of cities of different income levels, one finds that the higher a city's income level, the better its performance in economic vitality, technological innovation, quality of environment, social harmony, global linkages, cultural diversity, and governance. This is the key to a city forming sustainable competitiveness. Thus, even though high-income cities experienced slow or negative economic growth during the global financial crisis, their competitiveness still ranked higher. In middle-income cities and below, even though economic growth proceeded relatively rapidly, the relatively low level of these economies restricted competitive upgrading in aspects such as scientific and technological innovation. These cities will have a hard time matching high-income cities in the near term.

Table 5.1   Itemized Competitiveness Indices of Cities of Varying Income Levels

	High income	**Higher income**	**Middle income**	**Lower income**	**Low income**
Per Capita GDP	0.606	0.385	0.140	0.058	0.017
GDP Growth Rate	0.188	0.155	0.373	0.332	0.302
Quality of Environment	0.486	0.486	0.485	0.461	0.522
Social Harmony	0.957	0.964	0.862	0.906	0.922
Innovation	0.172	0.073	0.063	0.022	0.006
Global Linkages	0.271	0.208	0.181	0.110	0.112
Cultural Diversity	0.453	0.349	0.223	0.171	0.142
Governance	0.927	0.880	0.617	0.446	0.301
GUSCI	0.538	0.437	0.310	0.228	0.196

Note: The social harmony index is obtained from the reciprocal of the crime rate; the quality of environment index is calculated from the reciprocal of per capita carbon dioxide emissions.

DEVELOPMENT IN CITIES OF VARYING INCOME LEVELS

Sustainable Competitiveness Among High-Income Cities Is Mixed

Background: Most high-income cities are concentrated in developed countries, where development is more balanced. Although some cities show strong potential for sustainable development as sources of technological and scientific innovation, many cities are in danger of sluggish growth due to high welfare policies, while others have been greatly impacted by the financial crisis due to reliance on the virtual economy and excessive consumption.

Manifestation: Changes in sustainable competitiveness in high-income cities are greater. While some cities were severely weakened, other cities improved significantly.

One can see from Figure 5.4 that the magnitude of change in the GUSCI in 2013 in high-income countries was between -0.05 and 0.05, basically a normal distribution. Changes in ranking are mainly concentrated between -25 and 25 spots and sit slightly to the left of the graph. Changes to the GUSCI and competitiveness rankings show that the sustainable competitiveness of most cities declined. Looking at the rankings, the cities where sustainable competitiveness fell most were Toronto, Nashville, Las Vegas, Albuquerque, Buffalo, Munich, Malmo, Aarhus, Jackson Vail, Wichita, and Fort Worth, in that order. Their rankings declined 25 spots or more. The cities where sustainable competitiveness grew the most were Stockholm, Mannheim, Hamburg, Stuttgart, Cincinnati, Helsinki, and Austin, in that order. Their rankings rose 25 spots or more.

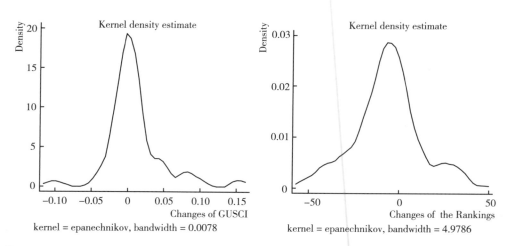

Figure 5.4   Kernel Density Curves for Changes of GUSCI and Competitiveness Rankings in High-Income Cities

Reason: Mainly that some cities had negative growth and deteriorating social order, but the number of patent applications grew rapidly.

High-income cities are generally in the post-industrial stage, with highly developed virtual economies and marginalized real economies. For example, among high-income cities in 2011, 45 percent were financial centers, while only 23 percent were manufacturing centers. Due to a lack of support from the real economy, the economic growth and total economic output of these cities with a high-degree of reliance on the financial industry fell under the impact of the financial crisis. Among them, Detroit and 18 others experienced the most serious slides, falling from high-income cities in 2011 to higher-income cities in 2013. The financial crisis not only pounded the financial system and dragged down the real economy, but also caused a deterioration of social order. Negative economic growth and the deteriorating social order ultimately resulted in the decline in sustainable competitiveness for high-income cities.

However, high-income cities are generally more developed cities, with high economic vitality, strong abilities to innovate, good ecological environments, extensive global linkages, and effective governance, providing favorable conditions for sustainable development and economic transformation after the financial crisis. From Figure 5.5 one can see that during the financial crisis, in high-income cities, regardless of whether sustainable competitiveness rose or fell, the number of patent applications grew. In Paris, New York, San Jose, Stuttgart, and Austin, the number of patent applications increased by large margins. In addition, high-income cities are mainly distributed amongst developed countries. After the financial crisis, developed countries began a new round of economic restructuring and achieved significant results. These changes have made important contributions to enhancing their sustainable competitiveness.

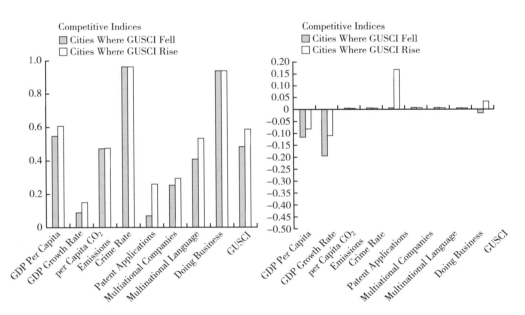

Figure 5.5   GUSCI Components and their Changes in High-Income Cities

Increases in Sustainable Competitiveness Are Slower in Higher-Income Cities

Background: Higher-income cities are "transitional cities" situated between middle-income cities and high-income cities. Although income levels are relatively high, they lag behind high-income cities in areas such as technological innovation and governance. In particular, higher-income cities have weak technological innovation abilities, and they have not yet formed the ability to support and lead economic development. These cities faced a severe test in the financial crisis.

Manifestation: Sustainable competitiveness increases slowly in higher-income cities, and there is a relatively large gap between them and high-income cities.

From Figure 5.6 one can see that the GUSCI for higher-income cities generally improved in 2013, with the index falling slightly in only a small portion. Declines were mainly between -0.025 and 0. However, in terms of the global sustainable competitiveness rankings, higher-income cities did not make significant progress.

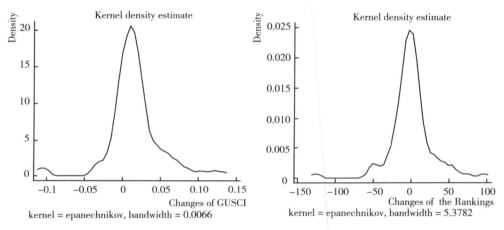

Figure 5.6   Kernel Density Curves for Changes of GUSCI and Competitiveness Rankings in Higher-Income Cities

Cause: Urban economic growth slowed, but technological innovation capabilities improved slowly.

During the financial crisis, although there are 11 cities that grew from higher-income cities in 2011 to high-income cities in 2013, overall, like high-income cities, economies in higher-income cities generally experienced negative growth, and economic growth rates in particular fell greatly. In contrast to high-income cities, higher-income cities have a lower ability for technological innovation, and under the impact of the financial crisis, the patent application index declined significantly in many cities. This index rose slightly in only a small number of cities. From this one can see that technological innovation capabilities are still weak in higher-income cities, which is a major bottleneck for rapid increases to sustainable competitiveness in higher-income cities.

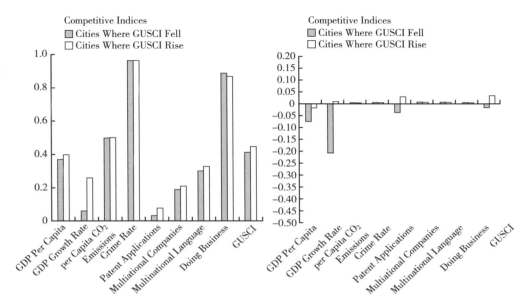

Figure 5.7   GUSCI Components and their Changes in Higher-Income Cities

Sustainable Competitiveness Improved Significantly in Middle-Income Cities

Background: Middle-income cities are mainly concentrated in emerging industrialized countries and are in the accelerated stage of industrialization and urbanization. In the context of globalization and information technology, the growth of these urban economies is rapid, but economic development models are generally factor-driven, shown in high factor inputs, low spatial agglomeration, low value-added trade, high consumption of natural resources, and environmental pollution. While the financial crisis brought opportunities to these cities, it also brought challenges.

Manifestation: Middle-income cities performed well during the financial crisis, but they face challenges in continuing to improve their sustainable competitiveness.

In 2013, in the context of slowing global economic growth, middle-income cities on average maintained economic growth of more than 6 percent, and their GUSCI generally rose significantly, as did their global competitiveness rankings. For example, Gyeongju in South Korea and Suzhou in China both saw their GUSCI rise more than 0.12, and their relative rankings rose more than 100 places. But this rapid growth is neither universal nor sustainable. Among middle-income cities, Chinese cities generally performed best. More than half of cities whose relative rankings rose were Chinese.

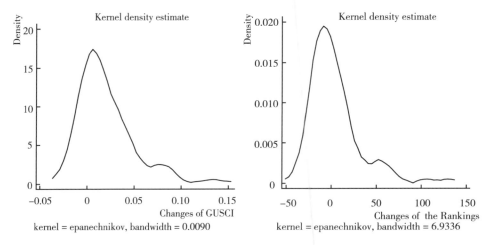

Figure 5.8   Kernel Density Curves for Changes of GUSCI and Competitiveness Rankings in Middle-Income Cities

Reason: The late-developer advantage is a favorable factor, but economic restructuring is a challenge.

Rapid economic growth is a major cause of the improvement to sustainable competitiveness among middle-income cities. The reason why middle-income cities did not lose growth momentum during the financial crisis may be related to the following two reasons: 1) Compared to high-income and higher-income cities, middle-income cities are relatively low in the multinational corporation index, and the external financial crisis thus had a weak effect; 2) Most middle-income cities are located in developing countries, the development stage of which determines that they are able to use their late-developer advantage to achieve economic growth for some time; 3) Governments interfere positively and effectively in the economy (for example, rapid economic growth among Chinese cities shows that the economic stimulus measures employed by the Chinese government during the financial crisis had a significant effect).

However, in the long-term, middle-income cities face some problems. For example, looking at per capita CO_2 emissions in 2013, environmental quality in middle-income cities is relatively poor. The middle-income-city development model of sacrificing the environment for economic growth is not sustainable. With the increasing economic level, being innovation-driven is increasingly important in maintaining sustained economic growth. But middle-income cities have weak abilities for technological innovation. In terms of the patent application index, middle-income cities are less than half high-income cities. Thus, growth transformation difficulties brought on by insufficient technological innovation capabilities may be the main factor restricting the formation of sustainable competitiveness in middle-income cities. In addition, middle-income cities face other serious social issues, such as high crime rates.

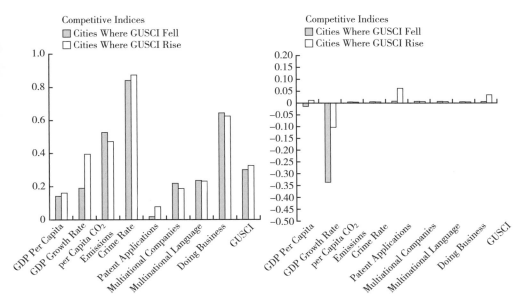

Figure 5.9   GUSCI Components and their Changes in Middle-Income Cities

Sustainable Competitiveness Must Improve by Leaps and Bounds in Lower-Income Cities

Background: Urban development takes the form of a "flying V," with lower-income cities mainly relying on developing industries that developed cities have eliminated for economic growth. Such development is not sustainable and has high social costs. Moreover, as technology in developed cities improves, the transferring industry becomes more and more technical, and lower-income cities must accelerate the pace of development.

Manifestation: When urban economic growth is accompanied by serious environmental pollution, the gap in sustainable competitiveness with cities of higher income levels grows.

The kernel density curve for the change to the GUSCI for lower-income cities in 2013 is clearly skewed to the right, indicating a general improvement in the competitive index. However, looking at the kernel density curve for changes to sustainable competitiveness rankings for lower-income cities, one can see that the relative rankings of lower-income cities declined. This is the case for cities such as Hohhot and Curitiba.

Cause: Economic and technological backwardness and low capacity for cultivating industry.

Due to the relatively abundant low-cost human capital and natural resources, lower-income cities take on the low-value-added and high-polluting industries of many developed cities in accordance with their comparative advantage. But this economic development model is not conducive to the long-term development of the economy. First is the harm to the environment. Looking at per capita carbon dioxide emissions for 2011 and 2013, environmental problems in lower-income cities are relatively serious. Second, this economic development model of reliance on exogenous comparative advantage is often not conducive

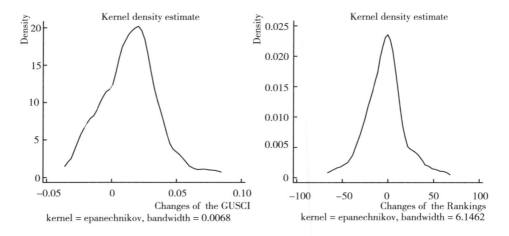

Figure 5.10   Kernel Density Curves for Changes of GUSCI and Competitiveness Rankings in Lower-Income Cities

to the formation of endogenous comparative advantage. The economic growth model of low-cost production of low-value goods restricts innovation-driven economic growth, which restricts the formation and development of high-tech industry.

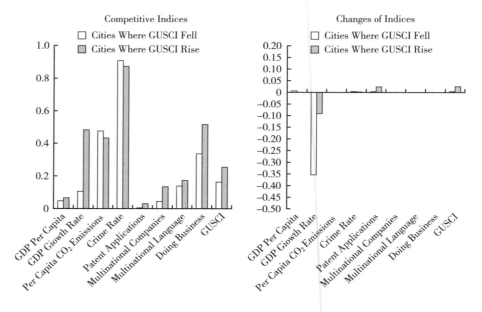

Figure 5.11   GUSCI Components and their Changes in Lower-Income Cities

Low-Income Cities Have a Hard Time Ensuring Rising Sustainable Urban Competitiveness

Background: For some time, low-income cities around the world have faced many challenges and vicious cycles resulting from low income levels. Global competition has made the sustainable development environment for low-income cities even worse.

Manifestation: Sustainable competitiveness is difficult for low-income cities to enhance significantly, and the financial crisis made development in many cities more unsustainable.

Although the GUSCI improved in low-income cities in 2013, this was mainly due to the good ecological environment. Looking at the sustainable competitive index, the sustainable competiveness of low-income cities is rather weak, and their global competitiveness rankings are low.

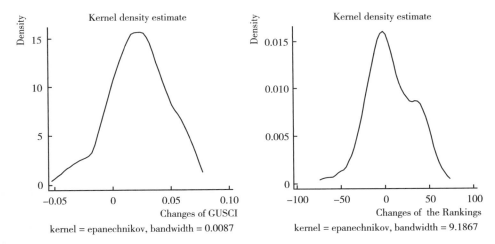

Figure 5.12   Kernel Density Curves for Changes of GUSCI and Competitiveness Rankings in Low-Income Cities

Cause: Backward economies restrict comprehensive and balanced development.

Low-income cities are still in the initial stages of urbanization. Not having formed real industrial economies in the urbanization process, they lack the economic means to resolve the issues of sustainable urban development. Their ability to withstand risks during crisis is also weak. During the crisis, economic growth in some low-income cities slowed significantly. Moreover, the low level of these economies is not conducive to the accumulation of other resources, restricting development in other areas. Low-income cities are weak competitors in economic vitality, technological innovation, global linkages, cultural diversity, and governance. This is particularly true in low-income cities in Africa. From the changes to the breakdown of the GUSCI for 2011 and 2013, one can see that whether in terms of cities whose GUSCI increased or those where it fell, low-income cities had no significant improvements in several components of the GUSCI.

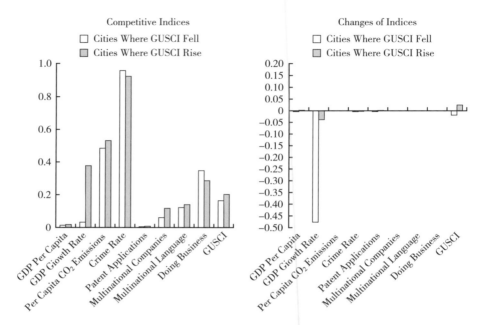

Figure 5.13   GUSCI Components and their Changes in Low-Income Cities

CASE STUDY

Mumbai and Shanghai are both Asian port cities and financial centers, and there are many similarities between the two. Because the stock markets of the two cities are booming, many people place Mumbai and Shanghai on par with each other, even calling Mumbai the "Shanghai of India." But Shanghai and Mumbai are also different. Shanghai is a rapidly developing, middle-income city, while Mumbai is a slowly developing, lower-income city. Therefore, this chapter will analyze Shanghai and Mumbai as typical examples of these categories of cities.

Shanghai: The Rise of a Middle-Income City

Shanghai, located at the mouth of the Yangtze River, is China's largest foreign trade port and largest industrial base, and is an economic, financial, trade, and shipping center with a population of more than 20 million people. Shanghai's global sustainable competitiveness ranking for 2013 rose 17 places over 2011, leaping to the 17th place worldwide. In 2013, Shanghai's per capita GDP was US$ 14,213, and its economic growth rate was 12.28 percent. Shanghai's economic development is related to its rapid development and its own strong competitiveness.

Looking at the various aspects of sustainable urban competitiveness, Shanghai's performance among middle-income cities is outstanding. Among them, technological innovation ranked ninth, global linkages ranked twelfth, cultural diversity ranked 33rd, and governance ranked 280th. More important, Shanghai shows good development prospects. In recent years, in order to build Shanghai into an internationally competitive economic, financial, trade, and shipping center with global influence, the local government has been accelerating the development of the modern service industry and advanced manufacturing industry, has gradually increased the degree of market openness and convenience of trade, and accelerated the construction of a world-class trade development environment. Thus, even during the financial crisis, Shanghai's global competitiveness ranking rose year after year.

Shanghai's development has also led to the development of surrounding cities. From a half-hour economic circle to a one-hour economic circle to a three-hour economic circle, the urban grouping with Shanghai at the center is expanding, and economic cooperation within the region is close. The one-city effect in the Yangtze River Delta economic circle has shown a great deal of power. Shanghai's nearby cities – Nanjing, Yangzhou, Suzhou, Hangzhou, Ningbo, Wenzhou, and Hefei – all exhibited strong competitiveness during the financial crisis, rising significantly in the global rankings.

Despite the wide gap between Shanghai and well-known international metropolises, Shanghai has made rapid progress in recent years, and the gap is narrowing. Shanghai's domestic and international competitiveness are fusing, and it is expected to become an economic and financial center for the Asia-Pacific region in the near future.

Mumbai: The Development Plight of the Low-Income City

Mumbai is a large city on India's western coast and the nation's largest port. It is home to the headquarters of numerous financial institutions and Indian companies. With 18 million people (2010), Mumbai is India's most populous city, and one of the world's most populous as well. In 2011 and 2013, Mumbai's global competitiveness rankings were around 300. Per capita income was only US$ 1,694.79. Because of the relatively large overall economy, Indian authorities proposed the city development goal of "letting the world forget Shanghai and remember Mumbai." But looking at the various competitiveness indicators, there is a great competitiveness gap between Mumbai and competitive cities.

Whether in terms of social harmony, technological innovation, or governance, Mumbai lags behind developed cities with higher incomes. From the 2013 sustainable competitiveness rankings, one can see that Mumbai is near the rear for the various rankings – 355th in crime, 234th in patent applications, 435th for business environment, at the end of the global list. Specifically, the factors constraining Mumbai's development are mainly manifested in short supply of urban public goods, lagging infrastructure, as well as urbanization problems such as urban slums and low-income housing supply. Mumbai's severe traffic jams have greatly influenced the development of the city. These are problems faced by many low-income cities in the development process.

On the financial level, Mumbai is home to the oldest stock exchange in Asia at 135 years old. This is wherein the city's competitiveness lies, and provides significant capital for the city to make progress. But if Mumbai cannot increase its ability to innovate, strengthen governance, and provide a good operating environment for the development of the urban economy, Mumbai will have a difficult time achieving long-term economic growth, and its financial development will be restricted. Therefore, we believe that there is still a long road to walk for low-income cities like Mumbai to catch up to high-income cities.

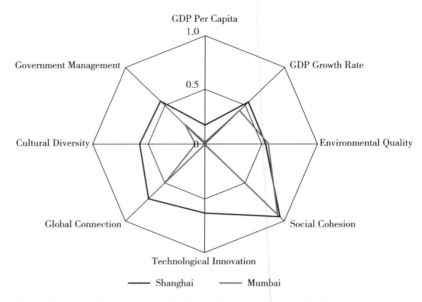

Figure 5.14   Various Competitive Indices for Mumbai and Shanghai

REFERENCES

Malecki, E. J. (2002), Hard and soft networks for urban competitiveness, *Urban Studies*, 39(5–6): 929–945.

McCann, P. (2013), *Modern Urban and Regional Economics*, Oxford: Oxford University Press.

Ni Pengfei (2013), *Report No, 11 on Chinese Urban Competitiveness*, Beijing: Social Science Documentation Publishing House.

Nie Yun (2011), Mumbai's pain: slums and housing difficulties, *Governance Digest*, (1): 49.

Taylor, P. J. (2011), *Global Urban Analysis: A Survey of Cities in Globalization*, London: Routledge Publishing.

Zhang Xunliang and Ning Yuemin (2011), Urban economic ties and international spatial development strategy for the Yangtze River Delta City Group, *Economic Geography*, 31(3): 353–359.

6. Global urban sustainable competitiveness and urban population size

Chao Li[1]

With the advance of industrialization, it is necessary to gather population and economic activity in a few areas in order to achieve economies of scale. The introduction to the World Bank's "World Development Report 2009" notes that half of the world's economic activity occurs on 1.5 percent of the world's land area. Overall, population density is higher in developed countries than in developing countries. This is because in the agricultural stage of development, land is immovable, and people have no choice but to be dispersed. But industry and services rely on capital. The service industry in particular requires face-to-face consumption, and therefore requires a higher concentration of population. Thus, in countries with more developed industry and services, the population is concentrated in fewer areas. Can such concentration of population effectively enhance the sustainable competitiveness of a city? This chapter will mainly discuss and analyze three aspects of this theme.

POPULATION SIZE AND GROWTH ARE REFLECTIONS OF URBAN SUSTAINABLE COMPETITIVENESS

Figures 6.1 and 6.2 show spatial distributions and correlation diagrams of the population sizes and levels of sustainable competitiveness of 500 sample cities in 2013. From the figures, one can see that among the top ten cities in the sustainable competitiveness rankings for 2013, with the exception of San Jose with a population of approximately 1 million, other cities all had populations exceeding 2 million. Population and sustainable competitiveness are significantly and positively correlated, indicating that the larger the population size of the city, the higher the level of urban sustainable competitiveness. At the same time, the higher the level of competitiveness, the stronger the attraction for additional population, and the higher a city's population concentration. Among cities in the top twenty for sustainable competitiveness, only Hong Kong, Seoul, Singapore, and Shanghai are located in emerging economies. The rest are located in developed countries.

Looking at the kernel density curves (such as Figure 6.3) for GUSCI and population size for the 500 sample cities, the two both appear to be inclined to the left rather than in a

---

1   Chao Li, Center of City and Competitiveness, CASS. No. 2 yuetanbeixiaojie, Xicheng District, Beijing, China, post code: 100836, Tel: 8610-68063478.
    Email: lichao202@163.com.

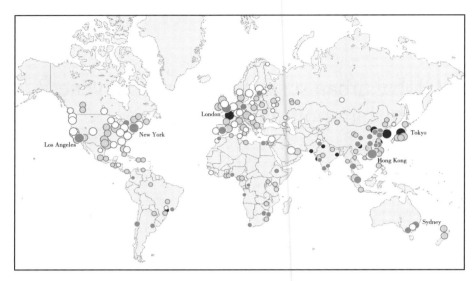

Figure 6.1   Spatial Distribution for Population Size and Sustainable Competitiveness for 500 Sample Cities in 2013

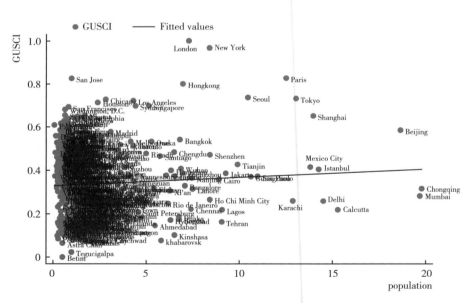

Figure 6.2   Correlation Diagram for Population Size and Sustainable Competitiveness in 500 Sample Cities in 2013

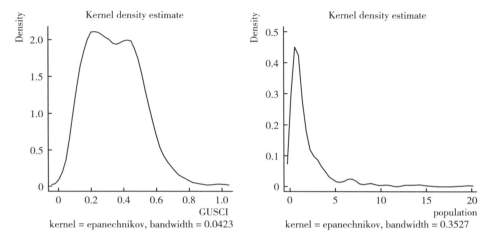

Figure 6.3   Kernel Density Curves for GUSCI and Population Size for 500 Sample Cities in 2013

normal distribution. The kernel density curve for GUSCI forms an "M" shape, while the kernel density curve for population size is clearly inclined to the left. Among the 500 sample cities, a large proportion has populations of around 1 million and a GUSCI level between 0.2 and 0.4.

AMONG DIFFERENT POPULATION SIZE SAMPLE GROUPS, RELATIONSHIP BETWEEN POPULATION SIZE AND SUSTAINABLE COMPETITIVENESS IS COMPLEX

1. Giant Cities

In 2013, there were 14 giant cities with populations above 10 million, flat with the number from the previous period. Among them, four were Chinese and three were Indian. In general, giant cities have high degrees of agglomeration, are highly concentrated, and economic activity within them is intensive. They are often political, economic, technological, and industrial center cities for their countries and have decisive influence in the world. By comparing data for 2013 and 2011, global recovery still does not enjoy significant momentum. As economic, professional, technological, and industrial agglomeration centers for their countries, giant cities are representative in that they bore the brunt of the impact. GDP growth rate and multinationals index scores both fell, and giant cities excelling in the multinationals index were likely to be hardest hit by the financial crisis. However, BRICS countries make up a high proportion of giant cities, so although some indicators fell, growth momentum for other indicators such as the patent index and business environment remained favorable.

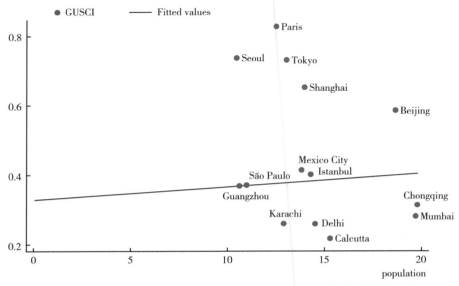

Figure 6.4   Relationship Fit Chart for Population Size and GUSCI for Giant Cities in 2013

Table 6.1   Changes to Various Indicators for Giant Cities

Year	Variable	Obs.	Mean	Std Dev.	Min.	Max.	CV
2013	GDP per capita	14	0.164	0.193	0.013	0.585	1.179
	GDP growth rate	14	0.374	0.181	0.097	0.700	0.484
	Inverse CO_2 emissions per capita	14	0.558	0.136	0.273	0.840	0.244
	Inverse crime rate	14	0.925	0.072	0.738	0.986	0.078
	Patent applications per 10,000 people	14	0.275	0.344	0.000	1.000	1.251
	Global network connectivity	14	0.578	0.240	0.192	0.957	0.415
	InterContinental Hotels Group PLC	14	0.232	0.174	0.083	0.583	0.747
	Doing business index	14	0.570	0.241	0.254	0.916	0.424
2011	GDP per capita	14	0.178	0.222	0.015	0.698	1.245
	GDP growth rate	14	0.483	0.149	0.196	0.666	0.309
	Inverse CO_2 emissions per capita	14	0.575	0.134	0.273	0.840	0.233
	Inverse crime rate	14	0.922	0.074	0.748	0.989	0.081
	Patent applications per 10,000 people	14	0.163	0.270	0.000	1.000	1.653
	Global network connectivity	14	0.602	0.239	0.192	0.957	0.396
	InterContinental Hotels Group PLC	14	0.250	0.170	0.083	0.583	0.679
	Doing business index	14	0.552	0.251	0.254	0.916	0.454

2. Very Large Cities

In 2013, there were a total of 79 very large cities with populations between 3 million and 10 million, thirteen more than in the 2011 period. The top six GUSCI scores (all 0.6 and above) went to London, New York, Hong Kong, Los Angeles, Singapore, and Sydney. Compared to 2011, with the exception of inverse crime rate and the patent index, which increased slightly, the average values of other indicators fell by varying degrees due to the higher number of cities in the "very large" group.

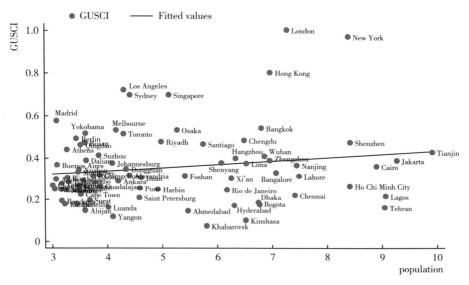

Figure 6.5   *Correlation Fit Diagram for Population Size and GUSCI for Very Large Cities in 2013*

Table 6.2   Changes to Various Indicators for Very Large Cities

Year	Variable	Obs.	Mean	Std Dev.	Min.	Max.	CV
2013	GDP per capita	79	0.136	0.173	0.000	0.787	1.277
	GDP growth rate	79	0.400	0.262	-0.183	1.000	0.655
	Inverse CO_2 emissions per capita	79	0.511	0.207	0.126	1.000	0.406
	Inverse crime rate	79	0.918	0.114	0.472	0.995	0.124
	Patent applications per 10,000 people	79	0.095	0.165	0.000	0.861	1.727
	Global network connectivity	79	0.277	0.230	0.012	1.000	0.831
	InterContinental Hotels Group PLC	79	0.268	0.229	0.083	1.000	0.853
	Doing business index	79	0.574	0.248	0.034	1.000	0.433
2011	GDP per capita	66	0.163	0.210	0.000	0.898	1.292
	GDP growth rate	66	0.484	0.180	0.166	0.884	0.372
	Inverse CO_2 emissions per capita	66	0.514	0.200	0.126	1.000	0.388
	Inverse crime rate	66	0.915	0.122	0.470	0.995	0.134
	Patent applications per 10,000 people	66	0.053	0.136	0.000	0.839	2.569
	Global network connectivity	66	0.308	0.237	0.027	1.000	0.768
	InterContinental Hotels Group PLC	66	0.283	0.238	0.083	1.000	0.841
	Doing business index	66	0.579	0.263	0.034	1.000	0.454

3. Large Cities

In 2013, there were 171 cities with populations between 1 million and 3 million, 12 fewer than in 2011.Chicago, Houston, Vienna, Dallas, Philadelphia, Dublin, and San Diego held the top 7 GUSCI spots with scores of 0.6 or more. Compared to 2011, among average values for various competitive indicators, the patent index, multinational contact index, multinational language index, and business environment index all rose to varying degrees. In contrast to other city groupings, the population and GUSCI fit curve for very large cities show a slightly downward trend.

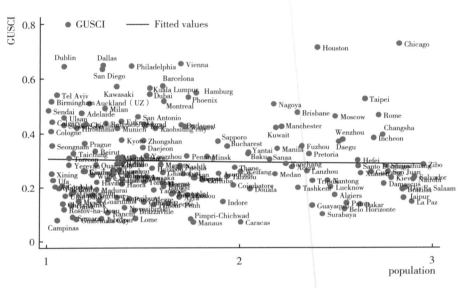

Figure 6.6   Fit Curve for GUSCI and Population for Large Cities in 2013

Table 6.3   Changes to Various Indicators for Large Cities

Year	Variable	Obs.	Mean	Std Dev.	Min.	Max.	CV
2013	GDP per capita	171	0.162	0.193	0.001	0.670	1.189
	GDP growth rate	171	0.323	0.232	-0.184	0.955	0.719
	Inverse CO_2 emissions per capita	171	0.496	0.203	0.000	0.923	0.409
	Inverse crime rate	171	0.918	0.104	0.204	0.995	0.113
	Patent applications per 10,000 people	171	0.042	0.101	0.000	0.706	2.415
	Global network connectivity	171	0.154	0.150	0.009	0.745	0.970
	InterContinental Hotels Group PLC	171	0.236	0.183	0.083	0.750	0.776
	Doing business index	171	0.535	0.277	0.000	0.990	0.517

Table 6.3   *(continued)*

Year	Variable	Obs.	Mean	Std Dev.	Min.	Max.	CV
	GDP per capita	183	0.166	0.212	0.000	0.909	1.277
	GDP growth rate	183	0.455	0.193	0.045	0.979	0.423
	Inverse CO_2 emissions per capita	183	0.500	0.200	0.000	0.923	0.400
	Inverse crime rate	183	0.925	0.101	0.204	0.998	0.110
2011	Patent applications per 10,000 people	183	0.023	0.050	0.000	0.318	2.197
	Global network connectivity	183	0.150	0.142	0.008	0.624	0.946
	InterContinental Hotels Group PLC	183	0.230	0.183	0.083	0.750	0.797
	Doing business index	183	0.528	0.273	0.000	0.990	0.518

4. Medium-Sized Cities

In 2013, there were 130 cities with populations between 500,000 and 1 million, basically even with the two previous years. San Jose, San Francisco, Washington D.C., Seattle, and Austin had the top five GUSCI scores, scoring 0.6 or higher. Compared to 2011, indicators including the CO_2 emissions index, patent index, and multinational contact index rose slightly, while other indicators declined. Similar to large cities, the GUSCI and population fit curve for medium-sized cities exhibited a downward trend, and a more significant one.

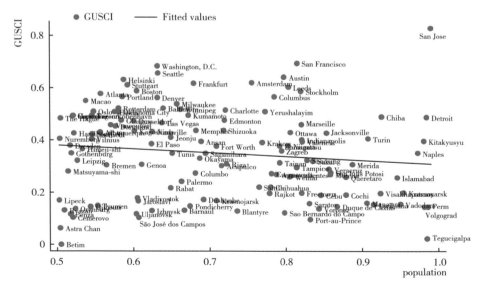

Figure 6.7   Fit Curve for GUSCI and Population for Medium-Sized Cities in 2013

Table 6.4   Changes to Various Indicators for Medium-Sized Cities

Year	Variable	Obs.	Mean	Std Dev.	Min.	Max.	CV
	GDP per capita	130	0.315	0.241	0.003	0.941	0.764
	GDP growth rate	130	0.206	0.190	-0.178	0.882	0.921
	Inverse CO_2 emissions per capita	130	0.471	0.161	0.095	0.845	0.341
2013	Inverse crime rate	130	0.918	0.134	0.000	1.000	0.146
	Patent applications per 10,000 people	130	0.072	0.156	0.000	0.999	2.185
	Global network connectivity	130	0.134	0.117	0.002	0.496	0.871
	InterContinental Hotels Group PLC	130	0.269	0.201	0.083	0.750	0.747
	Doing business index	130	0.700	0.294	0.034	0.984	0.421
	GDP per capita	132	0.353	0.276	0.003	1.000	0.781
	GDP growth rate	132	0.355	0.152	0.174	1.000	0.427
	Inverse CO_2 emissions per capita	132	0.465	0.173	0.076	0.845	0.371
2011	Inverse crime rate	132	0.922	0.135	0.000	0.999	0.146
	Patent applications per 10,000 people	132	0.029	0.048	0.000	0.322	1.667
	Global network connectivity	132	0.133	0.117	0.002	0.496	0.880
	InterContinental Hotels Group PLC	132	0.269	0.196	0.083	0.750	0.729
	Doing business index	132	0.716	0.276	0.034	0.984	0.385

5. Small Cities

In 2013, there were 106 cities with populations below 500,000, basically flat with 2011. Oakland, Palo Alto, and Doha had the top three GUSCI rankings, scoring 0.6 or higher. Compared to 2011, with the exception of slowing economic growth rate, other indicators saw only modest changes

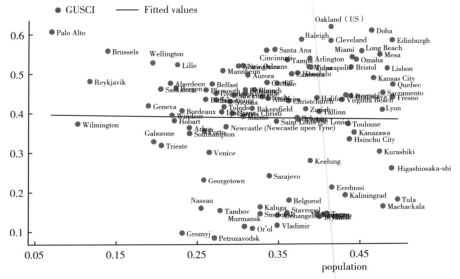

Figure 6.8   Fit Curve for GUSCI and Population for Small Cities in 2013

Table 6.5   Changes to Various Indicators for Small Cities

Year	Variable	Obs.	Mean	Std Dev.	Min.	Max.	CV
2013	GDP per capita	106	0.387	0.220	0.012	1.000	0.570
	GDP growth rate	106	0.141	0.161	-0.622	0.851	1.139
	Inverse CO_2 emissions per capita	106	0.472	0.154	0.076	0.923	0.326
	Inverse crime rate	106	0.942	0.086	0.164	0.995	0.091
	Patent applications per 10,000 people	106	0.058	0.082	0.000	0.478	1.403
	Global network connectivity	106	0.141	0.101	0.002	0.572	0.716
	InterContinental Hotels Group PLC	106	0.329	0.223	0.000	0.833	0.676
	Doing business index	106	0.784	0.264	0.228	0.990	0.337
2011	GDP per capita	105	0.449	0.248	0.007	0.974	0.551
	GDP growth rate	105	0.304	0.112	0.172	0.684	0.368
	Inverse CO_2 emissions per capita	105	0.470	0.148	0.161	0.923	0.314
	Inverse crime rate	105	0.948	0.082	0.211	1.000	0.087
	Patent applications per 10,000 people	105	0.023	0.030	0.000	0.142	1.286
	Global network connectivity	105	0.143	0.100	0.002	0.572	0.697
	InterContinental Hotels Group PLC	105	0.333	0.225	0.000	0.833	0.675
	Doing business index	105	0.782	0.272	0.119	0.990	0.348

THE "SPHINX RIDDLE" OF OPTIMAL CITY SIZE

Greek mythology contains the well-known story of the Sphinx asking passers-by a riddle, "What walks on four legs in the morning, two legs at noon, and three legs in the evening?" Before Oedipus guessed correctly that the answer was "man," those who guessed wrong met with disaster. The "Riddle of the Sphinx" emphasizes the morphological differences in the various stages of the human life cycle. In fact, the huge differences in city size also exist in the different stages of urban development. From the sustainable competitiveness index delineated by city size, one can see that, at different sizes, there are different linear relationships between city size and sustainable competitiveness. So, is there an optimal city size?

This question can be traced back to Plato in ancient Greece. Based on the plaza at the center as the standard, he said that the optimal size of a city was 5,040 people. In the mid-19th century, the utopian socialist thinkers Fourier and Owen said the ideal human commune would be 1,500-2,000 and 500-1,500 people, respectively. In 1898, Ebenezer Howard, the founder of modern urban planning theory, said the optimal size of a center city population was 58,000 people, and the optimal population of six surrounding Garden Cities was 32,000. In 1960, former Soviet engineering economist Davidovich said that the reasonable scale of an industrial and industrial transportation city was between 30,000 and 150,000, with a permissible size of 10,000 to 300,000. In 1977, American systems engineer Gibson said that from economic and other considerations, the optimal size of a city was between 800,000 and 1.2 million. Krihs (1980), analyzing from the perspective of the urban agglomeration economy, obtained an optimal size of around 6 million people through empirical research. Wang Xiaolu and Xia Xiaolin (1999), setting out from the benefits of scale and the relative external costs, said that the optimal range was between 1 million and 4 million people. Ma Shucai and Song Limin (2003) said that city size should be a dynamic equilibrium concept and that city size efficiency and urban sustainable development capability were greatest between 1 and 2 million people and 500,000 to 1 million people. Au and Henderson (2006) found that the peak value of the greatest agglomeration effect was between approximately 2.5 to 3.8 million, and that the peak value of the largest agglomeration effect would move upward with the proportion of a city's service industry.

1. Panel Data Model Test for Optimal City Size

On the basis of these previous studies, the following uses the panel data sets from 2011 and 2013 to test optimal city size for urban competitiveness. Before regression analysis, we first need to effectively distinguish an appropriate estimation method. The F-test and Breusch-Pagan test both reject the null hypothesis, that is, the panel data's individual effects are very significant, thus excluding the mixed OLS estimation method. Further, Hausman test results reject the null hypothesis of no systematic difference between the random effects model and fixed effects model. Therefore, synthesizing the results of these three tests, this paper employs the fixed effects model, whose estimation results were most ideal, as the main object of explanation, while at the same time carrying out a comprehensive comparison of regression results of the random effects model and mixed OLS model.

Table 6.6   Model Selection and Test Results

Test	Model (1)	Model (2)	Judgment
F test	87.86	84.31	Choose fixed effects, not mixed effects
Prob > F	0.000	0.000	
B-P test	477.48	468.38	Choose random effects, not mixed effects
Prob > x^2	0.000	0.000	
Hausman test	26.5	25.10	Choose fixed effects, not random effects
Prob > x^2	0.000	0.000	

Table 6.7   Panel Data Model Test for Optimal City Size

	Model (1)		Model (2)	
VARIABLES	Fixed Effects	Random Effects	Fixed Effects	Random Effects
Population	0.0021**	-0.0005	0.0014**	-0.0139**
	(0.004)	(0.004)	(0.009)	(0.007)
Population2	0.0002*	0.0004*	0.0003	0.0024**
	(0.000)	(0.000)	(0.001)	(0.001)
Population3			-0.0000*	-0.0001
			(0.000)	(0.000)
Constant	0.3293***	0.3327***	0.3299***	0.3446***
	(0.006)	(0.009)	(0.010)	(0.010)
Observations	1,000	1,000	1,000	1,000
R-squared	0.012		0.013	
Number of code	500	500	500	500

Note: Standard errors in parentheses, *** p < 0. 01, ** p < 0. 05, * p < 0. 1.

From the results of the panel data model test for optimal city size, one can see that the optimal fit result is the fixed effects model in Model (1). The fit results show for this model show that urban competitiveness and urban scale exhibit a positive "U"-shape correlation, and therefore do not support the optimal city size hypothesis. In Model (2), the triple regression coefficient is not significant, and the "law" of urban competitiveness and city size is also not true.

2. Study of Optimal City Size by Continent

From a study of samples broken down by their six continents, one sees that there is a positive correlation between city size and urban sustainable competitiveness in Europe, North America, Oceania, and Africa, which more or less exhibit a monotonically increasing hyperbolic relationship. Asia and South America exhibit a slightly downward sloping inverted "U"-shaped trend. But from the situations of the various continents, there is no clear, consistent inflection point. Therefore, the study by continent does not support the hypothesis of the existence of an optimal city size either.

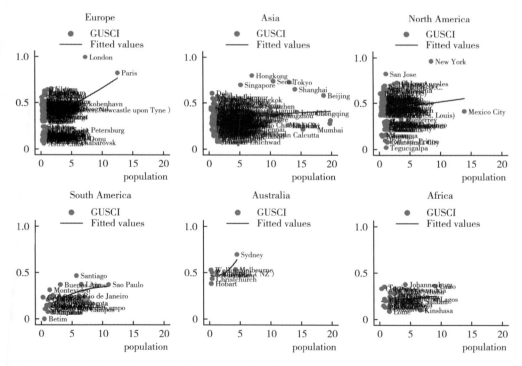

Figure 6.9   Correlation Fit Diagrams for City Population and Sustainable Competitiveness in Six Continents for 2013

3. Study of Optimal City Size by Function

From the study of optimal city size by city function, one finds that the relationship between city size and urban sustainable competiveness in seaport cities presents an inverted U-shaped curve, with the inversion point occurring around 10 million people. The relationship for non-seaport cities presents a clear U-shaped curve. The relationship in financial center function cities presents a monotonically decreasing hyperbolic curve, while the relationship in non-financial-center cities presents a clear U-shaped curve. Technology center function cities present a monotonically increasing hyperbolic curve, while non-technology-center function cities present a U-shaped curve. Tourism and non-tourism cities, capital and non-capital cities, manufacturing and non-manufacturing center cities all present varying degrees of U-shaped curves. Overall, there is no consistent inflection point among cities broken down by function. Therefore, the study results of cities broken down by function do not support the hypothesis of an optimal city size.

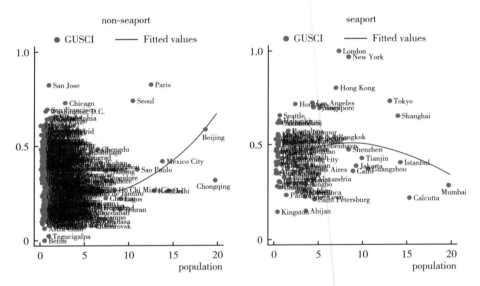

Figure 6.10   Correlation Fit Diagrams for Population and Sustainable
Competitiveness in Seaport and Non-Seaport Cities for 2013

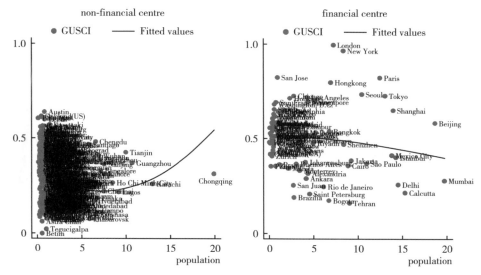

Figure 6.11   *Correlation Fit Diagrams for Population and Sustainable Competitiveness in Financial and Non-Financial Functional Cities for 2013*

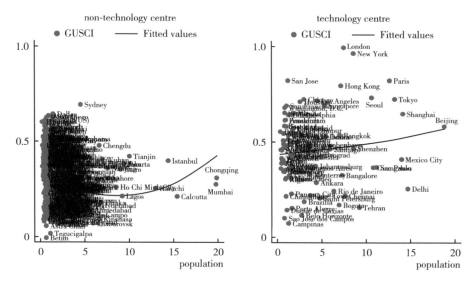

Figure 6.12   *Correlation Fit Diagrams for Population and Sustainable Competitiveness in Technology and Non-Technology Functional Cities for 2013*

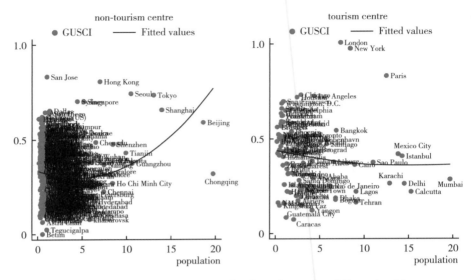

Figure 6.13   Correlation Fit Diagrams for Population and Sustainable Competitiveness in Tourism and Non-Tourism Functional Cities for 2013

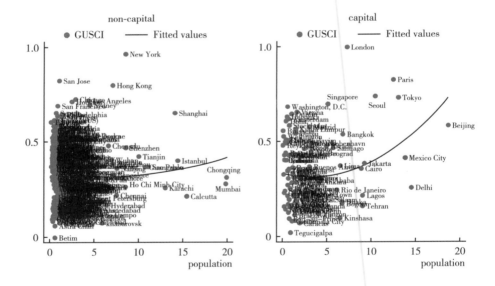

Figure 6.14   Correlation Fit Diagrams for Population and Sustainable Competitiveness in Capital and Non-Capital Cities for 2013

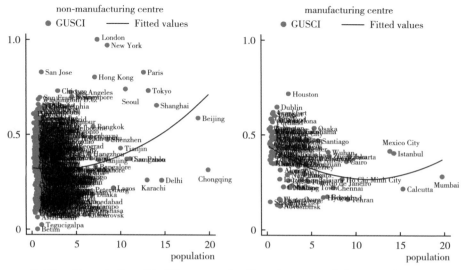

Figure 6.15   Correlation Fit Diagrams for Population and Sustainable Competitiveness in Manufacturing and Non-Manufacturing Functional Cities for 2013

CONCLUSIONS AND DISCUSSION

The city is a spatial carrier for highly concentrated economic activity and population. This section systematically analyzes the relationship between population size and competitiveness in 500 sample cities and, by further considering panel data and the breakdown of cities by continent and function, finds that there is no positive correlation between city size and competitiveness. The enhancement of competitiveness is a long-term, systemic process and cannot be achieved simply by increasing the size of a city. In cities of different sizes and different functional types, there are large differences in the key points of increasing competitiveness and the sequence of improving elements. Improvements to cities of different sizes should be made in a differentiated manner based on the specific endowments and characteristics of each city.

Because a city is a complex system made up of economic, political, historical, social, and environmental elements, coupled with differences in the analytical perspectives, periods of analysis, objects of analysis, and analytical tools, the best studies of city size cannot reach a consistent conclusion. After a long period of multidisciplinary exploration, we regret that we have not found an Oedipus to the unlock the Sphinx's riddle of optimal city size. Although theoretically there is a critical point of optimal size of a city, in real life, the influencing internal and external elements are extremely complex, and they change constantly. The development of a city's size is a process of dynamic equilibrium. In this sense, economics opens an inspirational door, encouraging the search for the answer to the "Sphinx's riddle" from the perspective of incrementally increasing benefits of size and the system of city strata. This will be beneficial to the better understanding of a long-term mechanism for the expansion of city size and the enhancement of urban competitiveness.

REFERENCES

Au, C. C. and Henderson, J. V. (2006), "Are Chinese Cities Too Small?", *Review of Economic Studies*, Vol. 73, pp. 549–576.

Au, C. C. and Henderson, J. V. (2006), "How Migration Restrictions Limit Agglomeration and Productivity in China", *Journal of Development Economics*, Vol. 3, pp. 1–45.

Calino, G. A. (1982), "Manufacturing Agglomeration Economies as Return to Scale: A Production Approach", *Papers of the Regional Science Association*, Vol. 50.

Chen, Zhuoyong (2008), "Theory and Empirical Study of Optimal City Size", *Urban Planning International*, Vol. 6.

Li, Pei (2007), "A Review of Studies on City Size", *Economic Commentary*, Vol. 1.

Lu, Ming, Xiang, Kuanhu, and Chen, Zhao (2011), "China's Urbanization and Adjustment to the City System: A Review of the Literature", *World Economy*, Vol. 6.

Ma, Shucai and Song, Limin (2003), "Analysis and Comparative Study of the Development in Size of China's Cities", *Statistical Research*, Vol. 4.

Wang, Xiaolu and Xia, Xiaolin (1999), "Optimizing City Size to Promote Economic Growth", *Economic Research*, Vol. 9.

7. Global urban sustainable competitiveness: characteristics of functional centers

Qingbin Li[1]

A city's value is reflected in its functional orientation. Not only are the functions of a city increasingly diverse, the values and roles of these functions are also increasingly different. In the context of globalization, cooperation and competition among cities unfolds around their similar and different functions. Analyzing and comparing the sustainable competitiveness of cities from the perspective of their functions is not without significance. From the sustainable competitiveness results for 2011 and 2013, this report conducts a specialized analysis centered on differences in both strength and direction of sustainable competitiveness in functional centers.

This report divides 500 global sample cities into seven functional centers: comprehensive center cities (100), financial center cities (100), science and technology center cities (100), political center cities (116), tourism center cities (89), manufacturing center cities (100), and shipping center cities (89). It should be noted that due to a variety of factors, such as development levels, economies of scale, agglomeration effects, etc., a city may fall under multiple categories.

Table 7.1 Seven Functional Centers

Functional Group	Number	Explanation
Comprehensive center cities	100	Control and decision-making centers within a specific area undertaking multiple functions, including financial, trade, and production services for the region; possess the ability to attract talent, radiate influence, and provide comprehensive services.
Financial center cities	100	Collection and circulation of funds within a country or region, price discovery for various financial products, and risk transfer, allowing social capital to be allocated effectively in accordance with market principles.
Technology center cities	100	Technology plays a core factor in driving economic growth, mainly its role in promoting and spreading industrialization and urbanization, as well as enhancing productivity.
Political center cities	116	Capital cities can better and more conveniently enjoy the rules government formulates for the economic activities among economic entities and the services it provides. Capital cities have a certain exclusive competitive advantage.
Tourism center cities	99	Tourism plays an important role in urban development. It is also an important channel by which to participate in the international division of labor and obtain economic interests, an important manifestation of soft power.
Manufacturing center cities	100	Manufacturing is a pillar of urban development, forming a huge industrial chain.
Shipping center cities	89	Relying on good natural harbors, shipping center cities are directly involved in competition in the international market.

1   Qingbin Li, Room B1215, Guohong Building, Muxudi, Xicheng District, Beijing, China, 100038.
     Email: Liqb03@gmail.com.

MORE IMPORTANT CITY FUNCTIONS EXHIBIT STRONGER SUSTAINABLE COMPETITIVENESS AND SMALLER INTRA-GROUP DIFFERENCES

1. More Important Functional Centers Show Stronger Sustainable Competitiveness

Due to different functional properties, different functional centers may have varying levels of sustainable competitiveness. Our results show that financial center cities have the most sustainable competitiveness, while political center cities have the least. In descending order, the others are: comprehensive centers, technology centers, shipping centers, tourism centers, and manufacturing centers. It should be noted that these results were consistent across the two periods. However, compared to the 2011 result, the competitive scores of center cities in the seven categories all increased in 2013, with most scores increasing at a level of 0.02, and manufacturing and shipping centers increasing by 0.01. This shows that the crisis has not had a significant impact on the sustainable competitiveness of global cities (as Table 7.2 and Figure 7.1 show).

The competitiveness rankings of functional centers basically comply with urban economic development laws and the current global situation. First, the rise of manufacturing brings with it population and capital and gradually leads to derivative producer services, consumer services, and financial services. Then, with changes to factors such as land prices, labor costs, and the environment, manufacturing centers slowly fade and transform into comprehensive center cities and financial center cities. Therefore, the development of a manufacturing center is a necessary path for almost any strongly competitive city to walk. Today, soft power is stronger than hard power in terms of competition among global cities, and manufacturing industry is no longer the dominant element for competitiveness. Instead, financial services, technology, and other elements provide more robust support for urban competitiveness. Correspondingly, cities with functions dominated by upstream financial services and R&D services rank at the top of the competitiveness index.

Table 7.2   Characteristics of Functional Cities

Functional Grouping	Number	Highest Value	Lowest Value	Average Value	Variation Coefficient
2013					
Comprehensive center cities	100	1.00	0.12	0.48	0.35
Financial center cities	100	1.00	0.16	0.51	0.31
Technology center cities	100	1.00	0.08	0.47	0.39
Political center cities	116	1.00	0.02	0.34	0.53
Tourism center cities	99	1.00	0.07	0.42	0.45
Manufacturing center cities	100	0.71	0.12	0.39	0.33
Shipping center cities	89	1.00	0.14	0.45	0.36
2011					
Comprehensive center cities	100	1.00	0.14	0.46	0.35
Financial center cities	100	1.00	0.15	0.50	0.30
Technology center cities	100	1.00	0.07	0.45	0.39
Political center cities	116	1.00	0.01	0.33	0.56
Tourism center cities	99	1.00	0.06	0.40	0.46
Manufacturing center cities	100	0.68	0.12	0.38	0.34
Shipping center cities	89	1.00	0.10	0.44	0.38

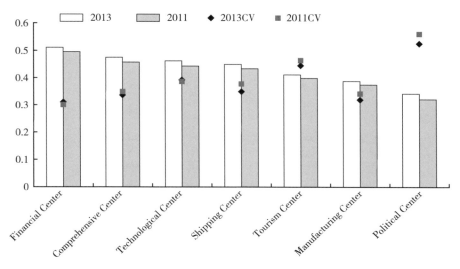

Figure 7.1   Competitiveness Scores of Functional Centers

2. Gaps Within City Sample Group Are Narrower with Stronger Sustainable Competitiveness

Discussing the dispersion among different functional centers in the city sample group is necessary. Functional centers with the highest score and small dispersion were most competitive. Interestingly, we found that the "strong are stronger." In terms of variation coefficients, financial center cities had the smallest, while political center cities had the largest. With the exception of manufacturing centers, the competitiveness of functional cities ranked high, and the degree of dispersion among them was small. One can see that the stronger the sustainable competitiveness, the smaller the gaps within the sample group.

   We believe that this characteristic is closely related to the nature of the functional center. Financial centers have little dependence on geography and history. Becoming a financial center requires the accumulation of financial resources and the development of a financial services industry. The threshold is higher, and homogeneity is strong. The gaps among cities are relatively small. Political centers and tourism centers are often of varying sizes, different levels of development, and more reliant on the political economy, geography, history, and culture, making them more heterogeneous. Thus, cities performing ordinarily in various aspects may become political or tourism cities, but would have a difficult time becoming financial centers.

Figure 7.2   Comparison of Competitiveness Rankings and Dispersion Rankings

MULTIPLE-INDICATOR DIMENSION RANKING AND OVERALL RANKING ARE CONSISTENT; SOCIAL COHESION IS AN ADVANTAGE; TECHNOLOGICAL INNOVATION IS A SHORTCOMING

1. Financial Centers

Financial center cities are concentrated in the eastern and western United States, Western Europe and East Asian coastal cities. They are most concentrated in Western Europe. The distribution of financial center scores is more in-line with the normal distribution, and there are more low-scoring cities than high-scoring ones. In 2011's result, scores were concentrated around the 0.55 level, while in 2013, scores were distributed evenly. Intermediate-level cities were greater in number; the number of high-scoring cities fell slightly; and the number of low-scoring cities increased slightly.

Financial centers ranked first in dimensions such as economic dynamic, environmental quality, technological innovation, global linkages, cultural diversity, and government management and rank second in social cohesion. Among all indicators, social cohesion had the highest score (0.93), and government management ranked second (0.78). Technological innovation had the lowest score (but was still the highest score among functional center cities). One can see that the advantage of financial center cities is social cohesion, while technological innovation is a clear constraining factor. At the same time, performance is even on several other dimensions (mostly around the 0.5 level).

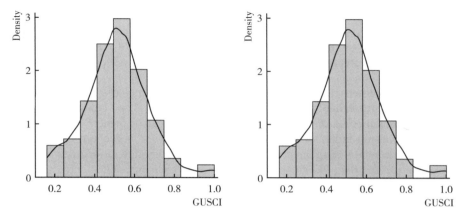

Figure 7.3   Sustainable Competitiveness Scoring Distribution: Financial Centers

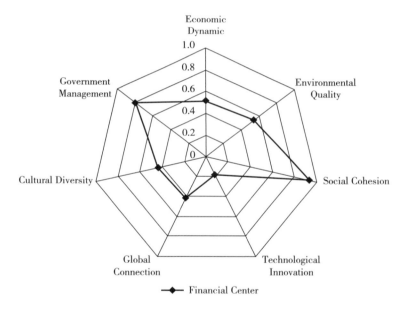

Figure 7.4   Scores for Various Indicators: Financial Centers[2]

2. Comprehensive Centers

Comprehensive centers are similarly concentrated in the eastern and western U.S., Western Europe, and coastal East Asia and are the most concentrated in Western Europe and East

---

2   The radar maps of several other centers and financial centers are similar and are not shown individually due to space limitations. Interested readers can request them from the author.

Asia. Scores for comprehensive centers are inclined to the left, with low-scoring cities more concentrated. In 2011, scores were concentrated in the intermediate range (0.35 to 0.55), while in 2013, they were in a more normal distribution and more tiered. The number of high-scoring cities increased slightly, while the number of low-scoring cities decreased slightly.

Comprehensive centers ranked second in five dimensions, including economic dynamic, environmental quality, technological innovation, global linkages, and cultural diversity. They ranked third in social cohesion and fourth in government management. Scoring was highest on the social cohesion indicator dimension (0.93) and lowest in technological innovation (0.16). The government management score was 0.73 and other dimensions were at the 0.4 to 0.5 level. One can see that, like financial centers, comprehensive centers have an advantage in social cohesion and a shortcoming in technological innovation.

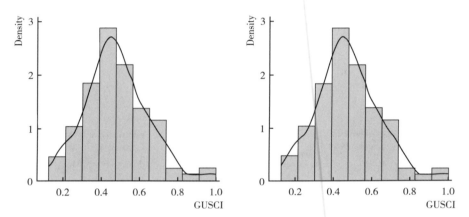

Figure 7.5   Sustainable Competitiveness Scoring Distribution: Comprehensive Centers

3. Technology Centers

Technology center cities are concentrated in the eastern and western U.S., Western Europe, and coastal East Asia and are most concentrated in Western Europe. In terms of scoring distribution, there are more low-scoring than high-scoring technology center cities. In 2013, the number of cities at the intermediate level of 0.4 increased significantly, expanding the distribution range of a majority of city scores.

Technology center cities ranked third in economic dynamic, technological innovation, global linkages, cultural diversity, and government management and ranked fifth in environmental quality and social cohesion. The highest indicator was likewise social cohesion (0.91), and the government management score was 0.75. However, although the functional orientation is that of a technology center, these cities ranked below financial centers and comprehensive centers in technological innovation scores.

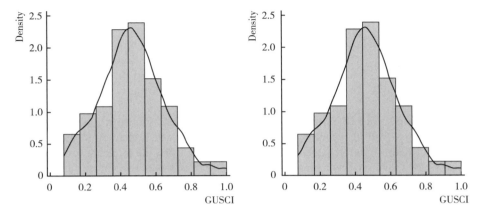

Figure 7.6   Sustainable Competitiveness Scoring Distribution: Technology Centers

4. Shipping Centers

Shipping center cities are concentrated on coasts. Geographically, they are still concentrated in the eastern and western U.S., Europe, and coastal East Asia. In terms of the scoring distribution, scores for 2011 were relatively evenly distributed in the intermediate area, while they were more dispersed in 2013, changing from evenly dispersed to concentrated. The number of low-scoring cities also increased slightly.

Shipping centers ranked second in government management, fourth in economic dynamic, social cohesion, and technological innovation, fifth in global connectivity and cultural diversity, and sixth in environmental quality. Among all indicators, social cohesion received the highest score (0.93), with government management second (0.78). Technological innovation scored lowest (0.11).

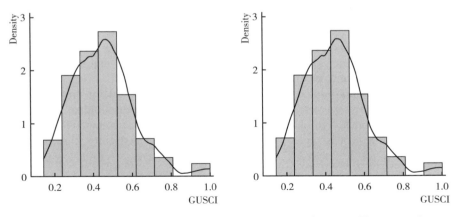

Figure 7.7   Sustainable Competitiveness Scoring Distribution: Shipping Centers

5. Tourism Centers

Tourism center cities are mainly concentrated in eastern and western U.S. and Europe, with some distribution in South America, Africa, and Southeast Asia. Each horizontal section is relatively evenly distributed, but also has an inclination toward the left. Few cities score high, at 0.7 or above. In 203, the situation improved, with the number of high-scoring cities increasing.

Tourism centers ranked third in environmental quality, fourth in global linkages and cultural diversity, fifth in technological innovation, and sixth in economic dynamic, social cohesion, and government management. Among all indicators, the highest-scoring was social cohesion (0.9). Government management ranked slightly lower than other functional cities (0.65), and technological innovation scored the lowest at 0.11.

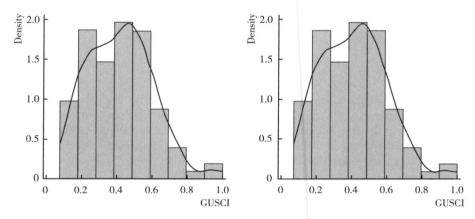

Figure 7.8   Sustainable Competitiveness Scoring Distribution: Tourism Centers

6. Manufacturing Centers

Manufacturing centers are mainly several cities in the eastern and western U.S., a portion of Western European cities, and southern Chinese cities. Scoring is concentrated at the intermediate level, with no cities at the low end or high end. At the same time, the highest score among manufacturing centers was not 1.It was 0.71 in 2011 and 0.68 in 2013.Scores tended more toward the intermediate area in 2013.

Manufacturing centers ranked first in the social cohesion indicator dimension, fifth in economic dynamic and government management, sixth in technological innovation and cultural diversity, and last in environmental quality and global connectivity. In indicator scoring, the advantage was social cohesion (0.94) and the constraint technical innovation (0.07).

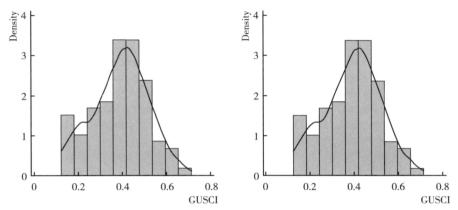

Figure 7.9   Sustainable Competitiveness Rankings Distribution: Manufacturing Centers

7. Political Centers

Political centers are the capital cities of countries. They are most concentrated in Europe, where they are also most competitive, second only to the Japanese, Chinese, and American political centers. Scoring for political centers is inclined seriously to the left, basically distributed in the low-scoring area, with few high-scoring cities. In 2011, scores were concentrated around 0.15.In 2013, the concentrated distribution level increased slightly, and the range expanded slightly.

Political centers ranked last in economic dynamic, social cohesion, technological innovation, cultural diversity, and government management. They ranked fourth in environmental quality and sixth in global connectivity. Looking at indicator scoring, continuing the previous rule, the advantage was social cohesion (0.9), and the restraint was technological innovation (0.06). At the same time, political centers scored low on multiple indicator dimensions, with government management in particular scoring only 0.54, the lowest among functional centers.

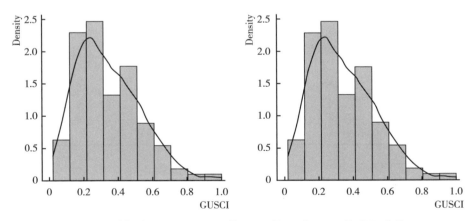

Figure 7.10   Sustainable Competitiveness Scoring Distribution: Political Centers

Overall, we found that functional cities have common characteristics, including:

- A majority of functional cities had sustainable competitiveness scores inclined to the "left," that is, there were relatively more low-scoring cities than high-scoring cities. At the same time, 2013 was generally an improvement over 2011, indicating improvement in the level of the score concentration area and an expansion of the range.
- Rankings on various indicator dimensions and sustainable competitiveness rankings remained consistent. This indicates that functional center cities with high sustainable competitiveness performed relatively well on each indicator dimension, with none "failing the class." The two remained consistent.[3]
- In indicator scoring, functional cities mostly maintained a similar ranking of indicator dimensions: social cohesion, government management, environmental quality, economic dynamic, global linkages, cultural diversity, and technological innovation. Social cohesion and government management are advantages, while technological innovation is a significant shortcoming. Thus, enhancing technological innovation is the key to enhancing the sustainable competitiveness of comprehensive centers.

Table 7.3   Sustainable Competitiveness Scoring Distribution and Trends for Functional Centers

Functional Centers	Scoring Distribution Characteristics (2011-2012)	Change Trend
Comprehensive Centers	Slightly to the left, distribution close to normal	Shift from concentration in the intermediate range to a more even distribution
Financial Centers	Slightly to the left, distribution close to normal	Shifting from highly concentrated to an even distribution, fewer high scores, more low scores
Technology Centers	Left, distribution close to normal	Expanding range of distribution concentration
Political Centers	Seriously to the left, concentrated in the low level area	Increasing level, expanding range of distribution concentration
Tourism Centers	Left, even distribution among horizontal segments	Some improvement, more high-scoring cities
Manufacturing Centers	Concentrated in the intermediate level	More inclined to the intermediate area
Shipping Centers	Even distribution at the intermediate level	Shifting from even to concentrated, more low-scoring cities

---

3   It should be noted that manufacturing cities, which ranked poorly in sustainable competitiveness, ranked first in social cohesion, estimated by the incarceration rate. This shows the differences between the functional orientation of manufacturing center cities and those of other functional centers. One possible explanation is that manufacturing centers are more labor-intensive, jobs are more abundant, and there is less income disparity, making for better social cohesion.

Table 7.4   Indicator Dimension Scores for Each Functional Center (2011-2012)

	Comprehensive Centers	Financial Centers	Technology Centers	Political Centers	Tourism Centers	Manufacturing Centers	Shipping Centers
Economic Dynamic	0.48	0.51	0.48	0.35	0.43	0.44	0.48
Environmental Quality	0.54	0.54	0.51	0.52	0.52	0.49	0.51
Social Cohesion	0.93	0.93	0.91	0.9	0.9	0.94	0.93
Technological Innovation	0.16	0.17	0.15	0.06	0.11	0.07	0.11
Global Connection	0.4	0.42	0.39	0.31	0.35	0.24	0.31
Cultural Diversity	0.39	0.44	0.38	0.3	0.38	0.32	0.37
Government Management	0.73	0.78	0.75	0.54	0.65	0.71	0.78

GLOBAL CENTER CITIES ALL POSSESS MULTIPLE IMPORTANT GLOBAL SERVICE FUNCTIONS

This report selects the top ten cities in overall sustainable competitiveness and the top ten cities of each functional center as global center cities for analysis. One can clearly see that the top ten cities have "multiple roles" in terms of functional orientation, generally four or five functional center properties. The number of functional centers and overall competitiveness ranking structure for the top ten cities are relatively consistent.

1. Overall Top Ten Cities: Multiple Roles – the More the Better

It is clear that the top ten cities play multiple roles in their functional positioning. At the most, they belong to six functional centers (such as London and Houston), and at the least they belong to two (such as San Jose). Other cities have four or five functional centers.

The number of functional centers and the overall competitiveness ranking structure of the top ten cities is consistent. The top ten are all financial center cities and technology center cities, and all but San Jose are comprehensive center cities. Six are tourism center cities and six are shipping center cities. Four are political center cities, and only one is a manufacturing center city.

Table 7.5   Breakdown of Top Ten Functional Center Cities (2011-2012)

Rank	City	Comprehensive Center	Financial Center	Technology Center	Political Center	Tourism Center	Manufacturing Center	Shipping Center	Total
1	London	•	•	•	•	•		•	6
2	New York	•	•	•		•		•	5
3	San Jose		•	•					2
4	Paris	•	•	•	•	•			5
5	Hong Kong	•	•	•				•	4
6	Seoul	•	•	•	•				4
7	Tokyo	•	•	•	•			•	5
8	Chicago	•	•	•		•			4
9	Los Angeles	•	•	•		•		•	5
10	Houston	•	•	•		•	•	•	6
Total		9	10	10	4	6	1	6	

2. Top Ten Cities by Functional Center: More Important Functional Centers Are More Leading in Nature

The top ten cities for financial centers and technology centers are the same as the overall top ten, but the top ten rankings of other functional centers have new entrants: manufacturing center cities numbers two through ten, political center cities numbers five through ten, tourism center cities numbers seven through ten, shipping cities numbers seven through ten, and comprehensive center cities number ten. This shows that the more important functional centers also basically occupy the lead spots in the top ten, making them more leading.

Table 7.6   List of Top Ten Cities for Each Functional Center (2013)

Comprehensive Centers	Financial Centers	Technology Centers	Political Centers	Tourism Centers	Manufacturing Centers	Shipping Centers
London	London	London	London	London	Houston	London
New York	New York	New York	Paris	New York	Dublin	New York
Paris	San Jose	San Jose	Seoul	Paris	Frankfurt	Hong Kong
Hong Kong	Paris	Paris	Tokyo	Chicago	Stuttgart	Tokyo
Seoul	Hong Kong	Hong Kong	Singapore	Los Angeles	Leeds	Los Angeles
Tokyo	Seoul	Seoul	Washington D.C.	Houston	Cleveland	Houston
Chicago	Tokyo	Tokyo	Vienna	San Francisco	Atlanta	Sydney
Los Angeles	Chicago	Chicago	Dublin	Washington D.C.	Barcelona	Singapore
Houston	Los Angeles	Los Angeles	Helsinki	Seattle	Portland	Seattle
Sydney	Houston	Houston	Amsterdam	Vienna	Arlington	Shanghai

CASE STUDY: LONDON AND HOUSTON

London is number one among six functional centers. Houston is the first among manufacturing centers. With these two cities as cases, we will further analyze their indicator dimensions.

1. London: A Leader Where Environmental Quality Is Still Lacking

London is the capital of England, the largest city in Europe, and the largest port. It is also Europe's largest metropolitan area. It is England's political, economic, cultural, and financial center, and a world-famous tourist destination. London is extremely diverse, home to people from all over the world. There are more than a hundred languages in use. It is a racial, religious, and cultural melting pot city. For this reason, London occupies the top spot in six functional categories, but not manufacturing.

By the results of our study, London ranked first in sustainable competitiveness, and it had near perfect scores in social cohesion, global linkages, cultural diversity, and government management. The relative shortcomings were technological innovation, economic dynamic, and environmental quality. London ranked fourth in the technological innovation dimension behind Paris, San Jose, and Seoul. It ranked ahead of New York. In economic dynamic, London ranked thirteenth. In environmental quality, London scored only 0.6, ranking it 119th. While the city long ago shook off the "smog capital" nickname, it is till a weak competitor in terms of ecological environment.

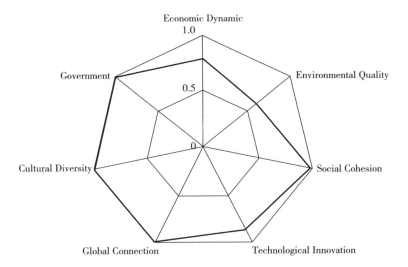

Figure 7.11   Indicator Dimension Scores: London

2. Houston: Comprehensive and Balanced Development Raises the Overall Level

Houston is the largest city in Texas, the fourth largest in the U.S., and the largest economic center of the Gulf Coast. Houston is known around the world for its energy (particularly oil), aviation industry, and canal. It is known as the "Oil Capital of the World" and "Space City." The Port of Houston has cargo throughput of 200 million tons. Located in Galveston on the northwest shore of the Gulf of Mexico, it is the largest international port in the U.S. and the world's sixth-largest. Houston is also an important international financial and trade center, with a large number of commercial banks, mortgage institutions, and securities exchange institutions. Houston is an international metropolis, and more than 70 countries have established consulates or honorary consuls there, making it second only to New York in the size of its consular group. Thus, it has all the functional center properties except that of a political center.

Houston ranks tenth in sustainable competitiveness and first among manufacturing center functional cities. Compared to other manufacturing centers, Houston's higher overall level pushes up its comprehensive score. In descending order, its functional center rankings are government management, social cohesion, cultural diversity, economic dynamic, technological innovation, environmental quality, and global linkages. The last two are its shortcomings. Houston ranks 225th in environmental quality with a score of 0.5.and ranks 48th in global linkages. In the future, efforts to enhance its sustainable competitiveness should strengthen. It is worth noting that ranks tenth in technological innovation, higher than Stockholm, San Francisco, Los Angeles, Chicago, and Shenzhen, but lower than Shanghai.

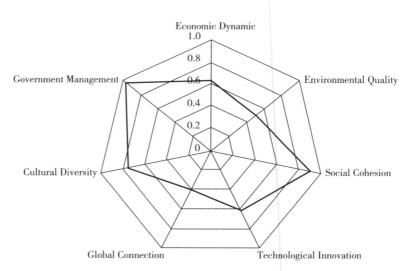

Figure 7.12   Indicator Dimension Scores: Houston

REFERENCES

Economist Intelligence Unit (2012), *Hot Spots: Benchmarking Global City Competitiveness*, The Economist Intelligence Unit Limited.

Institute for Urban Strategies (2011), *Global Power City Index 2011*, edited and published by The Mori Memorial Foundation.

Huggins, Robert, Hiro Izushi and Will Davies (2005), *World Knowledge Competitiveness Index*, Pontypridd: Robert Huggins Associates.

Ni, Pengfei (2013), *Annual Report on Urban Competitiveness No. 11*, Beijing: Social Science Documents Press.

World Bank (2012), *Doing Business 2013: Smarter Regulations for Small and Medium-Size Enterprises*, Available at: http://www.worldbank.org/en/news/press-release/2012/10/22/world-bank-ifc-report-finds-developing-countries-made-significant-progress-improving-business-regulations.

Part II

Specialized Analysis

8. The specialized differences: one key vector in urban competitiveness[1]

Saskia Sassen[2]

The specialized differences of cities matter much more in the global economy that began to take shape in the 1980s than is generally recognized. This goes against the common notion that economic globalization makes cities increasingly similar to each other. I will argue that this is based on confusion between the homogenizing of the state-of-the art built environment of cities worldwide, on the one hand, and, on the other, the actual economic activities that get done in those spaces.

This does require a far more finely grained analysis of the economies of global cities than the fact of specialized corporate services and headquarters. Once we recognize that what gives cities their strength can vary enormously, we can also see that global cities compete far less with each other than is commonly asserted. Finally, a focus on the specialized differences of cities allows us to capture the variable effects of economic globalization and of the current financial crisis on diverse types of global cities.

THE ACTUAL GLOBAL ECONOMY

There is no such entity as 'the' global economy. There are global formations, such as electronic financial markets and firms that operate globally. But the key feature of the current era is a vast number of highly particular global circuits that criss-cross the world, some

---

1   For a fuller development of the issues raised in this paper and extensive bibliography, see the author's following texts: "Analytic borderlands: economy and culture in the global city," in Gary Bridge and Sophie Watson (eds), *The New Blackwell Companion to the City*. Boston: Blackwell, pp. 210–20; "Novel spatial formats: megaregions and global cities," in J. Xu, and A. O. H. Yeh (eds), *Governance and Planning of Mega-City Regions: An International Comparative Perspective*. Routledge; *Cities in a World Economy* (4th fully updated edition), Thousand Oaks, CA: Sage.

2   Saskia Sassen, sjs2@columbia.edu, 713 Knox Hall, 606 W. 122nd Street, New York, NY, 10027 USA. T - 212.854.0790, F - 212.854.2963. Saskia Sassen is the Robert S. Lynd Professor of Sociology and Co-Chair, The Committee on Global Thought, Columbia University (www.saskiasassen.com). Her recent books are *Territory, Authority, Rights: From Medieval to Global Assemblages* (Princeton University Press 2008), *A Sociology of Globalization* (W. W. Norton 2007), and the 4th fully updated edition of *Cities in a World Economy* (Sage 2012). Among older books is *The Global City* (Princeton University Press 1991/2001). Her books are translated into over 20 languages. She is the recipient of diverse awards and mentions, ranging from multiple *doctor honoris causa* to named lectures and being selected as one of the 100 Top Global Thinkers of 2011 by *Foreign Policy* Magazine.

specialized and some not, that connect specific groups of cities. While many of these global circuits have long existed, what began to change in the 1980s was their proliferation and their increasingly complex organizational and financial framings. These emergent inter-city geographies begin to function as an infrastructure for globalization. And they increasingly matter for the competitiveness of cities.

Different circuits contain different groups of countries and cities. For instance, Mumbai is today part of a global circuit for real-estate development that includes investors from cities as diverse as London and Bogotá. Coffee is mostly produced in Brazil, Kenya, Indonesia, but the main trading place for futures on coffee is Wall Street, even though New York does not grow a single bean. The specialized circuits in gold, coffee, oil, and other commodities, each involves particular places, which will vary depending on whether it is a production circuit, a trading circuit, or a financial circuit. And then there are the types of circuits a firm such as Wal-Mart needs to outsource the production of vast amounts of products, including manufacturing, trading and financial/insurance servicing circuits. If we were to track the global circuits of gold as a financial instrument, it is London, New York, Chicago, and Zurich that dominate. But the wholesale trade in the metal brings São Paulo, Johannesburg and Sydney into the map, and the trade in the commodity, much of it aimed at the retail trade, adds Mumbai and Dubai. New York and London are the biggest financial centres in the world. But they do not dominate all markets. Thus Chicago is the leading financial centre for the trading of futures, and in the 1990s Frankfurt became the leading trader for, of all things, British treasuries. These cities are all financial leaders in the global economy, but they lead in different sectors and they are different types of financial centers.

Yet another pattern, the combination of global dispersal and ongoing spatial concentration of certain functions, becomes evident in the following cases. The 250,000 multinationals in the world together have over a million affiliates worldwide but they tend to keep their headquarters in their home countries. And so do the 100 top global advanced services firms which together have operations in 350 cities outside their home base. While financial services can be bought everywhere electronically, the major headquarters of leading global financial services firms tend to be concentrated in a limited numbers of cities and these are the ones which directly experience the unemployment crisis of the sector. Each of these financial centers is particularly specialized and strong in specific segments of global finance, even as they also engage in routinized types of transactions which need to be executed by all financial centres.

Not only global economic forces feed this proliferation of circuits. Migration, cultural work, and civil society struggles to preserve human rights, the environment, and social justice, also feed the formation and development of global circuits. Thus NGOs fighting for the protection of the rainforest function in circuits that include Brazil and Indonesia as homes of the major rainforests, the global media centers of New York and London, and the places where the key forestry companies selling and buying wood are headquartered, notably Oslo, London and Tokyo. There are particular music circuits that connect specific areas of India with London, New York, Chicago, and Johannesburg; and particular music circuits that connect parts of China with Los Angeles.

Adopting the perspective of one of these cities reveals the diversity and specificity of its location on some or many of these circuits. These emergent inter-city geographies begin to function as an infrastructure for multiple forms of globalization. The critical nodes in these intercity geographies are not simply the cities, but more specifically, the particular, often highly specialized capabilities of each city. Further, a critical trend is that, ultimately, being a global firm or market means entering the specificities and particularities of national economies. This explains why such global actors need more and more global cities as they expand their operations across the world. Handling these national specificities and particularities is a far more complex process than simply imposing global standards.

This process is easier to understand if we consider consumer sectors rather than the organizational/managerial ones addressed in this piece. Thus even such a routinized operation as MacDonald's adjusts its products to the national cultures in which it operates, whether that is France, Japan or South Africa. When it comes to the managerial and organizational aspects, matters become complicated. The global city contains the needed resources and talents to bridge between global actors and national specifics. Even a highly imperfect global city is better for a global firm or exchange than no such city. And this then explains why the many and very diverse global cities around the world do not just compete with each other but also collectively form a globally networked platform for the operations of firms and markets.

The network of global cities has expanded as more and more firms go global and enter a growing range of foreign national economies. The management and servicing of much of the global economic system takes place in this growing network of global cities and city-regions. And while this role involves only certain components of urban economies, it has contributed to a repositioning of cities both nationally and globally. But the formal governance frames, both national and local as well as international are mostly not able to accommodate this repositioning of cities, a repositioning that brings with it the multi-scalar dynamics that now run through cities.

THERE IS NO PERFECT GLOBAL CITY

While there is competition among cities, there is far less of it than is usually assumed. A global firm does not want one global city but many. However, given the level of specialization of globalized firms, what are preferred cities will vary according to the firm. Firms thrive on the specialized differences of cities, and it is this that gives a city its particular advantage in the global economy. This also points to the possibility of an urban global politics of reclamations among cities on similar circuits which confront similar corporate giants.

Recognizing the value of the specialized differences of cities and urban regions in today's global economy shows how the deep economic history of a place matters for the type of knowledge economy that a city or a city-region ends up developing. This goes against the common view that globalization homogenizes economies. How much this deep economic history matters varies, and partly depends on the particulars of a city's or a region's economy. It matters more than is commonly assumed, and it matters in ways that are not generally recognized. Globalization homogenizes standards – for managing, for accounting, for building state-of-the-art office districts, and so on. But it needs diverse specialized economic capabilities.

The capabilities needed to trade, finance, service, and invest globally need to be produced. They are not simply a by-product of the power of multinational firms and telecommunications advances. Different cities have different resources and talents for producing particular types of capabilities. The global city is a platform for producing such global capabilities, even when this requires large numbers of foreign firms, as is the case in cities as diverse as Beijing and Buenos Aires. Each of the 70 plus major and minor global cities in the world contributes to the production of these capabilities in its home country, and thereby functions as a bridge between its national economy and the global economy.

The other side of this dynamic is that for a firm to go global it has to put down its feet in multiple cities that function as entry points into national economies. This bridging capacity is critical: the multiple circuits connecting major and minor global cities are the live infrastructure of the global economy. It indicates that cities do not simply compete with each other. A global firm does not want one global city, even if it is the best in the world. Different groups of cities will be desirable, even if they have some serious negatives. This helps explain why there is no one 'perfect' global city. Today's global phase does not function through one imperial global capital that has it all.

A large study of 75 cities rates the top cities for worldwide commerce. Not one of them ranks at the top in all of the 100 factors, and not one gets the perfect score of 100.[3] The scores for the top two cities are 79 for London and 72 for New York. Further down, the 10th ranked city, for instance, Amsterdam, scores 60, followed by Madrid at 59. London and New York rank low in several aspects – neither is in the top ten when it comes to starting a business, or closing a business. If we consider a critical variable in the 'ease of doing business' indicator, part of which is 'ease of entry and exit', London ranks 43rd and New York ranks 56th. Perhaps most surprising is that London ranks 37th on 'contract enforcement' and 21st on 'investor protection'. It is Singapore that ranks number one in relation to all three variables. Less surprising is that New York ranks 34th on one of the data points for 'liveability': health and safety. In the global South, cities like Mumbai and São Paulo are in the top group for financial and economic services, but are brought down in their overall score by their low rankings in factors related to the ease of doing business and liveability, given their especially low levels of well-being for vast sectors of the population.

While much has been said about the global economy homogenizing national economies, these urban facts actually point in the opposite direction: different cities have different strengths. Global firms and markets, but also cultural enterprises, want many global cities because each of these cities expands the global platform for operations and because each is a bridge between the global and the particularities of national economies and societies. This also brings to the fore that global cities are built, developed, made.

I see in this growth of the numbers of global cities and in their differences the larger story of the rise of a multi-polar world. The loss of position of US cities is part of this shift: it mirrors the loss of position of the US as the dominant economic and military power. It is not that the US is suddenly poorer, it is that other regions of the world are rising and that there are multiple forces feeding their multi-sited economic, political, and cultural strengths.

---

3   The 2008 MasterCard Worldwide Centers of Global Commerce Index compiles 100 factors which cover a very wide range of conditions – from macro-level factors such as political and legal frameworks to the particulars of how easy it is to execute an import or export operation, how many days it takes to open and to close a firm, as well as liveability factors and a city's global recognition. The author is one of the experts on this project. See also ATKearney, Global Cities Index (2012) also found a similar group of cities at the top (London, New York, Paris, Tokyo, Chicago, etc.) and considerable variability on specific variables; unlike most of these types of studies, this one includes cultural dimensions.

URBAN/REGIONAL SPECIFICITY FEEDS THE KNOWLEDGE ECONOMY

The specific global circuits on which a city is located will vary from city to city, depending on a city's particular strengths, just as the groupings of cities vary on each circuit. All of this also shows us that the specialized differences of cities matter, and that there is less competition among cities and more of a global or regional division of functions than is commonly recognized. For example, the knowledge economies of São Paulo, Chicago and Shanghai all share a long history of servicing major heavy manufacturing sectors; theirs are economic histories that global cities such as New York and London never developed. Out of these specialized differences comes a global division of functions. Thus a steel factory, a mining firm, or a machine manufacturer that wants to go global will, depending on its location, go to São Paulo, Shanghai or Chicago for its legal, accounting, financial, insurance, economic forecasting, and other such specialized services. It will not go to New York or London for this highly particular servicing. Increasingly these urban economies are part of a networked global platform.

The deep economic history of a place and the specialized economic strengths it can generate increasingly matter in a globalized economy. This goes against the common view that globalization homogenizes economies. How much this specificity matters will vary, partly depending on that region's economy.

Establishing how a city/region becomes a knowledge economy requires highly detailed research. So let me use a case I researched, Chicago, to illustrate this. Chicago is usually seen as a latecomer to the knowledge economy – almost fifteen years later than in New York and London. Typically the answer is that Chicago had to overcome its heavy agro-industrial past: its economic history seen as a disadvantage compared to old trading and financial centers such as New York and London.

But I found that its past was not a disadvantage. It was one key source of its competitive advantage. This is most visible in the fact of its preeminence as a futures market built on pork bellies. The complexity, scale and international character of Chicago's historical agro-industrial economy required highly specialized financial, accounting, legal expertise. But these were/are quite different from the expertise required to handle the sectors New York specialized in – service exports, finance, and trade. It was Chicago's past as a massive agro-industrial complex that gave it some of its core and distinctive knowledge economy components and has made it the leading global futures financial center and global provider of specialized services (accounting, legal, insurance, etc.) for handling heavy industry, heavy transport, agriculture. Chicago, São Paulo, Shanghai, Tokyo, and Seoul are among the leading producers of these types of specialized corporate services, not in spite of their economic past as major heavy industry centers, but because of it. Thus when Boeing decided that it needed to enter the knowledge economy, it did not move its headquarters to New York, but to Chicago.

In brief, cities can generate kinds of 'knowledge,' both formal and informal, that go beyond the sum of recognized knowledge actors (e.g. in the economy, professionals and professional firms). This is a type of immaterial capital we can call 'urban knowledge capital.' One way of explaining it is that cities are fuzzy logic systems which enables scale-jumping – the switch from the mere sum of what is there to a third type of capability.

Particular processes, built environments and spatial forms in each city are the concrete and localized channels through which globalization exists and functions in these cities. These legible conditions of each city contain both parallels and differences with other cities. Density is a marker of the business centers of just about all major and minor global cities. But this does not mean they are all developing the same types of specialized economic capacities.

These differences also generate different types of strengths and vulnerabilities when there is a major financial crisis such as the current one. This is the subject of the next section.

GLOBAL FINANCE

A key characteristic of the current global crisis compared to other recent crises is the extent to which it is financial in a very generalized sense. The earlier crises of this global phase that began in the 1980s were banking and stock market crises, in addition to the real estate crises of the late 1980s and the so-called technology dot.com crisis. The sharp crisis to hit Asia in 1997-1998 was a banking crisis. (See generally Figures 8.1 and 8.2.)

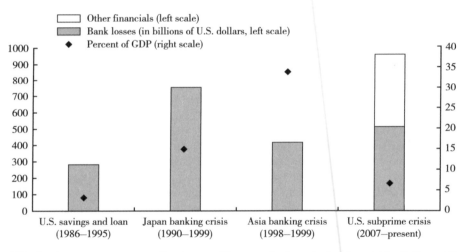

Note: US sub-prime costs represent staff estimates of losses on banks and other financial institutions. All costs are in real 2007 US dollars. Asia includes Indonesia, Korea, the Philippines, and Thailand.

Source: IMF (2008), p. 13.

Figure 8.1   Comparisons of Financial Crises

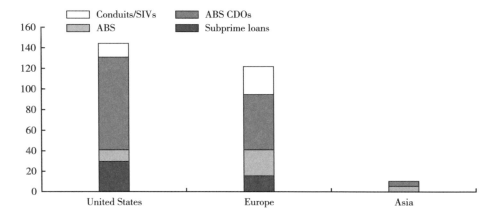

Note: ABS ¼ asset-backed security; CDO ¼ collateralized debt obligation; SIV ¼ structured investment vehicle.

Source: IMF (2008), p. 13.

Figure 8.2 Expected bank losses as of March 2008 (in billions of US dollars)

Figure 8.2 shows us the sharp differences in impacts on diverse regions before the credit-swap crisis led to the major financial collapse that begins in September 2009.Asia clearly is in a very different condition from Europe and, especially, the U.S., the originator of much of the crisis and the worst hit. But why did Asia eventually get so severely touched by the crisis?

The critical factor is the financializing of more and more sectors of the economy across the world. The financial deepening of economies has become one of the major dynamics characterizing advanced economies. The ratio of global financial assets to global gross domestic product was nearly 350 percent in 2006, a ratio that jumps to 450 percent in a growing number of highly developed countries, from the U.S. to Japan. More generally, the number of countries where financial assets exceed the value of their gross national product more than doubled from thirty-three in 1990 to seventy-two in 2006. Securitizing a broad range of types of debt is a key vehicle for this financial deepening. Even so, the depth of financializing by sectors will vary even among the highly developed countries, which can contribute to explain why the impact of the financial crisis though severe in most countries, is not the same in all countries. This is clearly, a continuously changing condition as the crisis evolves and the variable impact of government interventions also evolves.

At the heart of this financializing lie the extreme innovations of the late 1990s onwards and the also extreme practices of a growing number of financial services firms as well as the financial divisions of (traditional) banks.

The major global cities in the world are like factories or silicon valley's for the making of very complex and very risky financial instruments. This making requires large mixes of diverse specialized knowledge – the variety of financial instruments, law, accounting, software, forecasts about the economy. When a financial crisis hits, global cities can be in the forefront of the negative effects.

Some of the first professionals to be fired, often instantaneously, are financial experts and traders. When the first big financial crisis of the global era hit in September 1987 in New York, tens of thousands of high-paid professionals on Wall Street, New York's financial centre, were told from one day to the other that they no longer had their jobs. Many found out when they returned the next morning and boxes with whatever they had in their offices were given to them and they were asked to leave promptly.

It was a stock market crisis and it was largely contained within the financial sector. Few other cities in the US were as directly hit by that crisis as was New York, especially Wall Street. Much of the national economy was not affected. In fact, New York itself recovered rather quickly, because much of the city's economy was not that severely affected by the crisis. And even Wall Street recovered rather quickly: after a few years it was back inventing new financial instruments, hiring more financial experts and paying them even higher salaries. By 2005, the average heads of hedge funds earned 16,000 times more in income (and that excludes all the other sources of income, such as stock options) than the average American worker.

Today the impact on global cities is not just through the losses in the financial services as most commentators say. It is also because of this penetration of finance into all economic sectors. For instance, among the new inventions of finance was finding a way to making big profits from selling mortgages to low and modest income households – the much talked about sub-prime mortgages. The innovation was that they bundled as many of these mortgages as they could in order to sell them to financial investors; because this all moved very fast, the fact that those who got the mortgages were unable to keep paying them did not matter to the financiers. But it was devastating for those home buyers and for the cities where millions and millions of houses stand empty and abandoned. Cities have lost billions of dollars through this mortgage crisis alone. The economy of New York City in 2008 lost US$ 10 billion dollars due to these mortgages.

Subprime mortgages are one instance capturing the effect of some of the high-risk innovations directly on cities. The subprime mortgage market is the extreme step in a long development of mortgage securitization. It is extreme because the capacity to securitize large numbers of mortgages overrides the need for credit-worthiness of mortgage borrowers. We can capture this trend at very detailed local levels. Thus in the case of the United States, race and locality can make quite a difference. In New York City, African-American households and low-income neighborhoods showed a disproportionately high incidence of sub-prime mortgages as of 2006.

The current financial crisis is very different from the 1987 stock market crash, for two reasons. One is that the kind of financial innovations that were developed over the last ten years brought with them levels of risk and of leveraging never seen before. What had seemed extreme in the 1980s and 1990s was nothing compared to the new financial innovations. The second reason it is different is that, partly through those new innovations and partly through the aggressive practices of the financial sector, finance has penetrated all economic sectors. In the United States this is more extreme than in most other countries. As a result the crisis could not be confined to the financial sector as in 1987: it now affects the whole economy.

There are two ironies in this story of financial crisis and global cities. One is that through their "brilliant" inventions, financial experts have brought down themselves and the rest of the economy. The other is that most politicians have accepted the solution presented by financiers: a financial solution to the financial crisis – pouring taxpayers' money into the financial system. I think this is a bad idea. But it does mean that rescuing the financial crisis produced by financial innovations will require financiers to work at it. And there is no place for this like global cities. I already argued in the first edition of The Global City, in 1991, that finance, given all the effort to make innovations, is in permanent crisis. The current period has made this clearer than ever before.

CONCLUSION: FUTURE FORMATS – GLOBAL CITIES AND MEGAREGIONS

These major shifts in the scales, spaces and contents of economic activity are engendering novel spatial formats such as the Global City. But they are also engendering a second major new format: megaregions, Both are contributing to a whole series of old and new global intercity geographies. These shifts, in turn, call for shifts in our interpretations and policy frameworks to adjust to these novel spatial formats and maximize their benefits and distributive potential.

While megaregions and global cities are different formats, I find that analytically we can identify similar dynamics at work in both. Two such dynamics stand out. One is scaling and its consequences – in this case megaregional scaling and global scaling. The other dynamic is the interaction between geographic dispersal and new kinds of agglomeration economies, which in this case are operating, respectively, within a megaregion and in global cities. Specifying a common analytic ground for these two very diverse spatial formats should enable us to develop a sharper approach to empirical research and, possibly, policy. These diverse spatial formats also should help in assessing the extent to which policy decisions can encourage greater economic integration between a country's more globalized city (or cities) and its other areas currently performing subordinate functions within the national territorial hierarchy. In other words, taking a megaregional scale might help in connecting the 'winners' and the 'laggards. ' The megaregion then becomes a scale that includes both globalizing and provincial cities and areas. This raises a question as to whether this connecting of winners and laggards can also be extended to cross-border intercity networks by strengthening the connections between winners and laggards in the global political economy.

One consequence is that not only winners get privileged, as is typical with 'targeting' of resources to enable the formation of world-class cities and silicon valleys, but also laggards. More precisely, laggards can be enabled to become dynamically interconnected with winners within a megaregion in ways that replicate current practices at the global scale, notably outsourcing to low-cost areas, and in novel ways made possible because the low-cost area is within a megaregion. The hope would be that rather than pursuing the usual economic policies focused on the most advanced sectors, this would make a strong case for concentrating upon the poorer regions, not as charity but as a recognition that they are part of the advanced sectors; after all, when major firms outsource jobs to low-cost areas across the world, they are outsourcing some of their tasks. Many advanced economic sectors combine sufficiently diverse tasks that they have both a preference for lower-cost areas for some of these tasks, and for dense high-cost areas for other tasks.

To mention just one of several examples, this type of framing would bring value to poorer areas within the most developed countries as these might be developed to house activities that are now outsourced to low-wage countries. One key aim should be to avoid a race to the bottom as happens when these activities are off-shored, which might be simpler to ensure when both headquarters and low-wage activities are in the same country. A second aim should be to provide alternative or complementary development paths to what is today's prevalent path, i.e. the policy preference for high-end economic activities, such as bio-tech parks and luxury office parks.

Parallel to this effort to incorporate laggards, or less successful areas, into policy frames that today target mostly successful areas, is the effort to understand how cities in the middle range of urban hierarchies fit in today's global intercity geographies. In the case of the US, for instance, many of these mid-range cities are also part of megaregions. The analytic bridge between megaregions and intercity geographies is the fact that the operational chains of a growing number of firms today are part of both these spatial formats. This opens up a whole new research agenda about economic globalization and place, in addition to the existing global city scholarship.

REFERENCES

A. T. Kearney (2012), *Global Cities Index.*

Bridge, G. and Watson, S. (2011), *The New Blackwell Companion to the City*, Boston: Blackwell.

Sassen, S. (2012), *Cities in a World Economy* (4th fully updated edition), Thousand Oaks, CA: Sage/Pine Forge.

Sassen, S. (2008), *Rights: From Medieval to Global Assemblages*, Princeton, NJ: Princeton University.

Sassen, S. (2007), *A Sociology of Globalization*, New York: W. W. Norton.

Sassen, S. (2008), *The Global City*, Princeton, NJ: Princeton University.

The 2008 MasterCard Worldwide Centers of Global Commerce Index (2008).

Xu, J. and Yeh, A. (2011), *Governance and Planning of Mega-City Regions: An International Comparative Perspective*, London: Routledge.

9. Social and technological innovations in the competitiveness of cities

Banji Oyelaran-Oyeyinka[1]

INTRODUCTION

The process of urbanization has been closely associated with industrialization, which itself was founded on continuous innovation over a long historical period; and as urbanization unfolds, the primary role of the city has become more paramount. It is now widely acknowledged that the city represents a creative human construct which embodies complex human and technological innovations. It has built its success on the ability to generate, harness and access the advantages of localization and agglomeration. Whatever the historical genesis – be it military, political, religious, or communication, the central dynamic underlying the development of urban centres has been the quest for nurturing and improving avenues for generating prosperity. The city is therefore a human artifact, shaped, steered, and composed by engagements, transactions and interactions among people. It embodies human creativity and visions, needs and desires, as well as tensions and compromises.

For centuries the growth and evolution of the city has been driven by human inventiveness and nurtured in ways that foster prosperity, but above all, the city has been historically a locus of innovation, dynamism, transformation, increasing efficiency, productivity as well as value addition. It has also provided a platform for the realization of individual human aspirations, in the process improving the quality of life and promoting higher forms of aesthetic and cultural representation. In contrast to rural life, the city has increased social accommodation and fostered heterogeneity. Much of the societal surplus has been invested in cities and this, coupled with the increase in productivity, has promoted higher levels of affluence, albeit benefitting only a small segment of the urban population.

The relentless evolution of the city is evident in the fact that only a century ago, two out of 10 people in the world lived the urban life. In poorer countries, this proportion was as low as 5 per cent, as the overwhelming majority lived in rural areas. Since then, the world has urbanized rapidly and, in some countries and regions, at an unprecedented pace. It was only two years ago when the urban population outnumbered the rural population thus marking the advent of a new 'urban millennium'. By the middle of this century it is expected that seven

---

1   Banji Oyelaran Oyeyinka, Monitoring and Research Division, P.O. Box 30030, Nairobi, Kenya. Telephone: (254-2) 621234. Fax: (254-2) 624266/7.
Email: boyeyinka@hotmail.com.

out of every 10 persons on the planet will be urban dwellers.[2] The 21st century will therefore be known as the century of the city.

A city's competitiveness is closely associated with its capacity to generate prosperity and, as well, its ability to keep creating wealth for the greater good and well-being of the majority. Currently the main drivers of growth and prosperity for leading cities are global connectivity, technological adaptation, and the ability of local law and institutions to regulate life and business in ways that provide stability and a platform for investment, and human sense of security. The growing role of cities in accumulating wealth has increased the role and scope of governments at the state and municipal levels and it is imperative that increased local participation is complemented with citizenry awareness.

Table 9.1 shows the relative share of a group of selected cities from both developed and developing countries in terms of land, population and GDP relative to the country as a whole. In all cases, the economic output of these cities is several folds higher that the corresponding land inputs. In addition, all but one of these cities contributes a larger share of the country's GDP relative to their share of the population. Guangzhou and Brussels offer the most striking examples, with a GDP share that is 5 and 4.4 times higher, respectively, than that of their population.[3] The only exception is Sydney, which has a GDP share that is slightly below that of its share of the national population.

Table 9.1   Land, Population and GDP of Selected Cities as a Share of the Country Total

City	Percent of GDP	Percent of population	Percent of land	Relative share of GDP versus population
Bangalore	1.5	0.5	–	2.9
Guangzhou	2.9	0.6	0.1	5.1
Beijing	3.1	1.2	0.2	2.6
New Delhi	3.5	1.2	0.0	3.0
Mumbai	5.0	1.5	0.0	3.3
New York	8.5	7.8	0.1	1.1
Shanghai	13.6	1.9	0.1	7.1
Cape Town	14.0	6.1	0.2	2.3
Johannesburg	15.0	6.3	0.14	2.4
Sydney	23.5	24.4	0.02	1.0
Mexico City	26.7	23.9	0.1	1.1
Paris	27.9	21.2	0.5	1.3
Lisbon	38.0	26.3	3.2	1.4
Brussels	44.4	10.0	2.3	4.4
Budapest	45.6	25.3	0.8	1.8
Seoul	48.6	25.0	0.6	1.9

Sources: New York, Sydney, Mexico City, Paris, Lisbon, Brussels, Budapest, Seoul: OECD (2008); Bangalore, New Delhi, Mumbai, Guangzhou, Beijing, Shanghai: van Dijk (2007); Johannesburg, Cape Town: Naudé and Krugell (2004).

---

2   UN-DESA (2010), *World Urbanization Prospects: The 2009 Revision*, http://esa.un.org/unpd/wup/index.

3   These data should be interpreted carefully, as in some cases different data sources were used for each factor, for which there could be some discrepancy regarding the boundaries of cities.

The cities that are competitive at the global scale are as many and diverse as the factors that drive their dynamism. Transportation infrastructure, port capacity, manufacturing capabilities, cost, labour productivity, and financial clout were key determinants of a city's competitiveness during the 20th century. While these factors are still important, a number of other factors are becoming increasingly significant in determining a city's competitiveness in the 21st century, including technological ones, such as broadband availability and telecom infrastructure, and cultural characteristics, such as diversity and quality of life. Having maintained their historical advantages while, at the same time, continuing to develop new ones on other fronts, the traditional world cities – i.e., New York, Paris, Tokyo and London – are still considered to be the most competitive cities in the global economy in terms of a wide set of indicators. New York, for example, distinguishes itself for its intellectual capital and its capacity to innovate, which gives it a strong edge in terms of its ability to identify new opportunities and capitalize on them. Similarly, London continues to act as a magnet for global business as a result of its open business policies, its size, as well as its diversity.[4]

Some emerging cities, however, are playing an increasingly prominent role in the global economy. For example, Beijing ranks behind London and ahead of New York, Paris and Tokyo in transportation and infrastructure. Likewise, São Paulo, Dubai and Mumbai rank first in the world in the number of buildings under construction. Shanghai scores among the top cities in term of patents, reflecting an overall increase in the number of patents issued in China, particularly in relation to pharmaceutical and other medical devices. Singapore is considered to be the city most conducive to doing business, based on corporate taxation and regulatory factors.[5]

Competitive cities are entities that adapt to the needs of the times; for instance London gained prominence by adapting its locational advantages, over time, to manufacturing and services. Such cities implement bold initiatives to stay ahead in order to develop, sustain prosperity, and avoid regress. A competitive city pursues the main drivers of progress, which include global connectivity, technological adaptation, and strong governance; in addition, the development and attraction of human capital, and the incentivizing of new businesses, based on innovative technologies will maintain the city in a privileged position. Additionally, cities must identify and nurture their comparative advantage, utilizing the city's unique and important features peculiar to its stage of development. Cities should learn from one another, adopting policies that have proven success and steering clear of policies that may seem attractive but are unsustainable in the long run.

In addition to generating wealth, city growth is also pertinent to competitiveness. City growth means an enlarged local market for goods and services, spurring the increase of skilled and unskilled labour, opening more opportunities for learning and innovation, and reducing the cost of providing infrastructure; all of which further aid the growth of cities (Bogetic and Sanogo, 2005; Overman and Venables, 2005). The broader importance of the

---

4   Partnership for New York City and Price, Waterhouse, Coopers (2007), 'Cities of opportunity: business-readiness indicators for the 21st century' (http://www.pwc.com/en_US/us/cities-of-opportunity/assets/cities_of_opportunities.pdf). See also D. Nally and K. Wylder (2007), 'An open letter on cities in an interdependent world' (http://www.pwc.com/us/en/cities-of-opportunity/study-introduction.jhtml).

5   *Idem.*

city to the general economy is that the performance of the urban sector impacts the overall national economic growth.

The location and growth of a city are aided by a plethora of factors often working simultaneously to give particular areas comparative advantage to others. UN-Habitat analyses reveal that a combination of geography, demographic change (migration and natural increase), infrastructure development, government policies and other political and economic factors including globalization are responsible jointly or severally for city growth (Olokesusi, 2011).

In particular, city growth take on greater importance when particular areas are transitioning to a more developed state and United Nations projection show that cities of the developing world will absorb 95 percent of urban growth in the next two decades, and by 2030 will be home to almost 4 billion people or 80 percent of the world's urban population.

CITY COMPETITIVENESS: DETERMINANTS AND SIGNIFICANCE

Cities are becoming increasingly stratified, and differentiated by size and wealth creation capacity; ranging from small simple metropolises to larger megacities and more recently meta-cities.[6] This distinction is aligned most significantly with the size of the human population they house, as well as, increasingly, socio-economic and cultural leverages at local, regional and global levels. Of late, a number of cities have attained the elite status of 'global cities', although they tend to be in the developed world. This distinction is not based on population concentration, but rather by the influence they wield in global political and economic equations. The majority tend to be financial service centres such as London, Tokyo, New York, Bahrain, and Dubai, while others like Singapore and Amsterdam have carved distinct niches as transport and communications hubs. Cities in the developing world such as Cairo, Lagos, Kinshasa (in Africa), Shanghai, Mumbai, Dhaka (in Asia), and Buenos Aires, São Paolo, and Lima (South America) are rapidly growing in population size and regional importance, but not as rapidly in global significance, rather attaining the status of meta-cities.

The development of cities and subsequent wealth creation are driven largely by investment in myriad of assets such as Information and Communication Technologies (ICTs), Human Capital, Physical Infrastructure, and operating the right macroeconomic policies. As we noted earlier, the label of a city as either 'global', 'meta', or 'mega' is already instructive of certain features of the city. However, cities as loci of production and competition are measured by for more complex indicators and this paper will explore some of the measures with case studies and recommendations on how cities can be competitive in this era of continuous social and technological innovations.

---

6   Meta-cities are large urban agglomerations with human populations of 20 million people or more. This term is usually used to describe sprawling cities in developing countries with large population but incommensurate development.

BOX 9.1   ORIGIN AND CONCEPTS OF COMPETITIVENESS

Michael Porter first defined 'national competitiveness as an outcome of a nation's ability to innovate in order to achieve, or maintain, an advantageous position over other nations in a number of key industrial sectors' (Huggins and Izushi, 2008: 1). Although the focus has increasingly shifted from nations to cities in this era of borderless space, innovation to attain or preserve a competitive advantage remains the central motive.

   Increasingly, competitiveness is measured by the 'assets' of the business environment, which are human capital, innovative capacity and quality of local infrastructure, i.e. the factors which affect the city's ability to adapt to its growth and dynamic sectors (Huggins and Izushi, 2008: 1). City competitiveness can be altered, halted, or aided in many ways. Changes that positively affect the employment structure for example can fast track the process of city growth.

   It is important that a region nurtures the knowledge base of its economy, which is described as 'the capacity and capability to create and innovate new ideas, thoughts, processes and products, and to translate these into economic value and wealth' (Huggins and Izushi, 2008: 1). According to the World Knowledge Competitiveness Index 2008, the regions ranked number 1 and 2 were San Jose in Santa Clara and Boston in Cambridge, both American areas with a high density of world-class universities, some of which have strong emphases on innovation and technology. It is estimated that the high caliber research universities in Boston directly add US$7.4bn to the regional economic output, and this does not account for less quantifiable indirect impact. However, it noted that America has lagged of late in competitiveness, with regions in Europe and Asia in particular rapidly catching up (Huggins and Izushi, 2008: 9).

The power and potential of urban regions is more and more acknowledged, as over the last decade, more countries are relinquishing increasing power to municipal governments to design and implement locally relevant policy (World Bank, 2000). Consequently, cities are not just enlarging, but also 'gaining in economic and political influence' (Yeung, 2002).

RELATIONSHIP OF URBAN COMPETITIVENESS AND URBAN PROSPERITY

A significant number of countries that have realized high degrees of urbanization during the past century have also experienced a growing concentration of economic activity in and around their major metropolitain areas. For example, in the U.S., 83 percent of employment is in metropolitan areas. These areas account only for 24 percent of the total land area of the country (Chatterjee, 2003). Similar patterns are found elsewhere. To mention a few: in France, the metropolitan area of Paris accounts for 2.2 percent of the area of the country and 18.9 percent of the country's population, yet it produces 30 percent of GDP (Fujita and Thisse, 2002). Such phenomena are not peculiar to the western or developed world; data from Asia and Africa confirm the increasing economic importance of cities. For instance, in Korea, the capital region comprising Seoul, which has an area corresponding to 11.8 percent of the country and includes 45.3 percent of the population, produces more than 46 percent of GDP

(Fujita and Thisse, 2002). Similarly, Cairo's metropolitan area generates over half of Egypt's production while accounting for 0.5 percent of the country's land area. These data are similar to those in the recent McKinsey Report (2011), which suggests the following contributions of urban areas to GDP: China 74 percent, South Asia 31 percent, Latin America 68 percent, the Middle East 64 percent, sub-Saharan Africa 51 percent, while in the U.S. and Europe the figures were 82 percent and 59 percent, respectively. Clearly, people living in cities are more productive, but why is this so? Urbanization affects the creation and distribution of wealth in three ways.

First, through the effects proximity has, in the first instance, on the value of assets, and in the second instance, how the value of proximity, in turn, affects economic growth. This perspective has characterized notions of how cities work since at least the 1960s when Colin Clark wrote that 'all cities west of Budapest and east of Los Angeles' follow the same basic patterns with regard to density–that of density decreasing with distance from the city center. This pattern has significant implications for wealth and has intensified in recent years.

Second, the past twenty years – a period when the world's urban population increased by the over a billion people – witnessed the first shift in income distribution towards a more egalitarian distribution in the past 200 years. This shift in patterns of income distribution is the direct result of the rapid rates of economic growth experienced in countries, which previously attempted to change urbanization patterns in ways that prevented or severely discouraged migration – as did China's internal passports, India's 'license raj', and South Africa's apartheid system – all of which constrained industry and families from locating in cities.

And finally, urbanization affected the creation of wealth through improvements in health. As shown in the work by Yale economist William D. Nordhaus (2000), in the U.S., improvements in health, if correctly measured, in the post World War II period would have resulted in a doubling of per capita income growth. The health gains in the U.S. which produced these results were considerably smaller than those realized by the countries of the Global South as it urbanized since World War II. The so-called 'urban health premium' that results from the significantly healthier urban environments in the Global South translates into even greater gains in welfare than Nordhaus has found to be the case in the U.S. Urban residents have access to better health care facilities, doctors, and inoculations, higher literacy rates, and fewer children than do their rural colleagues. The result is a significant increase in life span, more than 8 percent longer in China, for instance, and less disability and sickness during their working years. A healthier, stronger, better educated workforce will obviously be more productive and will in a sense have a greater store of wealth implied by the higher expected lifetime earnings of urbanites. Clearly, investing in schools and health services yields potentially enormous increases in correctly measured wealth.

A UN-Habitat (2010) report points out that the factors that drive the growth and prosperity of cities are many and varied. Significantly, the synergy between and among these drivers produces the tangible changes that we see as outcomes. Factors that aid competitiveness range from security to institutional factors that shape the pattern of city growth. For instance, a series of planning reforms in Brazil that was experimented with in the city of Curitiba transformed the previously obscure city into a global exemplar. The better a city works, the more competitive it gets, and Curitiba is currently a centre of attraction to migrants and tourists, but also the beautiful bride of local and foreign investors.

Although cities tend to concentrate poverty, they also amalgamate the best tools for escaping it (UNFPA, 2007). This is due to the large efficiency gains derived from collecting a vast and broad range of capital together (Duranton and Overman, 2008). The transformation from town into city is accompanied by an accumulation of surpluses, which is reinvested to generate further prosperity. This prosperity manifests in the form of access to social amenities, higher wages, and improved social life, providing further incentive for rural-urban migration.

BOX 9.2 THE RESURGENCE OF SÃO PAULO, BRAZIL

The recent growth of São Paulo illustrates how an emerging economy city is making the transition to a prosperous international city through all three sources of service industry growth. Its success is increasingly reflected in international ranking and benchmarking indices, such as those of Mastercard and Mercer. First, the city is Latin America's financial powerhouse and has enjoyed strong recent growth in business services, particularly professional services, media, creative industries, research, and medicine. This is linked to the fact that it is the preferred location for Brazilian headquarters of companies in all major industrial, commercial and financial sectors. Second, São Paulo is becoming an important global outsourcing centre, specialising in animation, product development, infrastructure management services and multilingual call centres. This partly reflects the strength of education in the city, its cultural diversity and strong cosmopolitan character. Third, it is emerging as a strong commercial capital and consumer city, with a notable retail centre, diverse festivals and fashion events, rising tourism industry and growing cultural reputation. Economic success has also been accompanied by several important challenges, particularly in relation to human capital and infrastructure. Congestion is a problem because of continuing under-investment in urban infrastructure, and not enough has been done to upgrade the skills of the population in line with the improving economy.

Source: Greg Clark, personal correspondence.

Starting with the notion that the advantage of cities must outweigh its disadvantages, O'Flaherty (2005) somewhat likened cities to businesses using the two similar attracting advantages of increasing returns to scale and economies of scale. Increasing returns to scale occur when 'doubling all inputs more than doubles the output [and] an activity has economies of scale if doubling output less than doubles cost'. This agglomerating effect of cities means that resources are more ably utilized than in other settlement forms. This derives from the notion of Local External Economies tradition, which asserts that clustering of producers in a particular area yields advantages and likewise explains such clustering.

However, city growth is not determined solely by physical elements like size, population, economic growth, and infrastructure, but also depends on other intangibles such as liveability, social and cultural indices, and overall quality of life. Industrialization has played a large role in enhancing both levels of city growth. These intangible and tangible assets result in surplus value, part of which is redistributed in the form of higher wages on a personal level, and the provision of such social services as utility, healthcare, and education on a larger scale – aiding the comfort of city dwellers.

Cities often lose competitiveness when they fail to react to the dynamic nature of market, labour, and capital needs, i.e. the creators of wealth. The city of London is currently trying to find the best way to keep its position as a leading financial centre whilst enacting the necessary institutions as demanded by the public as a result of the 2009 global financial crash. Industrial production has epitomized the constant change cities must adjust to as the assembly line production of the Fordist era has given way to just-in-time production. Increased efficiency in transportation and telecommunications has also influenced industrial production, distribution and consumption. In a globalized world, cities are increasingly reliant on addressing industrial production techniques, shift in raw materials sourcing and a host of organizational restructuring activities to maintain their dynamism in a competitive world.

Cities, particularly big cities, tend to benefit from and also spur large agglomeration economies (Rosenthal and Strange, 2003). It is for this reason that city size tends to be an important determinant, not just of productivity growth, but also overall GDP and the wealth of the city. Not surprisingly, the contribution of some more advanced cities to the overall GDP of the country is disproportionately very large. Locational advantage, economies of scale and agglomeration economies, including lower prices for inputs, greater access to specialized services, lower transaction costs, and knowledge spillover contribute significantly to the efficiency gains and consumption benefits arising from agglomeration economies. Common services, specialized skills and new technologies are thus attracted to the city and in the more advanced and emerging economies these serve the high technology sectors such as pharmaceuticals, computers and ICT. Cities possess the clear advantage of promoting manufacturing depending on the above and also the ready availability of infrastructure such as transportation and communication. This is the area in which poorer developing countries lack competitive advantage.

Governments, Latecomer Countries and Competitiveness

The challenge of industrializing cities in developing areas is multifaceted and though often framed as one of simply acquiring the necessary investment for modern industrial plants and infrastructure, the issues tend to be far more complex. Cities and firms in both poor and emerging countries have to surmount three broad sets of challenges that determine to a large extent rate of development as well as the speed of urbanization. First, firms in these cities tend to operate in an environment that generates high transaction costs because of the unusually high costs of searching, screening and validation of information (related to suppliers, buyers, technologies and skills). In addition, weak knowledge bases mean that quite often enterprises have to invest their own funds in seeking information which, under normal circumstances in developed areas, are ordinarily available in the public domain. The second challenge to urban cluster manufacturing relates to the size and types of markets. The system of market exchange in which productive agents are embedded is overwhelmingly impersonal and often subject to high levels of uncertainty due to the equally uncertain nature of relational contract.[7] Amsden's (1977, 1985) insightful papers on the machine tools sector in the cities of Taiwan call attention to the ubiquitous ways in which the size and type of markets shape the pattern of consumption and production as well as the division of labour. The 'extent of market' or 'size of market' refers not to a

---

7   Today's modern industrial societies evolved from a system of personal to impersonal exchange and is now built on complex institutions and highly specialized knowledge (North, 2005; Mokyr, 2002). 'As increased specialization occurred with the growth of markets, individuals exchanged increased specialized knowledge at the expense of less "general" knowledge' (North, 2005, p. 122).

geographic area or large population but purchasing power, 'the capacity to absorb a large annual output of goods ...'.[8] Amsden makes a distinction between the notion of 'size' and 'type' of market. One may have two markets of equal purchasing power but qualitatively different in their capacities to consume large amounts of goods.[9] Markets in Africa and other poorer developing countries have relatively small size (thrive on personal exchanges of kinship relations, personal loyalty and social connections)[10] and fit in very many respects with the type of market that is characterized by low profitability, limited economies of scale and low intensity learning that slow long run technological capability building. Third, because states and governments are weak, there is a lack of effective state support, and in the absence of this important factor, private institutions have evolved to redress information asymmetry and enforce contracts informally. This is evident in the different types of clusters that we examine in this paper. Informal clusters are the predominant forms of industrial organization in developing countries while advanced and emerging coastal cities of China for instance concentrate high technology sectors.

There is a clear and emerging pattern: the nature of urban prosperity will become more and more uncertain, consistent with the nature of social and technological innovations; with all cities worldwide facing the same opportunities for prosperity and challenges of possible decline irrespective of location or level of development. There is now an increased onus on governments to create a competitive environment that attracts the right factors of production as enumerated below.

Government Regulation and Service

Government is the key coordinator of a city through regulations, service and rule of law. Cities in countries with strong legislation and judiciary are better able to attract businesses and encourage start-ups as there is greater business security. Particularly in the less developed nations, the role of the government is indispensable. The rapid growth of many Chinese cities can be directly attributed to well-planned government intervention through a 'visible hand'. In an increasingly global economy, well-governed cities can act as gateways for their countries and speed up the process of attracting capital and human resources.

Historically, the nations of the west industrialized and urbanized with the aid of strong government intervention, and the rapid rise of East Asian countries is continued testament to the need for government intervention in establishing the right business environment.

Macroeconomic Policies

Macroeconomic policies are important tools utilized by governments to influence the competitiveness of their cities. It is through these that they incentivize businesses through

---

8   Amsden (1977) cites Allyn Young's clarification of what an 'extent of market' is.

9   She illustrates: 'Assume market 100 economic units in market A with an income of $10,000. Assume 1,000 economic units in market B each with an income of $1,000 ... purchasing power in the two markets is equal, obviously a market of type A is a better candidate than a market type B for the absorption of non-essential goods with high unit costs, irrespective of how great increasing returns may be, and hence relatively high prices' (Amsden, 1977, p. 218).

10   Biggs and Shah (2006).

the creation of special designated areas such as special economic zones (SEZs) like export processing zones (EPZs), free trade zones (FTZs), industrial parks and technology incubation centres. This is done with the use of tax holidays and duty-free export of products from such areas to encourage investors, and often aided by complimentary infrastructure such as efficient, multi-modal transport network, uninterrupted power supply, and adequate security. For example, Shenzhen in China is a small city whose rapid growth over the last decade and a half can be attributed to its designation as a special economic zone. The formation of mostly export-oriented industries and services has brought about unprecedented economic growth.

Macroeconomic policies can take a variety of forms as long as they enable the government to control the activities in an area and provide as much advantage as possible to enhance city competitiveness. Macroeconomic policies are one method through which governments regulate their environment and another is through market mechanisms and policies.

Institutions, Market Mechanism and Policies

Firms require a combination of competitive capabilities, and working within the right sets of institutions in order to gain and sustain domestic and global competitiveness. While individual enterprises are learning how to compete in a changed and hostile economic environment, we posit that one of the greatest problems constraining the learning and competitive effort of enterprises is the absence of the right kinds of institutions. We follow the definition of institution provided by North (1996): 'Institutions are the rules of the game of a society or more formally the humanly devised constraints that structure human interaction. They are composed of formal rules (statute law, common law, and regulations), informal constraints ... and the enforcement characteristics of both'. However, as Nelson (2002) observes, to see physical and social technology as 'constraints' is problematic. He illustrates: 'A productive social technology is like a paved road across a swamp. To say that the location of the prevailing road is a constraint on getting across is basically to miss the point. Without a road, getting across would be impossible, or at least much harder.'

We take the view that institutions and continued technological innovations both, broadly defined, are central to the process of economic development and city competitiveness. Large numbers of cities in Africa have neither succeeded in acquiring technology effectively, nor built effective institutions to support technical change. Subsequently, the region has suffered the loss of competitiveness not only in manufactures but also in traditional commodity exports. Loss of opportunities in global trade and technology exchange has meant that African countries have so far benefited only marginally from globalization. For most sub-Saharan Africa (SSA) countries, manufactured exports, which remain a small proportion of global exports, declined over the years, while cities of Asia such as Shanghai, Shenzhen, Penang, and others have advanced very rapidly economically.

Policies and institutions provide a guarantee for investments and hence make cities with strong institutions more attractive. North (1996), asserts that market mechanism plays a crucial role in determining the incentives of individuals to invest and innovate. 'Through incentives, constraints, delimitation of property rights and transaction cost reduction, market mechanism can impact investment, innovation and efficiency, which in turn will affect economic growth' (Ni, 2012). The importance of institutions has been long and energetically debated in development economics and has been influential in explaining the success of developed nations; Saxenian (1994), Storper (1997) and Aron (2000) further reiterate the strong links between institutions, investment and growth.

The World Bank's 'Doing Business Report', which covered 100 regions and countries, shows a positive correlation between business regulations, implementation and per capita income. The improved business environment aided the growth of the local economies with places like Singapore, Hong Kong SAR, China, New Zealand (Wellington), the United States (New York), Denmark (Copenhagen), Norway (Oslo), the United Kingdom (London), and Korea, Rep (Seoul) standing out. Evidently, urban competitiveness is intricately linked with urban prosperity and institutions and governments play a large role in setting down the right tools and policies to attract wealth and investment and hence make their cities more competitive.

ANALYSIS OF GLOBAL CITY BEST PRACTICES

One of the most enduring social innovations that have changed the nature of cities is the agglomeration of firms and businesses and the ways it affects knowledge sharing. Bringing together large numbers of people facilitated the face-to-face interactions needed to generate, diffuse, and accumulate knowledge, especially in industries which experience rapid technological change, as described in Box 9.3 below.

BOX 9.3   THE ADVANTAGES OF AGGLOMERATION: SILICON VALLEY

Geographically situated in Northern California, Silicon Valley contains a thirty-mile by ten-mile strip of land in Santa Clara County between the cities of San Francisco and San Jose. Until the middle of the past century, this agriculturally rich region was known for its apricots and walnuts rather than for its 'Apples' (Rogers and Larsen, 1984). Even at the end of World War II, the predominant industry around San Jose was small-scale food-processing and distribution. A combination of regional advantages and historical accidents conspired to produce one of the greatest 'science parks' in the world. Observers have identified the following regional advantages: world-class academic institutions (Stanford University and the University of California at Berkeley), brilliant scientists, military procurements of semiconductors, and the pleasant climate of Northern California (Rogers and Larsen, 1984).

Many people have attributed the success of the Valley primarily to the influence of nearby institutions of higher education. Stanford graduates David Hewlett and William Packard commercialized the audio-oscillator in the late 1930s. After selling their first oscillators to Disney Corporation, they reinvested their earnings and expanded both their products and their range of customers (Rogers and Larsen, 1984).

In the 1950s William Shockley, a Cal Tech trained engineer, revolutionized electronics by developing the transistor to magnify electronic images and replace the much bulkier and energy-wasting vacuum tubes. At the same time, the relocation of a major military contractor, Lockheed, to California in 1956 brought federal defense dollars to the area. Semiconductors procurements by the defense agencies amounted to approximately two-fifths of total production.

This rapid rise of technology reflects itself in the organization of Silicon Valley. The people who began or were employed in these new firms considered themselves as technological trailblazers. The residents of this technological society were, originally at least, a strongly homogenous group: white, male, Stanford or MIT educated engineers who migrated to California from other regions of the country. As modern-day pioneers, they were especially responsive to risky ventures that had the potential for great rewards.

Along with sharing the same type of risks, the entrepreneurs also shared a camaraderie unsurpassed almost anywhere else in American industry. Even engineers and scientists who worked at competing firms during the work day remained close friends off the job. According to an account by Tom Wolfe (1983), the manager of one semiconductor firm would not hesitate to call a competitor for assistance on technical matters. After work, the engineers and programmers would meet at popular drinking establishments in the Valley to share high-tech 'war stories'. These after-hours discussions enabled the individuals to share industry gossip as well as facilitate employment searches in the region (Saxenian 1994).

Job mobility statistics show the extent of success of these networks: the average turnover rate for small-to medium sized firms was 35% and the average job tenure (in the 1980s) was approximately two years (Saxenian, 1994). Geography probably played as critical role in this rate as the informal social contacts. The spatial concentration of a large number of technology-based firms enabled people to change employers without altering other aspects of their lives. When a person left one firm in Palo Alto for another, there was no need to move one's residence or take one's kids out of a particular school district to enter a different firm. The attitude of the Vaey served as a catalyst for this risk-taking. In many cases, a small coterie of employees in a firm dissatisfied with their current place of employment would gather together after work to tinker around with some of their own ideas. They would then develop a business plan, acquire funds from venture capitalists, and seek advice from local academic sources. If they succeeded they were heroes. If they failed, many employers were located in the same town or in a neighboring community (Saxenian, 1994). Saxenian (1994) notes the motto of the region: 'competition demands continuous innovation, which in turn requires cooperation among firms'. In short, Silicon Valley's success is based on the promotion of collective learning and flexible adjustment among companies that make specialty products within a broad range of related technologies. 'The region's dense social networks and relatively open labor markets encourage entrepreneurship and experimentation' (Saxenian, 1994).

Adapted from Paul Mackun's article 'Silicon Valley and Route 128: Two Faces of the American Technopolis', accessed at http://www.netvalley.com/silicon_valley/Silicon_Valley_and_Route_128.html.

Sources: Rogers and Larsen (1984); Saxenian (1994).

This aspect of agglomeration economies affecting high tech firms has received less empirical attention, but as seen in the story of Silicon Valley, it has promised to be one of the more significant drivers behind dynamic growth in developing country cities.

Undeniably, the most important aspect of agglomeration economies is the cumulative effect generated by a growing number of agents that congregate in geographic spaces in order to benefit from the diversity of activities and a higher specialization (Fujita and Thisse, 2002). In other words, as national economies develop, there is an observed shift from subsistence-based agricultural production to higher-value manufacturing and services, spatial concentration rises and the beneficial effects of agglomeration increase. Simultaneously, the diversification of economic activity also increases. Small cities may tend to become specialized in fewer and more specialized industries. However, large metropolises like New York or Tokyo become both highly diversified as well as more specialized – as in the emergence of specialized restaurants that cater to the larger number of potential clients.

While there is less evidence on the role of agglomeration gains in cities of developing countries, poor transportation or communication systems could diminish the potential positive impact of clustering in a city. In such circumstances, while it is difficult to disentangle the empirical effects, locational advantages could be even more valuable, as suggested by Box 9.4, a discussion of the economy of Mumbai's largest slum area, Dharavi, even if it is more difficult to measure the gains.

BOX 9.4   AGGLOMERATION IN DEVELOPING CITIES: THE CASE OF DHARAVI

In his recent book *Welcome to the Urban Revolution: How Cities Are Changing the World*, Jeb Brugmann provides an interesting account on Dharavi in Mumbai, India.

Dharavi is no longer just a slum. It has a population equivalent to Nashville, Edmonton, Gdansk, or Leeds. Its GDP is far lower, but its economy is every bit as diverse and vibrant as those of Western cities – if not more so. While it remains one of the most densely populated areas of the world, in a matter of decades, it has matured into a global manufacturing and trading city built by hundredfold chains of migration from all over India. To use the jargon of western development, Dharavi has a number of export-oriented industry clusters. It has strong secondary and tertiary sectors. Primary industries are supported by networks of secondary suppliers and service businesses, many of which are also located in Dharavi itself. In a walk through the area, one finds a full range of retail shops, warehousing, goods transport, lawyers, accountants, expediters, pottery makers, tanners, hotel and entertainment businesses, health clinics, religious institutions, and local political organizations (Brugmann, 2009).

Altogether, Dharavi has an estimated GDP of $1.5 billion each year. In spite of its remittances to villages accross India, its continued economic growth, without significant external finance, suggests a very positive balance of trade. Nevertheless, whether Dharavi represents a more or less valuable locational advantage is not clear. Unquestionably, it is an area that has grown organically and is, in many ways, highly productive. On the other hand, however, it also grew up in a low-lying swampy area and has suffered from ambiguous land titles and building height restrictions that prevented development into a more high rise area. As a result, it sits in one of the most valuable pieces of land in the city. So, whether that land is being put to its highest and best uses is a question that is not answered by showing that Dharavi is productive. The question is, productive compared to what other uses?

In the end, the question of whether locational advantage has been achieved by a given usage of a property is in many cases very difficult to infer. In places where clear and unambiguous sales can be made, and transactions can be pursued transparently and without corruption, the most valuable locational advantage will be obvious, because it will be the highest price paid for the property. In most cities of the Global South this sort of judgment is perforce less obvious. As a result, it is not surprising that the evidence is lacking on agglomeration effects as we show in the next section.

Source: Brugmann (2009).

In sum, there are a variety of ways by which innovations in organizations and the emergence of institutions in cities do affect economic growth, most of them through the value people place on being near to each other. Proximity generates both ideas and much higher compensation, reflecting higher productivity. In fact, in the U.S. people who live in cities with more than 1 million people earn more than 50 percent more than do their counterparts in smaller cities (Glaeser, 2011). This wage premium, in turn, motivates others to migrate there, continuing the productive cycle. This sort of analytical angle has now entered into the lexicon of economic growth theorists who base much of their perspective, and optimism, on the fact that urbanization can have powerful effects on growth and welfare. We now turn to empirical analyses of the scale of these impacts.

However, the capacity to innovate and to benefit from social innovations varies with the characteristics of a city; according to Ni (2012) the factors influencing competitiveness for a sample of cities, including patent index (representing technological innovation) and freedom index (representing market mechanism), are very important to urban competitiveness and urban prosperity. The level to which individual factors affect cities though is linked to the current level of development of the city. For the high-income, upper-middle-income and middle-income groups, global connectivity and technological innovation are of the most crucial importance. Cities at other levels need a different focus; for the lower-middle-income group, labour productivity and technological innovation were of paramount importance for advancement. For the lowest-income group, labour productivity, infrastructure, and natural location were most important, showing they are perhaps the key to igniting urban prosperity, while technological innovation was needed to sustain it.

Sustainable urban development depends for its initiation on the advantage of natural location as the first factor determining a city's development and prosperity. However, business, politics, technology, culture, as well as military and natural factors and the ways they change and evolve tend to determine the direction of a city's prosperity or decline. For cities in historical perspective, there have always been other reasons that have affected their prosperity and development. Although location gives an area an initial advantage, other factors do become relatively more important over time in determining how this lead is sustained. Often locations change in significance, and the comparative advantage of a certain place can become obsolete.

Duranton and Puga (2001) point out that while large diverse metropolises could serve as nurseries, it is not always optimal to remain in such environments to foster a business. They postulate that cities are richer in information thereby encouraging the development of new products and processes. However, once these processes are developed, it is more prudent to relocate to specialized locations to benefit from localized economies. They cite evidence of firm birth and relocations across French metropolitan areas to prove their claim. Hence, while location might be of initial significance, innovation and technology are the true drivers of long term competitiveness.

INNOVATION AND TECHNOLOGY

Society has constantly been propelled by advancements in science and technology, with eras often defined by a particularly powerful invention, and this is a trend that is unlikely to change even in this era of globalization and urbanization. Solow (1957) identified the effect ('the residual') of technology on economic growth, and Gruber et al. (1967) argued that research and development is also a factor of production. Additionally, Romer, Porter, and Jacobs, amongst others, have emphasized the effect of technological spillovers in generating growth.

In addition to the effects of technology in fostering growth and therefore prospering cities, conversely cities are hotbeds for innovation (Bairoch, 1988). Jacobs (1984) argues that the increased number of interactions between people in cities spurs ideas and innovation, as knowledge spillovers are more widespread and evident. The speedy diffusion of knowledge and the subsequent wealth of information and ideas inspire innovation in knowledge-intensive production and service activities, which are increasingly key drivers of economic performance and growth (Ni, 2012).

Silicon Valley in the U.S., Tsukuba in Japan, Zhongguancun in Beijing, China, Bangalore in India, and a number of other places around the world with dense concentration of universities and research institutions provide evidence of the synergies that attend multiple nodes and agglomeration of technological research organizations.

BOX 9.5   BIOTECHNOLOGY CLUSTERS IN CHINESE PROVINCES

The growth of biotechnology clusters in Beijing, Shanghai and Shenzen/Guangdong, for example, results from several government policies going back to the 1970s. The first major policy change allowed more than 200,000 students to earn post-graduate science degrees abroad. Then in 1986, the government made plans to train hundreds of thousands of postgraduates in biotechnology. Next, they encouraged biotechnology professionals who had been working abroad to return home. Many did, and founded companies, drawing on the managerial and scientific expertise gained in their careers in the U.S. and elsewhere.

In biotechnology and in other clusters, company formation tends to proceed a little differently than in most Western market economies. Essentially, the Chinese authorities argue that entrepreneurship is less a function of spotting a profitable opportunity than it is an ability to form alliances with those who hold key assets.

The entrepreneur's social connections with government officials, for example, are often far more important than in the West. At the same time, working these connections is not simply a matter of gaining approvals by passing some envelopes under the table. Unlike arrangements in other emerging markets, analysts say that local governments in China today often add real value to local clusters by championing industry more generally rather than picking winners and losers among individual companies, as in the past. In Ningbo, for instance, the government began as a shareholder in some local firms, but now more often organizes trade and fashion shows, or coordinates local development.

> When this broader approach at coordination with industry works, as it seems to have in textiles and biotechnology, it adds effective state support to the initiative and energy of entrepreneurs. Some observers even argue that one key reason China is so much further ahead economically than Russia is that Chinese local officials tend to view business more as a source of long-term growth than a short-term revenue.

Significantly, innovation does not depend solely on R&D or necessarily frontier knowledge alone, but incremental innovation through technology adaptations is just as powerful a source of industrial progress for a city, particularly in a global knowledge-based era when the right policies by a government give a city the competitive edge through access to foreign technologies. Shenzhen in China is a good example of a city that has successfully applied foreign technology locally; Nanjing on the other hand has struggled to adequately translate its creativity to widespread growth (Ni, 2012).

However, the ability to adopt and adapt to innovation and technology varies across regions (Markusen et al., 1986; DeVol, 1999). The most prosperous regions in the world account for a majority of its technological innovation, with San Jose, where Silicon Valley is based, being a marker for sustainable growth and prosperity. Additionally, advances in transport technology and communications have greatly enhanced productivity, creating new pathways for prosperity as well as vast opportunities for employment.

The impact technology can make on the labour market, and hence city competitiveness, cannot be overstated. In addition to creating job openings, aiding research, allowing the easy sharing of best practices, and monitoring the implementation of policies, it can be used as a pulse for the labour market. Increasingly the world, driven by innovations underpinned by information technology, is moving from an industrial economy to one based on rapid communication and increased connectivity. Clearly transport and communication have become major social and technologically innovations that help bridge time and space in cities.

As early as 1991, Newton had divided companies engaged in information-based economy into four categories: knowledge and information production industries, information distribution and communication industries, information processing industries, and information infrastructure industries. Despite its skewed distribution and the well-known digital divide the impact and spread of the information economy is global. However, cities have advanced in prosperity based on their capabilities to adjust to industrialization, and their ability to take advantage of new opportunities and confront new threats arising for cities hinges on their adaptability to the information-based era.

Paramount to the success of knowledge economies, in which cities are increasingly the leading entities in a global world, is the availability of skilled labour that draws on a good world class education. A sound information and knowledge base enables cities to produce innovative techniques fuelled by a capable telecommunications infrastructure to keep them competitive. Studies show that cities that invest explicitly to accumulate and produce information tend to be more capable and tend to grow faster in all areas of terms and sectors. Additionally, such economies with ease of access to business information and innovation are more attractive to investors hence increasing their competitiveness.

BOX 9.6   DRIVERS OF INNOVATION SUCCESS

Innovation capacity building effort in latecomer countries has concentrated on three key components, which are: (1) R&D inputs including development of scientists and engineers (full time equivalent scientists and engineers in all sectors, FTES&T); (2) Cluster-specific innovation environment (specialization and private R&D), by which is meant highly specialized focus on key sectoral activities often geographically localized; (3) Drawing from accumulated knowledge capacity, meaning global pool of knowledge which latecomer countries have successfully exploited through learning and technological capability building in local firms and in or through public organizations.[11] This is in contrast to the experience of the OECD which builds innovation capacity on a wider range of sources. Patent as a means of building the knowledge stock for instance has only gained importance in East Asia since the mid-1980s.[12]

Source: Oyelaran-Oyeyinka (2010).

With increased integration of technology in the processes of production, the world economy, particularly advanced economies, are increasingly service-oriented.

Information and Communications Technology (software development), financial services, professional services (law, engineering) and other intangible components of the economy have increasing weight in the growth of global, national and city economies.

The convergence of services and technology has increasingly been exploited by the Newly Industrializing Countries (NICs) and now developing countries are beginning to adopt the policies used by their more advanced colleagues such as the creation of technopoles – industrial sites that bring together favourable institutions, human capital, and financial investment to become more competitive. These technopoles achieve this by encouraging the clustering of diverse businesses, research institutes and ancillary services, which are mutually beneficial. These are often referred to as special economic zones such as Export Processing Zones (EPZ), Free Trade Zones, Industrial Parks, Technology Incubation Villages and can be viewed from Lagos in Nigeria, Shenzhen in China, Kuala Lumpur in Malaysia to Bangalore in India, and increasingly across the globe.

Case Study: Tokyo – Transport Advantage

Often cities are given an initial advantage, which some sustain and others relinquish. These advantages vary from increased investment in better public services such as higher quality

---

11   See Hu and Mathews (2005) for a thoughtful analysis of the national innovation capacity of East Asian latecomers.

12   The findings by Hu and Mathews (2005) show two significant and contrasting (when compared with current highly advanced economies) determinants of innovation capacity in latecomers: the *extent of specialization* (in high tech activities) and the role of public R&D support. For instance econometric results show that when *public R&D funding* is added into the model of knowledge stock, *the effect of specialization rises by 110%* matching the level of contribution in the OECD. In contrast, innovation capacity of OECD countries is not limited to these few factors but depends broadly on the overall strength of national infrastructure, namely, R&D spending, IP protection, openness to international trade, private R&D spending, academic sector spending (particularly basic research), and linkages of public and private investment.

schools, to location, to resources or markets. They can take the form of favoured capital allocations to cities higher in a political hierarchy with China being a good example; the allocation of export or import licenses to favoured cities (Henderson and Kuncoro, 1996); the allocation of government owned enterprises such as heavy industry in Brazil; and the spatial provision of transport and telecommunications infrastructure as will be explored with Tokyo.

Tokyo is the largest metropolitan area in the developed world, and was the top destination for most businesses in the East. It was constructed through the use of both sub metro sub-centres and satellite cities, with strong interconnectivity achieved through well considered and strategically placed rail systems, and is an example of a well decentralized city (Sorenson, 2001: 10-12). A recent UN-Habitat (2010) survey found that investment in transport infrastructure enhanced the growth of hinterland cities relative to coastal cities. It was found that with such investment growth in mountain cities was 23 percent, dry land cities 21 percent, and coastal cities only 17 percent.

Polycentricism has traditionally referred to intra-urban agglomeration, i.e. the outward, diffusion from big cities to smaller cities within their urban fields or spheres of influence (Davoudi, 2003). Of late, it has also been used at interurban or interregional scales to denote polycentric urban regions (Kloosterman and Musterd, 2001) or megacity regions (Scott, 2001). This is usually accomplished with the help of a strategically and well-integrated transportation system, particularly rail.

In Tokyo, the authorities attracted capital for three main areas of Shinjuku, Shibuya and Ikebukuro, and made them huge rail intersections whilst providing incentives for their development. These areas quickly flourished as entertainment and restaurant districts developed to serve commuters switching trains on their way home, and these subcentres continued to further expand as, later, branch stores of the main downtown department stores and the major terminal department stores built by the private train companies also appeared (Honjo, 1978: 148). The case of Tokyo highlights the role of planners, as the initial development of the subcentres was largely a consequence of the inherent advantages of their location at busy commuter intersections.

Table 9.2   TMA Population and Employment Change, Core Areas, Subcentres, and Suburbs (1970-1995)

	Employment change	Average Employment change	Population Change	Average Population Change
All municipal areas	5 661 732	15 511.6	9 220 453	25 261.5
Tokyo core area	998 437	142 633.9	504 756	-72 108.0
Rest of 23 ward area (outside seven core wards)	379 064	23 691.5	367 809	-22 988.1
Suburban municipalities (outside Tokyo ward area)	4 284 231	12 527.0	10 093 018	29 511.7
All subcentres	1 953 372	65 112.4	2 184 117	72 803.9
Suburban subcentres	1 344 047	58 436. 8	2 704 483	117 586. 2

Source: Sorenson (2001: 22).

Table 9.2 shows the consequences of a long term plan in making the city competitive and increasing overall employment in the Tokyo Municipal Area by 5.66 million while the population increased by 9.22 million between 1970 and 1995. When we break it down, we see that while the population decreased in the congested central areas, more employment was created, highlighting the importance of planning and good transport linkages in creating a competitive city.

CHALLENGES OF THE GLOBAL CITY'S SOCIAL ENVIRONMENT

We have shown that the proximity and the consequent positive outcomes that cities are known for, also has its negative attributes that may challenge cities in significant ways. For example, density and concentration of activities may encourage creative socialization but it provides an environment that allows disease to spread more easily and quickly, creating situations where, as Glaeser (2011) shows, a young man in New York City at the beginning of the 19th century would expect to live 7 fewer years than his country counterpart. Now, in contrast, he can expect to live longer than his counterpart. Similarly, it is well-known that density is also correlated with higher levels of crime and pollution. However, a large literature has shown the importance of public programmes in combating these negative externalities through social and technological innovations. In what follows we highlight a few of the challenges.

Security and Social Harmony

The social environment has an important indirect influence on city development. Some cities such as Geneva and Singapore have thrived from a stern reputation whereas others like San Francisco have flourished through their liberality. Florida (2002) asserts that the quality of a place is a significant factor underlying its social dynamics, which in turn influences its economic performance.

Urban security for example depends in large part on the happiness of citizens, and how safe they feel working and living, which also influences entrepreneurial dynamics. It is a factor of transaction costs and a city's ability to recruit talent and investment. A city with lower rates of crime will be more attractive to business (Haughton et al., 2005); and da Mata et al. (2007) found that local crime and violence hindered Brazilian city growth between 1970 and 2000. Cities renowned for safety such as Luxembourg, Bern, Geneva, Zurich, Hong Kong and Singapore continually attract high calibre talents and investment, hence retaining their prosperity and competitiveness; while there are reported recessions and incidence of employment and negative growth rates for those embroiled in wars and turmoil, e.g. Abidjan, the economic capital of Cote d'Ivoire, Bangui, the capital of Central African Republic.

Social infrastructure and services are parts of physical capital. Importantly also, soft social capital such as adequate healthcare and primary education are crucial in moulding and retaining a city's top talents; whereas others such leisure activities are equally important for talent migration. Education is particularly important as it not only nurtures but also attracts talent. The rise of certain cities can be attributed to the presence of prestigious academic institutions, as in Boston, Silicon Valley, Oxford and Cambridge. City 'livability' and culture play an increasingly decisive role in city competitiveness particularly in this era of global production lines and an increasingly mobile workforce (Kitson et al., 2004).

We also find a shift of interest among the youth of the developed world from issues of national importance to concerns that have a more global texture and reach. 'It may therefore be argued that a cultural shift in political participation has occurred in many developed countries. Young people today may not be active in formal political circles, but they are passionate and proactive when it comes to advocating for environmental protection, human rights, gender equality and self-expression' (Inglehart, cited in Kovacheva, 2005). This means that the most globally inclined cities will attract the most attentive and expressive youth workforce.

Financial and Physical Capital

Physical capital plays a large role in deciding a city's fortunes, although as we move to a more knowledge-based era this is increasingly less so and the impetus placed on this form of capital has moved to better development of human capital which is still in short supply for many cities. Albeit slightly diminished in importance, material inputs are still crucial to servicing the needs of people and cities and are indispensable to city growth and development. The most common elements of physical capital include raw commodities such as gold, land (crucial to financing), soft commodities such as agricultural products, and the staples of industrial economies like plant and machinery.

Increasingly, financial accumulation is becoming less tangible as software, copyrights, stocks, and other such intellectual and financial components continually increase in prominence. This is important in a global economy where mobility of resources is paramount. Douglas Webster (2000) stresses the importance of local domestic capital to small and medium enterprises; an important set of actors for developing and developed countries alike. Countries in the middle income stage, e.g. China, India, have greater access to foreign and mobile capital, and this is reflected in the speed and quantity of investment in their major cities.

However, only a few cities have attained the level of truly global cities with full capabilities of information and human capital although still relying on industry and manufacturing, sectors that draw heavily on physical capital. Other places in the least developed regions are still slowly evolving into this phase and will be even more dependent on physical capital.

Overall, cities need to continuously accumulate financial resources for investment and also build the right human capital to utilize and manage physical capital. The resource curse has often plagued nations endowed with important raw materials but lacking in the right structures to best utilize and channel this wealth. Building a financial system, which attracts investment capital and uses knowledge to properly allocate the distribution of resources, minimizing transaction costs and maximizing capital utility, is key to the success of any city, so much so that many global cities have been built on the success of their financial centres, e.g. London and New York. When properly constructed, they become drivers of all other industries promoting investment, trade, consumption, and industry development. The growth of finance not only raises the aggregate output of the city, but also stimulates growth in various other industries.

Population and Human Capital

Education and the development of human capital are crucial elements in developing a city and increasing its competitiveness. These are not only crucial to instigating prosperity in a city, but also to sustaining it, and cities which find ways to do this tend to attract the most capable individuals. A study by Edward Glaeser and Alberto Ades (1995) concluded that there was a positive relationship linking initial schooling to income and population growth; this point was emphasized strongly in Oyelaran-Oyeyinka and Rasiah (2009).

The decline in economic stature and subsequent population drop of cities like Detroit highlight the crucial link of human capital to the long term fortune of the city. The link is not just quantitative but also qualitative. Rural-urban migration is a result of a lack of facilities and opportunities such as schooling in rural settings that 'pushes' the brightest from the villages to cities where they feel their potential may be best maximized. For most cities this becomes a big challenge as they struggle to provide for migrants with very low skills.

There is significant correlation between improved opportunities for education and enhanced access to and awareness of political functions. This is essential to give citizens exposure to the political process, making them aware of their role and rights. A populace ignorant of their privileges as citizens cannot make any significant contributions to the political pulse of their nation. As the SUYR2010 report states, 'education changes not just individuals' perceptions of society, but also provides them with the instrumental capabilities to shape society; in other words, education is both the means as well as the end of development'.

In both developed and developing countries, great strides have been made in providing educational opportunities. There is universal coverage of primary education, with equity in representation of the sexes. Ninety-eight percent of children complete primary education, but this figure is only 84 percent for the developing regions. This puts youth in developed nations in a privileged position for societal participation, particularly giving them an advantage in an increasingly globalized world.

The Challenge of Employment and Social Exclusion in Cities

There may not be a direct and simple, inevitable or linear relationship between urbanization and employment growth because cities can and do follow different growth paths and experience different rates of population and economic development. For instance, in contrast to the Asian experience, cities have proved to be weaker sources of growth in Africa. The composition and direction of economic growth can also have diverse consequences for the nature and quality of employment generated. Put simply, growth can be equalizing and inclusive, or divisive and exclusionary; this poses an enduring challenge to city managers.

Again, contexts do not remain constant and economic situations do change unexpectedly and for this reason the relationship can also vary over time, with cities going through different phases of growth and change. The great industrial cities of the past in Western Europe and North America began to experience absolute decline during the 1960s and 1970s. Decline was driven by suburbanization and deindustrialization, which left a costly legacy of surplus labour, out-dated skills, broken communities and physical dereliction. The phenomenon of 'shrinking cities' became more widespread during the 1990s, especially in Eastern Europe. It was driven by economic collapse, out-migration to Western Europe, declining fertility and rising mortality. In low-income countries the unemployment market is fuelled in large part by the migration of despair, the flood of the unskilled and the uneducated into cities without manufacturing and services.

Growth takes different forms and so do labour market conditions. Informal employment is particularly extensive in many Asian and African cities. In many cases it is growing at the expense of formal employment, and is often not considered to be productive or decent work. The informal economy is able to generate millions of jobs, incomes and livelihoods for poor urban residents partly because working conditions, labour standards and earnings are low. These are flexible, labour intensive operations with simple organizational and production structures and low levels of investment and technology.

Youth employment is a special challenge in cities around the world because of their youthful age structures. The global economic crisis has exposed the particular vulnerability of young people in the labour market. Youth who do not get integrated into the world of work after leaving school may experience long-term social and economic exclusion. They represent a wasted resource, a social hazard and a burden on the state to provide social assistance. Young people are also more likely than adults to be among the working poor in informal jobs. Being forced into precarious livelihoods by intense poverty and lack of social protection is a lost opportunity since they might otherwise attend school or college and acquire skills and competences that could raise their future productivity and earnings.

Location Challenge: Slums Formation and Ecological Environment

Regional agglomerations of industrial activity have long been recognized as potential sources of innovation as well as of general economic growth. At the turn of the 20th century, proximity was absolutely necessary for rapid communication and cooperation among firms. Thus it is not surprising that Marshall (1890, 1919) took great pains to explain the localization of particular industries and the benefits of industrial districts. Revolutions in transport and communication may seem to have reduced the need for firms to operate near one another, yet scholars continue to argue 'locality matters' (Schmitz, 2004).

Locality matters to industrial development in several different ways. Some observers have focused on the regional context in which industry operates, emphasizing the importance of local governance and in particular meso-level policy (Storper, 1997; Scott, 2002; Scott and Storper, 2003; Messner, 2004). The rich literature on industrial clusters highlights the availability of external economies and opportunities for joint action arising from proximity (Beccatini, 1990; Pyke and Sengenberger, 1992; Schmitz and Nadvi, 1999; Schmitz, 2004). Porter's (1990, 1998) slightly different use of the term 'cluster' underscores the importance of local synergy and rivalry as sources of industrial development. Attempts to examine the difference between developed and developing country clusters are yet another way of looking at the importance of locality. Schmitz and Nadvi (1999) pointed out that the former are frequently global leaders that play a decisive role in product design; further, they are standards makers, whereas firms in developing country clusters are standard takers and tend to work to specifications set elsewhere. While this dichotomy surely oversimplifies a wide range of cluster capabilities in both developed and developing countries, it serves to highlight the very important issues of industry leadership, product and process quality, and linkages between global standards and local realities. Nevertheless, locality does also seem to matter for innovation. Studies of innovation systems also point to the impact of local institutions in shaping patterns of innovation and technical change (Lundvall, 1992; Smale and Ruttan, 1997; Edquist, 1997).

Locality can be understood to mean anything from the whole of the developed or developing world to a very small local neighbourhood. We choose in this paper to focus on urban industrial clusters. These vary in size, but are most often sub-national in extent. We in turn articulate the role of cities as well as size on agglomeration economies and how particular cluster formations are determined by a host of policy and institutional factors.

In other contexts, rapid and uncontrolled urbanization can create problems of its own, including congestion, slum formation, pollution, pressure on natural resources, and higher labour and property costs in cities. These inefficiencies grow with city size, especially if urbanization is poorly managed, and if cities are deprived of essential public investment in infrastructure and services. The effect of dysfunctional systems may be to deter private investment, reduce urban productivity and hold back economic and employment growth. There is some evidence of this in Latin America's largest cities, such as Mexico City, São Paulo and Buenos Aires.

Although natural location as a direct factor of economic growth has significantly diminished over time, it still has significant effect on the costs of economic activities, by influencing the agglomeration of capital such as people, commodities, investment and trade, and hence on the sustaining of economic growth. The diminished influence of location can be attributed to improved communication and transport technologies. However, the history of advantageous ecological situations means coastal areas are the most urbanized, accounting for 65 percent of total city population (UN-Habitat, 2010).

Location related challenges vary in scope, scale and spread much in the same way that cities developed from different initial conditions. For instance, some cities took off and evolved on fertile agricultural land, trade route junctions, and at the heart of great cultures, valleys and deltas of great rivers, coastal lowlands, and high altitude areas with equable climate. Other cities emerged as centres of commerce, administration and defence. In Europe, for instance, cities such as Frankfurt, Cologne (Germany) and Lyon (France) are located in the valleys of the Rhine and Rhone Rivers, respectively, while Milan and Zurich are high-altitude settlements located on the Alpine passes. Venice, Bourdeaux, Amsterdam and London are all coastal cities. In Africa, cities like Lagos, Johannesburg, Cairo, Dar es Salaam, Dakar are coastal cities, while others like Timbuktu and Kano are great centres of commerce located along major trans-Saharan trade routes. Other developing country cities like Shezhen (China), Sirjan (Iran) and Nashik in India owe their location and growth to government policies that designate them as special economic zones (SEZs). It is clear therefore that a web of geographical as well as human factors plays a significant role in the location and growth of cities. In other words, settlement formation and consequent growth are often aided by an initial advantage usually associated with location and resources, however sustaining location harmony requires sustainable and progressive policies. Currently, the key factors of competitiveness deployed to overcome location disadvantages are mostly human capital, technological innovation, and global connectivity factors. The information era is not new but is still has to deliver its promise fully to large swathes of the cities of the developing world to resolve the development divide of the present time. Currently some stand out given a combination of historic location and continued favoured urban policies. They are primary cities and if governed properly possess great potential.

BOX 9.7   HANGZHOU, CHINA – USE OF GROWTH TRIANGLES

Globalization has enhanced the necessity for growth triangles, which have been properly exploited in Asia. Globalization, while creating stronger interdependence and linkages amongst the worldwide economy, also reinforces local advantage, as regions are forced to agglomerate to accommodate larger demands and position themselves as competent supply spheres. An example of one such growth triangle exists in Eastern China incorporating the Pearl River Delta (PRD), the Yangtze River Delta (YRD) and the Bohai Gulf region (BGR). However, coordinating such large spheres of influence does not imply a world of borderless space, but rather emphasizes the importance of localization as sub-national and regional governments are forced to assume greater responsibilities. 'Increasingly success or failure depends on the ability of municipal governments to capitalise on the assets of the local environment and to provide the modern infrastructure, enabling environment, and low-wage, flexible workforce demanded by modern businesses' (Cohen, 2004: 36). China spent about 15 percent of GDP on just infrastructure investment in the mid-2000s (McKinsey, 2010). One of the investments is the current fastest train in the world linking Shanghai, Nanjing and Hangzhou with an achievable speed of 487 km/h. Hangzhou in China is currently applying a process of mass agglomeration – incorporating smaller cities and towns into already flourishing economic hotspots (Sorenson, 2001; Yue et al., 2010). The benefits of this method are evident, as the region has achieved periods of rapid economic growth based on specialization, economies of scale, and other such advantages of agglomeration.

Some cities have flourished as a result of attaining primary city status, which is a large urban settlement that has grown so big and important it dominates other cities in terms of concentration of population and economic (and in many cases, political) powers (Olokesusi, 2011). This phenomenon is common in Africa, and many leading cities known as engines of growth for the national economy are primary cities. For instance, Lagos, Nigeria houses more than 5 percent of the country's population and more than 50 percent of the country's industrial and financial establishments and contributes over 30 percent of the GDP. These primary cities of Africa have the highest growth rates averaging 3.65 percent per year while some like Lome (Togo), Nairobi (Kenya), Niamey (Niger) have growth rates of 4 percent. These cities' advantage is derived from a legacy of the African colonial experience, which played a distinct role in urban spatial formations – specifically in carving dominant administrative centres (Stren and Halfani, 2001). However, primacy has its challenges, especially that these cities exhibit demographic and economic changes that are at variance with national performance. For instance, Cohen (2004) notes that the African urbanization experience seems to be partially decoupled from economic development, and that this could be further exacerbated as globalization plays a greater role in shaping cities, and isolates them from the realities of their national economies. Primary cities tend to exhibit large doses of all the negative manifestations of underdevelopment such as high unemployment, poverty, inequality, slum prevalence and crime wherever they are not properly managed.

BOX 9.8   CASE STUDY: LAGOS – A PRIMARY CITY

African countries often exhibit patterns of demographic polarization in favour of primary cities, particularly national capitals and/or coastal metropoles. In sub-Saharan Africa (SSA), Lagos in particular has witnessed a spectacular population explosion – being the only urban agglomeration in the region to make the UN top 30 list of megacities (United Nations, 2002: 45). In terms of competitiveness, Lagos, like some other primary cities in SSA, faces the problem of a dual city – one, a large port city serving as a window into sub-Saharan Africa for the world, and the other a congested centre of opportunity for migrants across the region. The first facet accords it a position seen as competitive in an increasingly globalized world (Dimitriou, 2010). This competitive advantage stems from the ability to conquer time and space through strong international communication channels and global-standard transportation infrastructure (World Bank, 2009). This usually awards the city the luxury of 'preferred types of land use, skilled labour, adequate capital and/or required infrastructure support' (Dimitriou, 2013: 21).

Among its African peers, Nigeria, and particularly Lagos, has relatively advanced infrastructure networks that cover the national territory quite extensively, and currently, extensive reforms are being implemented in the power, ports, ICT, and domestic air transport sectors (McKinsey Global Institute, 2010). Lagos is a megacity, signifying a city with a population surpassing ten million. Despite having a population that ranges between 13 and 15 million, it still possesses a high growth rate of 6% per annum. Mitric has pointed out that 'assisting such cities to become more productive, more liveable, and less polluted is equivalent to assisting entire countries in pursuit of such goals' (2008: 81). Lagos's primary city status means it will always attract human capital – a significant necessity in city competitiveness; the trouble comes in ensuring the work force is sufficiently educated. Although it has been suggested that in less democratic societies, the elites often favour national capitals or the larger cities (Ades and Glaeser, 1995; Davis and Henderson, 2003), this migration is not exclusive to the privileged, and national elites are not always globally competitive.

Additionally, although primary cities attract more foreign capital than other cities in the region, poor government planning leaves them globally hampered. As was earlier shown, at this stage in a city's development, the influence of governmental figures is of paramount importance, and although Lagos is currently enjoying what is largely seen as a regime of good governance, it remains to be seen for how long.

Notwithstanding numerous 'push-factors' there are 'pull-factors' entailing economic opportunities, attractive jobs, better education, and modern lifestyle in urban areas that are the main drivers of continued demographic movements (Kötter and Friesecke, 2009: 2-3), which drag people to large cities. Institutional factors such as type of economic system, legal system, extent of rule of law, property rights, system of government will continue to dictate city growth, and consequently competitiveness.

IMPROVING THE CITY'S SOCIAL ENVIRONMENT AND PROMPTING URBAN COMPETITIVENESS

Industrial Innovations through Agglomeration of Industries and Cities

How do we promote greater social and industrial dynamism in cities? First, there is a need to address the ubiquitous costs of transactions through investment in infrastructure, both physical and knowledge-based. The second is the need for city administrators to see cities as loci of wealth generation and therefore respond appropriately. Third, there is a need to strengthen formal and informal institutional to compensate for the evident lack of rules and enforcement in cities which often lead to crimes and push investment away. Cities with poor facilities tend to be associated with an industrial structure that is deficient in high level skills and capabilities and as well experience pervasive market failures. In short, cities and urban areas in less industrialized areas are characterized by poorly functioning markets, information asymmetries, poor division of knowledge and relative lack of specialization compared with advanced latecomers. Promoting greater agglomeration economies will require greater understanding of how precisely industrial clusters function. Governments are indispensable to markets, particularly in underdeveloped areas, because the price system of exchange is poorly developed and cannot be expected to solve the diverse problems, resulting in high transaction costs. The more backward a country is, the more critical the government role; this is clearly evident in the different cluster examples in this and other scholarly works (Oyeyinka and McCormick, 2007).

The prosperity of cities therefore is in large part about the progressive assimilation of modern infrastructure as well as about the institutions and markets that govern market exchanges. City prosperity is mediated in complex ways to generate efficiency and productivity growth. Despite agglomeration being the most basic feature of a city, some have used it to greater advantage than others such as Japan. Krugman (1991) points out that 'looking back, if we ask the most important geographical characteristics of economic activities, the simplest answer is of course agglomeration'.

There are many advantages of agglomeration and these have been documented in earlier sections, such as the ability of firms to share the same inputs, share labour pools, and improve productivity of labour (Henderson, 1986), influence enterprises' location choices (Head et al., 1995), existence of knowledge spillovers, increased number of new enterprises (Dumais et al., 2002), and improved employment prospects (Rosenthal and Strange, 2003).

Cities, particularly those that have sufficiently agglomerated surrounding areas, are better able to transfer information, benefit from knowledge spillovers, and attract those who can most benefit from extensive information flows (learning hypothesis).[13] In 2007, Global 150 Metropolitan accounted for roughly 12 percent of global population, but generated approximately 46 percent of global GDP. Megacities and urban agglomerations play an increasingly important role as centres of political and economic decisions for their

---

13	Glaeser (1999) finds that workers in New York, Chicago, and Los Angeles are 10 percent more likely to be college graduates than in other U.S. cities. Wheeler (2001) shows that increase in the size of a city increases the wage return to education and proportion of college graduates. Ciccone and Hall (1993) estimate that doubling of employment density increases productivity by 6 percent.

national economies. This is particularly true in an increasingly globalizing world. They serve as magnets for all forms of capital and are crucial for concentrating them and attracting the necessary investments to utilize them, making it impossible to understate their importance to their national economies and surrounding rural areas (Kötter and Friesecke, 2009: 4).

Additionally, economic growth will always be skewed in favour of certain areas where there are dense clusters of economic activities supported by key connectivity and network infrastructure. This is as true for firms seeking domestic competitiveness as those desiring greater global reach.

An important feature of the current urban transition is the fact that the nature and extent of urban growth is now more dependent on the global economy today than ever before. Without a doubt, globalization, i.e. the progressive integration of the world's economies, has accelerated over the past 30 years (Cohen, 2004: 34).

Globalization has enhanced the necessity for growth triangles, which have been properly exploited in Asia but have not translated to much economic advantage for sub-Saharan Africa. Globalization, while creating stronger interdependence and linkages in the global economy, also reinforces local advantage, as regions are forced to agglomerate to accommodate larger demands and position themselves as competent supply spheres. An example of one such growth triangle exists in Southern China, incorporating the Fujian and Guangdong provinces on mainland China, as well as Hong Kong and Taiwan. However, coordinating such large spheres of influence does not imply a world of borderless space, but rather emphasizes the importance of localization as sub-national and regional governments are forced to assume greater responsibilities. 'Increasingly success or failure depends on the ability of municipal governments to capitalise on the assets of the local environment and to provide the modern infrastructure, enabling environment, and low-wage, flexible workforce demanded by modern businesses' (Cohen, 2004: 36).

PROMOTING INDUSTRIAL INNOVATION

Connection and Infrastructure

Increased connectivity through more advanced forms of communication has positively affected the level of interaction among urban economic entities, garnering external capital and markets more effectively, increasing the dissemination of knowledge and innovation, and greatly reducing transaction costs and improving production efficiency.

There is increasing and robust evidence to support a view of the increasing significance of networks that ranks global connectivity as an important factor of competitiveness. This is particularly pertinent in an era of footloose multinationals where factors of production are increasingly mobile, and where there is increased efficiency from global value chains. Peter Taylor and Pengfei Ni (2010) show that of the global 500 cities, those with robust international connectivity also exhibited comparatively higher per capita income and increased urban competitiveness.

Infrastructure is a crucial element in city competitiveness as highlighted by the ease of access and mobility in Europe versus the abject lack thereof in Africa. Not only are companies involved in the development and dissemination important to their local economies, they are crucial in ensuring transaction and communications among the other diverse economic entities. Well-integrated and connected cities not only serve as attractions in themselves, they also provide those within with better access to external factors of production. Investment in infrastructure is hence not only crucial to a city's competitiveness but is in itself a form of capital for the city.

A UN-Habitat analysis of the 245 fastest growing cities in developing countries highlights the importance of investment in transport infrastructure as the most fundamental source of urban development, responsible for more than 1/3 of the cities' growth. Despite this, Oduwaye (2006) has elaborated the peculiar nature of cities of the developing world, including that rapid population growth is unmatched by growth in delivery of land for housing, services, utilities and infrastructure important to sustain a reasonable quality of life.

Paramount to the effective utilization of capital – human and otherwise – is a well-integrated infrastructure network, particularly in terms of telecommunication and transportation. They ensure the effective distribution of goods and services and facilitate smooth operations. Globalization and the eradication of borders in business terms has been largely aided by the rapid advances witnessed in the transportation and telecommunications industry. The use of mobile technology has revolutionized the business environment in Africa, and banking services, which had been notoriously difficult to penetrate are now being rapidly dispersed and adopted.

Across the seas, faster and more efficient vessels have reduced the costs (time and money) for shipping goods. The mass movement of people and goods is being better aided by modern rail systems, which have become faster and more comfortable, for example the Chinese high speed trains, the Bullet Train of Japan and the TGV of France can travel at incredible speeds of 300 kilometers per hour.

Other infrastructure of importance for the wellbeing of the citizens also plays a significant role in attracting firms to various cities, including pipe-borne water, electricity, security, which among others are important in location decisions of firms as well as migrants. Possibly of most importance is the establishment of power infrastructure particularly in determining the location of industrial centers and migrant destinations in most of the developing countries. Empirical evidence has proven that power availability is critical to industrial location decisions (Lall et al., 2003).

Investment in transport and related reforms in the sector, including finance and regulations, deliver major economic development benefits. In the UN-Habitat survey of fast growing cities in Asia, Africa and Latin America, two-fifths of the 245 sampled cities are found to have benefited from diversification and improvements in transport infrastructure. Many cities like Singapore and Abu Dhabi have developed as regional and global transportation hubs, handling a sizeable proportion of global sea and air cargo and passenger traffic.

The Role of National Governments in Supporting Cities

Government policy has an important role to play in harnessing the potential of cities to contribute to full and decent employment. National government has unique powers and resources to act strategically and set a positive legal and financial framework for economic development policy, including tax and incentives policy, industrial policy, investment in economic infrastructure, employment and training policy, and labour market regulation. It can help to build institutional capacity and encourage local municipalities to focus on developing the urban economy as well as delivering household services. It can work to align the functions of different government departments and state agencies, and strive to build cooperative relationships with regional and local spheres of government. It can also encourage local municipalities to forge partnerships with the private sector and civil society. Urban–rural interactions should be encouraged through shared city-region strategies that promote cross-boundary cooperation, trading linkages, transport connectivity and market integration.

Empowered city governments are perhaps more important than anything else to formulate and deliver the integrated strategies required to generate sustained employment growth and to connect workers to the work. Local municipalities can be more knowledgeable than national governments, and more responsive to conditions on the ground. Policies should be shaped by evidence and understanding of economic trends and forces, emerging markets and distinctive local assets and problems, rather than a wish-list of what people would like the city's economy to be. Municipalities can provide suitable land and property, business support to new and existing firms, public works programmes and training schemes. In low and middle income countries, city governments generally need to give financial and technical support from the centre to provide the investment in infrastructure and services required for accelerated economic development and job creation.

REFERENCES

Ades, A. and Glaeser, E. (1995), 'Trade and circuses: explaining urban giants', *Quarterly Journal of Economics*, 122, 195–228.
Amsden, A. H. (1977), 'The division of labour is limited by the type of market: the case of the Taiwanese machine tool industry', *World Development*, 5(3), 217–233.
Amsden, A. H. (1985), 'The division of labour is limited by the rate of growth of the market: the Taiwan machine tool industry in the 1970s', *Cambridge Journal of Economics*, 9(3), 271–284.
Aron, J. (2000), 'Growth and institutions: a review of the evidence', *The World Bank Research Observer*, 15(1), 99–135.
Bairoch, P. (1984), 'The Swiss economy in the European context', *Schweizerische Zeitschrift Fur Geschichte*, 34(4), 468–497.
Bairoch, P. (1988), *Cities and Economic Development: From the Dawn of History to the Present*, Chicago: University of Chicago Press.
Becattini, G. (1990), 'The Marshallian industrial district as a socio-economic concept', *Industrial Districts and Inter-firm Cooperation in Italy*, Geneva: International Institute for Labor Studies.
Biggs, T. and Shah, M. K. (2006), 'African SMEs, networks, and manufacturing performance', *Journal of Banking & Finance*, 30(11), 3043–3066.
Bogetic Z. and Sanogo I. (2005), 'Infrastructure, productivity and urban dynamic in Cote D' Ivoire', *Africa Region Working Paper*, Series No. 86.

Brugmann, Jeb (2009), *Welcome to the Urban Revolution: How Cities Are Changing the World*, New York: Bloomsbury Press.

Chatterjee, S. (2003), 'Agglomeration economies: the spark that ignites a city?', *Business Review*, 4, 6–13.

Ciccone, A. and Hall, R. E. (1993), 'Productivity and the density of economic activity', Working paper of National Bureau of Economic Research, No. 4313.

Cohen, B. (2004), 'Urban growth in developing countries: a review of current trends and a caution regarding existing forecasts', *World Development*, 32(1) 23–25.

Clark, Colin (1967), *Population Growth and Land Use*, London: Macmillan.

Da Mata, D., Deichmann, U., Henderson, J.V., Lall, S.V. and Wang, H.G. (2007), 'Determinants of city growth in Brazil', *Journal of Urban Economics*, 62(2), 252–272.

Davis, James C. and Henderson, J. Vernon (2003), 'Evidence on the political economy of the urbanization process', *Journal of Urban Economics*, 53(1), 98–125.

Davoudi, S. (2003), 'European briefing: polycentricity in European spatial planning: from an analytical tool to a normative agenda', *European Planning Studies*, 11, 979–999.

Derudder, B., Taylor, P., Pengfei Ni et al. (2001), 'Pathways of change: shifting connectivities in the world city network, 2000–08', *Urban Studies*, 47(9), 1861–1877.

DeVol, R.C. (1999), *America's High-Tech Economy*, Santa Monica, CA: Milken Institute.

Dimitriou, H. T. (2010), 'Transport and city development: understanding the fundamentals', in Dimitriou, H.T. and Gakenheimer, R. (eds), *Urban Transport in the Developing World: Perspectives from the First Decade of the New Millennium*, Cheltenham, UK and Northampton, MA, USA: Edward Elgar.

Dimitriou, H.T. (2013), *Global Report on Human Settlements 2013: Sustainable Urban Transport*, Nairobi: UN-Habitat.

Dumais, G., Ellison, G. and Glaeser, E.L. (2002), 'Geographic concentration as a dynamic process', *Review of Economics and Statistics*, 84(2), 193–204.

Duranton, G. and Overman, H. G. (2008), 'Exploring the detailed location patterns of U.K. manufacturing industries using microgeographic data', *Journal of Regional Science*, 48(1), 213–243.

Duranton, G. and Puga, D. (2001), 'Nursery cities: urban diversity, process innovation, and the life cycle of products', *American Economic Review*, 91(5), 1454–1477.

Edquist, C. (1997), *Systems of Innovation: Technologies, Organizations and Institutions*, London: Pinter.

Florida, R. (2002), 'The economic geography of talent', *Annals of the Association of American Geographers*, 92(4), 743–755.

Fujita, M. and Thisse, J. (2002), 'Agglomeration and market interaction', Core Discussion Paper from Université Catholique de Louvain, No. 2002011.

Glaeser, E.L. (1999), 'Learning in cities', *Journal of Urban Economics*, 46(2), 254–277.

Glaeser, E.L. (2011), 'The challenge of urban policy', *Journal of Policy Analysis and Management*, 31(1), 111–122.

Glaeser, E.L. and Ades, A.F. (1995), 'Trade and circuses: explaining urban giants', *Quarterly Journal of Economics*, 110(1), 195–227.

Glaeser E.L. et al. (1996), 'Crime and social interaction', *The Quarterly Journal of*

Economics, 111(2), 507–548.

Goodman, J.C. (2011), 'Triumph of the city: how our greatest invention makes us richer, smarter, greener, healthier, and happier', *Business Economics*, 07.

Gruber, W., Mehta, D. and Vernon, R. (1967), 'The R&D factor in international trade and international investment of United States industries', *Journal of Political Economy*, 20–37.

Haughton, Jonathan, Giuffre, Douglas, Barrett, John and Tuerck, David G. (2005), Comments on the Draft Environmental Impact Statement for the Cape Wind Project, Boston: Suffolk University.

Head, K., Ries, J. and Swenson, D. (1995), 'Agglomeration benefits and location choice: evidence from Japanese manufacturing investments in the United States', *Journal of International Economics*, 38(3), 223–247.

Henderson, J. (1986), 'The new international division of labour and urban development in the world system', in Drakakis-Smith, D. (ed.), *Urbanisation in the Developing World*, London: Routledge, pp. 63–82.

Henderson, J. Vernon and Kuncoro, Ari (1996), 'Industrial centralization in Indonesia', *World Bank Economic Review*, 10(3), 513–540.

Honjo, M. (1978), 'Trends in development planning in Japan', in Lo, F. and Salih, K. (eds), *Growth Pole Strategy and Regional Development Policy: Asian Experience and Alternative Approaches*, Oxford: Pergamon Press and UNCRD, pp. 3–23.

Hu, M. and C. Mathews, J. A. (2005), 'National innovative capacity in East Asia', *Research Policy*, 34(9), 1322–1349.

Huggins, H. and Izushi, H. (2008), *World Knowledge Competitiveness Index 2008*, Cardiff: Center for International Competitiveness.

Jacobs, M. (1984), 'Study of the genetic control and the evolution of fraction protein in the genus lycopersicon', *Advances in Photosynthesis Research*, 4, 551–554.

Kitson, M., Martin, R. and Tyler, P. (2004), 'Regional competitiveness: an elusive yet key concept?', *Regional Studies*, 38(9), 991–999.

Kloosterman, R.C. and Musterd, S. (2001), 'The polycentric urban region: towards a research agenda', *Urban Studies*, 38, 623–663.

Kötter, T. and Friesecke, F. (2009), 'Developing urban indicators for managing mega cities' (http://www.fig.net/pub/fig_wb_2009/papers/urb/urb_2_koetter.pdf).

Kovacheva, S. (2005), 'Will youth rejuvenate the patterns of political participation?', in Forbrig, J. (ed.), *Revisiting Youth Political Participation*, Strasbourg: Council of Europe Publishing , pp. 19–28.

Krugman, P. R. (1991), *Geography and Trade*, Boston, MAMIT Press.

Lall S. (2004), 'Reinventing industrial strategy: the role of government policy in building industrial competitiveness', Research paper for the Intergovernmental Group of Twenty-Four on International Monetary Affairs/United Nations Conference on Trade and Development, No. 28.

Lundvall, B. A. (1992), 'User-producer relationships, national systems of innovation and internationalisation', *National Systems of Innovation: Toward a Theory of Innovation and Interactive Learning*, London: Pinter, pp. 45–67.

Markusen, A. R., Hall, P. H. and Glasmeier, A. K. (1986), *High Tech America: The What, How, Where and Why of the Sunrise Industries*, Boston: Allen & Unwin.

Marshall, A. (1890), 'Principles of economics', *Mind*, 16(61), 110–113.

Marshall, A. (1919), *Industry and Trade*, London: Macmillan.

Mathew, K. M. (2006), *Manorama Yearbook 2006*, Malayala Manorama Press.

McKinsey Global Institute (2010), *Lions on the Move: The Progress and Potential of African Economies*, London: McKinsey Global Institute.

Messner, D. (2004), 'Regions in the world economic triangle', in Schmitz, H. (ed.), *Local Enterprises in the Global Economy*, Cheltenham, UK: Edward Elgar, pp. 21–52.

Mitric, S. (2008), *Urban Transport for Development: Towards an Operationally-Orientated Strategy*, Washington D.C.: World Bank.

Mokyr, J. (2002), *The Gifts of Athena: Historical Origins of the Knowledge Economy*, Princeton, NJ Princeton University Press.

Naudé, W. A. and Krugell, W. (2004), 'An inquiry into cities and their role in subnational economic growth in South Africa', WIDER Research Paper, Helsinki: UNU-WIDER.

Nelson, R.R. (2002), 'Bringing institutions into evolutionary growth theory', in V. Fitzgerald (ed.), *Social Institutions and Economic Development*, Dordrecht: Kluwer, pp. 9–22.

Ni, P. (2012), *The Global Urban Competitiveness Report – 2011*, Cheltenham, UK Edward Elgar.

Ni, Pengfei and Kresl, Peter Karl (2006), *Global Urban Competitiveness Report*, Beijing: Social Sciences Academic Press.

Nordhaus, W. D. (1969), 'Theory of innovation an economic theory of technological change', *American Economic Review*, 59(2), 18–28.

Nordhaus, W. D. (2000), 'New directions in national economic accounting', *American Economic Review*, 90(2) 259–263.

North, D. C. (1996), 'Institutions, organizations and market competition', Keynote Address to the Sixth Conference of the International Joseph Schumpeter Society, June, Stockholm.

North, D. C. (2005), 'Institutions and the process of economic change', *Management International*, 9(3), 1–7.

North, D. C. (2012), 'Economic performance through time', *Revista Universidad EAFIT*, 30(93), 9–18.

O'Flaherty V., Collins G., Fony C. McHugh S. (2005), 'Anaerobic biological treatment of phenolic wastewater at 15–18 degree C', *Water Research*, 39(8), 1614–1620.

Oduwaye, L. (2006), 'Effects of globalization on cities in developing countries', *Journal of Social Science*, 12(3), 199–205.

Olokesusi, F. (2011), 'Lagos: The challenges and opportunities of an emergent African Mega City', Paper Presented at the NISER Seminar, 5.

Organisation for Economic Co-operation and Development (2008), *OECD Environmental Outlook to 2030*, Paris: OECD.

Overman, H. G. and Venables, A. J. (2005), 'Cities in the developing world', Centre for Economic Performance, London School of Economics and Political Science.

Oyelaran-Oyeyinka, B. (2010), 'Technology and comparative advantage in the context of Vision 2010', in a paper presented at the Workshop of Vision.

Oyelaran-Oyeyinka, B. and Padmashree Gehl Sampath (2010), *Latecomer Development: Knowledge and Innovation for Economic Growth*, London: Routledge.

Oyelaran-Oyeyinka, Banji and Dorothy McCormick (2007), *Industrial Clusters and Innovation Systems in Africa: Institutions, Market and Policy*, UNU Press.

Oyelaran-Oyeyinka, Banji and Rajah Rasiah (2009), *Uneven Paths of Development: Innovation and Learning in Asia and Africa*, Cheltenham, UK and Northampton, MA, USA: Edward Elgar.

Pines, D. (2005), 'Economics of agglomeration: cities, industrial location and region growth', *Regional Science and Urban Economics*, 35(5), 584–592.

Porter, M.E. (1985), *The Competitive Advantage: Creating and Sustaining Superior Performance*, New York: Free Press.

Porter, M.E. (1990), *The Comparative Advantage of Nations*, New York: Free Press.

Porter, M.E. (1996), 'Competitive advantage, agglomeration economies, and regional policy', *International Regional Science Review*, 19, 85–90.

Porter, M.E. (1998), 'Clusters and the new economics of competition', *Harvard Business Review*, 76, 77–90.

Porter, M.E. (2000), 'Location, competition, and economic development: local clusters in a global economy', *Economic Development Quarterly*, 14, 15.

Pyke, F. and Sengenberger, W. (1992), *Industrial Districts and Local Economic Regeneration*, Geneva: International Institute for Labour Studies.

Rogers, E. M. and Larsen, J. K. (1984), *Silicon Valley Fever*, New York: Basic Books.

Rosenthal, S. S. and Strange, W. C. (2003), 'Geography, industrial organization, and agglomeration', *Review of Economics and Statistics*, 85(2), 377–393.

Saxenian, A. L. (1994), *Regional Advantage: Culture and Competition in Silicon Valley and Route 128*, Cambridge, MA: Harvard University Press.

Schmitz, H. (2004), 'Globalized localities: introduction', in *Local Enterprises in the Global Economy: Issues of Governance and Upgrading*, Cheltenham, UK: Edward Elgar, pp. 1–19.

Schmitz, H. and Nadvi, K. (1999), 'Clustering and industrialization: introduction', *World Development*, 27(9), 1503–1514.

Scott, A. J. (2001), *Global City-Regions: Trends, Theory, Policy*, Oxford: Oxford University Press.

Scott, A. J. (2002), 'Regional push: towards a geography of development and growth in low- and middle-income countries', *Third World Quarterly*, 23(1), 137–161.

Scott, A. and Storper, M. (2003), 'Regions, globalization, development', *Regional Studies*, 37(6–7), 549–578.

Smale, M. and Ruttan, V. (1997), 'Social capital and technical change: the Groupement Naam of Burkino Faso', in Clague, C. (ed.), *Institutions and Economic Development*, Baltimore, MD: Johns Hopkins, pp. 183–200.

Solow, R. M. (1957), 'Technical change and the aggregate production function', *Review of Economics and Statistics*, 39(3), 312–320.

Sorenson, A. (2001), 'Subcentres and satellite cities: Tokyo's 20th-century experience of planned polycentrism', *International Planning Studies*, 6(1), 9–32.

Storper, M. (1997), 'Territories, flows, and hierarchies in the global economy', in Cox, K.R. (ed.), *Spaces of Globalization: Reasserting the Power of the Local*, New York: Guilford Press, pp. 19–44.

Stren, R. and Halfani, M. (2001), 'The cities of sub-Saharan Africa: from dependency to marginality', in Paddison, R. (ed.), *Handbook of Urban Studies*, London: Sage Publications, pp. 466–485.

Taylor, P. J. and Ni, Pengfei (2010), *Global Urban Analysis*, London: Earthscan Press.

UN-Habitat (2010), *The State of African Cities 2010: Governance, Inequality and Urban Land Markets*, Nairobi: UN-Habitat.

United Nations (2002), *World Urbanization Prospects: The 2001 Revision*, New York: United Nations.

United Nations Population Fund (UNFPA) (2007), *State of World Population 2007: Unleashing the Potential of Urban Growth*, New York: UNFPA.

Van Dijk, M. P. (2007), 'The contribution of cities to economic development: an explanation based on Chinese and Indian cities', Inaugural Address as Affiliate Professor of Urban Management, 1 March 2007, Institution of Social Studies, The Hague.

Webster, F. (2000), 'Information, capitalism and uncertainty', *Information, Communication & Society*, 3(1), 69–90.

Wolfe, T. (1983), 'Wachovia is poised to grow dealer business', *Automotive News*, 5(4), 28.

World Bank (2000), *World Development Report 1999/2000: Entering the 21st Century*, New York: World Bank.

World Bank (2009), 'Transport costs and specialization', *World Development Report: 2009*, Washington, D.C.: World Bank.

World Gazetteer (2008), http://world-gazetteer.com/.

Yeung, Y. M. (2002), *New Challenges for Development and Modernization: Hong Kong and the Asia Pacific Region in the New Millennium*, Hong Kong: The Chinese University Press.

Yue, W., Liu, Y. and Fan, P. (2010), 'Polycentric urban development: the case of Hangzhou', *Environment and Planning*, 42(3), 563–577.

10. Green cities: examples of governing for green growth from OECD countries

Lamia Kamal-Chaoui,[1] Margo Cointreau[2] and Xiao Wang[3]

The motto for the 2010 World Expo in Shanghai, China captures the important role being attributed to the urban dimension of contemporary societies: "Better City, Better Life". While the oversimplified slogan can be interpreted in a myriad of sub-themes, no one will deny the importance of urban environmental sustainability in the heart of the discussion.

The scale of on-going urbanization across the globe has important economic and environmental implications. Today, more than half of the world's population (3.49 billion people) live in urban areas; by 2050, the figure will probably reach two-thirds (UN-Habitat, 2010). As key engines of the global economy, cities are responsible for the bulk of national output, innovation and employment, and they are strategic gateways of transnational capital flows and global supply chains (OECD, 2006). Cities are also major contributors to global warming and environmental problems. It is not surprising that cities account for an estimated 67% of global energy use and 71% of global energy-related CO_2 emissions (IEA, 2010). Urbanization also often entails a range of environmental pressures associated with the geographic concentration of people and economic activity, including severe air and water pollution, as well as the accumulation and inappropriate disposal of household and industrial waste (OECD, 2012b).

The OECD started the Green Cities Programme[4] in response to a call from mayors and ministers at the Third Annual Meeting of the OECD Urban Roundtable in Paris in 2010. The Programme aims to assess how urban green growth and sustainability policies can contribute to improve the economic performance and environmental quality of metropolitan areas, and thus enhance the contribution of urban areas to national growth, quality of life and competitiveness. "Green Growth", a highly debated term, is generally defined as a means to create jobs and economic growth while reducing costs and environmental impacts over the long run. The OECD has been an active participant in global efforts to advance green growth, evidenced by the release of the OECD Green Growth Strategy in May 2011.

---

1   Lamia Kamal-Chaoui, Head of the Urban Development Programme, OECD.2 rue Andre Pascal, 75775 Paris CEDEX 16, France. Email: Lamia. KAMAL-CHAOUI@oecd. org.

2   Margo Cointreau, Policy Analyst, Urban Development Programme, OECD.2 rue Andre Pascal, 75775 Paris CEDEX 16, France.

3   Xiao Wang, Policy Analyst, Urban Development Programme, OECD.2 rue Andre Pascal, 75775 Paris CEDEX 16, France.

4   For more information about the OECD Programme on Cities and Green Growth, see www.oecd.org/greencities.

Green growth is a key element of sustainable development and economic recovery. The concept emerged in response to the global recession and continued concern over climate change that call into question the ability of current models for economic growth to foster long term prosperity. Green growth offers a way forward towards a new sustainable development paradigm that will respond to the triple challenge of expanding economic opportunities while mitigating the environmental and social pressures that threaten our ability to seize these opportunities. Green growth fosters economic growth and development while ensuring that natural assets continue to provide the resources and ecosystem services on which our well-being relies. To do this it must catalyse investment, competition and innovation, which will underpin sustained growth and give rise to new economic opportunities. In that sense, green growth is not a replacement for sustainable development, but a means to help achieve it (OECD, 2011a; OECD, 2011c).

Cities have a unique role to play in advancing green growth. Cities have greater potential to create synergies between environmental and economic objectives because policies that respond to the negative effects of urban agglomeration address both environmental and economic growth priorities, for example road congestion charges, brownfield redevelopment or sustainable cost recovery for water and waste services. Moreover, attractiveness is a key factor in a city's economic growth and can be hampered by a poor environment. Congestion, pollution and public service constraints affect not only environmental quality, but also the efficiency of local economic activities and cities' ability to attract firms and skilled workers. Finally, the implementation of green growth at the local level can address social issues in a more direct way than at the national level. There are clear instances where green growth initiatives can provide social co-benefits simultaneously, such as reducing social exclusion through public transit enhancements and reducing households' energy costs through energy-efficiency retrofits or solar water heaters (OECD 2012b). Taking these examples into account, we define urban green growth as:

'Fostering economic growth and development through urban activities that reduce negative environmental externalities, the impact on natural resources and the pressure on ecosystem services. The greening of the traditional urban economy and expanding the green urban sector can generate growth (through increased supply and demand), job creation and increased urban attractiveness. These effects are in part the result of stronger interactions at the urban level among economic efficiency, equity and environmental objectives' (OECD, 2011a).

Cities also pose clear economic advantages for the pursuit of a green growth strategy. Urban areas in the OECD tend to feature higher income and productivity (Figure 10.1), due to specialization in higher value added activities (OECD, 2006). Just 2% of OECD regions, mainly the largest OECD urban areas, produce 1/3 of all growth in the OECD (OECD, 2011b). In both India and China, the five largest cities' economies contribute approximately 15% of national GDP – roughly three times their share of the population (UN-Habitat, 2010). As centres of innovation, cities play a disproportionate role in knowledge-generation, which will clearly play a critical role in strategies to address climate change and resource scarcity. By concentrating skills and firms, cities allow agglomeration economies to develop, thanks to effective urban infrastructure, knowledge spillovers, labour market pooling and input sharing, as well as demand and cost linkages.

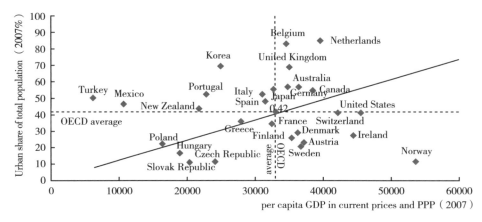

Notes: Share of total population in predominantly urban regions and per capita GDP in OECD countries. Urban share of total population by country refers to population in predominantly urban regions as a proportion of total population. Iceland and Luxemburg were not included in the sample as the OECD Regional Database does not identify predominantly urban regions in those countries. Switzerland was not included as GDP figures at sub-national level in that country are not available. Mexico's per capita GDP data refer to 2004; New Zealand's per capita GDP data refer to 2003; Turkey's per capita GDP data refer to 2001. PPP is purchasing power parity.

Source: Calculations based on data from the OECD Regional Database.

Figure 10.1   Urbanization and Income

While altering mature cities to reduce environmental footprint can be extremely costly, with urbanization still at a relatively early stage, developing countries have the opportunity to ensure that their cities continue to grow in a manner that will minimize the adverse environmental effects of urbanization. Here urban form – and lifestyle – matter. OECD research has found that the urban form is a critical factor that influences energy consumption and GHG emissions from transportation. CO_2 emissions from transport are likely to be greater in less densely populated areas than in more densely populated areas (Figure 10.2). As urban areas become denser and rely more on public transport, walking and cycling, CO_2 emissions from transport are likely to be greater in less densely populated areas than in more densely populated areas. When OECD functional urban regions within the same bracket for GDP per capita and national energy prices are compared, CO_2 emissions for lower-density cities can range up to roughly three times more than for cities with higher density (Figure 10.3). However, density is not the whole story. Other factors that come into play

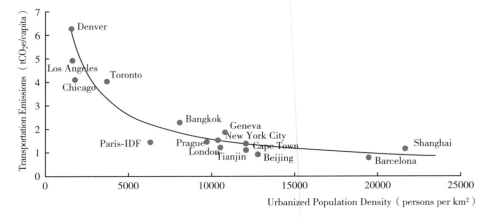

Figure 10.2   CO₂ Emissions from Ground Transportation in Large Metropolises

Notes:
1. The density of the urbanised land surface is calculated without including green areas.
2. Analytical units and reference years used for these calculations: Barcelona (city, 2006); Geneva (canton, 2005); London (Greater London, 2003); Paris-IDF (IDF region, 2005); Prague (Greater Prague, 2005); Chicago (Chicago Metropolitan Area, 2005), Denver (city and county, 2005); Los Angeles (county including 88 towns or cities, 2000); New York (city, 2005); Toronto (Greater Toronto, 2005); Bangkok (city, 2005); Beijing (province, 2006); Shanghai (province, 2006); Tianjin (province, 2006), Cape Town (city, 2006).

Source: Calculations adapted by C. Kennedy (personal communication), October 2011, using methodology from Kennedy et al. (2009b).

include availability of public transportation, lifestyle choices, and the proximity to industry, power generation and other potential sources of greenhouse gas emissions (OECD 2012a). Sprawling urban form also makes it difficult to build enough demand to efficiently deliver public services. For example, the cost savings by containing sprawl in the United States are estimated to be USD 12.6 billion for water and sewer infrastructure and USD 110 billion for road infrastructure (OECD, 2012a; OECD, 2002). In China, sprawling associated with the rapid expansion of the major metropolitan regions has become also a serious issue (Kamal-Chaoui et al., 2009).

National governments must understand that there is a clear economic advantage to meeting their emissions targets and pursuing green growth strategies through urban policies. The short term costs of urban environmental policies are lower than at the national level. An often sited example is local pollution, which increasingly impacts city attractiveness and

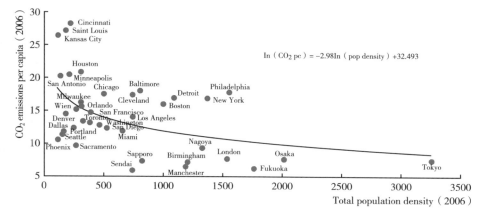

Note: Figure shows estimates of per capita emission for all sectors; variations from the curve can partly be explained by differences in emissions from electricity consumption.

Source: OECD Metropolitan Database 2011.

Figure 10.3   Population Density and Estimated CO$_2$ Emissions Per Capita in a Selection of Large Metropolitan Areas

competitiveness, especially in economies that are higher up the value chain. Results from the CGE model show, for instance, that if cities continue their current GHG emissions and lifestyle trends, by 2030 cities that could become more attractive will do so while also curbing local pollution (e.g. Ankara, Auckland, Barcelona, Krakow, Lille, Melbourne, Montreal, Monterrey, and Toronto). It also highlights that some metroregions risk losing attractiveness if their current pollution trends continue (e.g. Chicago, Los Angeles, New York, Osaka, Paris, Philadelphia, Seoul and Tokyo) (Kamal-Chaoui and Robert, 2009).

The myriad benefits of pursuing green growth at the local level can be observed in Kitakyushu, Japan where city government, under the leadership of Mayor Kenji Kitahashi has helped local industries invest in innovation and technology to reduce energy dependency and pollution with its Eco-Town Plan. During the rapid economic progress of the 1960s, Kitakyushu developed into one of the four largest industrial zones in Japan, with an economy based on heavy industry (steel, cement and chemical production). Environmental pollution, however, was so severe that the local Dokai Bay became known as the "Sea of Death". By implementing environmental policies, Kitakyushu managed to reduce its CO$_2$ emissions by more than 3% in the period from 1990 to 2002, while the overall rate for Japan registered an increase of more than 11%. The plan includes specific projects for recycling electric appliances, automobiles, plastic bottles and other recyclable wastes; advanced research on waste disposal and recycling technologies; and generating new industries from recycling resources and energy as city-wide activities. The opening of the special zone for recycling industries in the eco-town led to the creation of 1000 direct jobs. Having transformed itself from a "gray" polluted city to a progressive "green" one, Kitakyushu was commended by the central government in 2008 as "the environmental model City of Japan" (OECD, 2008).

Cities can also make the link between economic development and climate change mitigation link by focusing on making existing and new buildings more energy efficient. In U.S. cities, and to a certain extent, in European ones, buildings consume 70% of electric power, 39% of all power consumed, and create 39% of CO_2 emissions. A group of pioneering cities have capitalized on a "first-mover" advantage and witnessed the growth of renewable energy industries and employment. Freiburg, for instance, developed a citywide strategy as early as 1986 with environmental guidelines that served as a basis for its economic specialization in the solar energy industry. This included such policy measures as building city-owned solar projects; instituting a local ordinance requiring that 10% of the city's electricity be obtained from renewable sources by 2010; creating public subsidies; and pro-active research and economic development support. These efforts have led to the creation of about 10 000 jobs in the environmental and solar sectors. Philadelphia turned to the green economy as part of a strategy to revitalize its manufacturing basis and promote job creation. Using a mix of public policy tools, including grants to companies that invest in renewable industries, energy-saving production processes and alternative energy production, and renewable portfolio standards, the city has attracted major players in the wind-power industry, such as Iberdrola of Spain and the German solar conglomerate Conergy. Investment in energy efficiency can also promote employment, creating jobs in retrofitting and stimulating demand for new energy-saving and pollution-fighting products (Joan Fitzgerald in OECD, 2008).

Another success story is Toronto, Canada's largest city, whose mayor, David Miller, has argued that what is good for the environment is also good for the economy. Toronto has one of the smallest ecological footprints of large North American cities and better air quality than OECD cities of a similar size (OECD, 2010a). The city has achieved 40% reductions in greenhouse gas emissions by capturing methane from its landfill and using it to generate electricity. Its Better Buildings Partnership programme uses green building standards and a green fleet with plug-in hybrid cars and offers small loans for new creative ideas in this field. After the city took the initial step of instituting mortgages that encouraged green building, the market responded positively by creating its own instruments. It is now routine for builders in Toronto to observe the highest environmental standards, Mayor Miller noted, although making national building codes more stringent would speed the process. A major part of Toronto's efforts have been energy retrofits on its 2000 concrete-slab apartment towers constructed during the 1960s and the 1970s. The mayor's Tower Renewal Project has lowered total energy expenditure by 5%, created better living conditions in socially disadvantaged neighbourhoods and generated new jobs in a new building retrofit industry. The demonstration effect of this strategy should create jobs and investment opportunities.

Suttgart's leadership in environmental matters has been an excellent marketing tool for the city, thereby demonstrating how green growth can contribute to attractiveness. With 600 000 inhabitants (and around one million for the metropolitan area), Stuttgart is a world capital of the automotive industry, the city of Mercedes, BMW and Porsche. Although manufacturing jobs have been disappearing, climate change has also affected the city in its core business, and the city government is now fully aware of the importance of coupling the imperatives of the car industry with the protection of the environment – that is, of making Stuttgart's growth greener. Fostering a new culture of city development and housing, Stuttgart has reclaimed brownfields and recycled land to create communities that combine housing and employment, creating more sustainable communities. Working with the private sector, the city is now developing buses and cars that use new battery technologies with zero emissions and that need almost no fuel. The goal is to work with construction materials that are virtually 100% recyclable, Schuster said. The city has also launched many other interesting initiatives, including the establishment of a car-pool system, "Pendlernetz Stuttgart", generally recognised as the most innovative in Europe. It has also instituted green roofs in both municipal buildings and private houses, and realized further energy savings in public buildings. The city was awarded a Climate Star in 2004 by the Climate Alliance.[5]

These examples illustrate how cities' climate goals are increasingly aligned with their economic objectives. Efficiency, competitiveness and attractiveness concerns are coalescing in cities to make action against climate change a driver of urban economic growth. While the range of urban sustainable policies is large, policy makers can also refer to some policy examples based on an overview of the available data on capital costs of green urban infrastructure investment projects in different cities, specific to individual city contexts (Table 10.1).

Globally, green cities efforts will benefit from a "Race to the Top"[6] dynamism in which cities and regions compete to develop the most sustainable policies. As cities have already shown, successful policies can lead to job creation, increased competitiveness and attractiveness. Increased national support and guidance could improve returns on public investment and comparisons of policy options. In return, cities can serve as policy laboratories for testing and perfecting green growth strategies. Governments can and should enable a global "race to the top" to prevent the worst effects of climate change while fostering a sustainable economic recovery.

---

5   European Climate Star Award is a biannual award for showcasing its members' achievements. Stuttgart was one of about 20 municipalities awarded the Climate Star Award in 2004. Climate Alliance is an association of municipalities, regional governments, and NGOs, aiming for a reduction of greenhouse gas emissions. Since the foundation of the association in 1990, 1400 cities, municipalities and districts have joined the association. More than 50 provinces, NGOs and further organizations have also joined as associate members.

6   For example, in *Race to the Top: The Expanding Role of U.S. State Renewable Portfolio Standards* (2006, Pew Center on Global Climate Change, Arlington), Barry Rabe examines the proliferation of Renewable Portfolio Standards (RPSs) in American states. This policy tool establishes targets for growing the proportion of the local electricity supply that comes from renewable sources. He argues that "States are compelled to enact or expand RPSs for multiple reasons, and greenhouse gas emissions may or may not be central factors in prompting adoption. Instead, states consistently anticipate significant economic development benefits from promoting renewables, particularly given the promise of developing home-grown energy sources that could lead to instate job creation. In turn, states are also attracted to RPSs by the prospect of greater reliability of electricity supply in coming decades and the prospect of reducing conventional air pollutants through a shift toward expanded use of renewables."

Table 10.1   Capital Costs of Selected Green Projects in a Number of OECD Cities

Project	City	Annual GHG Savings (kt CO₂e)	Capital costs (USD million)	GHG Cost Effectiveness (tCO₂e/year/USD million)
Transportation				
Bus Rapid Transit	Vancouver	1.8	39.2	46
Congestion Charging	London	120	244	492
Bike Sharing	Paris	18	132	136
Buildings				
Solar Air Heating	Montreal	1.34	1.96	684
Energy				
Solar Centre Receiver Station	Seville	110	41	2683
Urban Wind Power	Toronto	0.38	1.21	314
Solid Waste				
Source-Separation and Methane Production	Sydney	210	75	2800
Incineration-Based CHP	Gothenburg	205	453	453
Water/Wastewater				
Biogas from Sewage	Stockholm	14	15	933

Source: Adapted from Kennedy et al. (2009a).

Like any competition, a "race to the top" will require clear rules and objectives. In other words, creating the conditions within which cities can unleash their green growth potential will depend on national and local governments' ability to work together to adapt institutions and modes of governance (Corfee-Morlot et al., 2009). In order to optimize urban policy's contribution to competitiveness and combating climate change, local governments need to make use of all regulatory modes of urban governance. One can indentify four modes of urban governance for implementing climate change policies (Alber and Kern, in Corfee-Morlot et al., 2009). The first, "self-governing: the municipality as consumer", relates to the capacity of local governments to govern their own activities, for example, to promote the energy efficiency of municipal buildings and the greening of public transport vehicles. This is the most widespread form of local action, driven in many cases by the financial benefits of energy savings. The city of Los Angeles presents an interesting case study. In 2008, after meeting its Kyoto targets of generating 10% of its energy from renewable sources, Mayor Villaraigosa announced that the city would raise the target to 20%, outstripping the Kyoto objectives and those set by the state of California.[7] These targets have been met so rapidly because the city controls a unique set of municipal assets, such as the Port of Los Angeles and the Department of Water and Power, which is the largest public utility in the United States (OECD, 2008).

A second mode of urban governance, "governing through enabling: the municipality as facilitator", refers to the different forms of co-ordination with private and community

---

7   *Financial Times*, 28 October 2008.

actors, such as the establishment of public-private partnerships for the provision of services and infrastructure. For example, the municipal energy plan of the City Council of Venice includes a series of intention protocols involving a number of joint venture projects between private companies, municipal transport companies, housing administrators' associations and associations of planners, architects and engineers. Under a third mode of urban governance, "the municipality as provider", the municipality can have a significant impact on local climate change action as the majority shareholder in the local utility companies for energy, transport, water and waste services. In many countries, local governments can resort to "governing by authority: the municipality as regulator", the fourth mode or urban governance, when they have the legal power in such important areas of planning responsibilities for energy, transport and land use. Examples include Barcelona's solar thermal ordinance; the introduction of regulations to reduce the fossil fuel standard for all new buildings in Santa Barbara, and restrictions on the use of cars in Munich and Paris. The extent of such a mode of authoritative governance, on a voluntary basis, remains limited. To maximize the impact of policies, it is crucial that local governments simultaneously employ multiple modes of governance.

National government engagement is another crucial element in fostering green growth in cities. For the moment, the state of vertical intergovernmental co-operation in climate-change mitigation and adaptation still appears ad hoc and subject to rapid evolution. The role of cities and the interactions between cities and national response policies is still largely unexplored, though some for effective and efficient responses to climate change can be cited. For example, Germany's 1997 guidelines for local climate protection (Leitfaden Kommunaler Klimaschutz) and the involvement of the United States National Oceanic and Atmospheric Administration in drafting environmental recommendations for the Seattle metropolitan region (Kern and Alber in OECD, 2008). Second, national governments can also be providers, by offering additional funding for local projects related to climate change, such as the Swedish Climate Investment Programme (KLIMP), which mainly funds municipal energy efficiency and transit projects. Even more importantly, national governments can serve as watchdogs, by establishing legal frameworks for local climate change action or creating national air and water quality standards, for example. But here again, success seems predicated on local planning capacity and budgetary resources. In the field of adaptation, national governments can facilitate timely and cost-effective action at the city scale, by providing mandates and incentives at the local level, financing regional climate scenarios and impact analysis to support decision-making, and raising awareness of businesses to integrate climate risks into business decisions. Regardless of the choice of models or the combination thereof, robust accountability standards will have to accompany these arrangements for public reporting. For the moment, bureaucratic processes are too unwieldy. Cities' initiatives would benefit from more co-ordinated and structured support from national governments.

As the global economic recovery begins to take shape, the green economy offers the opportunity to help cities and their inhabitants recover, which will, in turn, solidify the national economy. At this crucial stage, it is important to think in terms of synergies and opportunities outside the usual multiple-choice box of threats and priorities. Cities around the world have demonstrated that climate change is not so much a threat to be feared, but a challenge to be met. By pursuing green growth strategies, cities can generate opportunities to develop and sell the technologies that will be in demand in the markets of tomorrow. The underlying drivers such as drought, rising sea levels and increasingly extreme weather events, could fuel a new market demanding new services and products in areas such as energy efficiency, water infrastructure, modified crops, flood defences, new housing and commercial buildings. Climate change and related water challenges could become a catalyst that will anchor the runaway financial system to the basic and long-term needs of the real economy. Investment in renewable energy technologies and in the renovation of infrastructure vulnerable to climate change could serve as the backbone to a New Deal for public investment in cities. As currently being developed in many OECD countries, a green growth strategy for cities in China could be an efficient tool to reach the objectives of upgrading the economy whilst addressing equity and environmental quality. Attracting green industries, investing in green infrastructure and renewable technologies, and improving the eco-efficiency of existing industries and buildings could create a significant number of jobs in many cities and at the same time strengthen regional and national competitiveness.

REFERENCES

Corfee-Morlot, J., L. Kamal-Chaoui, M. G. Donovan, I. Cochran, A. Robert and P. J. Teashdale (2009), "Cities, Climate Change and Multilevel Governance", OECD Environmental Working Papers No. 14, Paris: OECD Publications.

Green-Weiskel, Lucia et al. (2009), "Building Carbon Inventories in China", Innovation Center for Energy and Transportation with Business for Social Responsibility and The Climate Registry, Innovation Center for Energy and Transportation, Beijing, China.

IEA (International Energy Agency) (2010), *World Energy Outlook 2010*, Paris: OECD/IEA.

Kamal-Chaoui, L., E. Leman and Z. Rufei (2009), "Urban Trends and Policy in China", OECD Regional Development Working Papers, 2009/1, Paris: OECD Publications.

Kamal-Chaoui, L. and A. Robert (2009), "Competitive Cities and Climate Change", OECD Regional Development Working Papers No. 2, Paris: OECD Publishing.

Kennedy, C. et al. (2009a), "Getting to Carbon Neutral: A Review of Best Practices", in D. Hoornweg et al. (eds), *Infrastructure Strategy in Cities and Climate Change Responding to an Urgent Agenda*, World Bank, Washington, D.C., pp. 242–263.

Kennedy, C. et al. (2009b), "Greenhouse Gas Emissions from Global Cities", *Environmental Science and Technology*, Vol. 43, No. 19, 7297–7302.

OECD (Organisation for Economic Co-operation and Development) (2002), *Impact of Transport Infrastructure Investment on Regional Development*, Paris: OECD Publications.

OECD (2006), *Competitive Cities in the Global Economy*, OECD Territorial Reviews, Paris: OECD Publications.

OECD (2008), *Competitive Cities and Climate Change: OECD Conference Proceedings*, Paris: OECD Publications.

OECD (2010a), *OECD Territorial Reviews: Toronto, Canada*, Paris: OECD Publications.

OECD (2010b), *OECD Territorial Review of Guangdong, China*, Paris: OECD Publications.

OECD/CRDF (2010), *Trends in Urbanisation and Urban Policies in OECD Countries: What Lessons for China*, Paris: OECD Publications.

OECD (2011a), "Cities and Green Growth: A Conceptual Framework", OECD Regional Development Working Papers, Paris: OECD Publications.

OECD (2011b), *Regional Outlook 2011: Building Resilient Regions for Stronger Economies*, Paris: OECD.

OECD (2011c), "Towards Green Growth", Green Growth Strategy Synthesis Report, Paris: OECD.

OECD (2012a), *Environmental Outlook to 2050: The Consequences of Inaction*, Paris: OECD.

OECD (2012b), "Mobilizing Investments for Urban Sustainability, Job Creation and Resilient Growth", Issues Paper for the OECD Roundtable of Mayors and Ministers, 8 March 2012, Chicago, Illinois, USA.

OECD (2012c), *The Compact City Concept in Today's Urban Contexts*, Paris: OECD.

UN-Habitat (2010), *State of the World's Cities 2010/2011*, UN-Habitat, Nairobi.

11. Institutions and urban competitiveness – a Doing Business perspective

Doing Business Group in the World Bank

COMPETITIVENESS AND INSTITUTIONS

In 2012, the Economist Intelligence Unit (EIU) – commissioned by Citigroup – published *Hot Spots: Benchmarking Global City Competitiveness*. The study ranks the competitiveness of 120 of the world's major cities, across eight distinct categories of competitiveness and 31 individual indicators.[1] While recognizing the importance of economic size and growth, the report also highlights factors such as the business and regulatory environment as key factors for a city's competitiveness.

Competitiveness studies often include institutional factors in their analyses, covering aspects such as the rule of law and the quality of political institutions and of public services.[2] Specific areas of institutional quality that are particularly often analyzed include the levels of property rights, governance and corruption. Michael E. Porter, a leading global authority on the competitiveness of nations and regions, considers social infrastructure and political institutions two of the most important inputs of firm productivity.[3]

It is therefore not surprising that governments committed to the economic health of their countries and cities also increasingly pay attention to the quality of laws, regulations and institutional arrangements that shape daily economic activity.

INSTITUTIONS, COMPETITIVENESS AND FIRM GROWTH

Small and medium-size enterprises are key drivers of competition, growth and job creation.

---

1   www.citigroup.com/citi/citiforcities/urban_exchange/eiu.htm.

2   One of the most comprehensive competitiveness studies in recent years is the World Economic Forum's annual Global Competitive Index. It defines the institutional environment – one its 12 pillars of competitiveness – as being determined by the 'legal and administrative framework within which individuals, firms and governments interact to generate wealth'. It emphasizes that the role of institutions goes well beyond simply setting up the legal framework: government attitudes towards markets and freedoms, and the efficiency and transparency of its operations (bureaucracy, red tape, public procurement, judicial procedures, etc.) may impose significant economic costs to business and slow the process of economic development. The proper management of public finances is also considered critical to ensuring trust in the national and local business environment.

3   Porter, M.E. *The Competitive Advantage of Nations*. New York: Free Press, 1990. (Republished with a new introduction, 1998.)

Policy makers worldwide recognize the important role that entrepreneurs play in creating economic opportunities for themselves and for others, and often take measures to improve the investment climate and boost productivity growth. Investments in infrastructure—ports, roads, telecommunications—are seen as a vital ingredient of private sector development and of broader competitiveness. Investments in education and training are also critical. However, these investments typically take time to bear fruit.

Entrepreneurs in low-income economies tend to encounter greater obstacles than their counterparts in high-income economies. Finding qualified staff and dealing with lack of adequate infrastructure are among the challenges, even in the main business cities in developing and emerging economies. Overly burdensome regulations and inefficient institutions that discourage the creation and expansion of businesses can unnecessarily compound the problem.

Excessive regulatory barriers partly explain why 80% of economic activity in low-income economies takes place in the informal sector. Firms are prevented from entering the formal sector by excessive bureaucracy and regulation. Even firms operating in the formal sector might not have equal access to transparent rules and regulations affecting their ability to compete, innovate and grow.

Research has confirmed that efficient business registration processes are associated with higher entry rates for new firms and a greater business density.[4] Where registering a new business is easy, businesses are also more likely to register in industries where the potential for growth is greatest, such as those that have experienced expansionary shifts in global demand or technology.[5] Reducing start-up costs for new firms was also found to result in higher take-up rates for education, higher rates of job creation for high-skilled labor and higher average productivity because new firms are often set up by high-skilled workers.[6]

Regulations should be efficient, striking a balance between safeguarding some important aspects of the business environment and avoiding distortions that impose unreasonable costs on businesses. Where business regulation is burdensome and competition limited, success depends more on whom you know than on what you can do. But where regulations are relatively easy to comply with and accessible to all who need to use them, anyone with talent and a good idea should be able to start and grow a business in the formal sector.[7]

---

4   Klapper, Lewin and Quesada Delgado. 2009. *Entry rate* refers to newly registered firms as a percentage of total registered firms. *Business density* is defined as the total number of businesses as a percentage of the working-age population (ages 18–65).

5   Ciccone, Antonio and Elias Papaioannou. 2007. "Red Tape and Delayed Entry." *Journal of the European Economic Association* 5 (2–3): 444–58.

6   Dulleck, Uwe, Paul Frijters and R. Winter-Ebmer. 2006. "Reducing Start-up Costs for New Firms: The Double Dividend on the Labor Market." *Scandinavian Journal of Economics* 108: 317–37.

7   Doing Business does not measure all aspects of the business environment that matter to firms or investors—or all factors that affect competitiveness. It does not, for example, measure security, corruption, market size, macro-economic stability, the state of the financial system, the labor skills of the population or all aspects of the quality of infrastructure. Nor does it focus on regulations specific to foreign investment. And even though Doing Business measures the institutional framework and efficiency of key regulatory processes, it does not cover all institutional aspects that may affect competitiveness at the national or local level (i.e. the political system, electoral process, fiscal structure).

COMPETITIVENESS AND DOING BUSINESS INDICATORS

Economies that do well on measures of competitiveness also tend to do well on the Doing Business Ranking. There is a high correlation between the rankings on the Ease of Doing Business and those on the World Economic Forum's Global Competitiveness Index, a broader measure of country competitiveness.

The Doing Business indicators—which have been published by the World Bank Group and International Finance Cooperation since 2003[8]—provide country level diagnostics of regulations affecting small and medium sized local businesses. Because the indicators are based on a reading of the laws and a description of the regulatory processes in individual countries, they can be of use to policy makers who are looking for solutions to the problems raised by perception and enterprise surveys.

A fundamental premise of Doing Business is that economic activity requires good rules. These include rules that establish and clarify property rights and reduce the cost of resolving disputes, rules that increase the predictability of economic interactions and rules that provide contractual partners with core protections against abuse. The objective: regulations designed to be simple and efficient in implementation and accessible to all who need to use them.[9]

Where regulation is burdensome and competition limited, success tends to depend more on whom you know than on what you can do. But where regulation is transparent, efficient and implemented in a simple way, it becomes easier for any aspiring entrepreneurs, regardless of their connections, to operate within the rule of law and to benefit from the opportunities and protections that the law provides. Not surprisingly, higher rankings on the Ease of DoingBusiness—based on 10 areas of business regulation measured by Doing Business—are correlated with better governance and lower levels of perceived corruption.[10]

Benchmarking exercises like Doing Business can uncover potential challenges and identify where policy makers can look for good practices. Because the indicators are based on standardized case studies, they provide important comparative data on best practices across the 183 economies included in the dataset.

---

8   The first Doing Business report, published in 2003, covered 5 indicator sets and 133 economies. The latest report, *Doing Business 2012: Doing Business in a More Transparent World*, covers 11 indicator sets and 183 economies. Ten topics are included in the aggregate ranking on the ease of doing business and other summary measures. The indicators presented and analyzed in Doing Business measure business regulation and the protection of property rights—and their effect on businesses. The indicators provide quantitative measures of regulations for starting a business, dealing with construction permits, getting electricity, registering property, getting credit, protecting investors, paying taxes, trading across borders, enforcing contracts and resolving insolvency—as they apply to domestic small and medium-size enterprises. They also look at the regulations affecting the employment of workers.

9   Accordingly, some Doing Business indicators give a higher score for more regulation, such as requiring greater disclosure to minority shareholders. Some give a higher score for a simplified way of implementing existing regulation, such as completing business start-up formalities in a one-stop shop.

10   The correlation coefficient between the ease of doing business ranking and the ranking on the Control of Corruption Index is 0.62, and that between the ease of doing business ranking and the ranking on the Transparency International Corruption Perceptions Index 0.77. The positive correlation is statistically significant at the 5% level.

DOING BUSINESS AND CITIES

To make the data comparable across countries Doing Business data is collected based on a standardized case. Each case assumes that a local business is either starting activity or is undertaking activity in the biggest business city of the country, the so called Doing Business city.[11] Hence, Doing Business data is not only about benchmarking economies but also about benchmarking cities.

The two best performing economies on the Doing Business ranking are both city-states (Singapore and Hong Kong, SAR, China) and 25 out of the 183 countries included in the annual Doing Business Report are countries where the business capital assessed accounts for at least 25% of the total population of the country.

In addition to the regular annual Doing Business Report, governments from 55 countries (including Brazil, China, Colombia, Egypt, India, Indonesia, Kenya, Mexico, Morocco, Nigeria, Pakistan, the Philippines, the Russian Federation) have requested sub-national Doing Business projects since 2005. These studies have covered a total of 365 cities.

And they are right to do so. Because even though regulations are usually designed at the national level, they are more often implemented at the regional and/or city level. The power to foster firm creation and job growth through more efficient regulatory processes is therefore often also in the hands of local governments and city mayors and not just in the hands of national parliaments.

BENCHMARKING CITIES CAN SPUR AND AID REFORM EFFORTS

National governments request sub-national Doing Business studies because they capture differences in business regulation and administrative processes across cities within the same economy or region. These sub-national studies usually cover the Doing Business indicators in which local governments and agencies play a large role in establishing and/or implementing the relevant regulations—starting a business, dealing with construction permits and registering property. In some cases, other indicators such as paying taxes, trading across borders and enforcing contracts are also included in the studies.

National governments also use the sub-national Doing Business data to monitor how efficiently the local branches of their agencies implement national regulations. Local governments can compare their regulations with those of their neighbors. The studies can also be used by national governments to start some healthy competition between regions and cities.

The example of Colombia is telling. *Doing Business in Colombia 2008* identified good practices in 13 cities, pointed out bottlenecks, and provided recommendations for business reform. Two years later, a new report tracked progress over time. The results were impressive. All 13 cities showed improvements in at least one of the areas measured, thanks to local-level reforms. Similarly, *Doing Business in India 2009* showed that nine out of ten Indian states benchmarked for the second time had introduced business reforms. As a result

---

11   For details on the city assumed for each country please refer to www.doingbusiness.org.

of these reforms, the average time to start up a company dropped from 45 to 35 days and the time to obtain a building permit was reduced by 25 days, on average.

Mexico is the economy with the highest number of sub-national studies since the beginning of the Doing Business reports, with four editions to date. Regulatory improvements there require the coordination of three levels of government: federal, state and municipal, and the support of the legislative and judicial bodies, as well as key stakeholders, such as notaries. In 2005, in an effort to examine this regulatory diversity, the Office of the President requested a study that would go beyond Mexico City, leading to the creation of the *Doing Business in Mexico* sub-national series.

Doing Business in Mexico 2012, the fourth report in this series, compares 31 states and Mexico City in the areas of starting a business, dealing with construction permits, registering property and enforcing contracts. The pace of reforms increased with each new report, and for the first time *Doing Business in Mexico 2012* showed improvements in 100% of the states. All of the states introduced reforms in at least one of the topics: 18 states made reforms in two indicators—mostly in starting a business and registering property—and six states implemented reforms in three indicators, including dealing with construction permits or enforcing contracts. One state, Colima, improved in all four areas and rose to the top of the ranking among Mexican states. Improvements in Colima (whose capital and main city share the same name) are the result of a wide reform plan that began in 2009 with a program that sought to turn Colima's government into "the most efficient in Mexico."[12]

In Asia-Pacific, large and decentralized countries such as the Philippines and Indonesia have also carried out several rounds of sub-national *Doing Business* studies, which have allowed the tracking of progress over time. *Doing Business in the Philippines 2011*, covering 25 cities (21 for the second time plus four new cities) across three areas of business regulations, found that Philippine cities actively reformed their business regulations in the two years following the first study. Sixty-five percent of the cities benchmarked for the second time show positive reforms in at least one of the areas measured. Many of these improvements came from re-engineering business processes rather than amending laws, with the aim of targeting unnecessary administrative requirements—a major breeder of corruption in cities across the country. While the economic outcomes directly linked to business reforms have yet to be measured, what is certain is that they have already simplified procedures and cut costs for local firms.

The results of sub-national studies often reveal that best practices in business regulations and their implementation, as measured by *Doing Business*, are scattered throughout a country rather than concentrated in a single city.

Take the example of the Philippines, a country of over 7,000 islands, where the Local Government Code of 1991 granted significant powers to the 80 provincial, 122 city, and 1,497 municipal governments—while retaining other powers within the central national government. In the Philippines, it is easiest to start a business in General Santos, obtain construction permits in Davao City, and register property in Valenzuela. The number of

---

12   Presentation by the Governor of the State of Colima, Lic. Mario Anguiano Moreno, Bogotá, Colombia, December 2011.

procedures required to start a business and deal with construction permits also show wide variation across the 25 cities included in the study of the Philippines.

Indonesia is another case in point. Despite its strong overall economic performance, Indonesia faces challenges that stifle private-sector development. Skilled labor shortages, poor infrastructure and an onerous regulatory framework are three major bottlenecks to business expansion.[13] The World Bank's Enterprise Surveys show that Indonesian firms identify the high rates of informality as one of the top 10 constraints to firm investment.[14] One of the key causes of this high rate of informality in Indonesia is the heavy regulatory burden borne by firms.

Improving economic competitiveness by creating a more salutary business climate is one of Indonesia's national priorities for 2010 to 2014.[15] Two subsequent sub-national reports have helped the policy makers in charge of reaching their 2014 goals establish if they are on track.

The *Doing Business in Indonesia 2012* report provided some encouraging signs that Indonesian cities are moving in the right direction. Twenty-two business reforms at the local level have made it easier to do business since the first sub-national report for Indonesia was conducted in 2010.

For starting a business, all 14 cities measured for the second time showed improvements. The average time and cost to start a business in Indonesian cities were reduced by more than 25% since the 2010 report. For dealing with construction permits, 10 out of 14 cities showed improvements. City performance in *Doing Business* indicators varies considerably across Indonesia as well. It is easiest to start a business in Yogyakarta, deal with construction permits in Balikpapan, and register property in Bandung and Jakarta. It is most difficult to start a business in Manado and register property in Batam. Dealing with construction permits is most burdensome in Jakarta.

CITIES AT THE HEART OF MANY REFORMS

City governments are at the heart of many business regulatory reforms. The most common business regulatory reforms observed by the *Doing Business Report* worldwide are regulatory reforms that are implemented at the city level like streamlining the rules for starting a business, registering property or dealing with construction permits. Hence, national governments who want to reform business regulatory institutions and increase their countries competitiveness have to work with local and municipal authorities.

Nine years of *Doing Business* Reports reveal important additional lessons for reformers.

---

13   International Monetary Fund. 2010. "Indonesia: 2010 Article IV Consultation." IMF Country Report No. 10/284.

14   World Bank. Enterprise Surveys. 2009. "Indonesia Country Profile." Available at http://www. enterprisesurveys.org.

15   The 2010–2014 National Medium-Term Development Plan (RPJMN 2010–2014) is the second phase of implementation of the 2005–2025 National Long-Term Development Plan (RPJPN 2005–2025).

Economies that have been successful at ensuring a place at the top of the Doing Business ranking or have been rising in the ranking in the last years have governments that share some important features:

- **They take a comprehensive approach to reform.** China, for example, implemented policy changes across 9 areas of business regulation in the years since 2005.The changes included a new company law in 2005, a new credit registry in 2006 and, in 2007, the first bankruptcy law regulating the bankruptcy of private enterprises since 1949.These reforms have made China one of the most improved economies among large emerging markets (Figure 11.2). More economies are taking this broad approach. In 2010/11, 35 economies implemented reforms making it easier to do business in 3 or more areas measured by *Doing Business*—12 of them in 4 or more areas. Four years before, only 10 reformed in 3 or more areas.
- **They periodically review and update business regulations as part of a broader competitiveness agenda.** In Korea the Presidential Council on National Competitiveness, created in 2008, identified regulatory reform as 1 of 4 pillars to improve the economy's competitiveness, along with public sector innovation, investment promotion, and legal and institutional advancement. Reviewing Korea's business regulations, the council found that 15% had not been revised since 1998.The council applied sunset clauses to more than 600 regulations and 3,500 administrative rules. Sweden undertook a systematic review of all regulations in the 1980s. Any unjustified requirements were cut in a "guillotine" initiative. (Mexico took a similar approach in the 1990s.)
- **They consider regulatory reform a continual process and create dedicated committees** or agencies such as Actal in the Netherlands and the Better Regulation Executive in the United Kingdom. These agencies not only routinely assess existing regulations. They also pay increasing attention to managing the flow of new regulations. More than 25 other economies have formed inter-ministerial committees which focus on improving the business environment, and in all these efforts DB is one source of input. These include India, Malaysia, Vietnam in East and South Asia; Yemen, UAE, Syria, Egypt, Saudi Arabia and Morocco in the Middle East and North Africa; FYR Macedonia, Georgia, Belarus, Kazakhstan, Kyrgyz Republic, Moldova and Tajikistan in Eastern Europe and Central Asia; Gabon, Liberia, Malawi, Kenya, Tanzania and Zambia in sub-Saharan Africa; and Mexico, Peru and Guatemala in Latin America.
- **They pay attention to transparent policy making.** The United Kingdom invites comment on regulatory proposals on the website of the Better Regulation Executive.[16] Canada and the United States publish guidelines on the evaluation process underlying the cost-benefit analysis of new regulations.
- **They learn from others.** Many countries have reached out to their peers to learn from them. Every year corporate registrars from 31 economies meet to discuss challenges and solutions. Representatives from Canada (Toronto), which ranks number 3 on the ease of starting a business, are now advising economies as diverse as Indonesia (Jakarta) and Peru (Lima). The Asia-Pacific Economic Cooperation (APEC) organization uses *Doing Business* to identify potential areas of regulatory reform, to champion economies that can

---

16   www.businesslink.gov.uk.

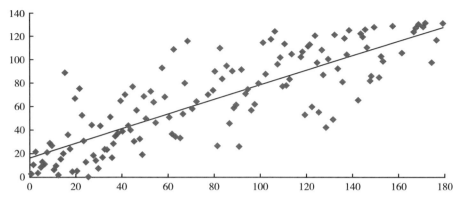

Figure 11.1   A Strong Correlation between Doing Business Rankings and World Economic Forum Rankings on Global Competitiveness

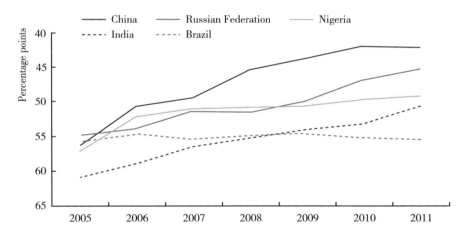

Figure 11.2   China Has Been Making Steady Progress Toward the Frontier

help others improve and to set measurable targets. In 2009 APEC launched the Ease of Doing Business Action Plan with the goal of making it 25% cheaper, faster and easier to do business in the region by 2015.[17]

---

17   Drawing on a firm survey, planners identified five priority areas: starting a business, getting credit, enforcing contracts, trading across borders and dealing with permits. APEC economies then selected six champion economies for the priority areas: New Zealand and the United States (starting a business), Japan (getting credit), Korea (enforcing contracts), Singapore (trading across borders) and Hong Kong SAR, China (dealing with construction permits). In 2010 and 2011 several of the champion economies organized

REFERENCES

Ciccone, A. and Elias, P. (2007), "Red Tape and Delayed Entry," *Journal of the European Economic Association*, 5 (2–3): 444–458.

Dulleck, U., Frijters, P. and Winter-Ember, R. (2006), "Reducing Start-up Costs for New Firms: The Double Dividend on the Labor Market," *Scandinavian Journal of Economics*, 108: 317–337.

International Monetary Fund (2010), "Indonesia: 2010 Article IV Consultation," IMF Country Report No. 10/284.

Porter, M. (1990), *The Competitive Advantage of Nations*, New York: Free Press.

World Bank Enterprise Surveys (2009), "Indonesia Country Profile", available at http://www.enterprisesurveys.org.

workshops to develop programs for building capacity in their area of expertise.

12. The challenge of world city network pattern changes on the world city network analysis

Peter J. Taylor[1]

INTRODUCTION

World city network analysis is an exciting field of research. However, it does have its depressing side. There is a relatively large constituency of interested parties who consider the results as just another ranking exercise – where is my city in the world pecking order and why isn't it higher? These city partisans, largely in the blogosphere, tend to evaluate research in terms of how it fits with their limited horizons: our world city network results are deemed 'controversial', meaning suspect, because we tend to rank US cities lower than bloggers would wish. This is all very depressing on several levels. The results are treated as just 'out there', available for discussion involving minimal effort: there appears to be little or no interest in how results are produced as if this had no relevance. It is part of a contemporary 'list-mania' where the ranking is all that matters. Ranking brings out the competitive spirit in commentators to replace reasoned thinking. And in the particular case of world city network analysis, the overall outcome is to spectacularly misunderstand what the research, and therefore the results, are all about. Networks are essentially about mutuality; analysing them reveals cooperative relations not competitive ones. No wonder city partisans find our results unappealing; actually it would be even more depressing if they embraced them!

I have begun with this little rant because it addresses challenges to world city network analysis at their most overt level. Of course, ill-informed discussion in the blogosphere is an easy target, but such academic smugness is not my intension here. Quite the opposite in fact: my purpose is to show that peer-reviewed knowledge is by no means immune from the basic assumptions underpinning list-mania. I have personally been caught up in this process through an early research project on how London related economically with other world cities. The latter had to be identified and a 'roster of cities' was devised by counting numbers of selected firms in a range of cities (Beaverstock et al. 1999). The variation in numbers was simplified by dividing cities into strata labelled alpha, beta and gamma. This essentially petty exercise, just a first step in investigating London's external links, has had immense influence: personally, it is my most cited article and, with hundreds of citations, it is the most cited article ever published in the journal *Cities*. I interpret this astonishing success as my 'alpha-beta-gamma misgiving'.

1   Peter J. Taylor, School of Built and Natural Environment, Northumbria University, Ellison Place, Newcastle upon Tyne, NE1 8ST UK. Tel: +44 (0)191 232 6002 (switchboard).
    Email: crogfam@yahoo.com.

Why a misgiving? This most successful paper is a very simple taxonomic exercise in which relational thinking is conspicuous by its absence. Hence we have made a major contribution to cities considered as merely separate entities to be ranked and compared. As all my subsequent writings show (deriving from Taylor 2001), such modes of thinking eliminate a crucial part of the complexity of cities and thereby misunderstand them. Hence the alpha-beta-gamma misgiving is just about as large a research embarrassment as can be imagined. What can we learn from it? Of course, there is nothing inherently wrong with simplification, in fact it is a necessity: simplifying complex reality is precisely the task of social science research as it tries to make sense of society continuously changing in myriad ways. However, in this basic pursuit, it is often relations between entities that are overlooked or largely ignored. To understand how such unhelpful simplification comes about requires thinking about the way research begins – what presumptions are brought to a subject?

Where to start is a generic conflict between activating social study through investigating attributes in situ, or investigating relations beyond the immediate situation. The latter is not a matter of adding 'context' to a study, rather it is a holistic argument: external relations are implicated in the very constitution of an entity. This argument occurs in many guises where study of individual units is confronted by systems, ecological or network thinking. Even with the most rigorous research on a unit or units, critical features will be banished from consideration leading, for instance, to subsequent identification of 'unintended consequences' in modern urban planning, or 'side effects' in modern pharmaceutical medicine. However well intentioned the motives, such practice based upon limited knowledge can be counter-productive: just so with cities when treating them as units rather than networks. This is the challenge to world city network analysis that is the subject matter of this chapter.

THE CITY HIERARCHY PRESUMPTION

Cities come in many sizes and central place theory was one very successful means of explaining why this should be so. First presented in 1933, Christaller (1966) modelled urban places as a hierarchy of central places so that size was a function of hinterland market. With the latter arranged in hierarchical order, it followed that cities servicing hinterlands were equally hierarchical, as represented by their different sizes. This idea of inter-city relations as hierarchical has become embedded in thinking about cities and is often generalized as city rankings. The link between hierarchy and ranking is that both imply city competition – a zero-sum game where hierarchies and ranking lists are there to be climbed.

I have documented the workings of this hierarchical presumption in urban economics (Taylor 2009) and it has been equally influential in the study of cities in globalization. The resulting emphasis on competition in inter-city relations has meant that with the coming of globalization, cities (city governments) were set a new task to climb Friedmann's (1986) 'world city hierarchy' so as to reach Sassen's (1991) 'global city' status at the top. In fact, when developing world city network analysis I never realized the degree to which 'competitive cities' were embedded in all thinking about cities. I totally underestimated the size of challenge that this represented. Who's got the biggest skyscraper has a very tangible answer – we can go and visit it, see a photograph of it, and read about its impressive physical dimensions. It is all about place, an attribute thereof. But relations between world cities are far less tangible; they can be seen as aerials for electronic communication on top of all large buildings but most have little or no impact on the observer on the ground, whether academic or blogger. This is all about myriad flows – ideas, information, knowledge, plans, instructions, advice, etc. from businesses in the buildings, all travelling via satellites in Castells's (1996) global space of flows. Gradually I came to appreciate that the key to pursuing a flows perspective on cities was to begin with process rather than place.

The way to remove a presumption is to change the question. The point about processes is that many can occur simultaneously in the same place. Thus the idea that a city is a cacophony of processes appears unexceptional but the key point is that it allows full reign to relational thinking. For instance, focusing on Frankfurt as a place we might ask whether it is truly a 'global city' with a debate rehearsing the pros and cons of this idea. But if we treat Frankfurt as a complex amalgam of many processes we bring forth a very different debate. To be sure, the process of global city formation occurs in Frankfurt, especially in its financial district, but only alongside many other important processes that are continually reproducing the city. The question is now about how global city processes relate to others, how important are they? I used Frankfurt as my example because its 'global city status' is seen as problematic, there is a debate about it, which I see as pretty pointless. Obviously there are global city processes operating there but they are less important than in London. But this archetypal 'global city' is equally complex with global city formation just one of many processes, albeit a relatively more important one. The message is simple: think flows as process before place as outcome. This is how I have treated my alpha-beta-gamma discomfort.

Let us look at the city process within globalization is more detail. The vibrancy of world cities derives from two distinct but related urban processes. Each generates an externality, a benefit beyond the market, a positive bonus for locating economic activity in the city. First there are dense patterns of intra-city relations that create agglomeration effects and cluster advantages. Second there are strong flows of inter-city relations that create network effects and connectivity advantages. All successful cities combine these agglomeration externalities and network externalities to maximise the bonus of an urban location. There is a massive and sophisticated literature on agglomeration effects (e.g. Fujita and Thisse 2002), but network externality effects have been much less studied. I have concentrated on the latter as part of the Globalization and World Cities (GaWC) research programme where the study of network externalities has been pioneered.

Introducing city networks directly addresses the question of city competition (Taylor 2012). Networks can only be reproduced through mutuality, that is to say they operate through cooperation rather than competition, win-win situations rather than zero sum games (Thompson 2003). In city networks, cities need each other and all contribute to the wellbeing of the network (Taylor 2004). One way of thinking about networks in relation to hierarchies is that the former encompasses all links across all cities whereas hierarchies focus on just specific 'vertical' links between cities at different levels: this argument has been theorized as a new 'central flow theory' that complements traditional central place theory (Taylor et al. 2010). Therefore, I accept that cities compete with one another; my concern is for the presumption that competitive behaviour is deemed to exhaust the possibilities of inter-city relations. The key point is that inter-city relations are more complex than this; in the more sophisticated studies of competitive cities, it is accepted that the competition exists alongside cooperative relations (Begg 1999; Sassen 1999). But this does not mean that they are of equal importance. The competitive process as hierarchy is so much simpler than the cooperative process as network. For instance, with a roster of 15 cities arranged as a hierarchy (1, 2, 4, 8) links are restricted to just 14 possible inter-city relations; a network of 15 cities encompasses a complete 105 possible links. Thus in this case, a hierarchical presumption would eliminate 91 links from consideration, that is to say, 87% of inter-city relations are ruled out of play before analysis begins. Of course, with larger numbers of cities, the percentage of inter-city relations that are missed rises appreciably through thinking hierarchically.

My conclusion is that the city hierarchy presumption (central place theory) should be replaced by a city network presumption (central flow theory). This means we treat city network processes as generic (it is how cities work), leaving city hierarchical processes as contingent. Examples of such contingency are cyclical downturns that enhance competition because of scarcity, and city gateway battles where there is only space for one city interfacing a region/country with the rest of a city network (Taylor 2012). Thus in today's cities in globalization there is a world city network with hierarchical tendencies, the latter enhanced by the current economic downturn and more generally by political boundaries. But this tendency cannot grow to dominate, that would destroy the mutuality of the network and thus its reproduction.

WORLD CITY NETWORK ANALYSIS

I draw on Castells's (1996) concept of 'network society' to theorize central flow theory and operationalize it as world city network analysis. Castells's (1996) network society is constituted as three spheres of flows: infrastructural (the logistics of communication and transport), social organizational (the work enabled by the network infrastructures), and transnational elite behavioural (billionaire leisure and wealth management). Network analyses have been conducted at each of these levels (Derudder et al. 2012); I focus on the second level in which cities are the critical places. I present this through three arguments: first I rehearse specification of network process, second I indicate and present basic results from such analysis, and third I consider the implications of this approach

SPECIFICATION: THE INTERLOCKING NETWORK MODEL

World city network formation is modelled as an inter-locking network. Networks usually consist of two layers, the net level and the node level, but in an interlocking network there is a third 'subnodal' level. For cities operating as key components of the global economy, it is advanced producer service firms operating at this third level that are the network makers; they create the world city network through their everyday practices linking offices across the world. The three layers of the world city network are therefore the net level of the global economy, the node level of cities, and the additional sub-nodal level of service firms. And it is the latter that define the critical level: this is where the agents of network formation are found. Thus for studying the world city network it is service firms that are investigated in order to understand the city network as the outcome. In other words, it is through studying the location strategies of firms that it is possible to measure and analyse the world city network.

Why focus on these service firms? In the 1970s two separate industries, computers and communications, merged their technologies to enable work to be coordinated worldwide based upon simultaneous connections. Early on Sassen (1994) spotted two contrasting economic geography effects: first, a dispersal of production to cheaper labour locales, and second, a contrary trend towards concentration of management and business service industries. The latter were required to organize the new worldwide production and were concentrated in cities. As Sassen (1991) originally argued, it is concentration of management alongside financial, professional and creative services that characterizes contemporary 'global cities'. Of course, service firms have always clustered in cities to provide such services to their clients but under conditions of contemporary globalization those specialised services became worldwide with fundamental implications for work practices. Firms need a multiple office policy across many cities to provide a seamless service and protect global brand integrity by keeping all work in-house.

This is how it came to be that from the 1980s onwards there have been hundreds of large service firms with trans-national office networks, many of them global in scope. Each firm had its own location strategy – which cities to have offices in, what size and functions those offices will be, and how the offices will be organized. It is the work done in these offices that 'interlock' various cities in projects that require multiple office inputs. Thus the inter-city relations in these servicing practices are numerous electronic communications – information, instruction, advice, planning, interpretation, strategy, knowledge, etc., some tele-conferencing as required, and probably travel for face-to-face meetings at a minimum for the beginning and end of a given project. These are the working flows that combined across numerous financial, professional and creative projects in multiple firms to constitute the world city network (Taylor 2001, 2004).

So we have to study service firms to describe and analyse the world city network but, unfortunately, there is no feasible way that data could be collected from firms on these working flows. As well as the obvious confidentiality issues with competing private firms, there is also a feasibility issue: the degree of research collaboration that would be needed from a large number of firms makes such a data collection exercise beyond reasonable social science research logistics. However, this is not a particularly rare situation in measurement practices: where direct measures cannot be obtained, there is the fall back position of carrying out indirect measurement. This requires access to more easily available data plus credible assumptions about how the firms operate.

As mentioned previously, service firms offer a seamless service across their office networks. This means that the geographical distribution of their offices, and their scope and range, are important selling points in attracting new clients. Hence such information is commonly available on service firms' websites. This has been the main source of data for measuring the world city network: for each firm, offices are assessed individually by asking what is the importance of this office in this city within the firm's overall office network? Answers to this question are termed the service value of a city to a firm. These values are coded and become the quantitative input into the study: the coding ranges from 0 (a firm having no office in a city) to 5 (a city housing the headquarters of a firm); standard or typical offices of a firm score 2, minor and major offices 1 and 3, respectively, leaving 4 for scoring cities housing exceptionally important offices such as regional headquarters. The credible assumption that is made is that the more important an office the more working flows it will generate. Therefore two important offices will generate a much higher level of flow between their respective cities than two minor offices between their respective cities. These data and this assumption are combined to generate estimates of inter-office working flow levels between cities for each firm; they are not actual working flows, but potential working flows, indirect measures derived from the data and the model assumptions. Aggregating all potential working flows for all firms located in a city generates estimates of its working flow relations with other cities; when this is done for all cities it constitutes the world city network.

Network connectivity is the main measure of importance of a city in this model (Taylor 2001). It is computed from the products of service values for the city with each other city for all firms. Thus assuming m advanced producer service firms and n cities we can define a service value for firm j in city i as v_{ij}. The basic relational unit of measurement is given by

$$r_{ab,j} = v_{aj} \cdot v_{bj} \tag{12.1}$$

which defines the relation between cities a and b in terms of firm j. This is an elemental city-dyad interlock for one firm. The aggregate city-dyad interlock is then given by

$$r_{ab} = \sum r_{ab,j} \tag{12.2}$$

For each city there are n-1 such aggregate city-dyad interlocks and the network connectivity for a city is given by their sum:

$$C_a = \sum r_{ai} \quad \text{(in which } a \neq i\text{)} \tag{12.3}$$

where C_a is the network connectivity of city a. This relates city a to all other cities within the network through its firms and measures the degree of integration of the city into the world city network.

The data collection to operationalize this model and provide the results reported below was carried out in 2010. Office networks were coded for 175 advanced producer firms chosen as leading firms in their respective sectors: the top 25 in accountancy, advertising, law and management consultancy, and the top 75 firms for financial services (banking, insurance and diversified finance). Their offices were scrutinized across 526 cities worldwide. The end result is a 526 cities x 175 firms matrix with each cell indicating the importance of a specific city in the office network of a specific firm, 92,050 service values in all.

From this large amount of customized data we compute network connectivities of cities as defined in equation (3) to show the degree of a city's integration into the world city network. The values computed from equation (3) are relatively large and therefore to make them easier to interpret we present them as percentages of the highest scoring city.

ANALYSIS: CHINESE CITIES IN THE WORLD CITY NETWORK

For the analysis I have chosen to focus on Chinese cities because they illustrate well the city network presumption operating in a network with hierarchical tendencies. As argued earlier, competition is enhanced through national boundaries; where there are many states there will be numerous 'gateway cities' to link the national economic jurisdictions to the world economy. This is the case for Europe. In contrast China has no such need for so many gateways. This contrast is shown in Table 12.1, in which are listed the leading 20 cities in China and Europe in terms of their global network connectivities. The top three in each case are relatively similar but thereon there is a marked contrast: the remaining 17 European cities are all much more connected than China's fifth ranked city Guangzhou. The latter, with Shenzhen, represent moderate integration into the world city network; the remaining 14 Chinese cities are only weakly connected. Clearly business service network flows are much more concentrated in China than in Europe, reflecting the latter's multiple states – 13 of Europe's top 20 are capital cities operating as gateways to their own 'national economies'.

Table 12.1   Top 20 Chinese and European Cities in the World City Network

World rank	Chinese city	GNC*	World rank	European city	GNC*
3	Hong Kong	73.8%	1	London	100.0%
7	Shanghai	64.1%	4	Paris	69.1%
13	Beijing	58.6%	12	Milan	60.1%
45	Taipei	41.8%	17	Madrid	55.7%
68	Guangzhou	36.4%	19	Amsterdam	54.4%
107	Shenzhen	28.6%	20	Frankfurt	54.2%
236	Kaohsiung	16.7%	25	Brussels	50.6%
271	Hangzhou	15.0%	30	Munich	46.7%
273	Nanjing	14.8%	32	Zurich	46.5%
278	Dalian	14.7%	33	Dublin	46.2%
286	Qingdao	13.8%	36	Warsaw	45.6%
291	Macao	13.5%	37	Vienna	45.1%
292	Chengdu	13.4%	40	Barcelona	43.5%
317	Suzhou	11.5%	47	Lisbon	41.4%
334	Hsinchu City	10.0%	48	Prague	41.3%
345	Chongqing	9.4%	49	Rome	41.1%
347	Xi'an	9.3%	51	Düsseldorf	40.5%
361	Xiamen	8.2%	52	Stockholm	39.8%
364	Ningbo	8.1%	53	Copenhagen	39.7%
370	Shenyang	7.8%	54	Hamburg	39.4%

Note: * Global network connectivity given as % of highest (i.e. London).

Thus, when comparing China and Europe in the world city network it is not that inland China is unconnected beyond the six leading eastern cities, but their levels are far lower than equivalent cities in Europe. This also reflects China's much more recent growth as part of the world economy which means that many of its dynamic cities have yet to develop a strong global business servicing presence.

However, it is unlikely that China will ever produce a national sub-network as multifarious as Europe's. This is because of China's sovereign unity, but the country's large size has an additional effect. Beyond Europe, economic globalization processes seemed to have favoured one city over its historic rival in several countries that traditionally had two leading cities – Sydney rising over Melbourne, Toronto over Montreal, Mumbai over Delhi, and São Paulo over Rio de Janeiro are all classic cases. But this does not seem to be happening in China; with three leading world cities, this country is apparently developing without such restriction. The case of Hong Kong is the archetypal example of how, without a mutuality presumption, commentators get cities spectacularly wrong. In 1997 Hong Kong reverted to Chinese sovereignty. The change of political authority was widely expected to result in the demise of Hong Kong as a major world city. In Pacific Asia generally, Singapore was identified as the main beneficiary, and within China, it was assumed that Shanghai would take over Hong Kong's role of linking the country to the rest of the world city network. Of course all this was surmised on the basis of inter-city relations being a zero-sum game: Hong Kong loses; other cities gain. But this is not how the world economy and the world city network work: as noted earlier the basic commercial process, as described by Jacobs (1992), operates through win-win market scenarios. Such a scenario has certainly unfolded for Hong Kong: since 1997 Shanghai, Singapore and Hong Kong have all massively prospered. The latter city, instead of declining, is consolidating its position as number three in the world city network, above Tokyo and Paris, and is even catching up London and New York (Derudder at al. 2010). It appears that Hong Kong has a deeply embedded niche that has grown to complement work done in Shanghai and Singapore; any competition between these three cities is simply not that important.

I will focus on Beijing and Shanghai to illustrate the mutuality alternative to competition. These are of general interest because they have been the top two cities growing their connectivities within the world city network since 2000 (Derudder et al. 2010). Here I will show that their respective increases in connectivity have not brought forth a competitive scenario, rather this appears to be another win-win process. Their growing complementarity is shown through two pieces of analysis that disaggregate their global network connectivities previously discussed in Table 12.1. The first disaggregation is by service sector and answers the question of which of Beijing and Shanghai is the more connected in each of five sectors? The second disaggregation is by other cities to depict each city hinterland and answers the question of which cities are more linked to Beijing and which to Shanghai? Both analyses set the two Chinese cities within the global network of world cites as global business centres.

The data upon which the connectivities are computed consist of five service sectors: financial services, legal services, advertising, accountancy, and management accountancy. Thus the overall connectivity can be broken down into these five component parts. When this is done we find that there are interesting differences between Beijing and Shanghai: in no cases are both cities ranked in the top ten, rather when one city has a top ten position the other is always outside the top ten. This means that the two cities are integrated into the world city network through different patterns of sector workflows based upon their different divisions of labour. The implication is that the two cities are more complementary than competitive in their global servicing relations.

Tables 12.2 and 12.3 show the evidence for this conclusion. The former table shows the two sectors where Shanghai is in the top ten: financial services and advertising. These are the modern core commercial services. Shanghai's highest ranking (7th) is as a global financial centre (Table 12.2) even though Beijing is the headquarters of the leading Chinese banks. In transnational financial terms, Shanghai is the place to be in China. Similarly, in advertising, Shanghai as China's leading commercial city is chosen by transnational advertising firms for their new offices resulting in 8th position (Table 12.2). In this case Beijing drops to a lowly 18th – it seems that in China today, government is not as big a market for advertising as it has been in western countries.

Beijing is in the top ten for the other three services (Table 12.3). Its highest ranking is 8th for accountancy (Table 12.3) for which Shanghai drops to 14th. For management services and law Beijing maintains a 10th ranking (Table 12.3) but for these services Shanghai fares very differently: its lowest ranking is for the former (a lowly 23rd) but it is nearly level with Beijing for law (in 11th position). It would seem that at this time, firms offering accountancy and management consultancy services are attracted by government (and the market it provides) to make Beijing more of a global priority than Shanghai. Law is more interesting because both Beijing and Shanghai are similarly attractive to these firms. As can be seen in other cities in Table 12.2, law firms service both financial centres and political centres; thus from Europe both Frankfurt and Brussels feature in Table 12.2. But overall, the key point is that firms in different sectors tend to use Beijing and Shanghai in different ways thus providing them with complementary roles in the world city network.

Table 12.2   Connectivities Where Shanghai is Stronger than Beijing

Rank	City	FS	Rank	City	AD
1	London	100%	1	New York	100%
2	New York	96%	2	London	75%
3	Hong Kong	93%	3	Paris	75%
4	Tokyo	82%	4	Hong Kong	73%
5	Singapore	82%	5	Tokyo	71%
6	Paris	79%	6	Singapore	70%
7	Shanghai	77%	7	Moscow	65%
8	Sydney	77%	8	Shanghai	64%
9	Seoul	70%	9	Warsaw	63%
10	Madrid	70%	10	Sydney	63%
12	Beijing	69%	18	Beijing	60%

Note: FS is financial services; AD is advertising.

Table 12.3   Connectivities Where Beijing is Stronger than Shanghai

Rank	City	AC	Rank	City	MC	Rank	City	LW
1	London	100%	1	New York	100%	1	London	100%
2	New York	79%	2	London	67%	2	New York	89%
3	Hong Kong	74%	3	Paris	65%	3	Paris	70%
4	Sydney	69%	4	Chicago	62%	4	Frankfurt	59%
5	Singapore	67%	5	Hong Kong	61%	5	Washington	58%
6	Milan	67%	6	Singapore	56%	6	Brussels	54%
7	Paris	66%	7	Tokyo	56%	7	Hong Kong	53%
8	Beijing	64%	8	Zurich	55%	8	Moscow	50%
9	Buenos Aires	63%	9	Madrid	55%	9	Tokyo	48%
10	Kuala Lumpur	62%	10	Beijing	53%	10	Beijing	45%
14	Shanghai	60%	23	Shanghai	44%	11	Shanghai	42%

Note: AC is accountancy; MC is management consultancy; LW is legal services.

Table 12.4   Comparing Beijing and Shanghai Hinter Worlds

Orientation	City	Link difference
	New York	52
	Tokyo	21
	Rome	17
	Los Angeles	10
BEIJING	Sydney	6
	Singapore	5
	Seoul	5
	Moscow	5
	Hong Kong	4

Table 12.4   (continued)

Orientation	City	Link difference
	São Paulo	-5
	London	-10
	Mexico City	-13
	Vienna	-15
	Jakarta	-15
	Frankfurt	-16
	Chicago	-16
	Bangkok	-17
	Toronto	-21
	Milan	-21
	Dublin	-21
SHANGHAI	Buenos Aires	-21
	Paris	-22
	Lisbon	-26
	Zurich	-27
	Amsterdam	-27
	Warsaw	-28
	Kuala Lumpur	-29
	Mumbai	-31
	Taipei	-37
	Stockholm	-42
	Brussels	-43
	Madrid	-44

Note: Link difference is Beijing's link to a city minus Shanghai's link to that city.

Complementarities between Beijing and Shanghai are also reflected in their respective hinterworlds. Hinterworlds are the non-local (i.e. beyond a city's hinterland) links cities have with other cities. Using data on the office networks of 175 leading business service firms, estimated working flows between pairs of cities are computed as the city-dyad interlock defined in equation 2. In Table 12.4 the inter-city links between Beijing and Shanghai are compared by subtracting Shanghai dyad interlocks from Beijing dyad interlocks. Where the result is positive Beijing has the stronger connections, where it is negative Shanghai has the stronger connections. The political and commercial roles of the two cities are reflected in this listing. Beijing is strongly connected to New York (United Nations HQ) and major neighbouring Pacific Rim cities (plus neighbouring Eurasian Moscow). Taipei is, of course, a special case with its commercial links to Shanghai but without political links to Beijing. The contrast between Beijing's links to Italy's capital city Rome compared to Shanghai's links to Italy's 'economic capital' Milan is particularly noteworthy. In fact, Rome (also with UN functions) is the only western European city where Shanghai does not have the stronger links.

Other Asian and American cities that are important commercial centres, such as Chicago and Mumbai, have closer connections to Shanghai. Thus do the hinterworlds of Beijing and Shanghai complement each other in the world city network.

The policy implications of such analyses are difficult to implement. City government has jurisdiction over its administrative area only; it is states that have ultimate authority for external relations. There are 'town twinning' and 'sister city' arrangements in place but these focus on transferring policy practice ('best-practice') with much less focus on commercial inter-city relations. The relations analysed above have not been developed through city governments but by business service firms interlocking cities to satisfy commercial needs. Some cities have been developing 'foreign policy' by locating 'development offices' in other cities but this is a minor process compared to world city network formation. What this analysis implies is that it is a city's Chamber of Commerce that should be forming alliances with other cities' Chambers of Commerce to explore and grow complementarities. This is to call for city-dyad economic governance practice in which city governments themselves would facilitate and monitor through democratic process.

CONCLUDING DISCUSSION: SPECIAL CITY-TRIAD CONNECTIONS

This paper has progressed as far as identifying the importance of city-dyads when thinking through world city network analyses. Of course, networks are much more than collections of nodal-dyads, just focusing on the latter itself presumes missing most network processes. This is where the analysis can become excessively complex. I will offer just one example of city-triads that suggest an important structure that appears to have evolved without any formal government policy prescription.

The development of the world city network seems to have involved creation of two city-triads each related to key stages of network formation and reproduction with respect to leading states. The initial globalizing impetus for network formation seems to have created a New York–London–Washington city triad with each city having a distinctive role. New York is the leading financial centre and Washington is the leading political centre (including finance governance of IMF and World Bank) both located within the leading state. London has the role of being the global platform outside the state's jurisdiction. The latter allows for certain processes that cannot occur in the leading state, for instance the creation of a 'Euro-dollar' market in London as an early step towards globalization. The latest impetus for network development seems to have created a very similar city-triad featuring Shanghai, Beijing, and Hong Kong. Shanghai is the fastest growing finance centre and Beijing the fastest growing political centre (including finance governance of state banks) both within the fastest growing country. Hong Kong has the role of being the fastest growing global platform outside the state's jurisdiction. Again, the latter allows for certain processes that cannot occur within the state, which is the reason for China's 'one country, two systems' policy and why Hong Kong continued to prosper after 1997. I think the parallel between the two city-triad processes is remarkable, suggesting a necessary underlying structure that could only be recognized using relational thinking about win-win situations.

REFERENCES

Beaverstock, J. V., Smith, R. G. and Taylor, P. J. (1999), 'A roster of world cities', *Cities*, 16, 445–458.

Begg, I. (1999), 'Cities and competitiveness', *Urban Studies*, 36, 795–809.

Castells, M. (1996), *The Rise of Network Society*, Oxford: Blackwell.

Christaller, W. (1966), *Central Places in Southern Germany*, Englewood Cliffs, NJ: Prentice Hall.

Derudder, B., Hoyler, M., Taylor, P. J. and Witlox, F. (eds) (2012), *International Handbook of Cities and Globalization*, Cheltenham, UK and Northampton, MA, USA: Edward Elgar.

Derudder, B., Taylor, P. J., Ni, P., de Vos, A., Hoyler, M., Hanssens, H., Bassens, D., Huang, J., Witlox, F., Shen, W. and Yang, X. (2010), 'Pathways of change: shifting connectivities in the world city network, 2000–08', *Urban Studies*, 47, 1861–1877.

Friedmann, J. (1986), 'The world city hypothesis', *Development and Change*, 17, 69–83.

Fujita, M. and Thisse, J.-F. (2002), *Economics of Agglomeration*, Cambridge: Cambridge University Press.

Jacobs, J. (1992), *Systems of Survival*, New York: Vintage.

Sassen, S. (1991), *The Global City*, Princeton, NJ: Princeton University Press.

Sassen, S. (1994), *Cities in a World Economy*, Thousand Oaks, CA: Pine Forge Press.

Sassen, S. (1999), 'Global financial centers', *Foreign Affairs*, 78 (1), 75–87.

Taylor, P. J. (2001), 'Specification of the world city network', *Geographical Analysis*, 33, 181–194.

Taylor, P. J. (2004), *World City Network: A Global Urban Analysis*, London: Routledge.

Taylor, P. J. (2009), 'Urban economists in thrall to Christaller: a misguided search for city hierarchies in external urban relations', *Environment and Planning A*, 41, 2550–2555.

Taylor, P. J. (2012), 'On city cooperation and city competition', in B. Derudder, M. Hoyler, P. J. Taylor and F. Witlox (eds), *International Handbook of Globalization and World Cities*, Cheltenham, UK: Edward Elgar, pp. 56–63.

Taylor, P. J., Hoyler, M. and Verbruggen, R. (2010), 'External urban relational process: introducing central flow theory to complement central place theory', *Urban Studies*, 47, 2803–2818.

Thompson, G. F. (2003), *Between Hierarchies and Markets: The Logic and Limits of Network Forms of Organization*, Oxford, UK: Oxford University Press.

13. Population aging and urban competitiveness

Peter Karl Kresl[1]

The GUCR continues to give us an excellent benchmarking study of the competitiveness of 500 of the world's cities. It offers us data on almost 50 economic and social variables that are utilized in this exercise. Thus is presents a rather comprehensive analysis of how we can determine and study the competitiveness of virtually all of the large cities in the global economy. One aspect of urban economics that cannot be taken into account in such a study, because of the fact that it is important only for a segment of these cities, is the age distribution of the population in a country. The data we have are for nations rather than for cities, but since the national age distribution and its development over time has such a powerful impact on individual urban economies, in addition to its impact on the finances and competitiveness of the nation, it is something that I would like to develop for the readers of GUCR 2013.

The aging of the population has been presented as a "ticking time bomb" which will have enormous financial and other consequences, especially for societies throughout the developed world. Expenditures on the retirement and health benefits of this cohort of the population will have to be covered by past contributions to the appropriate funds or by taxation of income earners at the time that the expenditures are made. Past governments everywhere under-taxed during previous decades so the funds in almost all countries are inadequate to meet the demands that will be placed upon them; hence, the burden on future taxpayers is looming both as an actual fiscal difficulty and as a potential taxpayer rebellion. While each national economy will have its own experience, in general they are all facing the same phenomenon with the same consequences. As will be shown, the aging of the population is principally a feature of the future of nations and cities in the industrialized world so it will not be necessary to examine the situation in all countries. Therefore, I will focus my attention principally on that of the country with which I am most familiar – the United States, but in the course of the study I will extend coverage to Canada, and the European Union. I will begin with an examination of some of the economic consequences of an aging population; then some policy considerations will be raised. This will be used as an introduction to the primary topic of this presentation, the impacts of aging on cities or urban economies. I will conclude with the possible consequences of an aging population on the competitiveness of cities.

THE DEMOGRAPHIC CHANGE AND SOME OF ITS ECONOMIC IMPACTS

Data for the US indicate that average life expectance will increase from 83 years today to

1   Peter Karl Kresl, Bucknell University, Lewisburg, PA, USA 17837. Tel: 570-490-5193.
     Email: kresl@bucknell.edu.

85 by 2035 and to 87 by 2075.[2] As a share of the population the over 65 cohort will double between now and 2030 to 71.5 million – twice the number in 2000 – or about 20 percent of the population.[3] These statistics are even more alarming, in the countries of the EU and the rest of the developed world. The data given in Table 13.1 show how devastating this demographic development will be for Japan and Western Europe, how the problem peaks for the USA and Canada in 2030 at a relatively manageable level, and how less affected will be the rest of the world, in particular for the less developed countries

Table 13.1   Population 65 and Older as a Share of National Population

Country	2000	2030	2050
USA and Canada	12.4	20.0	21.0
Japan	17.1	28.8	34.3
Western Europe	14.0	25.0	29.1
World	6.9	12.0	16.6

Source: 65+ in the United States: 2005, Washington: Department of Commerce, US Census Bureau, December, 2005, Table A-1.

Most importantly, demographic projections also tell us that the labor force should grow at a much slower rate than the retired population, since the relatively numerous "baby boom" generation is approaching retirement age. While the US labor force was growing by 16 percent between 2000 and 2010, this rate will fall to 6 per cent during the next decade and to 3 percent during 2020–2030. Over 46 percent of government workers in the US and over 31 percent of private sector workers are at least 45 years of age, and will therefore be eligible to retire during the next two decades. Obviously these figures will vary from country to country, but the situation should be even worse in countries which are, as shown in Table 13.2, less

Table 13.2   Immigrants as a Percentage of the Population, 2000

Sweden	11.2
France	10.7
Netherlands	9.9
Germany	8.9
Belgium	8.6
Ireland	8.1
United Kingdom	6.8
Spain	3.1
Italy	2.8
Portugal	2.3
United States	14.0

Source: Alberto Alesina and Francesco Giavazzi, *Goodbye Europa: Cronache di un Declino Economico e Politico*, Milano: Rizzoli, 2006, p. 57, and Census of the United States, Washington: Department of Commerce, US Census Bureau, 2006.

---

2   "The State of the Cities Report", Minneapolis: League of Minnesota Cities, 2006, ch. 4, p. 32.

3   "New Study Finds America's Communities Are Not Prepared for an Aging Population," CSRwire, Press Release, September 27, 2006.

able and/or willing than the US to accept immigration as a means of boosting the rate of population growth. It is anticipated that the number of immigrants in the EU will decline over the next three or four decades.[4] In a report for the OECD, Willi Leibfritz sees labor force growth stagnating or even falling in the other G7 countries.[5]

Cities are always powerfully affected by policies adopted by superior levels of government and immigration policy gives strong representation of this. While cities might very well wish to bolster their stagnating labor force with skilled immigrants, the closing of borders by national governments precludes that. As Alesini and Giavazzi write, this is particularly important with regard to relatively desirable and easily assimilated labor from Eastern and Central Europe.[6] When emigration becomes possible the most skilled workers are usually the most mobile and the first to leave. The unwillingness of countries of the European Union to suffer the consequences of inflows of "Polish plumbers" means that these skilled workers often opt for the immigrant friendlier United States, Canada and Australia. By the time the EU opened is borders in 2010, only relatively low-skilled workers were available. The cities will suffer because of this policy.

Many analysts have focused on the resulting "dependency ratio," the relationship between the retired population and the population that will be taxed to pay for their health care and retirement benefits. This ratio is projected to rise in G7 countries from 20–30 percent of the population that is aged 65 and older today to 35–50 percent by 2030 and to 40–70 percent by 2050. The Leibfritz study concluded that "the rapid increase in dependency ratios means that it will become harder to maintain continued increases in living standards, unless available labor resources are better mobilized."[7]

Increasing the rate of natality will help to moderate this problem in the long run – in the next two or three decades; in the short run increasing the labor participation rate among women, the retired or retirement eligible population, and allowing for more immigration are the principle palliatives. Increasing immigration has become a powerfully contentious issue of public policy in recent years as the pool of potential immigrants has become less homogeneous in terms of religious beliefs and more culturally and racially different from the dominant accepting populations. This has even become true in what have traditionally been immigrant societies, such as the US, as opposed to the emigrant societies of Europe and Asia, and we have already noted the unpromising expectation of immigration in the EU. While it is clear that immigration policy by the national government harms cities in that they cannot add to their dwindling working population through this reasonably efficient mechanism, a study of immigration policy would take us too far afield and will not be examined here. However, there are some more narrowly economic policy consequences that are more directly related that will now be considered.

4   Guillermo de la Dehesa, *Europe at the Crossroads*, New York: McGraw Hill, 2006, ch. 4.

5   Willi Leibfritz, "Retiring Later Makes Sense," *OECD Observer*, January 2003.

6   Alberto Alesina and Francesco Giavazzi, *Goodbye Europa: Cronache di un Declino Economico e Politico*, Milano: Rizzoli, 2006, p. 59.

7   "Ageing Populations: High Time for Action," Paris: OECD, background paper for the Meeting of the G8 Employment and Labour Ministers, London 10–11 March, 2005, p. 2.

SOME POLICY CONSIDERATIONS OF AN AGING POPULATION

For the OECD, the major culprit in the economic aspects and fiscal consequences of an aging population is the inducements that have been given to workers, throughout the industrialized world, for early retirement. This made sense when it was felt necessary to open access to jobs for a growing "baby boom" generation, but now that the demographic situation is so dramatically different the policy has become one that creates rather than resolves problems. The OECD noted that "increasing the participation rate of persons aged 55-64 years is one of the main objectives of social policy within the European Union under the Lisbon and Amsterdam Treaties." It is also the case that in many countries, various programs such as generous long-term sickness and disability benefits reduce the effective retirement age considerably below the "official" retirement age. Each early retirement shifts the financial burden to the remaining workers and the fiscal consequences create a situation in which the result is that while all workers should have a right to "retire decently and confidently ... without action, this right is being eroded" for future retirees.[8]

Clearly, this situation would not be as grave as it is if OECD economies had been able to generate adequate gains in productivity, such as those called for in the Lisbon Treaty of the EU. In a study for the C. D. Howe Institute, William Robson concluded that, for Canada, "raising growth in output per working-age person (from 1.5 percent) to 1.9 percent annually while holding growth in service intensity to 1.5 percent would make the net national implicit liability calculated here vanish. Program reforms, prudent fiscal policy, increases in productivity and rapid economic growth are four promising avenues to help Canadians deal with the demographic pressures on their public programs."[9] We can accept this analysis as having validity in the other economies of the developed or industrialized world.

Many observers also argue that it is necessary to bolster the labor force through a variety of measures ranging from better maternity leaves and child-care services to more opportunities for part-time employment and, perhaps most importantly, increased support for life-long learning, on-the-job training and skill-based adult education. These initiatives will both increase labor force participation and enhance the productivity, and employability, of workers as they progress through their working lives. This has become increasingly important as the pace of technological advance and the skill-levels of most jobs have become more rapid and inexorable – and as the work force ages and its skills become less relevant than in the past.

The conclusion is that at the level of the national economy, what are required are policies to raise labor participation rates and to increase the trend in productivity growth. Sadly, all of this is beyond the mandate or competence of city governments. But the OECD argues, in addition, that "what is needed now is a policy shift to reduce barriers to employment and work effort to promote more effective lifelong learning and thus increase the resources available to society."[10] It is here that urban governments have a contribution to make, since they generally do have a significant role to play when it comes to employment conditions and to training and education.

---

8   Willi Leibfritz.

9   William B. P. Robson, "Time and Money: Tracking the Fiscal Impact of Demographic Change in Canada," C. D. Howe Institute, e-brief, October 5, 2006

10   "Ageing Populations ... ," p. 3.

THE FISCAL BURDENS ON GOVERNMENTS OF AN AGING POPULATION

These phenomena generate fiscal pressures on governments and they need to adopt policies that will deal with them effectively. At this stage of the argument, representatives of the various levels of government will ask: How are we affected by this? A report done by a Canadian scholar highlighted four elements in the financial impacts of the aging of the population that affect the finances of governments: healthcare, education, elderly benefits and child and family benefits. For Canada, the smaller portion of the population that will be young means that between now and 2055 expenditures for both education and child and family benefits should fall as a percentage of GDP, expenditures for elderly retirement benefits will rise slightly until 2030 and fall back to their current level by the end of the period. Together they will fall from about 5.8 to 4.4 percent of GDP. The most significant element is health care that rises from about 6.2 percent of GDP to 12 percent during the same time period. In the aggregate, these four elements will rise from 15 percent to 19 percent of GDP by 2055.[11] If these figures are typical of the other industrialized countries, what gives each country a distinct structure of burden is the constitutionally mandated allocation of programmatic and financial obligations to each level of government. In Canada, education and health are provincial responsibilities while elderly and child and family benefits are covered by the federal government. The result for Canada is that for the period 2005–2050 the net burden on Canadian citizens is $810.6 billion, but with the provincial governments bearing a burden of $847.3 billion and the federal government a net gainer of $36.7 billion. In this instance the national government benefits and the sub-national governments bear the entire burden of the aging of the population. The impact on cities was not examined in this report. Again, this will be different for each national situation depending on the responsibilities that are mandated for each level of government.

It has often been the case that when faced with increasing fiscal burdens superior levels of government shift that burden to lower levels of government. Since fiscal responsibility at the national level seems to be in such short supply these days, cities should be prepared to be confronted with increased "unfunded mandates," and programmatic and funding obligations. This prospect has been raised by the League of Minnesota Cities in its *State of the Cities Report 2004*. It was suggested here that the federal government may: 1) choose to cut other areas of spending to pay for increasing Social Security costs, 2) decrease fiscal transfers to state and local governments, 3) decrease the rate at which it matches state funds for Medicare, and 4) find other ways "to shift the responsibility and cost of certain programs to sates or cities."[12] Thus lower levels of government, in this instance cities, have a powerful interest in seeing that national governments act responsibly with regard to their continuing budget deficits and excessive national debts.

Finally, some economists have concluded that when the dependency rate rises and the percentage of the population in working age declines, we should expect a lower savings rate, lower investment and more negative fiscal balance for government.[13] Hence, the aging of the

---

11   William B. P. Robson.

12   "The State of the Cities Report", p. 32.

13   Guillermo de la Dehesa, ch. 4.

population may be expected to have some negative macro-economic consequences that will have impacts on all levels of government with regard to tax revenues and the availability of funds for investments in infrastructure and other priority items.

THE IMPACT OF AN AGING POPULATION ON CITIES

How an individual city will be affected by an aging population will be primarily determined by a small number of variables. In this section of the presentation we will focus on the most important of them. On the one hand, population growth forecasts will suggest which cities would appear to have or to lack a fundamental attractiveness to those who are interested in moving their place of residence. On the other hand, we will be interested in the choices made by seniors with regard to what they do with their time and money. We can link these decisions to the economic strength and viability of an urban region.

The projected population growth of major US cities is quite diverse, and not entirely as one would imagine. Population is generally expected to grow most rapidly in the Sunbelt cities from Los Angeles through Dallas to Orlando to Atlanta-Charlotte-Raleigh, although New Orleans was expected to show a decline in population even before Hurricane Katrina. Many Northern and Rustbelt cities, such as Pittsburgh, Syracuse, and Buffalo should, as would be expected, experience declines in population. Other Northern cities such as Cleveland, Philadelphia, Detroit, Milwaukee and St. Louis will suffer loss of population loss in the city proper that will be offset by gains in the suburbs. Most surprising are the expected population gains that should be experienced by northern cities such as Seattle, Chicago and New York.[14] In other words, the impacts of demographic change, including ageing, will vary significantly from city to city.

Whatever the population experience will be for an individual city, its ability to gain revenues, jobs, taxes, and so forth, will be strongly determined by its stock of urban assets that will be attractive to the 55–80 year old population. This in turn will be determined by the characteristics of that population that will generate the demands they will place on urban centers and will govern their choice of residence and short-term visits. The US Census Bureau and the Commission of the European Union have both argued that tomorrow's seniors will be very different from their predecessors, living longer, being more mobile, achieving higher levels of education and being relatively wealthy. For example, Americans with a university degree rose from 3.4 to 17.4 percent of the population between 1950 and 2003 and this figure is expected to rise to more than 25 percent by 2030 and the Bureau links higher levels of education to "better health, higher income, more wealth and a higher standard of living in retirement."[15] These characteristics will continue to increase among the 65 year or older population. Finally, it should be noted that the poverty rate among Americans aged 65 and over has dropped since 1980 from almost 16 percent to 9.8 percent in 2004, a decline of

---

14   Peter Linneman and Albert Saiz, "Forecasting 2020 U.S. Country and MSA Populations," Zell-Lurie Real Estate Center, the Wharton School, the University of Pennsylvania, unpublished paper, April 2006, p. 15.

15   "Dramatic Changes in U.S. Aging Highlighted in New Census, HIH Report," Washington: Department of Commerce, US Census Bureau, March 9, 2006, pp. 1 and 2. For the original report see: *65+ in the United States: 2005*, Washington: Department of Commerce, US Census Bureau, December, 2005.

about 40 percent; this poverty rate for 1965 was 35 percent.[16]

This raises a new set of issues with regard to the impacts on cities of this aging population: Where do they choose to live?

What do seniors choose to do with their time?

What do seniors choose to do with their money?

In this section in which we examine the impacts of an aging population on cities we will take the subject population to be those individuals of between 54 and 80 years of age. The transition that occurs in people's lives as they age usually happens before they reach retirement age – roughly 65 years of age. By this age children have typically left the household to be on their own and their parents reconsider many of the basic dimensions of their lives, setting themselves up for the last active period of their lives, prior to settling into some sort of situation that is dominated by their health care requirements. Typically the population 75 years of age or more tends to be more sedentary and less actively engaged in the sorts of activities that will be highlighted below.

First, the choice of where to live. It is said that "life begins when the children leave home and the dog dies." For many this takes place in their late 50s, and for many of these seniors it offers an opportunity to reconsider their living accommodations – the location and type of housing in which they live. In the US, there seem to be four basic options. One, of course, is to make no change, in which case their home mortgage is paid off and their disposable income can be much higher than at any other time in life. Another option is to purchase the house or apartment they have wanted for some time but could not move into because of family obligations, employment, etc. Third, many move into retirement regions, such as the Sunbelt in the US. Finally, many cities in the US and Canada, as well as in the EU (Amesterdam, Hamburg and Malmö), are experiencing an inflow of seniors who move into apartments or condominiums in the city center. The attraction of the latter option is the complex of urban amenities that are to be found there, including theaters, concert halls, galleries and museums, as well as dining and shopping and, in general, an "urban ambience." This latter must include public transportation, public security/crime and the poverty rate. This has been the experience for many years of older cities such as New York, Boston and Chicago, but Denver has its Lo-Do (Lower Downtown) and Golden Museum Triangle areas, and there are similar districts in virtually all large cities. Even cities that are having difficulty such as Pittsburgh (with its Cultural District) and Philadelphia (with its Arts Avenue) are developing their cultural assets, in part to make their city centers more attractive to educated, relatively well-off seniors.

This brings us to the second of the three issues: what seniors do with their time. The city center offers them first class dining and evenings out, educational opportunities and cultural experiences that are to be found in museums, galleries, theaters and recital and concert halls – all of which are accessible by convenient public transportation and taxi and do not require long drives, often at night, in an automobile. Attendance at cultural events is positively correlated with income and education – and with age.[17] The first two are quite predictable and have

---

16 "The Myriad, Changing Faces of Poverty," *Fedgazette*, Federal Reserve Bank of Minneapolis, Vol. 18, no. 6, 2006, p. 2.

17 Bonnie Nichols, "Demographic Characteristics of Arts Attendance, 2002," Washington: The National Endowment for the Arts, The Nancy Hanks Center, Note #82, July 2003, p. 3; referring to Richard A. Peterson, Pamela C. Hull, and Roger M. Kern, *Age and Arts Participation: 1982–1997*, Washington: The National Endowment for the Arts, Research Division Report #42, ch. 4.

always characterized cultural participation, however, the age factor is promisingly important and worthy of attention.

A study of arts attendance in Southern California concluded that today, only 34 percent of seniors had not attended a Museum in the past twelve months (as opposed to about 50 percent twenty years earlier), and 54 percent had attended twice or more – the highest level of attendance by age group. The report concluded that "perhaps today's seniors retire earlier and/or are more affluent, leaving more time for artistic and cultural pursuits."[18] At the level of the US as a whole, while attendance at all cultural activities drops off for the 75 and older age cohorts, attendance for the 65–74 cohort exceeds their share of the population in classical music, opera and non-musical plays, and this is true for the 55–64 group in these same activities as well as in musicals.[19] The most active cohort is that of 45–54 year olds for which jazz is added to the interests of the 55–64 year old cohort. An important question for cities is whether this cultural activity for the 45–54 year old cohort will diminish to the levels of today's seniors as they age or whether their higher educational attainment and incomes will dominate so that cultural attendance will continue to increase during the coming decades. Similar figures are found when we consider actual participation in the arts, rather than just attendance. Whatever their experience will be, it is clear that seniors are an important and growing clientele for urban cultural institutions.

The same can be said of seniors and urban educational institutions. Participation among the 50 year and older population has increased from 40 percent to 44 percent during the past decade and there is no reason to think that participation will not continue to grow in the future. While participation in educational activities was 47 per cent among 50–54 year olds and 40 among 55–64 year olds, it was 23 percent among the 65 and older cohort. The same question must be asked here as was with regard to participation in cultural activities: will the younger cohorts continue their participation in educational activities past their 65th birthdays? The Institute for Retired Professionals, which conducts continuing education programs, now has 400 institutes across the country. As the director of one of the institutes said, "The boomers are the best-educated generation in the history of the universe. If early in life you learn to value education that stays with you through life."[20] This year, 160,000 seniors will enroll in 8,000 courses offered by Elderhostel, a nation-wide program for courses on university campuses for seniors.

Finally, what do seniors do with their money? The OECD noted that "retirees spend money rather than save it."[21] What they spend this money on is, of course, closely related to what they do with their time and, since each of these activities has just been discussed, their financial implications should be clear enough without much further discussion. Increased income and better health will result in more travel and, while cruises and exotic places have always been attractive to seniors, cultural tourism to cities with a wide range of urban amenities will also be favored. This travel will be both within the nation and international.

---

18 "Museum Attendance, Population Shifts, and Changing Tastes," The Ralph and Goldy Lewis Center for Regional Policy Studies, SCS Fact Sheet, Vol. 1, No. 7, May, 2005.

19 *2002 Survey of Public Participation in the Arts*, Washington: National Endowment for the Arts, Research Division Report #45, March 2004, ch. 3.

20 Abby Ellin, "No More Knitting. Older Students Want Enlightenment," *The New York Times*, November 11, 2006, p. B1.

21 Willi Leibfritz.

In a classic study done in 1993, the Port Authority of New York and New Jersey studied the economic impact of expenditures on cultural activities in the New York metropolitan region. Three of the findings are of interest when we consider the consequences for cities of an aging population that will have both the time and the money to attend cultural events. First, while there was capital investment in cultural facilities of $1.5 billion during the decade 1982–1992, only $313 million, or about 20 percent, was contributed by the City of New York – the rest came from other sources. Second, wages, salaries and royalties in the cultural sector were $3.5 billion while revenues of restaurants, hotels and retail shopping were $9.8 billion for the metropolitan region, of which $9.2 billion was for the core or center, New York City. Third, and of considerable importance, spending on cultural activities "grew solidly at a time of retrenchment in many other sectors of the economy."[22] While seniors are a minor share of the population that participated in cultural activities, we must remember that their expenditures must be multiplied by a relevant factor if we are going to be able to ascertain the full impact of their expenditures on the urban economy.

There have been numerous reports in newspapers in which the juxtaposition of artists and, among others, the information-communication technology sector specialists in certain districts of cities has led to collaboration in, and creation of, firms that specialize in animation, video games and advertising. In recent research, Ann Markusen and David King have examined the "artistic dividend," that is, the economic impact of artistic and cultural activity on a regional economy. In addition to the consequences that were highlighted in the report of the Port Authority of NY & NJ, they argue that: "the productivity of and earnings in a regional economy rise as the incidence of artists within its boundaries increases, because artists' creativity and specialized skills enhance the design, production and marketing of products and services in other sectors. They also help firms recruit top-rate employees and generate income through direct export of artistic work out of the region."[23] In my own research, a city's cultural assets have been identified and one of a small number of statistically verified determinants of urban competitiveness.[24] Hence any stimulus of cultural activity, including that of seniors, should be understood to have its impact on some of the industries that are considered to be central to the urban economy of the future; the contribution of seniors to the economic vitality of an urban region can be significant. We have seen that seniors are also active participants in educational activities. In the US, adult and continuing education is a $6 billion industry and it is projected to increase to $8 billion by 2011. It has been estimated that about one million Americans 55 years and older will enroll in university-offered continuing and professional courses, spending on average $920. As this evidence suggests, there is a significant impact on urban economies of seniors participating in a variety of educational activities, and we should expect to see this impact grow in coming decades. Many of these seniors will still be working, either in the companies in which they have been employed or as self-employed consultants, small business owners or entrepreneurs.

---

22 *The Arts as an Industry: Their Economic Importance to the New York–New Jersey Metropolitan Region*, New York: the Port Authority of NY & NJ, 1993, pp. 2 and 5, and chapter VI.

23 Ann Markusen and David King, "The Artistic Dividend: The Arts' Hidden Contributions to Regional Development," The University of Minnesota, Humphrey Institute of Public Affairs, July 2003, p. 3.

24 Peter Karl Kresl and Balwant Singh, "Competitiveness and the Urban Economy: Twenty-four Large US Metropolitan Areas," *Urban Studies*, Vol. 36, Nos 5–6, 1999, pp. 1017–1027.

When we put together the impacts, in a given city, on employment, incomes and tax revenues of the several sectors of urban economies that are going to be positively affected by the expenditure by seniors of time and money it can be projected to be a significant economic boost to the cities that are able to make themselves attractive to this growing segment of the population. Some state governments, such as Tennessee, are spending millions of dollars to attract seniors to in-migrate because they recognize the positive economic impacts, on cities and towns of all sizes, of an older population. Two researchers from the University of Michigan, in a study on the future of the Michigan economy, argued that after automobile and other manufacturing, tourism and knowledge-based industries the most important and most rapidly growing sector for the future was "high income ($60,000 or more in income) households headed by persons age 65 or older",[25] for the same reasons that are being highlighted here.

Beyond the financial consequences of the three choices of seniors, cities will also be affected by more general considerations. In most countries investments in whatever health care, cultural, educational and other infrastructure facilities may be constructed to meet the demands of seniors are done by national or sub-national governments, often with some degree of private sector participation, as was just noted with regard to cultural facilities in New York. In some instances cities may be required to issue bonds to participate financially in some other way. But whatever the financing scheme, the city will enjoy the benefits of construction jobs and incomes, as well as additional tax revenues.

These benefits may be offset to some degree by the burdens on cities of their own aging employees and their health care needs. Furthermore, they may be required to "reassess their policies, programs and services in the areas of transportation, housing, land use planning, public safety, parks and recreation, workforce skill development and volunteering/civic engagement." Some of these activities, such as skill development and volunteering/civic engagement, will bring benefits, some of which will be non-monetary, to the city in which they occur. What is disturbing for those who look to the future is the report issued by a group of concerned organizations that "only 46 per cent of US communities have begun planning to address the needs of the exploding population of aging 'baby boomers.'"[26]

SMART URBAN POLICY

Given what has been discussed above, it is clear that if a city or an urban region wants to capture the potential economic benefits from an aging population a certain ambience that is attractive to this cohort of the population must be put in place. This will require that certain policies and initiatives be adopted and that certain expenditures be undertaken. If done properly, the economic consequences of the aging of the population can significantly positive

---

25   George A. Fulton and Donald R. Grimes, *Michigan's Industrial Structure and Competitive Advantage: How Did We Get Into This Pickle and Where Do We Go from Here?* Institute of Labor and Industrial Relations, University of Michigan, March 14, 2006, pp. 20–21.

26   "New Study Finds America's Communities are not Prepared for an Aging Population," CSRwire, press release, September 27, 2006.

in their impacts. At this early stage in my research, I will simply enumerate the things that must be in place and the initiatives that must be undertaken. Of course, some cities or urban regions will have taken these steps years ago.

- A full complement of quality cultural institutions and activities.
- Universities and other educational institutions with special programs or privileged access for Seniors.
- Pedestrian streets and walk-ways.
- Parks and other green spaces.
- Policies to reduce poverty and exclusion.
- Public security, a feeling of safety and a low crime rate.
- Extensive opportunities for voluntary work with social, political and cultural organizations.
- An ombudsman to respond to issues raised by Seniors.
- Sustainable housing which integrates various age groups.
- A variety of restaurants and dining options.
- A full array of high quality health care facilities.
- A variety of living arrangements from individual houses or apartments, to group living, to assisted and full care living facilities.
- Initiatives to integrate Seniors into the life of the community with interaction with other age cohorts, for those who want this.

THE CONSEQUENCES OF AN AGING POPULATION ON A CITY'S COMPETITIVENESS

There are two primary linkages between an aging population and the competitiveness of an individual city: 1) the impact of the senior population itself, and 2) the labor force of that city. First, it has been demonstrated in this chapter that a population of seniors who are healthy, relatively wealthy, mobile and well educated can have beneficial impacts on the assets of a city and on its urban life. This cohort of the population spends much of its time and its income on activities – cultural events and education – that make any city increasingly attractive to a younger, educated, and highly skilled workforce that is crucial to a city's success in the economy of the 21st century. Hence, they have a positive impact on the city's competitiveness.

Second, the workforce that is required for a competitive urban economy must have the necessary skills and be sufficient in number to support a structure of firms in the sectors in which the city has a competitive advantage. While a large community of seniors will support competitiveness, while the population of any city at any moment in time may be aging, and while the share of young and skilled workers, other things being equal, may be diminishing, an attractive city with the necessary amenities and opportunities for satisfying work and family life will be able to add to its supply of these workers through inward migration from other less attractive cities.

FINAL COMMENTS

While superior levels of government are most likely to be negatively affected by the health and retirement costs of an aging population, seniors are most likely to spend their money on activities that are supplied by entities in cities, thereby adding to the total revenue base of urban workers and firms, and to their municipal tax income. The primary positive consequences will come from the participation of seniors in cultural, educational and tourism activities – all competitiveness-enhancing activities. While these are significant financial impacts today, given the education, income and health of the aging population, we must expect these positive consequences to increase in the coming years. This is due to the higher levels of income and education, and better health of seniors that will be seen in coming years. There should also be positive net impacts from the construction of new facilities to cater to the demands of the older population. Cities will have to ensure that the necessary facilities are in fact created or the increasingly mobile seniors will chose to retire in a more congenial city.

On the negative side, some health care activities will have to be provided by the city, and it will also have to provide for the increasing health care needs of its own aging workforce. Furthermore, cities cannot change their image or reputation over night, so cities that have not been giving attention to the needs of a aging population, 46 percent of US cities by one estimate, may not be able to turn things around in the foreseeable future; those cities, such as Pittsburgh and Buffalo in the US, will continue to lose out in relation to other, more favored or more activist, cities.

Finally, cities will be negatively affected by unfavorable policies by superior levels of government in areas such as immigration, and by the down-loading of program and funding responsibilities to them.

The aging of the population presents all cities with the possibility of net competitiveness benefits from this phenomenon but, as is almost always the case, capturing those net benefits will be dependent on the wisdom and vision with which city leaders are aware of these potential benefits, and take actions and implement policies that will position their city to be a net beneficiary.

Note: The central points of this argument have been developed more fully in: Peter Karl Kresl and Daniele Ietri (2010), *The Aging Population and the Competitiveness of Cities: Benefits to the Urban Economy*, Cheltenham, UK and Northampton, MA, USA: Edward Elgar.

REFERENCES

Alesina, A. and Giavazzi F. (2006), *Goodbye Europa: Cronache di un Declino Economico e Politico*, Milano: Rizzoli.
Arts Research (1993), *The Arts as an Industry: Their Economic Importance to the New York–New Jersey Metropolitan Region*, New York: The Port Authority of NY & NJ.

Bradshaw, T. (2004), *Survey of Public Participation in the Arts*, Washington: National Endowment for the Arts, Research Division Report.

CITI (2006), *The State of the Cities Report*, Minneapolis: League of Minnesota Cities.

CSRwire (2006), "New Study Finds America's Communities Are Not Prepared for an Aging Population," press release, 27 September.

Dehesa, G. (2006), *Europe at the Crossroads*, New York: McGraw Hill.

Ellin, A. (2006), "No More Knitting. Older Students Want Enlightenment," *The New York Times*. [Online] 11 November, p. B1, available from: https://www.nytimes.com (accessed 26 May 2014).

Fedgazette (2006), "The Myriad, Changing Faces of Poverty," *Federal Reserve Bank of Minneapolis*, 18 (6), 2.

Fulton, G. and Grimes, D. (2006), *Michigan's Industrial Structure and Competitive Advantage: How Did We Get Into this Pickle and Where Do We Go from Here?* University of Michigan: Institute of Labor and Industrial Relations.

Kim, H. (2005), "Museum Attendance, Population Shifts, and Changing Tastes," The Ralph and Goldy Lewis Center for Regional Policy Studies, *SCS Fact Sheet*, 1 (7).

Kresl, P. and Singh, B. (1999), "Competitiveness and the Urban Economy: Twenty-four Large US Metropolitan Areas," *Urban Studies*, 36 (5–6), 1017–1027.

Leibfritz, W. (2003), "Retiring Later Makes Sense," *OECD Observer*, January.

Linneman, P. and Saiz, A. (2006), "Forecasting 2020 U.S. Country and MSA Populations," Zell-Lurie Real Estate Center, the Wharton School, the University of Pennsylvania, unpublished paper, April.

Markusen, A. and King, D. (2003), "The Artistic Dividend: The Arts' Hidden Contributions to Regional Development," The University of Minnesota: Humphrey Institute of Public Affairs.

Nichols, B. (2002), "Demographic Characteristics of Arts Attendance," Washington: The National Endowment for the Arts, The Nancy Hanks Center.

NIH (2006), "Dramatic Changes in U.S. Aging Highlighted in New Census, HIH Report," Washington: Department of Commerce, US Census Bureau.

OECD (2005), "Ageing Populations: High Time for Action," Paris: OECD.

United Nations Human Settlements Programme (2006), *The State of the Cities Report*, Minneapolis: League of Minnesota Cities.

William, B. (2006), "Time and Money: Tracking the Fiscal Impact of Demographic Change in Canada," (n. p.): C. D. Howe Institute.

14. Driving factors of urban prosperity: an empirical analysis of global cities

Pengfei Ni[1]

PRESENTING THE ISSUE: THE CHARM OF URBAN PROSPERITY

The pursuit of a happier life has been almost an eternal dream of mankind, and cities are created as symbols of civilization through which humans can realize the happier life. "People come to the city for life and live in the city for the sake of a better life" (Aristotle, ancient Greek sage). However, citizens' happiness lies in the development and prosperity of the cities they live in, and achieving continued prosperity has been an eternal pursuit of many cities ever since they appeared in human history. Among different cities, some have prospered for long periods, others have prospered only briefly, while yet others have gone through rise and fall in their development.

In ancient times, Kaifeng in 1000 AD had a population of over 1 million and served as the political, economic, cultural, and communication center of the world. The book *Dream Record of the Splendor of the Eastern Capital* and the painting *Along the River during Ching Ming Festival* have both vividly depicted the city's prosperity, luxury, power, openness, richness and vitality, making it the most competitive and prosperous city of the era. Kaifeng and its grand momentum lasted nearly two centuries, until industrialization ushered in a new era of urban development and informatization that equipped cities with wings to fly on their way moving forward. Meanwhile they have also caused dramatic changes to the implicit meaning of urban prosperity. In modern times, New York in 2000 had a population of over 8 million and served as a global city, with important impacts on business and finance and influencing directly global media, politics, education, entertainment and fashion. Ever since its establishment in 1613, New York has experienced four centuries of development, two centuries of prosperity and one century of global leadership. Its development has created incredible prosperity and amazing civilization. From 2000 BC to 2000 AD, many cities have grown to become in one period or another world cities – centers of human civilization – including Ur, Memphis, Thebes, Babylon, Xi'an, Luoyang, Athens, Rome, Constantinople, Ctesiphon, Kaifeng, Hangzhou, Beijing, London, Paris, New York, Tokyo, Shanghai, etc. Having all dominated and led human development with their prosperity, these cities and their changes are inspiring people to think deeply.

---

1   Pengfei Ni is Director of the Center for City and Competitiveness at the Chinese Academy of Social Sciences (CASS) and a Professor at the Institute of Finance and Trade Economics at CASS. No. 2 yuetanbeixiaojie, Xicheng District, Beijing, China, post code: 100836, Tel: 8610-68063478. Email: ni_pengfei@163.com.

The prosperity of a city indicates its growth and development towards richness, diversity, and better prospects. According to Simon Smith Kuznets (1966), features of economic growth, which is almost synonymous with economic prosperity, include high production growth in proportion to population, high population growth, high productivity growth, and high speed at which economic structure is reformed as well as social and ideological structures. Traditionally, the key variables to reflect urban prosperity are population as well as residents' income and growth; while a more recent and comprehensive variable to indicate prosperity of a city is urban competitiveness, which in essence is the city's overall performance on a number of key factors. In addition, there is another single variable which is both vivid explicitly and reasonable implicitly: i.e. nighttime lights and their changes, since lights or use of electricity is closely correlated with production, consumption as well as wealth creation.

According to estimates and projections by the United Nations Population Fund on 2,000 cities worldwide, we can roughly get to know both the current and future situation of urban prosperity in the world. For Asia, most cities are growing at high speed and only a few are growing slowly; while the opposite applies to North America and Europe, where only a few cities are developing fast and most are growing at lower speed. In Latin America, some cities grow rapidly, some at normal speed, and some others more slowly. In Africa, some cities are developing quite rapidly. Among all the cities, those in China and India, especially in China, are growing the fastest in terms of urban population growth.

According to econometric research by the Global Urban Competitiveness Project on 500 sample cities (Table 14.1, Figure 14.1), we can understand the geographical distribution of worldwide urban economic growth. Most Asian cities are growing fast and some are growing at lower speed; while most North American and European cities are growing slowly, with only a few developing at faster speed; some cities in Latin America and Africa are growing quite rapidly, but most are only maintaining normal growth. Among all the cities, those in China and India, especially China, are growing the fastest, with 45 Chinese cities included in the top 50 fastest developing cities and 26 out of the 41 Indian sample cities included in the top 200.

A number of scholars (e.g. Xi Chen and William Nordhaus, 2010; Henderson et al., 2009) have researched the positive correlation among energy consumption, population growth, GDP growth and nighttime lights, and have attempted to estimate GDP with data on nighttime lights.

Table 14.1   Geographical Distribution of Worldwide Urban Economic Growth of 500 Cities

	Classification	1-50	1-100	101-200	201-300	301-400	401-500
Region	North America	0	4	18	16	47	22
	Europe	1	9	30	27	31	39
	Asia	48	78	35	32	10	32
	Other	1	9	17	25	12	7
Key Country	USA	0	0	1	10	36	18
	EU	0	0	5	12	31	39
	China	45	62	0	2	2	3
	India	0	5	21	15	0	0

Source: Ni (2012).

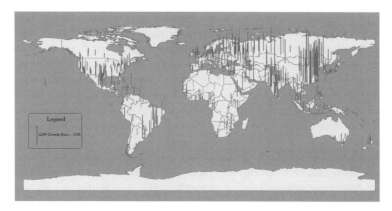

Source: Ni (2012).

Figure 14.1   Geographical Distribution of Worldwide Urban Economic Growth of 500 Cities

As a result of the "Global Nighttime Lights" Project,[2] the satellite images (as shown in Figures 14.2a and 14.2b) vividly present prosperity of global cities by showing changes of nighttime lights on earth from 1992–2009 (with white areas in the originals representing regions with no change, gray areas representing regions with increased lights at night, and black areas representing regions with decreased lights at night in the 17 years). It can be seen from the images that, "economically developed regions in Japan, West Europe, and on the east coast of the US are represented by purple and white showing declining prosperity and stable prosperity respectively. While India, in the South of Asia, and most regions in China are represented by yellow indicating prosperity and high economic growth. Regions in East Europe, especially in former Soviet Union, are mostly represented by purple, indicating a period of serious decline."[3]

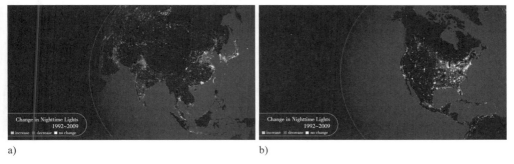

a)   b)

Source: http://www.nnvl.noaa.gov/MediaDetail.php?MediaID=803&MediaTypeID=1&MediaFileID=214.

Figure 14.2a   North America Change in Nighttime Lights 1992-2009
Figure 14.2b   Europe and Asia Change in Nighttime Lights 1992-2009

---

2   "Global Nighttime Lights" is a project by the U.S. National Oceanic and Atmospheric Administration (NOAA), in which it uses data returned by the U.S. Air Force's DMSP satellite to analyze global energy consumption.

3   The description is quoted from "Renewable Energy and the Lights of the World."
     http://www.nnvl.noaa.gov/MediaDetail.php?MediaID=803&MediaTypeID=1&MediaFileID=214.

The above two methods have shown the distribution of and changes in global urban prosperity: some of the world's top cities have been maintaining their prosperity, while others are experiencing gradual decline; some center cities in developed countries are continuing their prosperity, some are declining, and some others have renewed their prosperity after previous decline; some center cities in emerging countries are beginning to prosper rapidly yet some others have shown recession; some popular cities in emerging countries are beginning to emerge but others continue to develop at slower speed; and some cities in underdeveloped countries are beginning to change for the better, while some others have continued their fall.

This has shown a trending situation: the future of urban prosperity has become more and more uncertain, with each city worldwide facing the same opportunities for prosperity and challenges for decline no matter it is an emerging city or a declining city, a big city or a smaller one. For the future of cities, everything is possible. When pursuing a better life in cities and marveling at their prosperity, we have also come to see the fierce competition of urban prosperity and the uncertain future for a city's development. In a time when over 50% of world population are living in cities, who wouldn't like to explore the driving factors of lasting prosperity and the strategic key to maintain urban prosperity?

DRIVING FACTORS OF URBAN PROSPERITY: CONCEPTUAL FRAMEWORK

A city's growth, prosperity and decline are usually determined by various factors, coupling and overlaying with one another. In fact, the degree and contribution of the growth factors vary in different social and economic development stages for different cities. An observation of the thousands of years of urban development has shown that natural location is often the first factor in determining a city's development and prosperity. Business, politics, technology, culture, as well as military and natural factors and their changes can also cause a city to emerge, prosper and decline. For cities in history, there are always more reasons that have affected their prosperity and development. Based on the Cobb–Douglas production function, and combining it with New Growth Theory and thoughts on competitiveness, we could firstly decompose the factors affecting production efficiency A, and put these factors together with direct input factors K and L, then re-classify them into hard factors and soft factors. The soft factors are referred to as "string" and hard factors as "bow", with each category consisting of a number of detailed factors. Based on this, we have built the Bowstring Model to analyze the driving factors of urban prosperity.

Hard Factors Include:

Population and human capital
Population and labor force impact on a city's economic growth and prosperity from both aspects of supply and demand. Becker (1981) pointed out that "households are comprehensive economic players, since they are not only consumption units, but also production units and investment units".

Modern economic growth theory has regarded labor as one of the most fundamental factors of economic growth. Its size and growth affects the size and growth of output and its abundance determines the structure of industry, further affecting the city's attractiveness for capital as well as its development and prosperity. Although simple labor have become less important in urban economies of developed countries, abundant and low-cost labor in the large number of cities in developing countries are combining with the capital attracted to promote prosperity of the cities. In the comparison on economic growth among the 500 sample cities in 2000–2007, 45 out of the 50 fastest developing cities are in China,[4] and the prosperity that many Chinese cities are experiencing today is mainly driven by its labor force.

Human capital has become increasingly essential for urban economic development and prosperity. Improvement of labor quality has pushed along utilization efficiency of physical capital and technology, expanding input of physical capital and technology and making investment in human capital the most important factor for economic growth. Haughton et al. highlighted that human resources make a city attractive for business especially when the skilled labor force is densely concentrated, for this can lower the employment rate and makes it easy to access a widespread commitment to education, training and healthcare. Florida (2002) has argued the presence of such human capital in turn attracts and generates innovative and knowledge-based industries. More recent research (Glaeser et al., 1995; Glaeser, 1999; Simon, 1998) has empirically verified the role of human capital in urban regional growth. Da Mata et al. (2007) prove labor force quality had a strong impact on Brazilian city growth between 1970 and 2000. Abel and Gabe (2011) found that a one percentage point increase in the proportion of residents with a college degree is associated with about a 2% increase in metropolitan area gross domestic product per capita in US metropolitan areas. Edward L. Glaeser (1995) found that income and population growth were positively related to initial schooling between 1960 and 1990.

Population size and income level impact economic prosperity from the perspective of demand. Through the influence on local market size and capacity, they affect the division of labor and productivity, and cast further impacts on economic growth (Adam Smith, 1776). Porter (1990) held that more critical local demand can force local enterprises to improve quality and level of products, so as to enhance cost effectiveness and competitiveness of the products. Advancement of local demand determines enterprises' innovation and their access to super-normal profits. Krugman (1991) holds the view that local market demand is not only important to urban competition, but it is also likely to generate cumulative effects. Nalewaik et al. (2006) used panel data of US individual consumption and individual income for analysis and testing, and found that there is strong positive correlation between individual consumption and income growth. Da Mata et al. (2007) found that increases in market potential for goods had strong impacts on Brazilian city growth between 1970 and 2000.

The status of population and human capital are not only driving factors of a city's urban prosperity, but also an important representation of its prosperity. As rapid increase in wealth and income brings about urban prosperity, it will no doubt attract population and households to concentrate and reproduce. From ancient time to the present, urban population size and its positive or negative changes have always been a major measure of a city's development level as well as its rise and fall.

---

4   Pengfei Ni (2012), *Global Urban Competitiveness Report–2011*, Edward Elgar Publishing.

Financial and physical capital

Physical capital refers to material products serving as capital (including plant, machinery, equipment, raw materials, land, money, other securities, etc.), which are indispensable fundamental factors of urban economic growth and prosperity. Investment and accumulation of physical capital are important driving forces of economic development, and the classical theory of economic growth has emphasized the role of physical capital. Although capital is becoming increasingly mobile, availability of affordable local capital is still an important factor in competitiveness, particularly to small and medium-sized enterprises, especially domestic ones (Webster and Muller, 2000).

On the whole, general physical capital becomes less important in economic growth and competition in the era of the knowledge economy, yet for cities lacking high-end capital, physical capital is still very important to their economic growth and prosperity. However, with regard to specific cities, their local physical resources and product abundance are not directly related to the city's economic prosperity. In the course of human history, there have been cases of economic prosperity as a result of resource abundance, yet rich natural resources may also be a curse rather than a blessing for economic development. Many countries endowed with rich natural resources are developing at a slower pace than those with scare resources. The key lies in how to turn local resources into capital with investment or introduce external capital to achieve an increase in capital stock. And in both processes, financial services play a vital role.

Financial development is a key factor to promote economic growth (Levine et al., 2000; Levine, 1997). The financial system is very critical to enhance resource allocation efficiency, reduce transaction costs and improve capital utilization efficiency.

A sound financial service system can facilitate investment, thus enhancing a city's attractiveness for investment and promoting its growth. A good idea is not enough; businesses need to be able to mobilize financing for investment from the financial system. A sound financial service system can facilitate trade and enhance a city's attractiveness for products and services, so as to promote growth in trade. Similarly, a sound financial service system can also facilitate consumption and enhance a city's attractiveness in terms of consumption and promote growth. In addition, a sophisticated financial service system can also promote innovation and enhance a city's attractiveness for innovative factors. All these can promote economic growth and prosperity of a city, while financial repression, on the contrary, will hinder a city's development.

As a core industry of a city, the financial industry serves investment, trade and consumption as well as all industries and sectors. Its growth can not only result in increased aggregate output of the city, but also growth in various industries which can help optimize industrial structure and promote urban prosperity. According to a UN-Habitat analysis of the 245 fastest growing cities in developing countries, development of service-related sectors including finance, communications, and trade are the third largest contributor of urban development, explaining 16%[5] of urban economic growth.

Financial centers are key driving forces of urban prosperity. Kindleberger (1974) holds that there are economies of scale in financial market organization, forming clustering forces

---

5   South African Cities Network (2006).

among the financial market. And regional differences and local information are also major reasons for the agglomeration of financial markets. Concentrating financial organizations and related services as well as financial factors and activities, financial centers can not only help cities enjoy the agglomeration effect, external economies of scale, spillover effect and learning effect, but also achieve concentration of company headquarters, through which a city can command and control even the global economy and gain regional as well as global wealth. Ever since the 15th century, a number of cities have served as international financial centers and world economic centers, experiencing cycles of prosperity and decline. Among them, some of the better-known ones include Venice, Genoa, Florence, Amsterdam, London, New York, Paris, Zurich, Frankfurt, Tokyo, Singapore, Bahrain, the Bahamas, the Cayman Islands, Honk Kong and so on.

Innovation and technology

Advancement in science and technology has always been a key driving force in leading human progress, and hence a key dynamic in driving urban prosperity. Technological level can directly affect a city's productivity. Solow (1957) has noted the effect of technology on economic growth. Gruber et al. (1967) think that R&D is also a factor of production. Technological innovation is the source of urban economic growth and social progress. Recent theories of economic growth, including those of Romer, Porter, and Jacobs, have all stressed the role of technological spillovers in generating growth.

Some historians have argued that most innovations are made in cities (Jacobs 1969; Bairoch 1988). Jacobs (1969) argues that interactions between people in cities help them get ideas and innovate, since such knowledge spillovers are particularly effective in cities, where communication between people is more extensive. The creation and diffusion of new knowledge drives innovation in knowledge-intensive production and service activities, which in turn drives economic performance and growth.

Technological innovation belongs to all mankind. In addition to the effects of globalization and nationalization, it also presents the effect of localization, since research results are more often diffused, transformed and applied in local cities. Moreover, technological innovation can also generate greater attractiveness for human capital and physical capital. Regional knowledge stocks related to the provision of producer services and information technology are important determinants of economic vitality (Abel and Gabe, 2011). University activities, particularly knowledge-based activities, have been found to have substantial positive effects on a variety of measures of regional economic progress since the mid-1980s (Drucker and Goldstein, 2007). Sonn and Storper (2003) find that inventors cite local patents increasingly over time. Silicon Valley in the US, Japan's Tsukuba, Zhongguancun in Beijing, China, India's Bangalore and a number of other places around the world concentrated with universities and research institutions all serve as good examples where local high-tech industries are developed as a result of local applications of technological achievements. Meanwhile, such development has also attracted talents, technology and capital from outside the cities to better promote sustainable prosperity of local economies.

In the case of a specific city, technological innovation is not enough, and scientific research achievement is often more important in determining the city's prosperity. A city cannot realize its due growth and prosperity if it only excels in innovation but lacks the ability to transform such innovations, i.e. Daejeon of Korea and China's Wuhan, Nanjing, etc. On the contrary, a city with less creativity can still achieve outstanding growth and prosperity if it can successfully transform external scientific research results locally. Shenzhen of China is a good example, where a city lacking technological resources can still implement technology transformation to lead high-speed economic growth.

Some researchers have found considerable regional differences in the level and utilization of innovation and high-tech industry (Markusen et al., 1986; DeVol 1999). In fact, approximately 20 metropolitan regions account for most of the world's technological innovation. And they are also the most prosperous regions in the world, no matter whether in terms of nighttime lights or GDP statistics. As the global technological center, San Jose in Silicon Valley has always maintained sustainable prosperity and growth.

Connection and infrastructure

Connection is a basic human activity. As a central issue of communication, the degree of exchanges and ties among urban economic entities impacts the utilization of external capital and markets, learning and innovation, as well as transaction costs and production efficiency. Jacobs (1969) argues that these interactions between people in cities help them get ideas and innovate. Saxenian (1994) identifies Silicon Valley as a model industrial district, with high rates of growth and innovation flowing from its dense geographic networks of technology firms. Manuel Castells (1996) points out that a city "is not a place but a process", indicating that cities are interrelated global networks. Larsson and Lundmark (1991) and Angel and Engstorm (1995) all hold the view that global connection is even more important than local connection, since it is an essential way to improve and upgrade their own ability by participating in the global value chain. Research by Pengfei Ni and Peter Taylor has indicated that among the global 500 cities, those showing the strongest international connections are also the ones with comparatively higher per capita income and better urban competitiveness. Bathelt et al. (2004) conclude that innovation and new knowledge creation is best understood as a combination of local and global interactions.

Infrastructure is a major means to ensure transaction and communications among economic entities. Advanced and convenient infrastructure can not only enable a city to better utilize external markets and resources but also help enhance its attractiveness for talents, technology, investment, and trade, so as to improve production and transaction efficiency while reducing costs. Meanwhile, infrastructure such as railways, roads, harbors, airports, telecommunications, the Internet etc. are also part of a city's physical capital. Therefore, investment in infrastructure has dual impacts on a city's growth and prosperity. Aschauer (1989) and Borensztein et al. (1998) proved physical infrastructure's ability to facilitate wealth creation with empirical analysis. An UN-Habitat analysis of the 245 fastest growing cities in developing countries shows that investment in transport infrastructure is the most fundamental source of urban development, capable of explaining more than 1/3 of the cities' growth.

Agglomeration of industries and cities

Agglomeration is the most basic feature of a city. Krugman (1991) points out that "looking back, if we ask the most important geographical characteristics of economic activities, the simplest answer is of course agglomeration."

Spatial concentration of economic activities in a city leads to such concentration on an even larger scale due to reduced transaction and innovation costs, which further stimulates economic growth and widens the gap between center and peripheral regions. Spatial concentration and economic growth are essentially an endogenous process of mutual influence, in which different spatial concentration of economic activities is an important determinant of gaps in local economic growth and labor productivity, while the difference in economic growth also affects spatial concentration of the industries (Martin and Ottaviano, 1999, 2001; Fujita and Thisse, 2002; Baldwin et al., 2003). The highly correlated relationship between economic growth and agglomerate economy has already been widely recognized and proved by historians (Hohenberg and Lees, 1985).

Agglomeration implies that all innovation and most production activities take place in the core region: Population concentration facilitates the dissemination and exchange of knowledge and ideas, thus helping improve innovation and human capital. Population density enables better transfer of information and knowledge spillover that enhance growth and attract those who most likely benefit from extensive information flows (Jacobs, 1969; Glaeser et al., 1992; Audretsch and Feldman, 1996; Gehrig, 1998; Glaeser, 1999). A positive relationship exists between the density of creative workers and metropolitan patenting activity (Knudsen et al., 2007). Antonio Ciccone and Robert E. Hall (1993) found a doubling of employment density increases average labor productivity by around 6 percent using data across the United States.

Industrial agglomeration can enable firms to share the same inputs, share labor pools, and improve productivity of labor (Henderson, 1986), influence enterprises' location choices (Head et al., 1995), bring about knowledge spillovers, increase number of new enterprises (Dumais et al., 2002), and improve employment (Rosenthal and Strange, 2003). On the economic map of the world today, the large number of industrial clusters has formed a colorful and distinct "economic mosaic", creating most of the world's wealth within these blocks. Northeast and central Italy are dotted with small and medium-sized cities, which is closely related to the proliferation of industrial clusters. The rise of Prato into an important industrial town is exactly the result of hundreds of SME clusters in the region. In the US, the 380 cross-sector company clusters are employing 57% of the labor force and creating 61% of its national output. In the 1990s, four regional clusters gradually took shape in California, promoting strong economic growth for California and presenting a great example of regional prosperity for world attention. In Germany, clusters of enterprises specializing in automobile, electronics, information technology and software have promoted prosperity in Munich, Stuttgart, Nuremberg, the Rhine-Neckar Region, the Karlsruhe Region, the Darmstadt/ Starkenburg Region, the Cologne/Bonn Region, the Hanover Region, Berlin, Hamburg, etc. Clusters of SMEs for machinery and equipment manufacturing promoted a 38% employment growth in the Bodensee and Oberschwaben Region in 2000–2004. During the same time period, emerging biomedical clusters in the south of Germany promoted employment to grow 30% in the Ulm Region and 21% in the Nuremberg/Erlangen Region. In France, the 67 key industrial clusters of different levels are important factors determining the degree of urban prosperity. And in Finland, ICT industrial clusters are the propeller of its knowledge-based national economy.

The clustering of cities into mega-regions, urban corridors and city-regions operating as single economic entities sets in motion self-reinforcing, cumulative growth patterns that are making a significant contribution to the world's economic activity. Reduction in intercity-transport costs had strong impacts on Brazilian city growth between 1970 and 2000 (Da Mata et al., 2007). They point out that population density enables better transfer of information and knowledge spillover that enhances growth and attracts those who will most likely benefit from extensive information flows (learning hypothesis). Global 150 Metropolitan accounted for just under 12 percent of global population, but generated approximately 46 percent of world GDP in 2007 (Allard and Roth, 2010).

Location and ecological environment

Although natural location is not a direct factor of economic growth, it can affect the costs of economic activities, thereby affecting agglomeration of population, commodities, investment and trade and stimulating economic growth. Despite the fact that improved communication and transport technologies have reduced the importance of location to certain degree, a favorable natural location can help attract external population and capital, since locations near coastlines and navigable rivers can reduce transport costs to promote trade, a location near natural resources can help reduce production costs, and a location near major cities and urban agglomerations can get close to markets and factors of production (UN-Habitat, 2009). Throughout the history of urban development, we can see the first cities were often formed in better natural locations. Of course geographical factors are not the only reasons for urban growth and prosperity and some cities' prosperity may have nothing to do with their geographical advantages, yet a city established on the basis of relative geographical advantage can often prosper due to its economic agglomeration and good urban management.

Human activities need appropriate natural environment conditions, and the higher level talents and industries need higher quality of ecological environment. The attractiveness and condition of the natural environment are certainly important (Florida, 2002). Urban growth was described as a response to movements of people in search of consumer or lifestyle preferences, and amenities have an especially potent effect on the migration patterns of individuals endowed with high levels of human capital. Because of their advantageous ecological systems, coastal areas in the world are the most advanced in urbanization, with 65% of total population settling in cities (UN-Habitat, 2009). Climate environment affects health and lifespan of the population as well as concentration of population and industries. Tropical areas' relative underdevelopment lies mainly in factors concerning local temperature, soil and so on Bloom et al. (1998). World population is mainly concentrated in temperate and subtropical regions.

Quality of a city's air, water, soil and ecological environment affects the health of people and industries. And high-end talents are even more sensitive to environment, with environmental quality becoming increasingly important for development of high-end industries. Meadows et al. (1972) proved through empirical study that environmental pollution is an important factor affecting economic growth. The quality-of-life or urban amenities have been found to matter in the location decisions of high human capital households (Glaeser and Shapiro, 2001). An observation of cities promoting their prosperity with science and technological innovations shows that many also have the world's top ecological environment and quality of life, e.g. San Jose, Vienna, Stockholm, Helsinki, Seattle, Singapore, etc.

Soft Factors Include:

Security and social harmony

Social environment also impacts urban economic growth and prosperity in an indirect but important way. The underlying social dynamics of urban regions are particularly significant in shaping economic output (Bramwell and Wolfe, 2008). The quality of place is also a significant factor underlying the social dynamics of city regions and in turn influences their economic performance (Florida, 2002).

Urban security relates to happiness of the citizens as well as entrepreneurial dynamics. Meanwhile, it also affects companies' business costs and a city's attractiveness for talents and investment. A city will be more attractive to business if crime rate is low. Da Mata et al. (2007) find that local crime and violence impinged on Brazilian city growth between 1970 and 2000. Safe cities such as Luxembourg, Bern, Geneva, Zurich, Hong Kong and Singapore have become chosen destinations for talents and investment, with their cities prospering long term; while those undergoing wars and turmoil all suffer negative economic growth and recession, e.g. Abidjan, the economic capital of Cote d'Ivoire, the Central African Republic's capital Bangui, Lagos and Port Harcourt in Nigeria, and Colombia's capital Bogota.

Racial discrimination, income gaps, and social segregation not only hinder the free and frequent communications among urban residents, but also threaten social security. Edward L. Glaeser (1995) found racial composition and segregation was positively correlated with population growth in cities with large nonwhite community segregation between 1960 and 1990.

Social infrastructure and services are part of physical capitals, influencing the growth of a city's investment in human capital and materials. Scale, quality and constitution of medical, sports, entertainment, leisure services and facilities in a city are directly related to the citizens' physical and mental health. Such factors are also important in attracting and maintaining talent migration. For a city, education is essential not only for cultivating talents, but also for attracting talents and bolstering innovation. Development of Boston, Silicon Valley, Oxford and Cambridge clearly benefited from the presence of famous universities in these cities. In an era of an increasingly mobile workforce and industry, a city's urban culture and "livability" can impact on not only its existing residents and economy, but also potential future residents and businesses (Kitson et al., 2004). In Mercer's annual quality of living ranking, the best performing cities are also enjoying higher per capita incomes and faster economic growth and prosperity, such as Geneva, Zurich, Vancouver, Vienna, Frankfurt, and Munich.

Government regulation and service

Government plays an indispensable but challenging role in promoting urban prosperity, where it can help compensate for market deficiencies as a visible hand. Well-administered and well-governed cities that are open to new ideas, cultures and technologies can act as a host country's best catalyst of economic growth and human development.[6]

In fact, all governments have greater or lesser impacts on urban development, no matter whether it is the central, provincial (state) or municipal government or in terms of its political, economic, cultural or social functions. La Porta et al. (1999) believe that a region's economy can operate better when the local government establishes a fair competitive

---

6   *The State of African Cities 2010: Governance, Inequality and Urban.*

environment, when officials are more concerned with implementing rules of market orientation and efficiency promotion instead of maximizing bureaucratic budgets, and when the government is capable of providing enough resources to establish an economic environment with sufficient supply of public goods. Michael E. Porter (1990) pointed out that government should become "the dynamic source of driving force for enterprises' rapid innovation in technology and methods, as well as the nerve center to guide enterprises' development in appropriate directions". A city will be more attractive to business if public officials are trusted (Haughton et al., 2005).

History has amply shown that industrialization and urban productivity will progress faster where government takes a pro-active, enabling role. Europe, North America, Japan and, more recently, East Asia have all shown that successful socio-economic development follows proactive government assistance to urban-based industrial development, especially through enhanced transportation systems (UN-Habitat, 2009).

Market mechanism and policies
As the key to economic growth and development, market mechanism is a fundamental determinant of the incentives of private individuals to innovate and invest. Through incentives, constraints, delimitation of property rights and transaction cost reduction, market mechanism can impact investment, innovation and efficiency, which in turn will affect economic growth. The better market mechanism is usually accompanied by higher level of investment, faster technological progress and higher level of labor division. As a result, the faster productivity improves, the faster the economy can grow. There is a growing consensus that the institutional milieu is one of, if not the only, key factors in explaining the competitiveness of successful regions, particularly in more developed economies (Porter, 1990; Saxenian, 1994; Storper, 1997). There is the evidence for a link between the quality of institutions and investment and growth (Aron, 2000).

Market mechanism makes up a complete system. On the one hand, all institutions are interdependent, interactive, interchangeable and mutually exclusive, making up the institutional environment influencing investment, innovation and production efficiency. On the other hand, some related institutions also play a key role for economic growth.

Property rights system is a core aspect of economic systems, since a clear property rights system and an effective property rights protection system can motivate individuals to make efforts in directions close to both private benefits and social benefits, so as to promote economic development and technological innovation. A growing literature has documented the importance of good institutions that protect property rights for growth in the very long run (Acemoglu et al., 2005; Hall and Jones, 1999; Engermann and Sokoloff, 2000; and many others).

The quality of administrative institutions involving internal relationships between central and local governments can influence urban development. In an era characterized by economic globalization and global competition, local governments are enjoying more advantages than central governments in decision-making relating to urban development. A decentralized arrangement between central and local governments can stimulate local governments to better commit to urban economic prosperity. An increase in the degree of democracy leads to faster city formation, less of the national population growth being accommodated in bigger cities, and a reduction in the degree of spatial inequality. Democratization implies the election of regional representatives to a national assembly which leads to increased regional representation. According to a UN-Habitat analysis of the 245 fastest growing cities in developing countries, the special economic zone factor related to institutions can explain 20.8% of urban growth, and administrative changes can explain 12.2% of urban growth.

The quality of market regulations involving relationships between government and market can influence business cost and efficiency of an organization, and thus affect a city's attractiveness for investment. The World Bank's "Doing Business Report" on over 100 countries and regions worldwide measures local cities' business regulations and their implementation. The report shows cities with better business environment also enjoy higher per capita income and those with fastest improving business environment are also growing the fastest in their local economies, e.g. Singapore, Hong Kong SAR, China, New Zealand (Wellington), the United States (New York), Denmark (Copenhagen), Norway (Oslo), the United Kingdom (London), and the Republic of Korea (Seoul).

Culture and social values

Culture is an informal institution, and culture directly influences individual behavior through values and preferences (e.g. Akerlof and Kranton, 2000; Rabin, 1993). Drucker (1995) holds the view that culture is indeed the dominant resource and absolute decisive factor of production. Culture can be translated as the social norms and the individual beliefs that sustain Nash equilibrium as focal points in repeated social interactions (e.g. Schotter, 1981; Myerson et al., 1991; Greif, 1994).

As social morality and personal belief, culture can influence individual behavior and social order, which in turn determines the economic vitality. Porter (2000) stresses the rules, incentives and norms that encourage investment, vigorous competition, and sustained upgrading. Joseph Alois Schumpeter (1942) emphasized the proactive, adventurous, and failure tolerating entrepreneurial spirits that promote innovation under profit-making motives, while innovation determines economic prosperity. Saxenian (1994) stressed that an easy, tolerant, free, equal and carefree culture can create a favorable atmosphere for innovation.

ECONOMETRIC RESULT ANALYSIS[7]

Index Selection and Data Processing

Firstly, 500 sample cities are selected worldwide according to standards and methods provided in the Global Urban Competitiveness Report 2010, and then categorized into 5 groups, i.e. highest income group, high-income group, middle-income group, low-income group, and lowest income group, based on their GDP per capita (These are comparative

---

7   Econometrical analysis in this project is conducted by the Global Urban Competitiveness Group, whose members including Pengfei Ni, Chao Li, and Wei Liu.

groups based on the 500 sample cities and are different from income groups defined by the World Bank and others.)

Secondly, we selected GDP per capita as explained variables to reflect urban development and selected indexes in Table 14.2 as explanatory variables. We then extracted data from the "Urban Competitiveness Index Database" (Chinese Academy of Social Sciences) (uci.cass) for standardization.

Table 14.2   Factors Influencing Urban Prosperity and their Index Names

Index Name	Implication	Notation
Population Index	labor force	pop
Patent Index	technological innovation	pat
Freedom Index	market mechanism	free
Ratio of Central and Local Tax Revenue	economic institutions	tax
Number of Flights	infrastructure	fli
MNC Index	global connection	mnc
Education Index	human capital	edu
Multilingualism Index	diverse culture	lan
Distance to Sea	natural location	dis
CO_2 Emission	environmental quality	co2
Ease of Doing Business	government regulation	edb
Crime Rate	social security	cri
Bank Index	financial services	bank

Econometric Model

Based on the influencing factors, we establish a multi-factor econometric model for urban economic development,

$$pergdp = \alpha_1 + \beta_1 pop + \beta_2 pat + \beta_3 free + \beta_4 tax + \beta_5 fli + \beta_6 mnc + \beta_7 edu + \beta_8 lan + \beta_9 dis$$
$$+ \beta_{10} co2 + \beta_{11} edb + \beta_{12} cri + \beta_{13} bank + e$$

in which, α_1 is constant, β_n represents coefficient of various influencing factors, and e is stochastic disturbance.

Analytical Methods and Econometric Results

The first step is significance testing on influencing factors; the second step is analysis on influencing (contributing) factors of urban economic growth using fuzzy curve analysis method so as to indentify the most important factor; the third step is group analysis on influencing factors of economic growth in different income groups using fuzzy curve analysis method to identify the most important factor; and the fourth step is regression analysis on the most important influencing factor and urban GDP.

Table 14.3   Regression Results on Influencing Factors of Urban Prosperity for Different City Groups

Sample Variables	All Samples	High-Income Cities	Upper Middle-Income Cities	Middle-Income Cities	Lower Middle-Income Cities	Low-Income Cities
Pop	-0.117***				-0.191	0.063
Pat	0.157***	0.170	0.100	-0.077	0.367***	
Free	0.332***	-0.288**	0.313**	0.068		
tax	-0.291	0.072	0.058	-0.373***		51.75***
fli	0.050	-0.064	0.174	-0.205**		-52.709***
mnc	0.055*	0.085	-0.194	0.247***		
edu	0.262***		-0.017	0.538***		
lan	0.111***	0.296**		-0.023		
dis	0.056**					-0.026
CO_2	0.012				-0.091	
edb	0.243***					0.774
cri	-0.049*					
ban	0.035				0.133	
Samples of cities	499	99	101	107	88	105
F-test	145.25***	3.54***	2.23**	13.44***	2.90**	3.68**
Adjusted R^2	0.79	0.13	0.07	0.45	0.08	0.11

Note: ***, ** and * represent significant at 1%, 5% and 10% significance levels respectively.

Different Influencing Factors for Different Types of Cities

The above econometric analysis (Table 14.3) shows that influencing factors vary for different groups of cities each with their own features.

First, All Samples: Market Mechanism Represented by Economic Freedom is the Primary Factor of Urban Prosperity. The above econometric results show that labor force, technological innovation, market mechanism, economic institutions, infrastructure, global connection, human capital, diverse culture, natural location, environmental quality, government regulation, social security, and financial services are all important influencing factors. Among all the explanatory variables passing the significance testing, the three most influential factors are: freedom index > education index > ease of doing business. This suggests that market mechanism represented by economic freedom is the most important factor of urban prosperity. Increasingly improved market mechanism and higher degree of economic freedom can benefit a city's economic development; meanwhile improved education and increased accumulation of human capital in a city also presented obvious positive effects on urban growth. Better business environment has an invaluable effect on a city's ability to attract investment. In addition, technological innovation represented by patent licensing and diverse culture represented by multilingualism are both essential to a city's economic development. It is also worth noting that population index has a significant negative impact on urban development, indicating that with concentrating population and growing city size, the negative impact of population pressure on urban economic development will become more and more prominent.

Second, High-Income Cities: Diverse and Prosperous Culture is a Key Factor for Further Development and Excessive Liberalization Would Hinder Economic Growth. For high-income cities, technological innovation, market mechanism, economic institutions, infrastructure, global connection, and diverse culture are all important influencing factors. Among the two factors passing the significance test, freedom index has negative impact on urban growth, which is different from that for all samples. This suggests that when income moves up to a certain level, excessive liberalization would restrain instead of facilitate economic growth. The relationship between market mechanism and economic growth resembles an inverted U-shape curve, and the high-income countries have gone over the flex point. Meanwhile, diverse culture represented by multilingualism index is a key factor for high-income cities in their current development. Cultural diversity and inclusiveness is the fundamental driving force for development of high-income cities, when they have developed to a certain level.

Third, Upper Middle-Income Cities: Improved Market Mechanism is the Only Factor for Prosperity. It goes without saying that improving market mechanism would promote growth. For upper middle-income cities, technological innovation, market mechanism, economic institutions, infrastructure, and human capital are all important influencing factors, but the only one that passed the significance test is market mechanism represented by the freedom index. This shows that improved market mechanism and deepened market growth lie at the heart of urban development for upper middle-income cities in the current stage. For this type of city, many have experienced greater or lesser problems in the process of marketization, and resolving such problems is a primary consideration for upper middle-income cities.

Fourth, Middle-Income Cities: Human Capital Accumulation is Key to Development, but Imperfect Economic Institutions are Posing Serious Negative Influences. For middle-income cities, technological innovation, market mechanism, economic institutions, infrastructure, global connection, human capital, and diverse culture are all important factors for development. Among them, human capital represented by education index and business environment are both positively related and have passed the significance test. Education index, in particular, has the greatest influence on growth of this type of city, indicating that human capital accumulation, especially improvement of people's quality, is the current focus to drive growth. In addition, business environment can directly influence middle-income cities' ability to attract investment, showing an obvious positive role for economic growth. Furthermore, it is worth noting that inadequate infrastructure and imperfect economic institutions of middle-income cities are causing negative effects on their growth. For middle-income cities, it is critical to improve both their hard and soft environment to achieve future development.

Fifth, Lower Middle-Income Cities: Technological Innovation is the Soul of Current Development. For lower middle-income cities, labor force, technological innovation, environmental quality, and financial services are all important factors. However, the only one that has passed the significance test is patent index, indicating that technological innovation is the soul of urban prosperity for this type of city. The introduction and absorption of appropriate technologies as well as drawing on others' innovations and making independent innovations are the keys to development for lower middle-income cities in certain periods. Only by making leaps and bounds from manufacturing to creation can these cities promote their economic growth.

Sixth, Low-Income Cities: Lack of Infrastructure is A Primary Issue to Solve in Development. For low-income cities, labor force, economic institutions, infrastructure, natural location, and government regulation are all important factors, but only economic institutions and infrastructure have passed the significance test. Inadequate infrastructure can have a serious negative impact on economic growth, while economic institutions have positive impact on urban economic growth, indicating that the initial establishment of economic systems and improved local government autonomy can generate huge marginal contribution to urban growth in low-income cities. Yet this does not mean that low-income cities have already established complete and profound urban economic institutions.

CONCLUSION

In summary, prosperity factors for different types of cities follow the fundamental rule that influencing factors vary in different development stages, from hard environment to soft environment, from specific capital to cultural institutions, and from a basic mechanism of exogenous growth to endogenous growth, so the paper is of significant reference value for cities in different development stages.

Our study shows, firstly, global urban prosperity is not evenly distributed, and keeps changing; secondly, driving factors of urban prosperity are varied and complex, in which global connection, technological innovation, and institutional innovation are the most critical, yet such factors also differ in different stages in a city's development.

With deepening globalization, rapidly changing technology, and ever-intensified global competition, the global urban landscape is undergoing tremendous changes. Every city in the world needs to get into action if it wants to achieve rapid development, sustain prosperity and avoid decline and marginalization. Such efforts may include: firstly, seize key factors in common, i.e. making full use of external factors, markets and opportunities to expand global connection, actively developing education to foster human capital, providing sustained incentives for technological innovation, and continuing to implement institutional innovation; secondly, utilize unique and important factors, i.e. seeking, nurturing and using unique and important factors to stimulate self growth according to its own specific development stage and urban features; and thirdly, make up appropriate development strategies, i.e. forming a unique and adequate urban prosperity strategy on the basis of previous successful experience.

BIBLIOGRAPHY

Aaker, David A. (1991), *Managing Brand Equity: Capitalizing on the Value of a Brand Name*, New York: The Free Press.
Abel, J. R. and Gabe, T. M. (2011), 'Human capital and economic activity in urban America', *Regional Studies*, 45(8), 1079–1090.
Acemoglu, D., Johnson, S. and Robinson, J. A. (2005), 'Institutions as a fundamental cause of long-run growth', in Aghion, P. and Durlauf, S.D. (eds), *Handbook of Economic Growth*, Vol. 1, Amsterdam: Elsevier, pp. 385–472.
Akerlof, G. A. and Kranton, R. E. (2000), 'Economics and identity', *Quarterly Journal of Economics*, 115(3), 715–753.
Allard, S. W. and Roth, B. (2010), 'Strained suburbs: the social service challenges of rising suburban poverty', Brookings Institution Metropolitan Policy Program.
Angel, D. P. and Engstrom, J. (1995), 'Manufacturing systems and technological change: the US personal computer industry', *Economic Geography*, 79–102.
Anholt, Simon (2005), 'The Ahholt–GMI City Brand Index: how the world sees the world's cities', *Place Branding*, 2(1), 18–31.
APEC 2004 (2004), 'Realizing Innovation and Human Capital Potential in APEC', Singapore.
Arcy, E. D. and Keogh, G. (1999), 'The property market and urban competitiveness: a review', *Urban Studies*, 36, 917–928.
Aron, J. (2000), 'Growth and institutions: a review of the evidence', *The World Bank Research Observer*, 15(1), 99–135.
Arrow, Kenneth J. (1970), *Public Investment, the Rate of Return, and Optimal Fiscal Policy*, Baltimore: The Johns Hopkins Press.
Arto, E. W. (1987), 'Relative total costs: an approach to competitiveness measurement of industries', *Management International Review*, 27, 47–58.
Aschauer, David Alan (1989), 'Is public expenditure productive?', *Journal of Monetary Economics*, 23, 177–200.
Audretsch, D. B. and Feldman, M. P. (1996), 'R&D spillovers and the geography of innovation and production', *The American Economic Review*, 86(3), 630–640.
Austrian Embassy, China (2006), 'Australian Government information and services', http://www.china.embassy.gov.au/bjing/australia.html (accessed 27 March 2008).
Bairoch, P. (1988), *Cities and Economic Development: From the Dawn of History to the Present*, Chicago: University of Chicago Press.
Baldwin, R., Forslid, R., Martin, P., Ottaviano, G. and Robert-Nicoud, F. (2003), 'The core-periphery model: key features and effects', *Public Policies and Economic Geography*, Princeton: Princeton University Press.
Barro, R. J. and Sala-i-Martin, X. (1996), *Economic Growth*, New York: McGraw-Hill.
Bathelt, H., Malmberg, A. and Maskell, P. (2004), 'Clusters and knowledge: local buzz, global pipelines and the process of knowledge creation', *Progress in Human Geography*, 28(1), 31–56.
Becker, G. S. (1981), 'Altruism in the family and selfishness in the market place', *Economica*, 48(189), 1–15.

Becker, Gary S. (1962), 'Investment in Human Capital: A Theoretical Analysis', *The Journal of Political Economy*, 70, 9–49.

Begg, I. (1999), 'Cities and competitiveness', *Urban Studies*, 36, 795–809.

Begg, I. (2000), *Urban Competitiveness: Policies for Dynamic Cities*, Bristol: Policy Press.

Begg, Iain (1999), 'Social exclusion and social protection in the European Union: policy issues and proposals for the future role of the EU'.

Berg, L.V. D. and Braun, E. (1999), 'Urban Competitiveness, Marketing and the Need for Organising Capacity', *Urban Studies*, 36(5), 987–999.

Bloom, D. E., Sachs, J. D., Collier, P. and Udry, C. (1998), 'Geography, demography, and economic growth in Africa', *Brookings Papers on Economic Activity*, 2, 207–295.

Boddy, M. (1999), 'Geographical Economics and Urban Competitiveness: A Critique', *Urban Studies*, 36(5), 811–842.

Boddy, Martin and Michael Parkinson (2004), *City Matters: Competitiveness, Cohesion and Urban Governance*, Bristol: Policy Press.

Borensztein, E., José De Gregorio and Jong-Wha Lee (1998), 'How Does Foreign Direct Investment Affect Economic Growth?', *Journal of International Economics*, 45, 115–135.

Bovee, C. L. and W.F. Arens (1992), *Contemporary Advertising*, 4th edn, Homewood, IL: Irwin.

Bramwell, A. and Wolfe, D. A. (2008), 'Universities and regional economic development: the entrepreneurial University of Waterloo', *Research Policy*, 37(8), 1175–1187.

Budd, L. and Parr, J.B. (2000), 'Financial Services and the Urban System: An Exploration', *Urban Studies*, 37, 593–610.

Burgess, E. (1928), 'Residential Segregation in American Cities', *Annals of the American Academy of Political and Social Science*, 140, 105–115.

Burgess, E. W. and Harvey J. Locke (1945), *The Family, From Institution to Companionship*, New York: American Book Company.

Camagni, R. (2002), 'Urban Studies on the Concept of Territorial Competitiveness: Sound or Misleading?', *Urban Studies*, 39(13), 2395–2411.

Camagni, Roberto (2002), 'Urban mobility and urban form: the social and environmental costs of different patterns of urban expansion', *Ecological Economics*, 40, 199–216.

Castells, M. (1996), *The Rise of the Network Society*, Volume 1, The Information Age: Economy, Society and Culture, Oxford: Blackwell.

Cellini, R. and A. Soci (2002), 'Pop Competitiveness, Banca Nazionale del Lavoro', *Quarterly Review*, 55(220), 71–101.

Chen, X. and Nordhaus, W. D. (2010), 'The value of luminosity data as a proxy for economic statistics', NBER Working Paper No. 16317.

Chen, Zhaofeng (2006), 'Shenzhen innovative urban construction of regional innovation system of competitive advantage', *Science & Technology and Economy*, 4, 3–8.

Chenery, H.B., S. Robinson and M. Syrquin (1986), *Industrialization and Growth: A Comparative Study*, Washington D.C.: A World Bank Publication.

Cheshire, P., Carbonaro, G. and Hay, D. (1986), 'Problems of Urban Decline and Growth in EEC Countries: Or Measuring Degrees of Elephantness', *Urban Studies*, 2, 131–149.

Cheshire, P.C. and Malecki, E. J. (2004), 'Growth, development, and innovation: a look backward and forward', *Regional Science*, 83(1), 249–267.

Cheshire, Paul C. and Ian R. Gordon (1998), 'Territorial Competition: Some Lessons for Policy', *The Annals of Regional Science*, 32(3), 321–346.

Chussil, M. (1991), 'Does market share really matter?', *Planning Review*, 19, 31–37.

Ciccone, A. and Hall, R. E. (1993), 'Productivity and the density of economic activity', NBER Working Paper No. 4313.

City of Toronto Culture Division (2005), 'Culture plan progress report', http://www.toronto.ca/ (accessed 18 February 2008).

Clark, T. and V. Hoffmann-Martinot (eds) (1998), *The New Political Culture*, Lightning Press.

Corfee-Morlot, J., L. Kamal-Chaoui, M.G. Donovan, I. Cochran, A. Robert and P. J. Teasdale (2009), 'Cities, Climate Change and Multilevel Governance', *OECD Environmental Working Paper*, No. 14.

Cortright, Joseph (2002), 'The Economic Importance of Being Different: Regional Variations in Tastes, Increasing Returns, and the Dynamics of Development', *Economic Development*, 16, 2–16.

Da Mata, D., Deichmann, U., Henderson, J.V., Lall, S.V. and Wang, H.G. (2007), 'Determinants of city growth in Brazil', *Journal of Urban Economics*, 62(2), 252–272.

Deal, Terrence E. and Allan A. Kennedy (1982), 'Corporate Culture', *The American Economic Review*, 56–58.

Dee, P. and K. Hanslow (2000), 'Multilateral Liberalization of Services Trade', *Productivity Commission Staff Research Paper*.

DeVol, Ross C. (1999), 'America's High-Tech Economy: Growth, Development, and Risks for Metropolitan Areas', Santa Monica: Milken Institute, 13 July.

Dong-Sung Cho (2007), 'Korea city competitiveness report', working paper 2007.8, Seoul: Institute for Industrial Policy Studies.

Dong-Sung Cho and Hwy-Chang Moon (2000), *From Adam Smith to Michael Porter, Evolution of Competitiveness Theory*, Singapore: World Scientific.

Dreyer, J., (1997), 'Beyond the Great Wall: urban form and transformation on the Chinese frontiers', *Journal of Asian Studies*, 56(4), 1086–1088.

Drucker, J. and Goldstein, H. (2007), 'Assessing the regional economic development impacts of universities: a review of current approaches', *International Regional Science Review*, 30(1), 20–46.

Drucker, P. F. (1995), *People and Performance: The Best of Peter Drucker on Management*, Routledge.

Drucker, Peter F. (1955), *The Practice of Management*, Burlington: Elsevier Ltd.

Dumais, G., G. Ellison and E.L. Glaeser (2002), 'Geographic Concentration as a Dynamic Process', *Review of Economics and Statistics*, 84, 193–204.

Dunning, John H. and Sarianna M. Lundan (1987), 'The Geographical Sources of Competitiveness of Multinational Enterprises: An Econometric Analysis', *International Business Review*, 7(2), 115–133.

Einwalter, D. (1996), 'Urban spaces in contemporary China', *Comparative Economic Studies*, 38(4).

Engermann, S. and Sokoloff, K. L. (2000), 'Institutions, Factor Endowments, and the Path of Development in the New World', *Journal of Economic Perspectives*, 14(3), 217–232.

Fisher, R. C. (1997), 'The Effects of State and Local Public Services on Economic Development', *New England Economic Review*, 53–82.

Florida, Richard (2002), *The Rise of the Creative Class*, New York: Basic Books.

Friedmann, J. (1995), 'Where we stand: a decade of world city research', in P.L. Knox and P.J. Taylor (eds), *World Cities in a World System*, Cambridge: Cambridge University Press.

Fujita, M., Thisse, J. F. (2002), *Economics of agglomeration: Cities, Industrial Locations, and Regional Growth*, Cambridge: Cambridge University Press

Fukuyama, Francis (1996), *Trust: The Social Virtues and The Creation of Prosperity*, New York: Free Press.

Gardiner, B., Martin, R. and P. Tyler (2004), 'Competitiveness, productivity and economic growth across the European regions', *Regional Studies*, 38(9), 1045–1067.

Gaubatz, P. (1999), 'China's urban transformation: patterns and process of morphological change in Beijing, Shanghai and Guangzhou', *Urban Studies*, 36 (9), 1495–1521.

Gehrig, T. (1998), 'Competing markets', *European Economic Review*, 42(2), 277–310

Glaeser, E. (2011), *Triumph of the City: How Our Greatest Invention Makes US Richer, Smarter, Greener, Healthier and Happier*, London: Pan Macmillan.

Glaeser, E. L. (1995), 'The Case for Competition among Local Governments', *Policy*, 11, 16–19.

Glaeser, E. L. (1998), 'Are cities dying?', *The Journal of Economic Perspectives*, 139–160.

Glaeser, E. L. (1999), 'Learning in cities', *Journal of Urban Economics*, 46(2), 254–277.

Glaeser, E. L. (2000), 'The new economics of urban and regional growth', *The Oxford Handbook of Economic Geography*, 83–98.

Glaeser, E. and J. M. Shapiro (2001), 'City Growth and the 2000 Census: Which Places Grew, and Why', Brookings Institution, 5.

Glaeser, E. L., Kallal, H. D., Sheinkman, J. A., and Shleifer, A. (1992), 'Growth in Cities', *Journal of Political Economy*, 100(6), 1126–1152.

Glaeser, E. L., Scheinkman, J. and Shleifer, A. (1995), 'Economic growth in a cross-section of cities', *Journal of Monetary Economics*, 36(1), 117–143.

Gordon, I. and Cheshire, P. (2001), 'Locational advantage and lessons for territorial competition in Europe', in B. Johansson, C. Karlsson, and R. Stough (eds), *Theories of Endogenous Regional Growth. Advances in Spatial Science*, Berlin, Germany: Springer.

Greif, A. (1994), 'Cultural beliefs and the organization of society: a historical and theoretical reflection on collectivist and individualist societies', *Journal of Political Economy*, 102 (5), 912–950.

Griliches, Zvi (1957), 'Hybrid Corn: An Exploration in the Economics of Technological Change', *Econometrica*, 25(4), 501–522.

Gruber, W., D. Mehta and R. Vernon (1967), 'The R&D Factor in International Trade and International Investment of United States Industries', *Journal of Political Economy*, 25(1), 20–37.

Gugler, J. (2004), *World Cities Beyond the West: Globalization, Development and Inequality*, Cambridge: Cambridge University Press.

Hall, R. E. and Jones, C. I. (1999), 'Why do some countries produce so much more output per worker than others?', NBER Working Paper No. 6564.

Han Fengchao and Zhang Dongfeng (1998), 'The Experiences in Transformation of Economic Growth in the Four Tigers of Asia', *Economy and Management*, 2, 28–29.

Harvey, D. (1989), 'From managerialism to entrepreneurialism: the transformation in urban governance in late capitalism', *Geografiska Annaler. Series B. Human Geography*, 3–17.

Haug, Peter (1991), 'The Location Decisions and Operations of High Technology Organizations in Washington State', *Regional Studies*, 25, 525–541.

Haughton, Jonathan, Giuffre, Douglas, Barrett, John and Tuerck, David G. (2005), *Commentson the Draft Environmental Impact Statement for the Cape Wind Project*, Boston:Suffolk University.

Hautamaki, Antti (2006), 'Innovation ecosystem in city policy: the case of Helsinki', *Helsinki Quarterly*, 4/2006, 17–21.

He Xiaowei (2007), 'Shenzhen City: construction of innovation system, create innovative atmosphere', *Newspaper of Chinese Academy of Social Sciences*, 17 July.

Head, K., J. Ries and D. Swenson (1995), 'Agglomeration Benefits and Location Choice: Evidence From Japanese Manufacturing Investments in the United States', *Journal of International Economics*, 38, 223–247.

Heckscher, Eli F. (1919), 'The Effect of Foreign Trade on the Distribution of Income', *The Scandinavian Journal of Economics*. Retrieved January 20, 2011, from http://www.jstor.org/action/downloadSingleCitation?format=bibtex&include=abs&singleCitation=true.

Henderson, J. V. (1986), 'Efficiency of Resource Usage and City Size', *Journal of Urban Economics*, 19, 47–70.

Henderson, J. V., Storeygard, A. and Weil, D. N. (2009), 'Measuring economic growth from outer space', NBER Working Paper No. 15199.

Hohenberg, Paul, M. and Lees, L. H. (1985), *The Making of Urban Europe, 1000–1950* Cambridge, MA: Harvard University Press.

Huang Zhihong (2000), 'The experiences in developing vocational education cause in Singapore', *Education and Vocation*, 6, 51–54.

Huggins, R. (2003), *Global Index of Regional Knowledge Economies 2003 Update: Benchmarking South East England*, Cardiff, UK.

Huggins, Robert, Hiro Izushi and Will Davies (2005), *World Knowledge Competitiveness Index*, Pontypridd: Robert Huggins Associates Ltd.

Iyer, S., Kitson, M. and Toh, B. (2005), 'Social capital, economic growth and regional development', *Regional Studies*, 39, 1015–1040.

Jacobs, J. (1969), *The Economy of Cities*, New York: Vintage.

Jarvenpaa, Sirkka J. and Leidnar, Dorothy E. (1998), 'An Information Company in Mexico:Extending the Resource-based View of the Firm to a Developing Country Context', *Information System Research*, 9(4), 342–361.

Jin Zhongfan (2002), *Urban Development Policy in Korea*, Shanghai: Shanghai University of Finance and Economics Press.

Juha, K. (2002), *Urban Economic Development Policy in the Network Society*, Acta Electronica Universitatis Tamperensis, 197.

Kindleberger, C. P. (1974), 'An American Economic Climacteric?', *Challenge*, 16(6), 35–44.

Kitson, M., Martin, R. and Tyler, P. (2004), 'Regional competitiveness: an elusive yet key concept?', *Regional Studies*, 38(9), 991–999.

Knudsen, B., Florida, R., Gates, G. and Stolarick, K. (2007), 'Urban density', *Creativity and Innovation*, May.

Kresl, Peter Karl (1995), 'The determinants of urban competitiveness', in P. K. Kresl and

G. Gappert (eds), *North American Cities and the Global Economy: Challenges and Opportunities*, London: Sage Publications, pp. 45–68.

Kresl, Peter Karl and Pierre-Paul Proulx (2000), 'Montreal's place in the North American economy', *The American Review of Canadian Studies*, 30(3), 283–314.

Kresl, Peter Karl and Balwant Singh (1999), 'Competitiveness and the urban economy: the experience of 24 large U.S. metropolitan areas', *Urban Studies*, 36(May), 1017–1027.

Krugman, P. (1996a), *Pop Internationalism*, Cambridge, MA: MIT Press.

Krugman, P. (1996b), 'Making sense of the competitiveness debate', *Oxford Review of Economic Policy*, 12, 17–35.

Krugman, P. R. (1991), *Geography and Trade*, MIT Press, p. 142. Retrieved October 23, 2010, from http://books.google.com/books?id=AQDodCHOgJYC&pgis=1.

Kuznets, S. (1966), *Modern Economic Growth: Rate, Structure and Spread*, New Haven, CT and London: Yale University Press.

Kuznets, S. S. (1971), *Economic Growth of Nations: Total Output and Production Structure*, New York: Belknap Press.

Kyoji, A. Saito (2006), 'Evolution and Economic Theory', *Journal of Political Economy*, 58, 211–221.

La Porta, R., Lopez-de-Silanes, F., Shleifer, A. and Vishny, R. (1999), 'The quality of government', *Journal of Law, Economics, and Organization*, 15(1), 222–279.

Lan Zhiyong (2005), 'Governance and innovation strategy for local government: a case study of the City of Phoenix, US', *Southeast Academic Research*, 1, 30–37.

Larsson, S. and Lundmark, M. (1991), 'Kista: företag i nätverk eller statusadress?: en studie av Kistaföretagens länkningar', Uppsala University.

Leavy, Brian (1999), 'Organization and Competitiveness: Towards a New Perspective', *Journal of General Management*, 24(3), 33.

Leibenstein, Harvey (1966), 'Allocative efficiency vs. "x-efficiency"', *The American Economic Review* 56(3), 392–415.

Lever, W. F. (1999), 'Competitive Cities in Europe', *Urban Studies*, 36(5), 1029–1044.

Lever, W. F. (2002), 'The knowledge base and the competitive city', in I. Begg (ed.), *Urban Competitiveness: Policies for Dynamic Cities*, Bristol: Policy Press, pp. 11–31.

Lever, W. F. and Turok, I. (1999), 'Competitive Cities: Introduction to the Review', *Urban Studies*, 36(5/6), 791–794.

Levine, R. (1997), 'Financial development and economic growth: views and agenda', *Journal of Economic Literature*, XXXV, 688–726.

Levine, R., Loayza, N. and Beck, T. (2000), 'Financial intermediation and growth: causality and causes', *Journal of Monetary Economics*, 46(1), 31–77.

Liang Longnan (1998), 'A study on urban planning and development of Korea', *Urban Planning Overseas*, 2, 35–41.

Linnamaa, R. (2001), 'The Role of the City Government in the Urban Economic Development Network', *Professionals and Public Expectations*, 22–25.

Liu Xiaodi (2004), 'Reasons and inspirations of economic advancement and economic recession in Singapore', *Contemporary Finance & Economics*, 9(238), 87–90.

Logan, J. and H. Molotch (1987), *Urban Fortunes: The Political E-conomy of Place*, Berkeley: University of California Press.

Lucas, Robert E. (1988), 'On the Mechanics of Economic Development', *Journal of*

Monetary Economics, 223–242.

Malecki, E. J. and Moriset, B. (2007), *The Digital Economy: Business Organization, Production Processes, and Regional Development*, London: Routledge, Taylor & Francis, p. 274. Retrieved January 20, 2011, from http://books.google.com/books?id=mCKlYwhr82EC&pgis=1.

Mao Yong (2002), 'On talent strategy of Singapore and its promotion to economy', *Around Southeast Asia*, 9, 21–24.

Markusen, A. R., Hall, P. H. and Glasmeier, A. K. (1986), *High Tech America: The What, How, Where and Why of the Sunrise Industries*, Boston: Allen & Unwin.

Martin, L., E. van Duren, R. Westgren and M. Le Maguer (1991), 'Competitiveness of Ontario's agrifood sector', Prepared for the Government of Ontario, May.

Martin, P. and Ottaviano, G. I. (1999), 'Growing locations: industry location in a model of endogenous growth', *European Economic Review*, 43(2), 281–302.

Martin, P. and Ottaviano, G. I. (2001), 'Growth and agglomeration', *International Economic Review*, 42(4), 947–968.

Mattoo, A., R. Rathindran and A. Subramanian (2001), 'Measuring Services Trade Liberalization and Its Impact on Economic Growth: An Illustration', *World Bank Working Paper*, No. 2655.

McGregor, Douglas M. (1960), *The Human Side of Enterprise*, San Diego: Pfeiffer and Company.

McKinnon, Ronald I. (1976), *Money and Finance in Economic Growth and Development: Essays in Honor of Edward S. Shaw, editor and contributor*, New York: Marcel Dekker.

Meadows, D. H., D. L. Meadows, J. Randers, W. W. Behrens, and Rome Club (1972), *The Limits to Growth*, New York: Universe Books.

Molotch, H. (1976), 'The city as a growth machine: toward a political economy of place', *American Journal of Sociology*, 82, 309–330.

Montgomery, C. A. and M. E. Porter (eds) (1991), *Strategy: Seeking and Securing Competitive Advantage*, Boston, MA: Harvard Business School Press.

Myerson, R. B., Pollock, G. B. and Swinkels, J. M. (1991), 'Viscous population equilibria', *Games and Economic Behavior*, 3(1), 101–109.

Nalewaik, Chen J., Roussel, M. and Sherr, C. (2006), 'The product of the c-fms proto-oncogene: a glycoprotein with associated tyrosine kinase activity', *Science*, 228, 320–322.

Nelson, Richard R. and Sidney G. Winter (1982), 'The Schumpeter Tradeoff Revisited', *The American Economic Review*, 72(1), 114–132.

Nye, Joseph (1990), 'Soft Power', *Foreign Policy*, 80, 165–168.

O'Sullivan, Arthur (2007), Urban Economics, Irwin, IL: McGraw-Hill.

OECD (2006), *OECD Territorial Reviews, Competitive Cities in the Global Economy*, Paris: OECD Publications.

OECD (2008), *Competitive Cities and Climate Change: OECD Conference Proceedings*, Paris: OECD Publications.

Parkinson, M., Hutchins, M., Simmie, J., Clark, G. and Verdonk, H. (2004), *Competitive European Cities: Where Do the Core Cities Stand?* Final Report, October 2003.

Parr, J. B. (1979), 'Regional economic change and regional spatial structure: some interrelationships', *Environment and Planning A*, 11, 825–837.

Parr, J. B. (2002), 'Missing Elements in the Analysis of Agglomeration Economies', *International Regional Science Review*, 25, 151.

Pengfei Ni (2001–08), 'China urban competitiveness report', Report Series by Social Sciences Academic Press, China.

Pengfei Ni and Peter Karl Kresl (2006), 'Global urban competitiveness report', report series by the Global Urban Competitiveness Project, Social Sciences Academic Press, China.

Petroni, Alberto (2000), 'The Future of Insurance Industry in Italy: Determinants of Competitiveness in the 2000s', *Futures*, 32(5), 417–434.

Porter, M. E. (1985), *The Competitive Advantage: Creating and Sustaining Superior Performance*, New York: Free Press.

Porter, M. E. (1990), *The Comparative Advantage of Nations*, New York: Free Press.

Porter, M. E. (1996), 'Competitive Advantage, Agglomeration Economies, and Regional Policy', *International Regional Science Review*, 19, 85–90.

Porter, M. E. (1998), 'Clusters and the New Economics of Competition', *Harvard Business Review*, 76, 77–90.

Porter, M. E. (1999), 'The Microeconomic Foundations of Economic Development and Competitiveness', *Wirtschaftspolitische Blätter*.

Porter, M. E. (2000), 'Location, Competition, and Economic Development: Local Clusters in a Global Economy', *Economic Development Quarterly*, 14, 15.

Porter, M. E. (2001), 'Innovation: Location Matters', *MIT Sloan Management Review*, 4, 42.

Posner, Michael V. (1961), 'International trade and technical change', *Oxford Economic Papers*, 13(3), 323–41.

Prahalad, C.K. (1990), and Hamel, G. (1990), 'The core competence of the corporation', *Harvard Business Review*, 68(3), 79–91.

Rabin, M. (1993), 'Incorporating fairness into game theory and economics', *The American Economic Review*, 83(5), 1281–1302.

Romer, Paul M. (1986), 'Increasing Returns and Long Run Growth', *Journal of Political Economy*, October, 67–68.

Rondinelli, Dennis A. (1998), 'The Changing Forces of Urban Economic Development: Globalization and City Competitiveness in the 21st Century', *Cityscape*, 3(3), 71–105.

Rosenthal, S. S. and W. C. Strange (2003), 'Geography, Industrial Organization, and Agglomeration', *Review of Economics and Statistics*, 85(2), 377–393.

Sassen, S. (1994), *Cities in World Economy*, London: Pine Forge Press.

Saxenian, A. (1994), *Regional Advantage: Culture and Competition in Silicon Valley and Route 128*, Cambridge, MA: Harvard University Press.

Schotter, A. (1981), 'Why take a game theoretical approach to economics? Institutions, economics and game theory', Discussion Paper No. 81-08.

Schultz, Theodore W. (1962), *Investment in Human Beings*, Chicago: University of Chicago Press.

Schumpeter, J. A. (1942), *Capitalism, Socialism and Democracy*, New York: Harper & Row.

Schumpeter, Joseph (1911), *The Theory of Economic Development: An Inquiry into Profits, Capital, Credit, Interest and the Business Cycle* New York: Oxford University Press.

Scott, A. and Soja, E. (1986), 'Los Angeles: the capital of the twentieth century', *Environment and Planning, D: Society & Space*, 4, 201–216.

Sha Hong (2004), 'The strategy of Singapore's education and talents', *Journal of Tianjin*

Academy of Educational Science, 12, 6.

Simon, C. J. (1998), 'Human capital and metropolitan employment growth', *Journal of Urban Economics*, 43(2), 223–243.

Smith, A. (1776), *An Inquiry into the Nature and Causes of the Wealth of Nations*, London: George Routledge and Sons.

Solow, R. M. (1957), 'Technical change and the aggregate production function', *The Review of Economics and Statistics*, 39(3), 312–320.

Sonn, J. W. and Storper, M. (2003), 'The Increasing Importance of Geographical Proximity in Technological Innovation', paper prepared for the conference 'What Do We Know about Innovation', Sussex, 13–15 November.

Sotarauta, M. and Linnamaa, R. (2001), 'Urban competitiveness and management of urban policy networks: some reflections from Tampere and Oulu', *Technology, Society and Environment*, 2.

South African Cities Network (2006), 'State of the cities report'.

Stone, C. (1989), *Regime Politics: Governing Atlanta, 1946-1988*, University Press of Kansas.

Storper, M. (1997), *The Regional World: Territorial Development in a Global Economy*, New York and London: Guilford Press.

Tang Hua (2000), *U.S. Government Management – Phoenix as an Example*, Beijing: Renmin University Press of China.

Taylor, Frederick Winslow (1911), *The Principles of Scientific Management*, New York: Harper & Brothers.

Taylor, P.J. (2004), 'Competition and Cooperation Between Cities in Globalization', *GaWC Research Bulletin*, 351 (A).

Taylor, P.J. (2004), *The World City Network*, London: Routledge.

Taylor, P. J. and Pengfei Ni (2010), *Global Urban Analysis*, London: Earthscan Press.

Thompson, G.F. (2003), *Between Hierarchies and Markets: the Logic and Limits of Network Forms of Organization*, Oxford: Oxford University Press.

Thünen, J. H. V. (1966), *Isolated State; an English edition of Der isolierte Staat*, Oxford, New York: Pergamon Press.

UN-Habitat (2009), 'Global report on Human Settlements 2009', London: Earthscan.

United Nations Human Settlements Programme (2008), 'Enhancing urban safety and security: global report on human settlements 2008', London: Earthscan.

Van den Berg, Leo and Antonio Paolo Russo (2007), *The Impacts of Culture on the Economic Development of Cities*, Rotterdam: EURICUR

Verikios, G. and X.-G Zhang (2001), 'Global Gains from Liberalizing Trade in Telecommunications and Financial Services', *Productivity Commission Staff Research Paper*.

Weber, A. (1909), *Theory of the Location of Industries*, Chicago: The University of Chicago.

Webster, D. and Muller, L. (2000), 'Urban competitiveness assessment in developing country urban regions: the road forward', World Bank, Washington D.C.

Weiss, Charles (2003), 'Scientific Uncertainty and Science Based Precaution', *International Environmental Agreements: Politics, Law and Economics*, 3, 137–166.

World Bank (2007), 'Doing Business 2007: How to Reform', Washington D.C.: World Bank.

World Bank (2008), 'Doing business 2008', www.doingbusiness.org (accessed 13 July 2007).

Xiao-Guang Kang and Qing-bin Ma (2005), 'Relationship between urban eco-environment and competitiveness with the background of globalization: statistical explanation based on industry type newly classified with environment demand and environment pressure', *Journal of Environmental Sciences*, 17.

Ye, L. (2004), 'Is Shanghai really a global city?', International Conference on Globalisation and Urban Change, Chicago.

Zhang, L. and Zhao, X. B. (2001), 'The impact of state resource allocation on urbanization in socialist China', *Post-Communist Economies*, 13(4), 505–524.

Zhang, T. (2000), 'Urban sprawl in China: land market force and government's role', *Cities: The International Journal of Urban Planning and Studies*, 17(1).

Zhao Guang (1994), 'Looking at China's urban history from a macroscopic perspective', *Social Science in China*, 15(3), 171–179.

Zhu, J. (1999), *The Transition of China's Urban Development: From Plan-controlled to Market-led*, London: Praeger.

Zhu Yu (2007), 'China's floating population and their settlement intention in the cities; beyond the Hukou Reform', *Habitat International*, 31(1), 65–76.

Zweig, D. et al. (2006), 'Rewards of Technology: Explaining China's Reverse Migration', *Journal of International Migration and Integration*, 7(4), 449–471.

15. Patterns of the global cities: present and future
Pengfei Ni[1] and Peter Karl Kresl[2]

In order to have a thorough and deep understanding to the pattern of the global cities and their opportunities and challenges, the subject group conducted a questionnaire. First of all, Professor Ni proposed questions and the final 10 questions were formed after taking the advice of Peter Karl Kresl from Bucknell University. Since the beginning of 2012, the project group sent emails to experts, researchers, and some officials and collected their responses before collating the deep and thought-provoking opinions on this topic (see Table 15.1).

Table 15.1   Information on Foreign Experts Taking Part

Name	Title
Richard T. Legates	Professor of San Francisco State University
Peter Taylor	Professor and Dean of Geography and Environmental Sciences in Northumbria University, in charge of GAWC
Peter Viducis	Official from Toronto in Canada
Chris Webster	Professor and Dean of City and regional planning in Cardiff University
Andrea Frank	Senior Lecturer from City and regional planning in Cardiff University
Tatsuaki Kuroda	Professor of Nagoya University
Mark Brown	Official of London
Ron Van Oers	Official from UNESCO World Heritage Centre
Ding Chengri	Maryland university urban studies and planning, Assistant of president of Lincoln Institute of Land Policy
Daniel You	Korea Culture and Contents Agency Minister

Q1. What are the new phenomena, new challenges and hot topics in global city development? These questions include global financial crisis, natural resources, city development and people's livelihoods. The answers are as follows.

Peter Taylor: On the current matters facing global/world cities the overriding issues relate to the current world are the economic crisis and how it unfolds in the next few years. If the

1   Pengfei Ni, Center of City and Competitiveness, CASS. No. 2 yuetanbeixiaojie, Xicheng District, Beijing, China, post code: 100836, Tel: 8610-68063478.
    Email: ni_pengfei@163.com.

2   Peter Karl Kresl, Bucknell University, Lewisburg, PA, USA 17837. Tel: 570-490-5193.
    Email: kresl@bucknell.edu.

worse case scenarios are correct, it may well be that city resilience rather than city growth becomes the key policy goal.

Richard T. Legates: Energy and resources are the new problems; potential competition lies in countries. What I am concerned more is that is China experiencing a housing or more general "bubble"?

Peter Viducis: Tall buildings; 20 years ago few residential buildings in Toronto went higher than 20-25 stories. Now many developers want to go 40+ stories. How to cope with increasing energy costs and (possibly) global warming, implications for built form e.g. low rise sprawl vs. medium rise apartment neighborhoods. Making the transition from a place where people live in houses (small city) to one where many people live in apartment units (large city). Gentrification is a valuable tool for revitalizing neighborhoods, but it may also lead to displacement of low income people. How to fund cities infrastructure needs and operating expenses? Large cities are very productive places, but they are also more expensive to maintain compared to smaller centers.

Mark Brown: The main challenge will be how growth in the long run will be accommodated.

Q2. What key elements are influencing global cities' development, and how? What is the effect of the global financial crisis on the cities?

Economic growth and population movements are the key elements. Globalization is creating more chances for global city development and exerting different influence on it. Answers are as follows.

Peter Viducis: Economic growth and population movements are the key influencing factors.

Mark Brown: To the extent that we define global cities as the interface between national and international markets, the key influence for these cities will be whether the world will continue its process of economic integration. The significant imbalances in the global financial system combined with what appears to be two financial crises in quick succession (the first driven by the housing market and the second by sovereign debt) suggests to me that there may be a near term slowdown in world trade that will affect global cities. The depth of this effect, however, is open to question.

Globalization and urban development are closely tied. Once countries begin to industrialize the twin effect of the application of capital to agriculture and the growing demand for labor in cities as a result of industrialization leads to the mass movement of labor to cities. China's recent economic history is, of course, a good example of this process; albeit I am unsure home much more capital is being applied to agriculture now than before.

Peter Viducis: Interdependence is increasing, e.g., the recent Japanese Tsunami, which stopped assembly lines in North America, because of just-in-time inventory practices. For Toronto, the effect has been largely positive, because our banks did not have the same problems that most global banks experienced. The financial crisis is an opportunity for Canadian banks to increase their presence in US and other markets.

Richard T. Legates: Differentials in strong European countries (Germany, France) and weak ones (Greece, Portugal, Italy, Spain, Eastern European countries).

Q3. What will be the major changes in the hierarchy of global cities in the industrialized, emerging and less developed countries? In particular, are there individual cities you believe are on the rise or the decline?

Today, some cities in developing countries have the tendency of dropping, while cities in developing countries are rising. These cities' development levels are getting closer. The economic change of pattern will lead to a change in the world city pattern, in which case, the world is shifting to advanced industrialized countries.

Andrea Frank: Global cities in the industrialized countries will remain relatively stable in terms of population and they will decline in importance relative to global cities in Asia (emerging countries). While many cities in less developed countries will grow in population their development will be so chaotic that they will not really become important as economic hubs as in the classical 'global' cities debate.

Chris Webster: Industrialized cities will lose out to emerging cities as the economy shifts eastwards. The urban economy in Europe will shrink and focus on the North. London may maintain advantage as a USA–Europe centre of transactions. Peripheral European cities will shrink in economy. Madrid may retain an advantage as link between emerging economies in Latin America and Europe. Warsaw will rise in importance as a free market oriented large European economy. If the Euro survives and it joins, it could be a major player in drawing the centre of gravity of a split euro-zone northwards. In the longer term, a northwards shift in the European economy aligned with the opening up of the Arctic shipping routes, could have a profound effect on the spatial economy of Europe–Russia–Scandinavia. Tokyo and Japanese cities will bounce back as foreign investment flows into its undervalued stocks and industrial and financial structural problems are addressed by Italian and Greek style technocratic emergency governments to move the country out of twenty years of recessive activity.

Emerging: Jakarta and Yangon (Rangoon) will grow in importance in SE Asia. Jakarta could dominate the region in 20 years time. HCMC and other Vietnamese cities will work their way up within 10 years as the constraints on the Vietnamese political economy gradually ease out. Bangkok will continue to dominate and will stabilise politically to retain its position as friendly entreport for SE Asia. Give three years to overcome effects floods. Istanbul will grow in importance in Europe and Mid East – as Europe's low cost manufacturing centre and as gateway between rising Mid-East block and Europe. Watch for a possible Mid-East economic block over next 20 years as economic benefits cooperation overcome sectarian differences in the Muslim block. An attack on Iran's nuclear facilities will galvanise disparate Muslim nations and could stimulate the creation of a Mid-East trading block approaching the size of Europe, with the gulf as its finance centre and Turkey its manufacturing centre and North Africa suppliers of natural resources and cheap labor and Iran defense and manufacturing. This would put Istanbul in an even more pivotal position. Mexico City could have a similar role to Istanbul – low cost manufacturing partner to US economy and gateway between Latin and North America.

Tatsuaki Kuroda: Due to the rapid growth of economies in developing countries, transition of comparative advantages among countries or global cities is becoming very fast. In addition, the progress of fragmentation changes the trade pattern or "division of labor" among countries as well. While most global cities are not specialized in any specific industries but concentrated with many kinds of service industries, some parts of them would be damaged by the changes (e.g., in the past, garment industries in downtowns of NYC, Osaka or Nagoya). Urbanization of developed countries is decelerated since it is around 80% or more. Yet, in developing countries, especially China or India, many mega-cities would emerge soon.

Ron Van Oers: Big cities have their own advantage, likewise in small cities and advanced cities and new emerging cities. Human capital is the key to advanced ones, while the production factors and market are crucial to new industries cities. In emerging and less-developed countries cities up to 200,000 inhabitants have an advantage as they can provide for the proper infrastructure and services needed to be competitive, whereas the large metropolises will always have to struggle with a backlog in this.

Mark Brown: It seems to me that we can divide global cities into two groups. Those in places that have already passed through the process of industrialization that brought with it large migration flows from rural to urban areas. These cities are slow growing, but function as important centers for the exchange of information within and across industries. These are cities that are more specialized in service industries than manufacturing. To the extent that the development of human capital and the exchange of knowledge continue to increase in importance, these cities will grow in significance. The remainder is global cities in places that are at various stages of industrialization. These cities face significant challenges accommodating growth, while also establishing themselves as important players in global markets. They are, in a sense, control and entry points into these emerging markets, and major centers of production.

Daniel You: Communication through the Internet. On the rise, I wish to point the city of São Paulo and on the decline, the cities of the UK and the most European cities could be the ones.

Q4. What issues of cities in the world that will be important or crucial in the future are we not yet thinking about?
The important or key questions include natural resources, racial problems, population movement and so on. In the age of globalization and information, internet development enables resources movement to be more convenient and the interaction to be more frequent and competition more severe, which will cause some unexpected problems. The answers are as follows.

Andrea Frank: Energy and water will be the issues.

Chris Webster: First, a religion-influenced Mid-East trading block could have an impact on the relative position and alignment of cities across the globe. Like COMECON. The Islamic economy already has its international influences on the world's city system – e.g. links between Turkey and Western Indonesia (regional development of the latter), Saudi influence in Islamic cities across the globe. With a rise in Protectionism due to reaction against globalism, new alignments will emerge and religion will be one of them.

Second, income inequality will become an efficiency issue rather than an equity issue. This will lead to a different kind of urban inequality policy and countries more able to address inequality may do better than those unable to.

Third, democracy will continue to be re-shaped by the economic success of state-led capitalism models. The current European crisis governments will strengthen the acceptability of non-democratic capitalism. This will be matched in the next 20 years by urban government policies in pursuit of urban reconstruction.

Fourth, continued rise in environmental totalitarian tendencies will also threaten democracy as we know it.

Fifth, the impact of a major terrorist attacks.

Tatsuaki Kuroda: Composition of races in each city and its effects for creativity and social stability in the city.

Ron Van Oers: 1) How electronic networks will actually shape cities, in terms of the use of SMART technologies in direct planning and design (as opposed to indirect by means of improved information and communication among its citizens; 2) How increased mobility of people will affect livability and competitiveness of cities and their choices as regards investments in infrastructure, housing and services, including preservation of local culture and heritage.

Daniel You: Water supply is the issue.

Peter Viducis: The issue of how to integrate immigrants. It seems that immigrants are having a harder time integrating than before. This problem seems to be very acute in European cities e.g. Paris banlieues, where there seem to be large concentrations of disadvantaged people.

Q5. How are global cities responding effectively to the fiscal constraints of their national governments and the reduction in fiscal transfers?
A country should empower more authority on managing local affairs. The cities should strengthen their governance accordingly. More answers are as follows.

Chris Webster: there will be a continuation of the trend towards private urban governance (I have published many papers and books on this subject), with urban public goods being increasingly provided through contractual neighborhood governments. We shall see a federation movement among these to supply goods and services with higher thresholds.

Tatsuaki Kuroda: Since global cities enjoy agglomeration economy burdening rural areas with no scale economy, they should transfer the surplus to those areas. Otherwise, the country as a whole becomes unstable or unhappy.

Ron Van Oers: My most recent book, *The Historic Urban Landscape – Managing Heritage in an Urban Century* (2012), puts forward some observed trends in this regard, such as ongoing decentralisation with a transfer of significant measures of autonomy from national to city governments, also in terms of running their own budgetary affairs and revenue streams, which will allow for the planning and design of specific attributes at the local level to boost the performance of cities. In addition, place marketing and place branding for cities and regions have emerged in recent years to manage internal and external opportunities and to transform them into competitive advantage.

Ding Chengri: There are different kinds of government structure. In United States, it is the federalism that cities may or may not be affected by national government's fiscal difficulty. City's fiscal conditions more rely on local tax structure.

Daniel You: Enforcing with the local taxes.

Q6. What problems are most necessary to research?
There are many aspects that are worthy of researching. For example, improving the city's sustaining development, city comprehensive management, preserving local culture and upgrading environment. More answers are as follows.

Andrea Frank: Maintaining good quality of life and sustainability.

Chris Webster: Private neigborhood governance and its co-evolution with public urban governance, spontaneous regional governance (networks of private interests collaborating in more bespoke and efficient regional scale coordination over infrastructure investment).

Tatsuaki Kuroda: The importance and roles of face-to-face communication and social network with respect to the growth of global cities.

Ron Van Oers: Of crucial importance will be how local culture, which is an infinite but place-bound resource, can be harnessed in directing human and urban development. Inclusion and representation of all social, religious and ethnic groups in society, with equitable distribution of opportunities, facilities and services is certainly one such topic, as disregard for this issue will disrupt society and compromise its competitiveness.

Ding Chengri: There are many different kinds of cities in terms of government involvement. In the case of strong government involvement, the implementation and responsible behaviors of local officials with long term version are critical.

Daniel You: Pollution and restructuring.

Q7. What impact on the competitiveness of individual cities in the world are technological change and the green economy having?
Technological change and green economy are both playing a role in strengthening and sustaining competitiveness in technology and energy and resources, which will significantly affect competitiveness. Answers are as follows.

Andrea Frank: They both have.

Chris Webster: Not too much at present but green technology will become a major basis for competition in the years to come, giving advantage to cities in advantageous positions with respect to green credentials, energy and so on, and perhaps favoring medium size cities or mega cities configured in a particular way (like Chongqing).

Tatsuaki Kuroda: Transition of comparative advantages among countries or global cities is becoming very fast. As a result, some parts of global cities would be damaged by the technological changes as well. I myself do not believe that CO_2 is the origin of global warming, yet resource constraints such as shortage of oil and gas deposits might be crucial for maintaining mega cities in the near future.

Ron Van Oers: Cities with a lean and effective government, a strong local culture, an active civic engagement and supported by an entrepreneurial environment with R&D facilities and start-up companies, will be able to rapidly introduce SMART technologies and create more sustainable city environments, and thereby attract the brightest and smartest among the young people.

Daniel You: Being equipped with high speed Internet.

Q8. To what extent can the planning of global cities control or influence the course of their development?
It exerts a significant influence on the future development of a city. In the process of planning and development, the force the city has is very crucial, but still needs more joint efforts. More answers follow.

Andrea Frank: Good level ... but not entirely (30-50%).

Chris Webster: City leadership and high level strategy is important. Much urban and economic planning is ineffective in changing a city's fortunes.

Tatsuaki Kuroda: It is the matter of course that provision of infrastructure and necessary regulations in urban planning has vital role for promoting global cities. For example, subways should be provided for more development of Manila, I guess. However, market mechanism shall determine the way of development in the global economy after all.

Ron Van Oers: In my view, planning will remain important, but more as a way of governance and civic engagement than to produce planning documents ("plans").

Daniel You: The initiatives shall become greater but I don't believe the cities themselves control everything in the near future.

Q9. What are the principal threats and opportunities for the cities in the world with which you are most familiar? Please recommend a few cities which you think strong in some aspects or have a strong comprehensive level, and give me your reason.
Apart from major issues concerning politics, military, security and natural disasters, the current threat the world is facing is much agglomeration and lack of reform. More answers are as follows.

Chris Webster: Principle threat = security. A nuclear/dirty bomb threat is plausible. National response must therefore include an analysis of risk and contingency plans, which, logically, should involve decentralization of London's capacity. There is an obvious tension here. Research question: is it possible to devise resilience strategies that involve decentralization and dispersal without compromising the size and centralization effects that make a global city like London great? Is there a new form of dispersed centralism? Can the internet model (which developed under precisely this goal) be applied to the urban economy and physical city?

Tatsuaki Kuroda: In some countries, too much agglomeration is dangerous against natural disasters such as big earthquake, tsunami, typhoon, flood, etc. In terms of opportunities, there are so many advantages as suggested by Jane Jacobs. London: financial markets are really important in the global economy. In that sense, London is the first runner in the field rather than NYC, although many companies and workers there are non-natives. Shanghai: if Chinese economy and public institutions would be more liberalized, Shanghai has a huge potential power for many kinds of activities as a center of East Asia.

Ron Van Oers: A principal threat is inertia, by way of city size as well as governance, which can lead to a complete breakdown once physical and social structures start to fall apart. The flipside to that coin is a rapid response facility at the city government level to shift resources to areas in need of assistance, which will facilitate a quick recovery and subsequent regeneration of the city. NYC under Mayor Bloomberg has managed to reinvent itself according to a lean business management structure at City Hall level; Boston has shown several periods of down fall and regeneration, based on internal strengths related to vision, governance and enabling environment; Curitiba in Brazil has been hailed for years as a progressive and innovative way of city governance; Singapore remains an example of continuously shifting gears to stay at the forefront of city development currently fueled by strong investments in R&D facilities and further upgrading of infrastructure and services, to name a few classic ones. As emerging cities, I don't see anything (yet) coming up in the Arab States that seems sustainable (not Dubai nor Abu Dhabi); in Africa perhaps Kampala in Uganda, which has made a remarkable recovery in the last 20 years, or Windhoek, Namibia.

Daniel You: Traffic is the major threat. Shanghai, Kuala Lumpur, Nairobi and São Paulo have a relatively high comprehensive level.

Q10. What are the governments of worldwide cities doing? And what changes are happening and will happen in global urban structure?

All governments of cities are dealing with different problems. The rise of emerging cities may bring a change to the structure of global cities. The infrastructures are particularly important. More answers are as follows.

Richard T. Legates: China is doing more than most other countries. The US and Europe want to do more, but are economically troubled.

Peter Viducis: Different solutions in different circumstances. For example, Detroit and several other northern US cities are faced with declining populations. Other cities (like Toronto) are trying to cope with population increases.

Mark Brown: The main challenge will be how growth in the long run will be accommodated. Infrastructure investment now will have lock-in effects well into the future. Los Angeles, which was built around the automobile, will never look like New York and New York, built around mass transit, will never look like Los Angeles. They have effectively obtained different spatial equilibriums. Which is better is open to question.

Peter Viducis: Europe's cities may become less important in the world as their banks face challenges. Chinese, Indian and other emerging markets cities will become more important.

Mark Brown: The planning and infrastructure decisions being made now will have profound effects on the urban structure of global cities moving forward.

Part III

Index Report

16. The state of sustainable competitiveness of 500 cities

Global Urban Competitiveness Assessment Team

City	Ranking	Economic Dynamic		Environ-mental Quality	Social Cohe-sion	Techno-logical Innov-ation	Global Conne-ction	Cultural Diversity	Govern-ment Manage-ment
		GDP per capita (dollar)	GDP growth rate (%)	CO₂ emissi-ons per capita (kg)	Crime rate (%)	Patent applica-tions	Global network connec-tivity	Language multina-tionality index	Doing business index
London	1	64701.48	0.006	0.010	1.735	32956	0.966	13	0.984
New York	2	57157.59	-0.046	0.000	5.781	28961	1.000	10	0.979
San Jose	3	77401.91	0.053	0.019	9.946	38209	0.342	8	0.979
Paris	4	47857.55	0.007	0.010	1.519	38256	0.847	6	0.860
Hong Kong	5	34363.19	0.103	0.000	0.919	6765	0.959	8	0.995
Seoul	6	23720.54	0.017	0.000	2.934	33053	0.728	3	0.916
Tokyo	7	48170.93	0.024	0.008	0.864	15445	0.957	5	0.905
Chicago	8	48283.78	-0.053	0.001	6.354	19749	0.370	10	0.979
Los Angeles	9	62122.85	-0.033	0.012	6.525	19980	0.428	9	0.979
Houston	10	55123.75	-0.053	0.045	8.094	23603	0.407	10	0.979
Sydney	11	41005.75	-0.001	0.025	1.295	1435	0.634	13	0.950
Singapore	12	34469.11	0.087	0.492	0.102	6500	0.976	8	1.000
San Francisco	13	72127.01	0.036	0.751	8.276	20297	0.359	9	0.979
Washington D.C.	14	63777.63	-0.020	0.032	7.987	11940	0.403	10	0.979
Seattle	15	59588.06	-0.001	0.378	6.858	16707	0.301	10	0.979
Vienna	16	50696.13	0.000	0.000	1.045	3722	0.525	8	0.826
Shanghai	17	14213.69	0.123	0.022	4.153	24468	0.717	8	0.562
Dallas	18	52324.25	-0.037	0.040	6.878	16567	0.340	9	0.979

City	Ranking	Economic Dynamic		Environ-mental Quality	Social Cohe-sion	Techno-logical Innov-ation	Global Conne-ction	Cultural Diversity	Govern-ment Manage-ment
		GDP per capita (dollar)	GDP growth rate (%)	CO_2 emissi-ons per capita (kg)	Crime rate (%)	Patent applica-tions	Global network connec-tivity	Language multina-tionality index	Doing business index
Philadelphia	19	54678.15	-0.009	0.002	5.781	6697	0.234	10	0.979
Dublin	20	48252.97	-0.011	0.030	1.324	4978	0.570	9	0.956
Austin	21	43281.73	-0.010	2.753	6.076	32153	0.275	8	0.979
San Diego	22	51707.00	-0.019	1.645	6.176	27002	0.289	8	0.979
Helsinki	23	68152.66	0.123	0.015	2.647	9408	0.403	4	0.934
Amsterdam	24	56991.52	-0.011	0.032	1.270	4120	0.496	9	0.837
Oakland (US)	25	67368.35	-0.015	0.039	8.726	7381	0.182	10	0.979
Frankfurt	26	41467.70	0.012	0.008	0.944	9476	0.414	8	0.882
Stuttgart	27	37825.17	-0.041	0.078	1.134	25158	0.230	8	0.882
Doha	28	51556.14	0.168	0.001	4.210	20	0.278	9	0.725
Palo Alto	29	37718.07	-0.015	0.026	5.920	11885	0.163	11	0.979
Leeds	30	63958.93	-0.001	0.041	1.440	1738	0.181	10	0.984
Boston	31	63192.93	-0.003	0.211	7.910	6752	0.341	8	0.979
Stockholm	32	48949.65	-0.030	0.352	1.320	21553	0.464	4	0.927
Raleigh	33	45279.36	-0.036	0.001	5.523	7692	0.155	8	0.979
Beijing	34	8105.12	0.122	0.001	4.194	17747	0.849	3	0.562
Edinburgh	35	58021.17	-0.001	0.006	2.778	2252	0.196	8	0.984
Cleveland	36	46642.76	-0.051	0.026	5.074	6438	0.223	10	0.979
Madrid	37	32374.16	-0.015	0.001	1.349	4540	0.725	5	0.731
Atlanta	38	42667.52	-0.049	0.002	6.343	6965	0.327	7	0.979
Barcelona	39	37496.57	-0.015	0.000	2.558	4322	0.453	6	0.731
Kawasaki	40	48017.61	0.230	0.006	0.258	2804	0.117	6	0.905
Kuala Lumpur	41	9937.13	0.012	0.000	4.103	217	0.581	7	0.889
Portland	42	42426.94	-0.054	0.004	6.385	16251	0.246	5	0.979
Columbus	43	44895.39	-0.028	0.018	5.849	7520	0.243	8	0.979
Denver	44	53910.78	-0.005	0.004	6.618	5044	0.252	6	0.979
Santa Ana	45	28446.07	-0.016	0.000	6.593	3989	0.132	9	0.979

City	Ranking	Economic Dynamic		Environmental Quality	Social Cohesion	Technological Innovation	Global Connection	Cultural Diversity	Government Management
		GDP per capita (dollar)	GDP growth rate (%)	CO_2 emissions per capita (kg)	Crime rate (%)	Patent applications	Global network connectivity	Language multinationality index	Doing business index
Cincinnati	46	40471.34	-0.045	0.911	5.332	18270	0.241	8	0.979
Brussels	47	43617.38	-0.010	0.264	1.358	2110	0.572	8	0.866
Long Beach	48	53251.41	-0.021	0.021	6.591	2913	0.167	9	0.979
Macao	49	38466.83	0.195	0.000	-0.309	41	0.165	5	0.821
Hamburg	50	40744.34	0.003	0.006	1.260	10167	0.328	5	0.882
Mesa	51	41363.06	-0.015	0.011	5.251	7265	0.144	8	0.979
Dubai	52	45005.78	0.022	0.001	1.425	91	0.556	4	0.781
Tel Aviv	53	31223.19	0.022	0.017	2.343	3468	0.224	10	0.844
Miami	54	40711.18	-0.046	0.370	5.949	7660	0.380	8	0.979
Bangkok	55	12254.24	0.037	0.052	16.483	506	0.710	9	0.900
Arlington	56	45011.64	-0.015	1.133	7.201	10883	0.195	9	0.979
Milwaukee	57	44264.62	-0.033	0.003	6.334	4024	0.191	7	0.979
Omaha	58	49408.72	-0.002	0.005	6.220	2473	0.156	7	0.979
Tampa	59	35125.95	-0.039	0.048	4.892	2597	0.216	10	0.979
Melbourne	60	35947.68	-0.002	6.365	1.246	2989	0.354	11	0.950
Phoenix	61	36686.62	-0.043	2.522	4.800	12330	0.277	9	0.979
Osaka	62	39281.51	0.044	0.002	0.060	9478	0.373	2	0.905
Wellington	63	48903.62	0.012	0.408	1.578	2208	0.247	8	0.990
Taipei	64	28205.38	0.084	0.006	12.420	2581	0.601	5	0.821
Lille	65	26396.82	-0.015	0.000	1.434	794	0.167	7	0.860
Rotterdam	66	42917.12	-0.012	0.030	0.928	5444	0.200	8	0.837
Baltimore	67	46015.05	-0.021	0.332	5.510	6739	0.209	8	0.979
New Orleans	68	48642.85	0.013	1.044	7.362	2099	0.175	10	0.979
Nottingham	69	48049.64	-0.001	0.014	1.861	2400	0.108	7	0.984
Montreal	70	54046.82	0.014	0.578	1.887	39.3	0.332	7	0.967
Yokohama	71	33663.16	0.016	0.011	0.056	2283	0.178	8	0.905
Winnipeg	72	43904.08	0.014	0.000	1.679	22.75	0.132	5	0.967

City	Ranking	Economic Dynamic		Environmental Quality	Social Cohesion	Technological Innovation	Global Connection	Cultural Diversity	Government Management
		GDP per capita (dollar)	GDP growth rate (%)	CO_2 emissions per capita (kg)	Crime rate (%)	Patent applications	Global network connectivity	Language multinationality index	Doing business index
Birmingham	73	39582.63	0.005	0.015	1.474	3184	0.233	6	0.984
Minneapolis	74	52607.15	-0.037	0.159	7.115	9083	0.222	6	0.979
Toronto	75	4566.84	0.002	0.016	1.642	35.92	0.507	8	0.967
Bristol	76	46642.50	-0.001	0.111	1.007	4053	0.180	7	0.984
Tulsa	77	48088.30	0.019	0.082	5.074	3751	0.175	7	0.979
Charlotte	78	43503.98	0.012	0.079	5.955	3622	0.234	7	0.979
Lisbon	79	29751.33	-0.013	0.012	2.112	180	0.385	8	0.832
Auckland（NZ）	80	36905.29	0.012	2.022	0.918	1663	0.380	8	0.990
Oslo	81	56634.45	-0.030	23.469	0.126	4052	0.440	7	0.961
Yerushalayim	82	24437.97	0.022	0.007	2.489	2529	0.097	10	0.844
Oklahoma City	83	42767.67	0.012	0.009	5.024	2893	0.164	6	0.979
Mannheim	84	44802.56	0.003	0.199	0.597	7325	0.117	8	0.882
Nagoya	85	52592.09	0.005	0.003	0.742	1418	0.246	4	0.905
Essen	86	45427.43	0.004	0.031	1.305	3925	0.088	8	0.882
Honolulu	87	49368.52	-0.022	0.003	6.180	1225	0.180	5	0.979
Canberra	88	45536.71	-0.001	0.322	2.075	98	0.157	9	0.950
Aurora	89	56741.56	-0.015	0.129	7.394	6130	0.119	6	0.979
Kumamoto	90	34109.86	0.238	0.000	-0.394	159	0.076	2	0.905
Hannover	91	33980.56	-0.005	0.014	0.479	4278	0.161	7	0.882
Berlin	92	32035.16	0.022	1.042	0.407	13506	0.415	4	0.882
Tucson	93	28337.48	-0.024	0.007	3.254	6243	0.159	6	0.979
Copenhagen	94	47599.48	-0.033	0.620	1.720	3266	0.416	5	0.972
Milan	95	37546.05	-0.034	0.098	0.840	1868	0.591	8	0.556
Chiba	96	42731.36	0.100	0.001	0.198	1669	0.121	3	0.905
Kansas City	97	46977.51	-0.004	0.405	5.542	2960	0.205	7	0.979
Detroit	98	35468.41	-0.079	0.635	5.026	2754	0.280	9	0.979
Sendai	99	47053.24	0.104	0.001	0.131	473	0.129	2	0.905

City	Ranking	Economic Dynamic		Environmental Quality	Social Cohesion	Technological Innovation	Global Connection	Cultural Diversity	Government Management
		GDP per capita (dollar)	GDP growth rate (%)	CO₂ emissions per capita (kg)	Crime rate (%)	Patent applications	Global network connectivity	Language multinationality index	Doing business index
The Hague	100	46921.22	-0.011	0.332	0.987	5724	0.119	8	0.837
Chengdu	101	6167.96	0.212	0.000	2.071	10339	0.288	3	0.562
Reykjavik	102	58419.97	-0.029	0.018	0.105	460	0.137	5	0.922
Brisbane	103	31420.36	-0.002	0.300	0.985	1171	0.229	8	0.950
Riyadh	104	18225.50	0.019	0.028	0.900	172	0.294	7	0.945
Cardiff	105	51494.87	-0.001	0.414	1.652	1577	0.097	7	0.984
Aberdeen	106	47874.11	-0.001	0.068	2.957	2180	0.099	6	0.984
Nice	107	31586.32	-0.015	0.001	1.192	1077	0.153	6	0.860
Adelaide	108	31947.38	-0.002	0.102	1.538	582	0.166	8	0.950
Glasgow	109	47954.88	-0.026	0.006	2.046	1906	0.223	3	0.984
Edmonton	110	54059.69	0.014	1.357	2.402	245.21	0.169	7	0.967
Belfast	111	56965.66	-0.001	0.180	1.660	619	0.167	5	0.984
Busan	112	16526.94	0.002	0.000	1.956	2665	0.160	4	0.916
Dusseldorf	113	36029.93	-0.005	0.256	0.228	203	0.241	8	0.882
Shenzhen	114	13565.89	0.135	4.551	5.858	18805	0.327	8	0.562
Quebec	115	47098.13	0.014	0.009	1.514	40.08	0.240	3	0.967
Rome	116	31335.98	-0.034	0.013	1.356	1362	0.426	8	0.556
Santiago	117	10935.17	0.008	0.037	1.606	326	0.523	7	0.765
Las Vegas	118	38314.65	-0.085	0.000	6.562	2682	0.211	3	0.979
Bergen	119	58504.66	0.003	3.588	0.073	1538	0.101	7	0.961
Moscow	120	35333.00	-0.031	0.003	14.390	7302	0.745	5	0.315
Qingdao	121	10489.58	0.203	0.002	5.270	3311	0.198	7	0.562
San Antonio	122	31632.95	-0.047	0.039	5.044	4872	0.175	6	0.979
Saskatoon	123	34204.45	0.013	0.001	1.424	81.27	0.079	4	0.967
Plymouth	124	28831.67	-0.002	0.600	1.329	4566	0.086	8	0.984
Bonn	125	32754.48	0.003	0.256	0.239	2651	0.128	8	0.882

City	Ranking	Economic Dynamic		Environ-mental Quality	Social Cohe-sion	Techno-logical Innov-ation	Global Conne-ction	Cultural Diversity	Govern-ment Manage-ment
		GDP per capita (dollar)	GDP growth rate (%)	CO$_2$ emissi-ons per capita (kg)	Crime rate (%)	Patent applica-tions	Global network connec-tivity	Language multina-tionality index	Doing business index
Marseille	126	31586.32	-0.015	0.002	0.877	1572	0.176	5	0.860
Pittsburgh	127	42978.65	-0.049	0.080	5.179	5130	0.257	4	0.979
Ulsan	128	50420.75	0.006	0.003	5.036	851	0.074	4	0.916
Vancouver	129	39411.59	0.014	5.482	1.918	171.34	0.310	7	0.967
Dortmund	130	42281.26	-0.001	0.027	0.306	2406	0.122	5	0.882
Riverside	131	22926.77	-0.064	0.017	3.594	3074	0.123	7	0.979
Gyeongju	132	82201.81	0.009	0.779	0.976	415	0.036	4	0.916
Sacramento	133	39094.45	-0.042	2.199	5.341	2673	0.181	8	0.979
Stockton	134	25390.52	-0.045	0.000	3.384	1652	0.127	3	0.979
Fukuoka	135	34347.00	0.009	0.005	1.007	742	0.161	4	0.905
Liverpool	136	33107.03	-0.026	0.028	1.337	961	0.164	5	0.984
Calgary	137	46984.67	0.014	55.814	2.006	40.86	0.236	8	0.967
Bratislava	138	15200.60	-0.025	0.039	0.562	318	0.397	7	0.770
Athens	139	25300.80	0.088	0.004	0.872	1547	0.505	5	0.394
Utrecht	140	36203.46	-0.012	1.391	0.305	1595	0.121	9	0.837
Fresno	141	27878.18	-0.035	0.001	3.401	1322	0.137	3	0.979
Belgrade	142	5650.34	0.011	0.000	3.341	99	0.255	8	0.506
Halifax	143	38872.43	0.014	0.011	2.018	107.03	0.087	4	0.967
Anaheim	144	28623.22	-0.016	1.816	5.792	3943	0.138	8	0.979
Shizuoka	145	49735.32	0.172	0.209	0.325	827	0.123	2	0.905
Memphis	146	42704.36	-0.061	0.289	5.082	3440	0.203	5	0.979
Chichibu	147	38023.29	0.112	0.297	0.455	1230	0.083	5	0.905
Buffalo	148	35676.09	-0.111	0.719	4.920	3536	0.142	8	0.979
Strasbourg	149	31421.48	-0.015	0.012	0.766	1517	0.161	5	0.860
Virginia Beach	150	42982.41	-0.030	0.007	5.661	1130	0.149	3	0.979
Kagoshima	151	42532.32	0.184	0.185	0.756	148	0.090	3	0.905
Budapest	152	19765.76	0.042	1.477	2.094	2844	0.576	5	0.747

City	Ranking	Economic Dynamic		Environmental Quality	Social Cohesion	Technological Innovation	Global Connection	Cultural Diversity	Government Management
		GDP per capita (dollar)	GDP growth rate (%)	CO_2 emissions per capita (kg)	Crime rate (%)	Patent applications	Global network connectivity	Language multinationality index	Doing business index
Suwon	153	14979.92	-0.010	0.019	1.323	16712	0.045	3	0.916
Christchurch	154	34631.83	0.012	6.041	1.059	565	0.113	8	0.990
Kobe	155	42516.65	0.095	0.032	1.036	1056	0.163	2	0.905
Nashville	156	39749.30	-0.083	0.431	5.559	2609	0.207	6	0.979
Sofia	157	5600.04	-0.003	0.000	3.802	436	0.368	5	0.720
Nicosia	158	23784.72	0.011	0.005	0.608	227	0.221	5	0.799
Albuquerque	159	36685.85	-0.071	0.004	5.306	3188	0.161	3	0.979
Ottawa	160	43851.63	0.014	15.975	2.212	83.03	0.284	6	0.967
Warsaw	161	13186.97	-0.088	0.000	2.046	1064	0.624	2	0.612
Jacksonville	162	37636.22	-0.067	31.404	5.068	2993	0.182	9	0.979
Manchester	163	31682.73	-0.026	0.542	1.013	4585	0.252	4	0.984
Tianjin	164	8721.52	0.188	0.028	3.104	6621	0.291	5	0.562
Hamilton (CA)	165	46204.83	0.014	0.142	1.969	16.08	0.114	4	0.967
Sheffield	166	34249.92	-0.002	0.039	1.260	1705	0.091	4	0.984
Kuwait	167	8180.59	0.000	0.001	0.864	18	0.182	8	0.590
Hiroshima	168	50543.31	0.106	0.783	0.600	329	0.148	3	0.905
Kaohsiung City	169	21547.23	0.063	0.023	13.819	287	0.165	7	0.821
Munich	170	40170.18	-0.025	18.376	1.946	1750	0.378	6	0.882
Geneva	171	63803.04	0.014	0.016	0.820	1521	0.351	4	0.344
Toledo	172	38047.70	-0.043	0.011	4.444	4099	0.150	2	0.979
Mexico City	173	13867.12	0.026	0.011	18.340	2724	0.633	2	0.810
Suzhou	174	10336.03	0.232	0.590	6.354	18270	0.243	3	0.562
Bakersfield	175	34571.32	0.011	0.125	3.488	1386	0.127	4	0.979
Zurich	176	57021.87	0.001	0.044	0.418	2203	0.430	4	0.344
Gwangju	177	17190.14	0.003	0.000	2.096	718	0.074	3	0.916
Cologne	178	30730.55	-0.030	0.012	0.985	128	0.164	4	0.882
Wuhan	179	7233.44	0.185	0.002	2.997	5329	0.245	3	0.562

City	Ranking	Economic Dynamic		Environmental Quality	Social Cohesion	Technological Innovation	Global Connection	Cultural Diversity	Government Management
		GDP per capita (dollar)	GDP growth rate (%)	CO_2 emissions per capita (kg)	Crime rate (%)	Patent applications	Global network connectivity	Language multinationality index	Doing business index
Lyon	180	33135.71	-0.015	0.812	1.473	5372	0.267	4	0.860
Bordeaux	181	30156.46	-0.015	0.012	1.143	1033	0.138	4	0.860
Turin	182	25325.13	-0.034	0.000	0.719	84	0.163	6	0.556
Nuremberg	183	47301.03	0.005	0.373	0.608	69	0.145	4	0.882
Ljubljana	184	39182.50	0.052	0.363	1.215	684	0.253	4	0.770
Tallinn	185	27984.20	0.210	2.680	7.581	224	0.283	3	0.911
Istanbul	186	6763.77	-0.023	0.010	2.569	960	0.495	5	0.641
Vilnius	187	26212.88	0.122	0.713	16.143	116	0.302	5	0.877
Corpus Christi	188	34026.92	-0.018	0.030	3.626	1013	0.126	3	0.979
Indianapolis	189	49487.86	-0.034	6.533	6.288	6196	0.226	3	0.979
Hangzhou	190	8751.05	0.239	0.164	4.245	9831	0.204	4	0.562
Kitakyusyu	191	41000.73	0.108	0.114	0.379	11	0.084	2	0.905
Changsha	192	9867.56	0.263	0.002	3.567	2807	0.126	3	0.562
Windsor	193	28573.67	0.013	0.316	0.634	34.19	0.091	5	0.967
Valencia	194	31978.21	-0.015	0.225	1.269	1988	0.179	6	0.731
Ansan	195	23737.34	0.012	0.013	2.564	1455	0.052	4	0.916
Malmo	196	37960.74	-0.031	0.012	0.815	255	0.128	2	0.927
Krakow	197	17179.87	0.189	0.100	1.131	143	0.128	6	0.612
Dalian	198	11230.10	0.174	0.046	4.656	3507	0.243	5	0.562
Bologna	199	33605.38	-0.034	0.139	1.327	1708	0.147	8	0.556
Zhengzhou	200	2682.64	0.182	0.000	2.260	3981	0.125	3	0.562
Jakarta	201	3733.68	0.029	0.015	2.205	112	0.568	7	0.326
El Paso	202	31108.39	-0.024	0.024	3.772	1150	0.152	2	0.979
Incheon	203	21057.40	0.022	0.085	1.648	2931	0.085	4	0.916
Wichita	204	39549.08	-0.045	0.320	5.412	2666	0.152	3	0.979
Hobart	205	46679.73	-0.001	0.103	1.021	130	0.071	2	0.950

City	Ranking	Economic Dynamic		Environ-mental Quality	Social Cohe-sion	Techno-logical Innov-ation	Global Conne-ction	Cultural Diversity	Govern-ment Manage-ment
		GDP per capita (dollar)	GDP growth rate (%)	CO$_2$ emissi-ons per capita (kg)	Crime rate (%)	Patent applica-tions	Global network connec-tivity	Language multina-tionality index	Doing business index
Dresden	206	28688.08	-0.014	0.175	0.706	3034	0.102	4	0.882
Saint Louis	207	40563.31	-0.040	0.731	5.084	3547	0.217	2	0.979
Wenzhou	208	5865.39	0.187	0.000	4.167	5159	0.095	2	0.562
Johannesburg	209	6549.87	0.009	0.046	43.324	1171	0.442	8	0.815
Kyoto	210	47369.25	0.074	43.414	0.041	1476	0.142	4	0.905
Niigata	211	26531.87	-0.060	0.017	0.048	164	0.079	4	0.905
Shenyang	212	8152.30	0.149	0.320	3.313	3105	0.192	7	0.562
Hamamatsu	213	43903.85	0.110	0.870	1.036	1	0.093	2	0.905
Zhongshan	214	13761.11	0.168	0.038	3.429	4342	0.106	5	0.562
Fort Worth	215	39925.22	-0.015	2.147	7.112	3678	0.172	3	0.979
Wilmington	216	32473.24	-0.091	10.934	6.313	12816	0.200	3	0.979
Lima	217	5734.90	0.051	0.299	3.980	634	0.330	5	0.804
Sapporo	218	35526.91	0.035	0.121	0.482	211	0.126	2	0.905
Toulouse	219	29978.19	-0.015	1.073	0.611	2689	0.202	4	0.860
São Paulo	220	7794.20	0.036	0.031	23.564	1101	0.726	7	0.292
Daegu	221	15120.85	0.028	0.082	1.421	2735	0.065	4	0.916
Guangzhou	222	10423.86	0.136	0.135	5.222	8081	0.409	2	0.562
Buenos Aires	223	16967.21	0.036	0.001	13.678	835	0.660	2	0.360
Newcastle	224	36508.20	-0.001	0.519	0.910	1981	0.109	2	0.984
Himeji-shi	225	43765.05	0.091	14.687	0.537	170	0.069	4	0.905
Prague	226	23010.69	0.035	3.357	2.376	176	0.527	4	0.652
Arhus	227	49894.39	-0.033	0.473	1.835	47	0.078	2	0.972
Nanjing	228	6772.65	0.132	0.198	3.076	4816	0.253	5	0.562
Cairo	229	2067.45	0.021	0.005	0.817	174	0.468	4	0.479
Zagreb	230	15060.20	-0.021	0.219	1.413	473	0.324	7	0.534
Seongnam	231	13357.36	0.006	0.029	1.386	3349	0.047	3	0.916
Porto	232	14725.00	-0.014	0.068	0.725	690	0.174	4	0.832

City	Ranking	Economic Dynamic		Environ-mental Quality	Social Cohe-sion	Techno-logical Innov-ation	Global Conne-ction	Cultural Diversity	Govern-ment Manage-ment
		GDP per capita (dollar)	GDP growth rate (%)	CO_2 emissi-ons per capita (kg)	Crime rate (%)	Patent applica-tions	Global network connec-tivity	Language multina-tionality index	Doing business index
Fuzhou	233	7014.71	0.141	0.003	2.677	2018	0.176	3	0.562
Bucharest	234	7461.08	-0.001	1.235	2.045	395	0.401	6	0.686
Kanazawa	235	37507.50	0.003	0.328	0.844	332	0.111	2	0.905
Southampton	236	39005.16	-0.001	0.754	1.298	1975	0.115	1	0.984
Gothenburg	237	33279.39	-0.031	0.295	0.897	219	0.167	2	0.927
Daejeon	238	16824.56	0.017	0.270	1.337	4961	0.062	3	0.916
Naples	239	14089.30	-0.035	0.012	0.619	520	0.102	7	0.556
Tunis	240	4347.56	0.037	0.009	1.673	29	0.204	4	0.697
Sagamihara	241	31585.94	-0.036	0.037	1.040	140	0.080	2	0.905
Dongguan	242	12466.08	0.148	0.093	3.110	8093	0.133	3	0.562
Xuzhou	243	4359.76	0.140	0.001	3.183	1742	0.068	3	0.562
Manila	244	1763.35	-0.023	0.002	9.272	126	0.457	8	0.175
Beirut	245	9830.47	0.087	0.001	1.136	41	0.273	3	0.371
Hsinchu City	246	23330.04	0.044	0.060	10.915	643	0.101	3	0.821
Monterrey	247	17270.11	0.026	0.001	23.273	308	0.140	2	0.810
Yantai	248	10226.33	0.160	0.046	4.362	2249	0.096	4	0.562
Okayama	249	34909.16	0.024	1.447	0.914	476	0.090	2	0.905
Bangalore	250	2683.27	0.172	0.000	7.584	373	0.325	2	0.254
Gaborone	251	9607.44	0.034	0.009	15.070	1	0.108	5	0.714
Taichung	252	20403.34	0.093	0.075	14.127	514	0.083	3	0.821
Baku	253	2613.13	0.092	0.064	1.775	69	0.154	4	0.702
Pretoria	254	5965.21	0.008	0.029	38.792	839	0.126	8	0.815
Shaoxing	255	6762.71	0.115	0.127	3.717	11192	0.057	3	0.562
Leipzig	256	31331.02	-0.014	0.618	0.561	780	0.099	2	0.882
Trieste	257	27905.05	-0.034	0.012	0.805	532	0.072	4	0.556
Yangzhou	258	6969.31	0.158	0.012	3.532	2003	0.072	3	0.562
Sakai	259	28354.33	-0.110	0.294	0.945	1933	0.074	3	0.905

City	Ranking	Economic Dynamic		Environmental Quality	Social Cohesion	Technological Innovation	Global Connection	Cultural Diversity	Government Management
		GDP per capita (dollar)	GDP growth rate (%)	CO$_2$ emissions per capita (kg)	Crime rate (%)	Patent applications	Global network connectivity	Language multinationality index	Doing business index
Changchun	260	7162.99	0.171	0.143	3.141	1814	0.117	4	0.562
Alexandria	261	1999.98	0.021	0.002	0.785	3604	0.113	4	0.479
Penang	262	6969.63	0.010	1.146	2.223	633	0.168	4	0.889
Foshan	263	11710.20	0.161	2.020	4.038	10677	0.100	3	0.562
Minsk	264	3076.99	0.014	0.009	4.238	353	0.185	4	0.624
Amman	265	5680.38	0.046	0.218	1.447	44	0.272	7	0.382
Chongqing	266	2692.50	0.178	1.813	1.662	4820	0.192	4	0.562
Alamaty	267	7687.68	0.016	0.052	12.627	6	0.205	5	0.675
Lahore	268	1098.66	0.023	0.000	9.542	11	0.099	2	0.540
Hanoi	269	2162.62	0.094	0.011	4.476	15	0.314	2	0.567
Tainan	270	18288.59	-0.019	0.014	11.474	262	0.064	3	0.821
Montevideo	271	9059.06	0.055	0.015	7.126	410	0.259	6	0.310
Torreon	272	15096.74	0.026	0.001	18.599	13	0.030	2	0.810
Riga	273	9827.08	-0.115	0.300	4.696	329	0.325	3	0.871
Jinan	274	7184.61	0.141	0.296	3.354	4571	0.167	3	0.562
Wuxi	275	10830.58	0.168	0.450	6.028	5028	0.125	3	0.562
Merida	276	13097.99	0.026	0.001	16.680	18	0.023	2	0.810
Sanaa	277	1481.41	0.000	0.001	6.520	3	0.114	6	0.416
Genoa	278	25718.12	-0.034	0.108	1.356	139	0.095	5	0.556
Xi'an	279	4526.40	0.278	2.620	1.625	3285	0.217	2	0.562
Bremen	280	27361.46	-0.014	8.255	0.157	1329	0.109	3	0.882
Kurashiki	281	22514.92	0.024	1.030	0.738	116	0.065	2	0.905
Venice	282	28780.14	-0.034	0.359	0.942	354	0.113	5	0.556
Acapulco	283	9742.41	0.026	0.003	10.754	23	0.029	2	0.810
Hefei	284	6870.81	0.158	0.024	4.052	1307	0.127	2	0.562
Leon	285	12326.58	0.026	0.003	16.177	454	0.047	2	0.810

City	Ranking	Economic Dynamic GDP per capita (dollar)	GDP growth rate (%)	Environ- mental Quality CO₂ emissi- ons per capita (kg)	Social Cohe- sion Crime rate (%)	Techno- logical Innov- ation Patent applica- tions	Global Conne- ction Global network connec- tivity	Cultural Diversity Language multina- tionality index	Govern- ment Manage- ment Doing business index
Addis Ababa	286	425.09	0.097	0.000	8.980	1	0.120	2	0.422
Tampico	287	14591.28	0.026	0.004	15.921	30	0.020	2	0.810
Rizhao	288	5730.30	0.240	0.359	1.492	734	0.051	3	0.562
Ningbo	289	9247.61	0.240	14.560	5.668	9882	0.137	2	0.562
Ankara	290	7335.34	-0.023	0.115	2.304	589	0.189	4	0.641
Zhuhai	291	10655.23	0.114	0.116	4.476	1797	0.110	3	0.562
Nanchang	292	7339.28	0.139	0.037	2.271	869	0.109	2	0.562
Veracruz	293	14308.91	0.026	0.005	19.420	36	0.038	2	0.810
Maputo	294	473.95	0.013	0.000	8.889	0	0.108	5	0.299
Quanzhou	295	6743.36	0.153	0.267	0.882	2045	0.079	3	0.562
Yerevan	296	1168.10	-0.048	0.055	0.880	66	0.114	4	0.736
Taiyuan	297	5689.97	0.135	0.118	2.482	1421	0.087	3	0.562
Nashik	298	6212.25	0.221	0.000	12.976	19	0.016	2	0.254
Zibo	299	9105.17	0.149	0.160	3.611	1408	0.059	3	0.562
Mumbai	300	1694.79	0.090	0.017	6.247	573	0.510	2	0.254
Matsuyama-shi	301	26780.89	-0.112	0.585	0.934	236	0.072	2	0.905
Shijiazhuang	302	6043.98	0.161	0.315	2.047	1317	0.083	3	0.562
Keelung	303	19116.92	0.101	1.624	12.230	68	0.030	3	0.821
Santo Domingo	304	7419.44	0.042	0.000	45.129	18	0.169	4	0.601
Puebla	305	11543.46	0.026	0.016	15.308	60	0.040	2	0.810
Tangshan	306	8352.61	0.225	0.417	2.265	710	0.071	2	0.562
San Luis Potosi	307	13136.80	0.026	0.020	18.247	20	0.061	2	0.810
Thane	308	1058.64	0.166	0.000	2.771	92	0.017	2	0.254
Accra	309	871.18	0.013	1.087	4.225	15	0.139	6	0.630
Columbo	310	2199.53	0.038	0.004	9.856	264	0.144	4	0.434
Huizhou	311	7624.83	0.123	0.712	2.734	1011	0.071	4	0.562
Cuernavaca	312	11150.18	0.026	0.021	14.499	73	0.024	2	0.810

City	Ranking	Economic Dynamic		Environ-mental Quality	Social Cohesion	Techno-logical Innov-ation	Global Conne-ction	Cultural Diversity	Govern-ment Manage-ment
		GDP per capita (dollar)	GDP growth rate (%)	CO$_2$ emissions per capita (kg)	Crime rate (%)	Patent applica-tions	Global network connec-tivity	Language multina-tionality index	Doing business index
Aguascalientes	313	14165.51	0.026	0.018	18.803	14	0.019	2	0.810
Morelia	314	12206.21	0.026	0.015	17.571	30	0.012	2	0.810
Changzhou	315	8089.03	0.147	1.358	3.445	2536	0.100	3	0.562
Kunming	316	4831.60	0.107	0.079	2.053	1400	0.108	2	0.562
Ho Chi Minh City	317	1960.83	0.104	1.268	5.700	18	0.378	2	0.567
Liuzhou	318	6603.96	0.168	0.087	3.710	406	0.048	2	0.562
Tijuana	319	11812.80	0.026	0.049	16.462	55	0.061	2	0.810
Guadalajara	320	10618.76	0.026	0.097	14.848	120	0.090	2	0.810
Jiaxing	321	5646.51	0.128	0.588	3.300	3163	0.057	3	0.562
Ciudad Juarez	322	14327.46	0.026	0.051	18.265	10	0.045	2	0.810
Karachi	323	1257.97	0.023	0.021	9.460	14	0.284	2	0.540
Higashiosaka-shi	324	21704.79	-0.263	0.137	0.874	30	0.068	3	0.905
Weihai	325	9146.75	0.132	0.701	4.033	1079	0.077	3	0.562
Lanzhou	326	4531.22	0.133	0.097	1.388	598	0.062	2	0.562
Weifang	327	4735.28	0.183	2.153	2.181	2586	0.055	3	0.562
Delhi	328	2571.48	0.118	0.168	5.195	166	0.498	2	0.254
Queretaro	329	14270.89	0.026	0.071	19.840	81	0.060	2	0.810
Ghaziabad	330	1800.02	0.183	0.000	2.486	14	0.010	2	0.254
Durban	331	6698.66	0.009	0.157	43.139	321	0.110	6	0.815
Islamabad	332	1117.22	0.023	1.187	9.108	902	0.156	6	0.540
San Juan	333	3809.63	0.000	0.020	20.610	1789	0.140	2	0.742
Guiyang	334	3478.67	0.144	0.259	1.818	1052	0.089	2	0.562
Pune	335	1234.72	0.214	0.022	2.850	131	0.200	2	0.254
Xining	336	4138.80	0.187	0.450	1.673	137	0.068	2	0.562
Asuncion	337	1614.80	0.007	0.004	17.125	7	0.127	5	0.411
Kalyan	338	1752.18	0.200	0.001	4.089	4	0.016	2	0.254
Harbin	339	6130.84	0.147	19.179	2.114	2400	0.104	4	0.562

City	Ranking	Economic Dynamic		Environ-mental Quality	Social Cohe-sion	Techno-logical Innov-ation	Global Conne-ction	Cultural Diversity	Govern-ment Manage-ment
		GDP per capita (dollar)	GDP growth rate (%)	CO_2 emissi-ons per capita (kg)	Crime rate (%)	Patent applica-tions	Global network connec-tivity	Language multina-tionality index	Doing business index
Urumqi	340	4844.42	0.182	0.924	2.126	378	0.098	2	0.562
Xiamen	341	8696.04	0.123	12.292	3.112	2330	0.179	3	0.562
Varanasi	342	991.32	0.184	0.001	1.421	3	0.016	2	0.254
Medan	343	4436.99	0.026	0.000	1.643	18	0.080	2	0.326
Casablanca	344	2201.75	0.050	0.120	0.846	47	0.283	3	0.366
Rio de Janeiro	345	6239.91	0.036	0.292	18.650	513	0.324	6	0.292
Wuhu	346	6391.81	0.197	1.123	2.526	1006	0.046	2	0.562
Hohhot	347	9412.24	0.155	3.432	2.989	505	0.078	3	0.562
Nanning	348	4239.32	0.172	3.443	1.363	488	0.082	3	0.562
Sarajevo	349	4509.44	0.004	0.027	2.386	27	0.198	3	0.389
Palermo	350	15724.19	-0.035	0.244	0.153	344	0.081	3	0.556
Lusaka	351	1384.90	0.012	0.056	1.575	2	0.139	2	0.579
Taizhou	352	5411.54	0.125	6.668	2.865	4811	0.056	3	0.562
Quito	353	4845.12	0.036	0.009	24.234	48	0.171	6	0.276
Bhopal	354	4543.43	0.087	0.000	10.643	2	0.038	2	0.254
Salvador	355	2701.62	0.034	0.001	13.921	41	0.122	3	0.292
Nagpur	356	1661.83	0.221	0.011	2.520	17	0.046	2	0.254
Kiev	357	1979.62	-0.010	0.017	4.386	697	0.370	3	0.191
Panama City	358	4958.68	0.064	1.085	16.585	699	0.297	2	0.601
Georgetown	359	1195.77	0.020	0.002	17.934	4119	0.072	2	0.445
Srinagar	360	1142.95	0.085	0.000	3.624	6	0.016	2	0.254
Ufa	361	4223.18	0.021	0.000	6.791	74	0.009	2	0.315
Nairobi	362	1468.53	0.020	0.016	18.019	44	0.200	3	0.456
Curitiba	363	6150.43	0.036	0.101	18.737	109	0.082	7	0.292
Cape Town	364	5827.14	0.008	0.150	39.253	774	0.241	2	0.815
Nantong	365	3624.73	0.112	11.591	4.522	4102	0.082	3	0.562

City	Ranking	Economic Dynamic		Environmental Quality	Social Cohesion	Technological Innovation	Global Connection	Cultural Diversity	Government Management
		GDP per capita (dollar)	GDP growth rate (%)	CO_2 emissions per capita (kg)	Crime rate (%)	Patent applications	Global network connectivity	Language multinationality index	Doing business index
Tripoli	366	5968.19	0.023	0.001	1.770	234	0.123	2	0.152
Toluca	367	11736.98	0.026	1.215	15.978	210	0.040	2	0.810
Chennai	368	774.26	-0.117	0.000	7.302	95	0.216	2	0.254
Chihuahua	369	20030.79	0.026	0.997	25.202	131	0.042	2	0.810
Havana	370	21985.31	0.021	0.047	8.334	81	0.050	2	0.416
Saltillo	371	17999.52	0.026	0.945	22.265	96	0.025	2	0.810
Lagos	372	1606.91	0.031	0.008	4.936	30	0.211	5	0.034
Calcutta	373	1898.76	0.093	0.040	4.873	4	0.246	2	0.254
Rabat	374	2477.74	0.050	0.270	0.429	20	0.088	4	0.366
Meerut	375	644.51	0.176	0.011	1.884	2	0.022	2	0.254
Harare	376	567.60	0.031	0.002	8.385	37	0.152	4	0.124
Haora	377	413.89	0.061	0.001	1.383	0	0.009	2	0.254
Ordos	378	13744.15	0.228	42.466	5.037	80	0.036	2	0.562
Damascus	379	2085.61	0.045	1.898	3.477	215	0.144	7	0.197
Saint Petersburg	380	6590.07	0.008	1.068	9.990	180	0.227	5	0.315
Coimbatore	381	3124.73	0.117	0.014	2.348	14	0.057	2	0.254
Cordoba	382	11733.32	0.036	0.463	8.334	85	0.095	4	0.360
Allahabad	383	2423.35	0.187	0.056	1.095	2	0.014	2	0.254
Baotou	384	12191.92	0.186	144.578	4.411	251	0.045	3	0.562
Lucknow	385	1317.10	0.199	0.219	2.798	7	0.092	2	0.254
Krasnoyarsk	386	5980.75	0.007	0.001	10.105	7	0.008	2	0.315
Freetown	387	748.06	0.042	0.004	4.314	14	0.053	3	0.202
Dar Es Salaam	388	1101.94	0.067	0.002	19.440	2	0.140	2	0.287
Visakhapatnam	389	4263.38	0.156	0.046	5.227	7	0.043	2	0.254
Tashkent	390	1225.09	0.069	0.026	4.952	75	0.162	3	0.164
Surat	391	989.16	0.090	0.006	4.436	4	0.030	2	0.254
Yinchuan	392	4871.74	0.181	26.411	2.888	411	0.050	2	0.562

City	Ranking	Economic Dynamic		Environ-mental Quality	Social Cohe-sion	Techno-logical Innov-ation	Global Conne-ction	Cultural Diversity	Govern-ment Manage-ment
		GDP per capita (dollar)	GDP growth rate (%)	CO_2 emissi-ons per capita (kg)	Crime rate (%)	Patent applica-tions	Global network connec-tivity	Language multina-tionality index	Doing business index
Rajkot	393	1256.53	0.110	0.012	2.232	3	0.019	2	0.254
Bandung	394	418.65	0.015	0.013	0.927	12	0.068	2	0.326
Madurai	395	2039.95	0.117	0.036	1.282	10	0.045	2	0.254
Kaliningrad	396	3839.29	-0.033	0.015	6.865	39	0.018	4	0.315
Douala	397	2282.21	0.039	0.110	2.725	4	0.127	5	0.112
Brazilia	398	8488.47	0.036	0.134	29.249	27	0.189	5	0.292
Cochi	399	7086.54	0.146	0.076	4.110	22	0.018	2	0.254
Yaounde	400	1513.00	0.010	0.008	2.620	12	0.080	4	0.112
Cebu	401	1977.24	0.036	0.001	8.278	63	0.082	2	0.175
Dhaka	402	1142.75	0.058	1.820	6.482	1	0.250	2	0.405
Trivandrum	403	4104.07	0.146	0.101	3.027	5	0.014	2	0.254
Tula	404	5643.01	-0.008	0.013	9.056	46	0.003	3	0.315
Kanpur	405	1132.23	0.160	0.093	4.893	9	0.027	2	0.254
Medellin	406	2892.35	0.023	0.178	39.978	31	0.096	2	0.787
Belgorod	407	5397.55	0.059	0.029	8.577	25	0.034	2	0.315
Vladivostok	408	4134.80	0.036	0.073	6.466	59	0.023	3	0.315
Kampala	409	983.90	0.079	0.019	18.818	2	0.119	2	0.321
Bogota	410	6679.41	0.024	18.358	47.824	247	0.402	2	0.787
Kazan	411	4110.16	0.009	0.063	6.177	142	0.028	3	0.315
Faridabad	412	822.86	0.077	0.033	2.262	11	0.022	2	0.254
Dushanbe	413	771.86	0.073	0.194	2.835	6	0.086	3	0.225
Amritsar	414	4526.16	0.076	0.062	2.057	5	0.017	2	0.254
Hyderabad	415	1035.07	0.019	0.094	5.480	180	0.187	2	0.254
Haikou	416	3751.50	0.124	107.876	1.160	257	0.092	2	0.562
Algiers	417	3165.35	0.018	0.213	0.697	6	0.182	2	0.242
Lipeck	418	4384.09	-0.026	0.006	7.431	5	0.013	2	0.315
Krasnojarsk	419	3246.24	0.019	0.025	4.640	5	0.006	2	0.315

City	Ranking	Economic Dynamic		Environ-mental Quality	Social Cohe-sion	Techno-logical Innov-ation	Global Conne-ction	Cultural Diversity	Govern-ment Manage-ment
		GDP per capita (dollar)	GDP growth rate (%)	CO$_2$ emissi-ons per capita (kg)	Crime rate (%)	Patent applica-tions	Global network connec-tivity	Language multina-tionality index	Doing business index
Ulan Bator	420	760.86	0.013	24.342	18.108	17	0.076	5	0.596
Jaroslavl	421	3673.92	-0.048	0.022	6.138	10	0.015	3	0.315
Machackala	422	2064.82	0.084	0.177	3.385	4	0.010	2	0.315
Kaluga	423	3787.67	0.029	0.051	5.660	15	0.015	2	0.315
Agra	424	1291.36	0.116	0.191	1.767	2	0.014	2	0.254
Luanda	425	1783.14	0.032	0.004	8.735	6	0.134	2	0.090
Tehran	426	3856.46	0.019	0.553	5.933	57	0.206	2	0.281
Ekaterinburg	427	4849.73	-0.057	0.117	8.595	8	0.037	4	0.315
Jaipur	428	888.06	-0.028	0.018	2.757	3	0.079	2	0.254
Nassau	429	17436.45	-0.034	0.035	14.193	524	0.102	2	0.228
Managua	430	2211.91	0.064	0.298	1.826	6	0.140	4	0.034
Porto Alegre	431	5728.52	0.036	0.145	17.107	134	0.083	3	0.292
Saratov	432	2835.06	0.013	0.062	3.802	87	0.003	2	0.315
Vadodara	433	2598.65	0.110	0.558	2.927	22	0.049	2	0.254
Tambov	434	7076.57	0.020	0.051	10.740	11	0.009	2	0.315
Ludhiana	435	2732.91	0.076	0.300	3.803	0	0.057	2	0.254
Guarulhos	436	7439.92	0.036	0.057	30.166	13	0.037	4	0.292
Abijan	437	2127.33	0.030	0.060	0.215	0	0.066	2	0.164
Tyumen	438	2631.17	-0.028	0.039	4.073	7	0.006	2	0.315
Stavropol	439	2216.01	0.005	0.107	3.604	14	0.014	2	0.315
Pondicherry	440	1856.56	0.086	0.249	3.192	6	0.008	2	0.254
Mysore	441	2036.21	0.049	0.210	1.008	8	0.021	2	0.254
Ahmedabad	442	939.91	-0.102	0.015	5.733	47	0.130	2	0.254
Duque de Caxias	443	12759.28	0.036	0.279	44.273	14	0.051	6	0.292
Tver	444	2623.73	-0.026	0.050	4.626	36	0.007	2	0.315
Djibouti	445	759.26	0.051	0.051	0.300	0	0.066	2	0.119
Smolensk	446	3835.17	0.001	0.094	6.553	24	0.016	2	0.315

City	Ranking	Economic Dynamic		Environ- mental Quality	Social Cohe- sion	Techno- logical Innov- ation	Global Conne- ction	Cultural Diversity	Govern- ment Manage- ment
		GDP per capita (dollar)	GDP growth rate (%)	CO_2 emissi- ons per capita (kg)	Crime rate (%)	Patent applica- tions	Global network connec- tivity	Language multina- tionality index	Doing business index
Indore	447	3682.69	0.087	0.352	8.316	4	0.058	2	0.254
La Paz	448	954.26	0.047	0.013	14.931	79	0.137	2	0.124
Kingston	449	8985.21	-0.006	0.001	75.937	3625	0.122	2	0.551
Conakry	450	1159.38	0.022	0.006	1.077	6	0.085	2	0.000
Volgograd	451	2998.24	-0.056	0.115	5.203	24	0.009	3	0.315
Perm	452	4875.15	-0.029	0.050	7.749	70	0.011	2	0.315
Ivanovo	453	4503.63	-0.045	0.034	7.847	28	0.015	2	0.315
Archangelsk	454	6011.43	0.003	0.113	9.559	10	0.020	2	0.315
Patna	455	635.05	-0.034	0.029	2.495	2	0.023	2	0.254
Recife	456	4878.89	0.035	0.060	18.148	21	0.053	2	0.292
Kursk	457	3566.59	-0.013	0.096	5.981	19	0.003	2	0.315
Orenburg	458	4112.77	-0.019	0.097	6.280	11	0.005	2	0.315
Chelyabinsk	459	5448.06	-0.074	0.020	10.106	4	0.014	2	0.315
Dakar	460	638.72	0.025	1.003	1.763	57	0.147	3	0.152
Bryansk	461	2002.10	-0.038	0.096	3.721	11	0.020	2	0.315
Voronez	462	2646.04	0.002	0.191	4.396	5	0.003	2	0.315
Phnom Penh	463	676.52	-0.013	0.151	5.078	871	0.145	2	0.180
Guayaquil	464	3767.47	0.035	0.106	21.404	20	0.115	2	0.276
Ryazan	465	3166.89	-0.029	0.122	5.398	31	0.002	2	0.315
Omsk	466	4942.76	-0.005	0.339	7.357	42	0.031	2	0.315
Barnaul	467	1693.43	-0.037	0.124	3.744	24	0.004	2	0.315
Izhevsk	468	3297.45	-0.031	0.163	5.431	28	0.011	2	0.315
Blantyre	469	485.05	0.037	22.379	0.305	60	0.072	4	0.259
Novosibirsk	470	3752.57	-0.040	2.363	12.941	506	0.061	4	0.315
São Bernardo do Campo	471	12641.74	0.036	0.114	43.456	45	0.038	4	0.292
Yangon	472	402.32	0.000	0.291	3.613	314	0.097	2	0.180
Belo Horizonte	473	5565.51	0.036	0.668	16.765	111	0.077	2	0.292

City	Ranking	Economic Dynamic		Environ-mental Quality	Social Cohe-sion	Techno-logical Innov-ation	Global Conne-ction	Cultural Diversity	Govern-ment Manage-ment
		GDP per capita (dollar)	GDP growth rate (%)	CO_2 emissi-ons per capita (kg)	Crime rate (%)	Patent applica-tions	Global network connec-tivity	Language multina-tionality index	Doing business index
Uljanovsk	474	6667.73	-0.037	0.225	11.031	6	0.009	2	0.315
Penza	475	2323.21	-0.007	0.774	3.794	16	0.003	2	0.315
Rostov-na-Donu	476	2492.27	-0.027	0.648	4.846	50	0.027	2	0.315
Vladimir	477	3977.92	-0.032	0.345	6.995	35	0.005	2	0.315
Brazzaville	478	1860.53	0.064	0.031	24.790	1	0.063	2	0.175
Murmansk	479	6225.49	-0.053	0.233	10.859	15	0.019	2	0.315
Or'ol	480	4404.78	-0.055	1.335	7.696	122	0.003	3	0.315
Ranchi	481	512.65	-0.086	0.202	1.642	2	0.030	2	0.254
Cemerovo	482	4157.42	-0.037	0.742	7.426	14	0.002	2	0.315
São José dos Campos	483	13741.17	0.036	0.072	41.035	58	0.046	2	0.292
Surabaya	484	4178.79	0.011	76.306	0.098	95	0.114	2	0.326
Kinshasa	485	200.79	0.000	0.076	19.125	1	0.097	2	0.175
Groznyj	486	1839.50	-0.025	2.098	4.568	2	0.012	2	0.315
Port-au-Prince	487	1783.45	0.017	0.036	22.265	13	0.101	2	0.096
Samara	488	4400.45	-0.096	0.662	8.931	63	0.021	2	0.315
Petrozavodsk	489	3725.05	-0.097	0.743	7.408	2	0.002	2	0.315
Lome	490	246.69	0.024	1.804	2.890	3	0.073	2	0.107
Jabalpur	491	480.23	-0.111	0.497	1.259	0	0.017	2	0.254
Pimpri-Chichwad	492	957.97	-0.117	0.385	3.815	4	0.027	2	0.254
Guatemala City	493	7930.75	0.019	1.558	72.277	16	0.161	5	0.439
Campinas	494	7895.71	0.036	6.116	22.940	171	0.051	2	0.292
Khabarovsk	495	396.15	-0.070	2.171	7.414	8	0.012	2	0.315
Caracas	496	9114.39	-0.033	62.381	34.644	622	0.375	5	0.040
Manaus	497	9208.32	0.036	5.066	28.306	22	0.062	2	0.292
Astra Chan	498	2795.17	-0.033	28.417	4.266	2	0.004	2	0.315
Tegucigalpa	499	2368.28	0.008	0.018	90.887	5	0.118	4	0.270
Betim	500	17339.53	0.037	1.428	72.528	3	0.040	2	0.292